TRACED

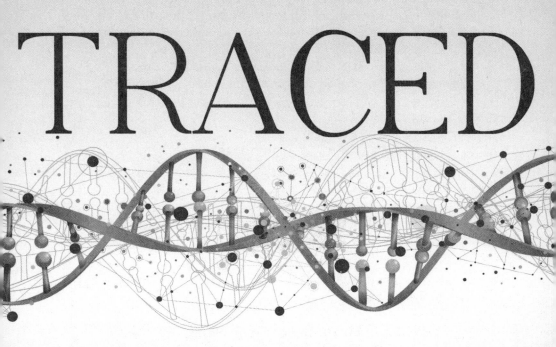

Human DNA's Big Surprise

Nathaniel T. Jeanson

with illustrations by Cameron Suter

First printing: March 2022
Fourth printing: August 2022

ISBN: 978-1-68344-291-2
ISBN: 978-1-61458-793-4 (digital)
Library of Congress Control Number: 2021948815

Cover by Diana Bogardus

Unless otherwise noted, Scripture quotations are from the New King James Version (NKJV) of the Bible.

Please consider requesting that a copy of this volume be purchased by your local library system.

Printed in the United States of America

Please visit our website for other great titles:
www.masterbooks.com

For information regarding promotional opportunities, please contact the publicity department at pr@nlpg.com.

Master
Books®
A Division of New Leaf Publishing Group
www.masterbooks.com

For David, Billy, and Axel
And all those who long for the "rest of the story"

Advance Praise for *Traced*:

. . . a ground-breaking book . . . likely to become a classic.
Ola Hössjer, PhD, Professor of Mathematical Statistics, Stockholm
University, Sweden

. . . extremely well researched.
Emerson Thomas McMullen, PhD, Emeritus Associate Professor of History,
Georgia Southern University

*. . . a profoundly intriguing book. It throws a new light on ancient history
and will leave the reader eager to learn more.*
Steven E. Woodworth, PhD, Professor of History,
Texas Christian University

*. . . pulls the curtain back further on the mystery of early human history
using genetics, history, and linguistics . . . goes a long way toward
reconstructing the origins of the human family.*
Les Bruce, PhD, retired research specialist,
Summer Institute of Linguistics International

*Jeanson will take you on a tour of human history like you
have never seen before.*
Joe Owen, Director, Answers in Genesis Latin America

Table of Contents

EPILOGUE

Introduction

1

The Hiddenness of History

In the late 1990s, I was a high school student living in small-town southeastern Wisconsin and driving a '93 green Mercury Tracer past farmers' fields to a tiny Christian school 25 minutes away. For two of those semesters, world history class lifted me far away in time and space from my modern parochial home. And it left me with nagging questions.

In broad brushstrokes, I learned a history that went something like this: The first civilizations arose half a world away from Wisconsin. In ancient Mesopotamia, the Sumerians appeared. To the southwest in Africa, the ancient Egyptians also emerged. To the west and northwest in the Mediterranean, the first European civilizations (the Minoans and Mycenaeans) ascended.

As history progressed, it focused on this same small geographic triangle. One kingdom rose and fell after another, including ancient Assyria, Babylon, and Persia. However, these Asian empires eventually gave way to a European one. Alexander the Great rushed his armies through Persia to create, at that time, the world's largest empire.

The focus of my class then shifted to Europe. We learned that the ancient Greeks were eventually overrun by the Romans. For several hundred years, the Romans dominated the Mediterranean and western Europe. Then they fell to Germanic tribes of barbarians, sending Europe plummeting into the Dark Ages.[1]

---

1. Now known as the Early Middle Ages.

Europe awoke from the Dark Ages to the rising culture of the Renaissance. The continent recovered some of the glory of the great Greek and Roman ideals. Then the Reformation shook the European world. Eventually, the inevitable march of technological progress pushed Europe to venture out in the Age of Exploration, ushering in an era which brought together East and West, Old World and New World, into one global enterprise.

This was the story I was taught. Like many students, I learned the required facts and recited them on tests. But the experience left me unsatisfied.

Who did the ancient Sumerians come from? From whom did the Egyptians arise? What about the Minoans? Mycenaeans? Greeks? Romans? When these empires were overthrown, what happened to the people of these ancient civilizations? Did they just recede into the shadows of history? Did they go extinct? Are they still with us today?

My history education never answered these questions. It was as if civilizations popped into existence and then disappeared into oblivion.

I knew this couldn't be true. But I had nothing to offer in its place.

The narrow focus of this history also nagged at me. Along the way, I'm sure we learned something about historical India and China. We may have touched on the Aztecs and Mayans in the Americas. But if we did, I didn't retain much of their histories.

In other parts of the globe, large gaps in the timeline remained in my mind. We learned next to nothing about what was going on north of the Rio Grande before Europeans arrived. My course left the pre-European history of sub-Saharan Africa as a large void. The pre-European peoples of Australia and of the Pacific had no story — at least none that was taught to me. Central Asia — the vast landmass between Europe and China and above the Middle East — was hardly discussed, except to highlight the massive Mongolian empire of Genghis Khan.

What had happened in these places? In these locations, the indigenous peoples had no narrative to explain their existence. Their history seemed a big blank slate.

Again, I knew this couldn't be true. Again, I had nothing to offer in its place.

I never thought that one day I'd be personally uncovering the answers to these questions.

The Hiddenness of History

****

By training, I'm a biologist. I did my Bachelor of Science at the University of Wisconsin-Parkside. Officially, my degree was titled *Molecular Biology and Bioinformatics*. In more understandable terms, my training involved looking at life at the tiniest levels — the microscopic and chemical levels (the *Molecular Biology* part of the degree). And it involved analyzing the results with computers (the *Bioinformatics* part of the degree). I learned these skills in the classroom and in the lab, where I worked with single-celled algae. My goal — or, I should say, the goal of the lab in which I trained — was to understand the larger question of how plants genetically control photosynthesis, the process by which they turn sunlight into useful energy.

For my PhD, I moved to Massachusetts and studied at Harvard. Originally, I planned on working in a cancer lab. At the time, little did I know that the field of cancer research was taking a sharp turn in a new direction. Prior to arrival in Boston in 2003, I had acquired an interest in stem cells — the cells that are responsible for replacing old cells in the body as they die. I soon discovered that these cells had unexpected relevance to cancer. I realized this connection much more fully during the years I spent working on my thesis in an adult blood stem cell lab. My experiments produced no great breakthroughs, just average scientific advances.

But immersion in the wide-open world of how cells develop, change, and mutate produced lasting effects on my career — in ways I never anticipated.

After graduation in 2009, I began a journey in an entirely different direction — one that would unexpectedly tie all my scientific pursuits together and lead back to the history of the ancients.

In the fall of 2009, I began developing a research program on the origin of *species* — different types of creatures. I was part of a team that tried to tackle the problem from as many angles as possible. The field of genetics — the study of inheritance at the DNA level — became key.

In 2013, I published the first of several papers on the origin of species. Rather than study the DNA of species directly, I compared their genetic sequences indirectly. *Proteins* are encoded by DNA, and comparison of protein sequences among species is a useful way to gain insights into their DNA differences. I compared the protein sequences from more than 2,700 different species, and I used the results to predict the function of the similarities and differences among these sequences.[2]

At the close of the paper, I examined another type of DNA finding: the rate at which DNA sequences change from generation to generation. The rates for a particular type of DNA[3] were known for only four types of creatures. Of the four, three were animal species. The fourth was our own species — humans. At the time, I treated the human data as a clue to the larger animal questions. But as I dove deeper into the data, the human connection grew.

In 2015, I published the next set of findings in two papers. One paper examined the patterns in which new types of animals formed from preexisting types.[4] The second paper focused exclusively on humans and again on the rate at which DNA sequences change from generation to generation.[5]

In 2016, this cycle repeated itself. I published a large paper on the mechanism by which new animal, plant, and fungal species form.[6] Then I published a second paper, digging even deeper into the question of the speed at which DNA changes in humans.[7]

By this time, the potential impact of these findings on the history of civilization was hard to miss. So I began to ask questions of the dataset that focused on events from the history of humanity.[8]

In 2020, the answers exploded. From the family trees I was exploring, the echoes of the history of civilization were jumping out. Here, right in front of me, were the marks of the Mongol conquest of Asia and Europe, of the Russian expansion from eastern Europe to the Pacific, of the long isolation of African and Chinese civilizations, and of so much more. Even more tantalizing were the histories of places whose story, to date, had consisted largely of pre-history[9] — such as the pre-Columbian Americas and pre-colonial Australian, Papua New Guinea, and the Pacific.

---

2. Jeanson (2013).
3. Specifically, for mitochondrial DNA.
4. Jeanson (2015a).
5. Jeanson (2015b).
6. Jeanson and Lisle (2016).
7. Jeanson (2016).
8. Jeanson (2019); Jeanson and Holland (2019); Jeanson (2020).
9. I.e., the time period before written records were created to document historical events.

Most shocking were the connections among the various civilizations — and the implications for human ethnic identity.

****

In this book, we'll explore some of the answers I've begun to uncover — answers you won't find anywhere else. These answers are also just the tip of the iceberg. Of the billions of people who roam our planet, we have public access to the DNA from only thousands of them. The conclusions you will find in this book are based on these sequences. These conclusions will likely be updated and may change as more data comes in.

Some readers might find that last sentence unsettling. It's actually a distinguishing feature of science. By definition, scientific ideas must be open to change and even to direct disproof. Uncertainty, rather than certainty, is the rule in science.

However, despite this uncertainty, scientific conclusions can still be useful. The ultimate standard in science is whether something *works*. We invoke gravity because it works. It successfully explains and predicts activity in the physical world. The ultimate test of the conclusions of this book is whether they work — whether they successfully explain the history we know, and whether they successfully predict future historical-genetic discoveries. I'll leave it to you, the reader, to decide whether the conclusions in this book meet this standard.

In communicating where the project is right now, I hope to give you a taste of the wild and emerging field of historical genetics. I also hope to inspire the next generation of budding historians, archaeologists, geneticists, linguists, and anthropologists to dive in and take the research even further.

For everyone else, my hope is that you'll wonder and marvel at the story of humankind — in ways you've never dreamed of marveling before.

The 30,000-foot View

Before we take our journey together, let's sketch the outline of our path.

In chapters 2 through 4, I lay out some of the background findings to these recent genetic discoveries. I do so because these recent genetic discoveries are shocking — so shocking that you might be tempted to dismiss them. The background of chapters 2 through 4 is needed context for what we'll encounter. In one sense, these chapters are a reminder to me: I frequently invoke these conclusions in my own mind as I evaluate and reevaluate the unexpected implications of genetics.

In chapters 5 through 12, we'll focus our historical and genetic searches on seven ancient or prehistorical (i.e., pre-written records) civilizations — those of the ancient Egyptians, the ancient Romans, the ancient Persians, the earliest Indians (i.e., from South Asia, not the Americas), the ancient Chinese, the indigenous Easter Islanders, and the Native Americans. We'll explore their rise and fall through the DNA of modern peoples. We'll take DNA from modern Egyptians, modern Italians, modern Iranians, modern Indians, modern Chinese, modern Easter Islanders, and modern Native Americans. And we'll compare their DNA to DNA from modern peoples around the globe.

For chapters 13 and 14, we'll look deep into the past and then into the future. Using genetic clues from one of the smaller but well-known ancient Near Eastern peoples, we'll uncover how the human story began. Then we'll step back to evaluate the bigger picture. Once we identify the biggest outstanding historical mysteries, we'll gaze into the future and assess our chances of solving them.

If I had read the previous paragraphs just a few years ago, I probably would have been disappointed. Yes, Native Americans and Easter Islanders are groups outside the emphasis of the typical world history class. But Egyptians, Romans, and Persians? We hear about them all the time. Why not explore the history of sub-Saharan Africa before the arrival of Europeans? Or northern Europe before the time of the Romans? Hearing again the history of the tried-and-true historical locations would have seemed tiresome and unhelpful. At least, it would have seemed so until recently.

In our journey, we'll discover that, in trying to tell the stories of these seven civilizations, we'll end up telling the story of the whole world.

How to use this book

Whether you're a lay reader or a technical reader, I think you'll find this book unlike any that you've read before. In light of this prospect, I've included the following tips to help you navigate it and make the most of your journey.

First, a picture is worth a thousand words. This adage is especially true when exploring the hidden parts of human history. This history is locked away in our family trees and in the geography of our ancestors; the color plates are where this information jumps out. I recommend that, while you read the text, you keep a finger in the section containing the illustrations. This way you can easily move back and forth between text and color plates, and the conclusions will make more sense.

Another reason to keep your finger in the illustrations section is that I've deliberately designed the color plates as memory aids. The details of the genetic history of humanity can easily become overwhelming. In the color plates, I've color-coded the details to make them easier to remember.

Second, a brief heads-up on the pacing and scope of the scientific detail: In Part I (chapters 2 through 4), you'll likely find the content to be leisurely and light. The subjects are familiar, but the conclusions are not. These chapters take straightforward topics and give them an unexpected twist.

In Parts II and III (chapters 5–14), the pacing and scope shifts. Instead of tackling familiar themes, these chapters blaze new trails. They read more like a detective story. I anticipate that you'll find the material in these chapters to be less familiar and more intense. I synthesize evidence from geography, languages, written records, and DNA to derive the rest of the story of history — the part of history that my high school class never covered. If at any time the path becomes hard to find, just skip to the end of the chapter where I've written short chapter summaries in bullet point format. Then, armed with this information, you can return to the section that you were just reading. Alternatively, you might start each chapter by reading the summaries, and then going through the chapter text.

Third, for technical readers and for skeptical ones, Appendix A has the technical details on my conclusions as well as pointers to more in-depth papers and online tables. If you're looking for the step-by-step answers to *How did he derive that conclusion?* then Appendix A is the place to start.

On a related note, Appendix B deals with contemporary origins controversies, like the creation/evolution debate, and how this book relates to these disputes.

Fourth, in the spring and summer of 2020, I recorded a video series describing early stages of this research. During and after the completion of the video series, I received many questions from viewers who wanted to find out their own history with genetic testing. Appendix C walks you through the steps to answer that question. It also contains the key findings from chapters 5 through 14 for those who want a quick reference for what the results of their genetic tests mean.

I hope these tips will make your search for the hidden history of humankind as exciting as the search has been for me.

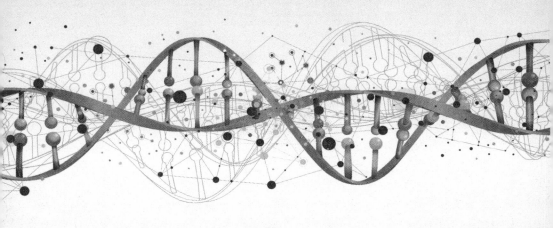

Part I: Early Clues

2

Smaller Than We Think

On February 25, 2012, in a small church in the center of Birmingham, Alabama, I married the love of my life. Growing up, I wasn't sure that this day would come. My ethnic and cultural background had raised questions for which I didn't have ready answers.

Despite being born in the heart of the Midwest, I grew up bilingual. My American dad had enlisted in the military, met a German woman while overseas, married her, and settled in the U.S. Wisconsin was a thoroughly English-speaking context in which to raise a family. Yet my mother made sure to teach German to my siblings and me so we could speak to our German relatives.

Culturally, Wisconsin wasn't the only influence on my upbringing. Almost every year, I would see my German relatives for weeks at a time. Usually, we would fly to Germany and stay with my grandparents. Part of our time together would include seeing tourist sites. But most of the trip was simply living with my German grandparents, doing what they did alongside them: Going to German grocery stores, bakeries, and butchers; eating what Germans eat; driving what Germans drive; and playing what Germans play — *Fußball* (soccer). We created rich memories together. For this American son, the other side of the Atlantic became, over time, a home away from home.

As I matured toward marrying age, I began to wonder how my heritage would affect my family prospects. I asked my mother if she thought I should look for a German spouse rather than an American one. Or, I thought, maybe a wife from either country would create problems. After all, I had my feet in both worlds.

Eventually, I recognized what years of living in the United States had produced: A thorough-going American with German ties. My now-wife, a southern belle who had been born in Italy to missionary parents, didn't have German ties. But I felt at ease marrying her. For both of us, English was our first language; American was our primary culture.

Implicit in my little marriage dilemma was a fact we all take for granted: Linguistic heritage and cultural heritage naturally direct our choices in mates. I thought my bilingual and bicultural upbringing would add extra constraints to my marriage prospects. In the end, I followed the path that most Americans do: Marrying someone who shares the same primary language and traditions.

These types of constraints exist all around the globe, but they are felt more acutely when different cultures exist in close geographic proximity. For example, today, modern Greeks and Egyptians reside only a few hundred miles apart on the Mediterranean Sea (**Color Plate 1**). Yet they exist in dramatically different worlds. Greek nationals belong to a country that is a member of the European Union. Egyptians are geographically African. Greeks speak the language that gives them their name and that ties them back to Alexander the Great. Most Egyptians speak the language of the nation's Muslim conquerors — Arabic. In terms of religious practice, faithful Greeks attend churches — Greek Orthodox ones. Faithful Egyptian Muslims frequent mosques.

Naturally, these differences preclude much mixing between these two peoples. I can't imagine many single Greek men spending their time looking for *hijab*-clad spouses. And why should they? If a Greek man wanted to marry someone outside his nationality, why choose Egyptian? Why not French? Or Spanish? German? Serbian? Perhaps Romanian or Swedish? Or Irish? Turkish? How about Pakistani? Nigerian? Angolan? Chinese? Vietnamese? Samoan? Peruvian? The world is a big place — too big to assume that any two of the vast numbers of peoples will regularly intermingle. There are just too many options.

For that matter, why go looking outside Greece at all? With a population of more than 10 million, Greece must surely offer the single Greek man plenty of options for a wife. Similarly, why send Egyptian men beyond the borders of Egypt to find a spouse? With a population of nearly 100 million, Egypt must surely offer the average Arabic-speaking man a litany of choices for potential nuptials.

But what about the Greeks and Egyptians of ancient times? Would the same rules have applied? Would they have lived in separate worlds, never to intermingle or mix their family trees?

Politically and culturally, ancient Egypt and ancient Greece looked as different from one another as do modern Egyptians and modern Greeks. In Egypt, the Pharaohs commissioned elaborate pyramid tombs, built the Sphinx, and etched their histories in engravings and art forms that are unmistakably Egyptian. The Greeks built the Parthenon. Egyptians were ruled by Pharaohs. The Greeks gave us democracy. Linguistically, Egyptian hieroglyphics were as different from the Greek script of Aristotle as you can get.

On their face, these differences suggest that these ancient peoples kept to themselves. This is the default conclusion I grew up with. And it's one I've since learned to reject.

Full

Take a look at a current political map of the globe (**Color Plate 2**). I'm guessing that it's pretty familiar to you. Even if you don't look at maps on a regular basis, you probably still have an image like this burned into your mind. Even if parts of your mental map are fuzzy, I'm sure you have a sense for how high and wide the major landmasses are.

Furthermore, I'm sure that your mental map is *full*. We visualize a map in which every square inch of the globe is claimed by someone. No blanks exist. Fuzzy parts, yes. For example, in homes in the West, the former Soviet republics in Central Asia — Kazakhstan, Uzbekistan, Kyrgyzstan, Turkmenistan, and Tajikistan — are not the typical topics of dinnertime conversations. Neither are the fine details of Southeast Asian countries — Laos, Cambodia, Thailand, Malaysia, Brunei. But we know that even the fuzzy parts are political entities ruled by someone, even if we don't know the details of who the someones are.

Naturally, when we think about the beginning of human civilization, this modern map subconsciously nags at our thinking. Today, we know that all the land on the globe has been claimed. Yet at the beginning of human history, the map was drastically different.

Cradles of Civilization

The earliest human civilizations were born in places that we term *cradles*. The ancient Aegeans (the Minoans and Mycenaeans) and the ancient Egyptians created two of them. Mesopotamians, South Asians, East Asians, and Central Americans also birthed the earliest human civilizations (**Color Plate 3**).

But why in these places? Or, to put it in terms that nagged at me while growing up, what was going on in the rest of the world? Why didn't the people in the rest of the world also create civilizations? What were they doing?

Consider the vast geographic region of Russian Siberia (**Color Plate 2**). We know that the people of Siberia came from...someone. Yet the first human civilizations never touched Siberia. As another example, a great diversity of people roam modern Europe — Irish, British, French, Spanish, Portuguese, German, Swiss, Norwegian, Danish, Swedish, Finnish, Italian, Polish, and on and on the list of modern nationalities goes. Again, we know that these peoples must have come from someone. Yet the maps of the earliest stages of human history show a big blank in these regions. In ancient times, no civilizations formed there.

On other continents, the same questions arise. Who did the Sudanese come from? Who gave rise to the Ethiopians? The Kenyans? The Zambians? The Nigerians? How about the Australian Aborigines? Who were their ancestors? What about the Navajos of North America? The Guaraní of South America?

The more you look at the details of the modern globe, the bigger the mystery of early human history.

Perhaps you can understand my shock, then, when I first saw a map of modern population density (**Color Plate 4**). Do you see how much of the world is virtually empty of people? Remember: This map shows the modern era. Civilization is largely absent from large chunks of the globe *today*.

Notice how much of Canada and Russia are blank. With few exceptions, North and Southwest Africa are equally empty. In **Color Plate 4**, Australia looks almost uninhabited. The Arabian Peninsula is sparsely populated, as is the Amazon in South America and the Rocky Mountain region of North America. In modern China, the land of more than 1 billion people, the population is concentrated in just half of the total landmass.

Historical Population Density

Now let's expand our horizons to the past. How did the map of peoples — not polities — look in the ancient past?

Take a look at population density in 1000 B.C. (**Color Plate 5**). In sub-Saharan Africa, few people exist. Similarly, the Americas show little sign of human occupation. The Olmec civilization exists in Mexico. But most of the rest of the Americas are empty. In Southeast Asia, in Australia, in the Pacific, and in Central Asia, few people reside, and so history books don't cover them. Instead, they focus on the densely populated regions like India, China, and the Mediterranean lands.

But wait, you might say. Couldn't our understanding of population densities simply be a consequence of the presence or absence of historical records? In other words, isn't the evidence behind the population density map of 1000 B.C. an artifact of what we know or don't know from historical records? Maybe many people *did* roam these regions, but we just haven't discovered the evidence for them yet? Perhaps.

But population densities are determined not solely from written historical records — records like the ancient Roman and Chinese censuses. Archaeology also fills in the gaps. For example, some of the sites without written records, like pre-Roman northern and western Europe, still show strong population sizes (**Color Plate 5**).

More importantly, if you compare the map of population density to other maps of earth, the absence of peoples makes sense. Siberia and Canada are mostly empty because they're some of the coldest places on earth (**Color Plate 6**). North Africa holds few people; it also holds the largest desert in the world — the Sahara (**Color Plate 7**). Deserts stretch across Southwest Africa and the Middle East, and the dry outback covers most of Australia. The Rocky Mountains slice through much of western North America, and the landmass connecting the Middle East to India — i.e., Iran, Afghanistan, and Pakistan — is covered with mountains. Few people have tried to call these areas home. Similarly, few have tried to eke out an existence in the thin air of the Tibetan plateau. The absence of peoples at these heights is understandable.

These features would have been present in 1000 B.C. It makes sense that these same factors would constrain population densities in the ancient past.

Let's watch how this ancient map matures. One thousand years later (A.D. 1), little has changed (**Color Plate 8**). Sub-Saharan Africa, the Americas, Southeast Asia, Australia, the Pacific, and Central Asia remain mostly empty. In contrast, where people are concentrated, history books make mention — Egypt, the Mediterranean, and the Middle East (all under Roman rule); Central America (under Mayan rule); India (under various rulers); and China (under Han Dynasty rule).

Fast forward another thousand years to A.D. 1000 (**Color Plate 9**), and previously sleepy regions begin to wake. For example, in Southeast Asia and West Africa, people begin to concentrate. Consequently, history books mention the Khmer empire in Southeast Asia and the Ghana empire in West Africa. As another example, in the Americas, the previous loci of peoples expand. Though the Classic Mayan civilization has just collapsed, Central America is just a few hundred years removed from the rise of the Aztecs, and South America is anticipating the rise of the Incas.

In the rest of the map, the human story continues to march forward at the traditional foci of activity. Europe's population continues to grow, despite the raids of the Vikings. In the Middle East, the Arab Muslim conquerors continue to dominate. Far to the east in China, the Song Dynasty reigns, and to the south in India, multiple kingdoms cover the landscape.

Moving forward in time from A.D. 1000 (**Color Plate 9**) to the present (**Color Plate 4**), the map undergoes a noticeable change. Yellow intensifies to red, as population densities suddenly increase in China, Southeast Asia, India, Europe, and parts of Africa. The Americas also show sudden signs of life. In the previous population density maps, the changes didn't look quite this dramatic (compare **Color Plates 5, 8, and 9** to one another). The color transitions between maps were smoother. Why?

Explosion

When King David was on the throne of Israel around 1000 B.C., the entire world population was around only 50 million people.[1] A thousand years later (A.D. 1), this number had more than tripled to

---

1. McEvedy and Jones (1975); also for the rest of the paragraph and subsequent paragraphs.

almost 170 million. However, in the coming centuries, several factors kept the rate of population growth low. For example, by the A.D. 500s, the western Roman Empire had fallen, and China had experienced its own tumult. Consequently, from A.D. 1 to A.D. 1000, the world population grew more slowly. In fact, it didn't even double in size. By A.D. 1000, the world population sat at 265 million.

The world population took a hit when the Black Death swept through parts of Asia and then into Europe. Pre-Black Death, in A.D. 1200, the world population had reached 360 million. Because of the Black Death, it dipped to 350 million in A.D. 1400.

And then the population took off.

Today, nearly 8 billion people roam the earth. In other words, in just 600 years, the world population has grown over *20-fold*. This is a remarkable rate of increase. By contrast, the 2,400 years prior to A.D. 1400 saw an increase of only 7-fold (**Color Plate 10**). The arrival of modern medicine and of improvements in agriculture and technology have combined to produce an explosion in human population size.

This explains why the history of the world looks so empty for most of the past several thousand years. Only in the last few hundred years has the human population grown to such an extent that nations have extended their political reach across every terrestrial part of the globe.

In other words, we live in a unique era of human history.

The Ancient World

In the simplest sense, we know that everyone — including the ancients — came from...*somebody*. But the history of human population growth casts this fact in a new light. You don't have to go far back in history to see that there were far fewer *somebodies* alive then, than are alive today. Just a few hundred years ago, the peoples of the globe were fewer in number and more limited in their geographic reach. Eligible bachelors had a much smaller pool of potential spouses from which to pick.

Let's make that statement more concrete.

Say you're browsing a dating website today, and it reports 100 people who might be a good match to you. Just six hundred years ago, an analogous process would have returned only 5 matches — because, back then, the world population was 20-fold smaller than today. And going back even further in history, the pool would have been even smaller. The single men would have gone looking for spouses and found the list of candidates to be small.

When for millennia — uninterrupted — you face slim pickings, at some point you have to settle for someone who might be a fourth cousin. Or closer. Or you might go looking outside your ethnic group.

Choose the latter, and you've begun to bring the genealogies of the world together.

This is the situation that faced the ancient Aegeans and Egyptians. Ancient Greece didn't have 10 million people. Instead, in 1250 B.C., about 1 million resided there.[2] Ancient Egypt wasn't populated by 100 million people. In 1200 B.C., around 3 million called the Nile Valley home.[3]

In terms of eligible bachelors, ancient Greece would have had far fewer than 1 million. Assuming a 50:50 split of males and females, only 500,000 males would have lived in ancient Greece. If we assume a 1:1:1 breakdown of children versus marriable adults versus elderly, then less than 170,000 men were looking to start families in 1250 B.C. In other words, modern New York City has 50 times[4] as many people as *the entire land* of ancient Greece had men of marriable age.

How often did the peoples of ancient Greece and ancient Egypt intermix? Much more than we expect — because the ancient world was much smaller than we think.

---

2. McEvedy and Jones (1975), p. 110.
3. McEvedy and Jones (1975), p. 226.
4. https://www.census.gov/quickfacts/fact/table/newyorkcitynewyork/PST045219.

Chapter 2 Summary:

- Normally, language and culture constrain our choices in mates.

- Political maps of the globe imply that a multitude of languages and cultures exist across the entire surface of the earth. From this perspective, it's hard to imagine that these diverse groups regularly mixed.

- Population density maps of the globe show that languages and cultures have a much narrower geographic distribution. From this perspective, it's easier for these diverse groups to intermix.

- Compared to the present, populations in the ancient past were even more geographically restricted, and their numbers were far lower.

- Fewer people meant fewer options for mates.

- Fewer options for mates would have brought the genealogies of the world together, making the ancient world smaller than we think.

3

More Connected Than We Think

In 1492, Columbus completed a voyage with monumental implications for the world. Several hundred years earlier, the Viking Leif Erickson had landed on the shores of modern Canada. Nevertheless, it was Columbus, not Leif Erickson, who brought the Old and New Worlds together for the first time in a lasting way (**Color Plate 11**).

Or so we've been taught.

Growing up, I had little reason to question this narrative. Surely Native Americans and Europeans had lived separate lives for millennia in their own continents, never to mix until the European Age of Exploration.

On the surface, all the evidence pointed to the vast gulf between these peoples. For example, before Columbus, European empires never ruled the New World. The reverse was also true. Politically, the Americas had no relevance to the rise and fall of kingdoms in Europe.

Culturally, the contrast between the European colonists and the Native Americans is the stuff of infamy. Neither side seemed to understand the other. Linguistically, they couldn't communicate. And culturally, the cotton-garment, glass-window-house, horse-drawn-carriage, firearms-protected European way of life was foreign to the Native Americans, just as much as the buffalo-robed, animal-skinned-tipi, horse-less,[1] bow-and-arrow-protected Native American way of life was to the Europeans.

---

1. They were horseless before Europeans arrived.

But do these differences tell the whole story? Before Columbus, how disconnected were the genealogies of the peoples of the Old and New Worlds? How far apart were the Mayans and the Germans? The Sioux and the Vikings? How long ago had their family lines separated? Did Leif Erickson leave a genealogical legacy in the New World? Did any Europeans before him? Did any Native Americans leave descendants in Europe?

Too Many Ancestors

To answer these questions, let's not turn to written records or DNA sequences. Instead, let's turn to math. Not to complicated math, but to basic addition, subtraction, and multiplication.

Let's start by picking an average Native American man and then tracing his ancestors back in time. We don't need any names or locations of the ancestors. Just numbers. To make our illustration more concrete, let's say that this individual is a warrior from the Sioux tribe. Watch what happens:

We know that every person has two biological parents. Each of these parents also comes from two parents. Which means that this particular Sioux individual had four grandparents.

So far, so good.

Each grandparent also comes from two parents. Now we're up to eight great-grandparents. Double eight to get sixteen great-great-grandparents. See the pattern? We double the number of ancestors at each generation. This Sioux warrior would have had thirty-two great-great-great-grandparents.

Now let's put these numbers in a concrete historical context.

To keep the math simple, let's say the Sioux warrior was born in A.D. 900 — before Leif Erickson and Columbus arrived. Let's also say that, in each prior generation, people married and bore children at age 25. Thus, to go back a generation, just subtract 25 years. His parents would have therefore been born in A.D. 875, his grandparents in A.D. 850, his great-grandparents in A.D. 825. How many ancestors would he have had in A.D. 625 — two hundred years before his great-grandparents were born?

In A.D. 625 in North America, the ancestors of our Sioux warrior would have represented the great-great-great-great-great-great-great-great-great-grandparent generation. And there would have been 2,048 of them. This is a large number. But now compare it to something more familiar. At this time in history, Europe was in the Dark Ages. The population of all of Europe was around 26 million. Compared to this number, the number of Sioux warrior ancestors is tiny — only 0.008% of the total population in Europe.

What if we step back in time another 200 years to A.D. 425? The ancestors of our Native American would have been his grandparents with seventeen "great" prefixes. Numerically, there would have been 524,288 of them. Now compare this number again to something more familiar. At this time in history, the western Roman Empire was at its end. Tribes of Germanic barbarians had already breached the borders and had begun sacking the empire. The population of all of Europe was around 31 million. Compared to this number, the number of Sioux warrior ancestors is just a small fraction — only 1.7% of the total population in Europe.

Drop back another 100 years to A.D. 325, and the numbers get wild. For context, at this stage of history, the Roman Empire across the ocean had not yet been overthrown. The population of Europe was around 33 million. The ancestors of our Sioux man would have represented the grandparents with twenty-one "great" prefixes. And there would be more than 8 million of them — about one-fourth of the total people in Europe.

If we go back to A.D. 125, the population of Europe remains about the same. But the ancestors of our Sioux warrior (i.e., the grandparents with twenty-nine "great" prefixes) do not. More than 2 *billion* in number, these ancestors would have exceeded, not just the entire population of Europe, but the entire population of the globe, which was around 180 million.

Surely this cannot be true.

Before we attempt to solve our little mathematical dilemma in the Americas, let's reflect on the situation across the ocean in Europe. Take your average European. In A.D. 900, this European could have been a Viking. The math for the ancestors of this Viking works the same way and produces the same result as it did for the Sioux warrior. In A.D. 625, this Viking would have had 2,048 great-great-great-great-great-great-great-great-great-grandparents. In A.D. 325 he would have had 8 million ancestors, and 2 *billion* ancestors in A.D. 125.

In fact, for every person alive back then — not just our Sioux warrior and Viking — the math works out basically the same way. What's the solution?

Let's approach the problem visually.

As we draw the theoretical family tree of our Sioux warrior, the number of branches increases with the number of his ancestors (**Color Plate 12**). We know from the math we just explored that the number of ancestors eventually exceeds the number of people in the globe. Since the branches reflect this, they must also eventually explode in number. How do we stop this from occurring?

The solution is simple: *Connect the ancestral branches* (**Color Plate 13**).

At some point, *the paternal lineage of the Sioux warrior must connect to his maternal lineage.* This solves our math problem by reducing the number of ancestors. And it still fulfills the biological requirement of each person having two parents.

Recent Ancestors

When would these genealogical connections — between the paternal and maternal lineages — have occurred? In 2004, a group of scientists ran computer simulations to explore the global family tree of humanity.[2] Running realistic versions of these scenarios would have required enormous amounts of computing power. So they started with an unrealistic, simplistic scenario and then worked outward from that.

The scenario they conceived deliberately ignored the geographic and language complexities of our globe. Language barriers obviously make inter-ethnic marriages challenging. Most people marry spouses they can talk to. (Wouldn't you?) Also, in earlier eras of human history, technological sophistication wasn't what it is today. Geographic separation made marrying a distant bride more challenging. The 2004 team pretended these language barriers and geographic hurdles didn't exist — at least for the initial rounds of their simulations.

In these initial rounds, the researchers employed a math formula to calculate how long ago the common ancestor of everyone lived. I'll omit the complex math details and just give the results. In a nutshell, the scientists modeled how family trees come together and connect — similar to what we just uncovered in our own calculations. But they

---

2. Rohde, Olson, and Chang (2004).

ran these calculations for everyone, not just one person like the Sioux warrior or Viking.

To illustrate what they found, we need to decide on the size of the population for which we want to run the formula. We can pick whatever size we like, and the formula will tell us how long ago the ancestor of *everyone in that population* lived.

For example, let's say we specify the global population in A.D. 900 as being 1,000 people in size. Obviously, it wasn't 1,000 people; it was around 200 million. But the number 1,000 is a good place to start to see how this formula works. (Again, we're assuming that no geographic or language barriers existed among these 1,000 people. Anyone can marry anyone else.) When did this ancestor live? According to the formula, about 250 years prior. Subtracted from the year A.D. 900, this puts the date for this person around A.D. 650.

What if the global population were 100,000 people in size? Again, same assumptions — no geographic or language barriers existed among these 100,000 people. When did their ancestor live? According to the formula, about 415 years prior. Subtracted from the year A.D. 900, this puts the date for this person around A.D. 485.

Let's run the formula again, but this time with 10 *million* people. When did the ancestor of these 10 million people live? According to the formula, only about 580 years prior. Subtracted from the year A.D. 900, this puts the date for this person around A.D. 320.

Do you think the dates drop much more into the distant past for 200 million people? The ancestor for this group would have lived around the year A.D. 210.

Just to clarify, this calculation does not imply that *only one person was alive in A.D. 210.* Instead, it's saying that many people were alive in A.D. 210, but that one person alive back then *could have had all those alive in A.D. 900 — from North America to Europe and beyond — as his direct descendants.*

You might ask, "But we've assumed away geographic and language barriers, haven't we?" The answer is yes. And if you make migration harder, the family tree connections happen more slowly.[3]

Nevertheless, *all it takes is a single wanderer to leave his homeland and venture out to a foreign land to make the family trees connect.* Or to put it differently, only a stubborn line of division — a tenaciously

---

3. Kelleher et al. (2016).

uncrossable barrier to migration — would have kept the genealogies of the pre-Columbian Old and New Worlds apart.

These principles apply to more than just the question of Old and New World relationships. They apply to every ancient culture that existed. Without a stubborn line of division, the genealogies of ancient Egyptians would have mixed with ancient Greeks. The ancient Romans would have mixed with the ancient Chinese. The ancient Israelites would have mixed with the early peoples of the Pacific. Each group would have mixed with all the rest. Only an uncrossable barrier could have kept them apart.

The genealogies of the ancients were more connected than we think.

Chapter 3 Summary:

- We've been taught that Old World and New World peoples didn't meet until Leif Erickson and Columbus landed in the Americas.

- Basic biology allows us to calculate the number of ancestors for every person alive before Erickson and Columbus.

- Less than 1,000 years before Erickson, the theoretical number of ancestors for any person alive in his day would have exceeded the global population size — a mathematical impossibility.

- The solution to this mathematical impossibility is to connect the paternal and maternal branches of each person's family tree — or to connect the branches of a person's family tree to the branches of another person's family tree.

- This mathematical result raises the possibility that Old World and New World peoples may have met and married before Erickson and Columbus arrived.

4

Faster Than We Think

In central China during the third century B.C., Qin Shihuangdi ("First Sovereign Emperor"[1]) prepared a tomb for himself unlike any the world had seen before — or since. It lay hidden for millennia until, in 1974, his terracotta army was unearthed (**Color Plate 14**).

On their own merits, the lifelike features of these thousands of soldiers impress the viewer. Upon reflection, they also raise intriguing questions. To any observer, these soldiers bear the obvious ethnic features of East Asians (**Color Plate 15**). The shape of their eyes and faces, together with their straight hair, all recall characteristics common among East Asians today. Does this mean East Asians have always looked this way?

In ancient Egypt, the Pharaohs also memorialized themselves. They did so through statues, reliefs, and other forms of art. They also depicted their non-Egyptian neighbors. One such neighbor was shown as very dark-skinned; Egyptians represented themselves as lighter-skinned. From this perspective, ancient Egyptians appear to have had features more in common with modern Arabs than with modern sub-Saharan Africans. Does this mean that Egyptians have always looked this way — never dark-skinned?

In other words, if you're once a lighter-skinned Egyptian, are you always a lighter-skinned Egyptian? If you once bear East Asian features, do you always bear East Asian features?

---

1. https://www.britannica.com/biography/Qin-Shi-Huang.

Have the ethnicities of antiquity been preserved in modern peoples who roam the geographic realms of the ancients?

Among living peoples, the bushmen, or *Khoisan* (**Color Plate 16**), of southwestern Africa have become scientific rock stars of sorts. They possess some of the greatest genetic diversity of any people group alive today. In mainstream science, they're also considered one of the earliest people groups to have arisen on earth.

Linguistically, they stand apart from the rest of Africa. Their vocabulary includes a series of clicks and other sounds foreign to the Western ear. In terms of language classification, they belong to a group that is restricted largely to southwestern Africa, with a few scattered locations elsewhere in Africa. They do not belong to the language groups that dominate West, Central, and North Africa.

At first glance, you might not notice anything unusual about their physical features. While lighter-skinned than a typical Sudanese, they still have a brown skin tone. Their tightly curled hair is also unmistakably associated with sub-Saharan Africa.

But their eyes seem to tell a different story. Their shape does not resemble the common appearance of eyes among West and Central Africans. The Khoisan look different. In fact, they look more at home in East Asia — among the Chinese.

Who did the Khoisan come from?

****

In 2015 upon moving to Kentucky, I purchased a home in a middle-class subdivision on the edge of rural farmland. My wife and children and I had lived there for only a few years when a pair of window salespeople came to our door. Being a nerdy geneticist, I naturally turned our conversation to ancestry and heritage. (Yes, I have these conversations with random strangers.)

Both of the window salespeople were African-American. One was a student studying anthropology, and she let me guess her heritage based on her features. The shape of her eyes and cheekbones reminded me strongly of the Khoisan. So I guessed that her ancestors came from southwestern Africa or someplace with similar-looking people.

I was wrong. She said her mother was African-American. And her dad was Pakistani. The marriage between Africa and Asia had produced her unique physical characteristics.

From a genetics perspective, this result was not at all surprising. To understand why, all you need is the simple genetics that you learned in high school — Punnett Squares.

To keep our discussion easy to follow, let's oversimplify. Let's designate the genetic information for light skin with lowercase letters — *a* and *b*. To designate the genetic information for dark skin, let's use uppercase letters — *A* and *B*.

What happens when a light-skinned man marries a dark-skinned woman? What will their children look like? If you personally know families of mixed ethnicities, then you've already witnessed the answer (e.g., see **Color Plate 17** where the ethnicities of the parents are reversed, but the outcome is the same).

Now let's derive it from basic genetic principles. In fact, let's derive an answer from the genetic extremes. Let's examine the hypothetical marriage of a very light-skinned man to a very dark-skinned woman. We'll make the man as light-skinned as your average Finnish male. And we'll make the woman as dark-skinned as the average Sudanese female.

The genetics of the skin tone of this couple would match their physical appearances. The light skin of the Finnish man would be genetically encoded by all lowercase letters. We would represent him as *aabb*. Conversely, the dark skin of the Sudanese woman would be genetically encoded by all uppercase letters. We would represent her as *AABB*.

I've doubled up on each letter for a reason. We all have two copies — and sometimes two versions — of our genetic information because each of our two parents contributes the information to us. The Finnish man has two copies (but identical versions, both lowercase) of the *a*'s and two copies (but identical versions, both lowercase) of the *b*'s. The same is true for the Sudanese woman — two copies (but identical versions, both uppercase) of the *A*'s and two copies (but identical versions, both uppercase) of the *B*'s.

To predict the skin tone of their children, we can use a Punnett Square (**Color Plate 18**). This predicts the children to all be middle brown in their skin tone (i.e., *AaBb*), just like what we see in today in families of mixed ethnicities (i.e., **Color Plate 17**).

Once these children grew up and married spouses, what would their children (i.e., the grandchildren of the Finnish-Sudanese couple) look like? It depends on who they married. Let's say that they were living in Sudan. Presumably, they would marry dark-skinned individuals. If so, we can predict the skin tone of their children (i.e., the grandchildren of the original Finnish-Sudanese couple) with a Punnett Square (**Color Plate 19**). As you can see, on average around a fourth of them would return to the skin tone that was as dark as the original Sudanese mother/grandmother.

Alternatively, this scenario may have played out in Finland. Here, the children presumably would have grown up and married light-skinned individuals. Again, we can predict the skin tone of their children (i.e., the grandchildren of the original Finnish-Sudanese couple) with a Punnett Square (**Color Plate 20**). Around a fourth of them would return to the skin tone that was as light as the original Finnish father/grandfather.

In other words, ethnic change can happen quickly. Though I've oversimplified this particular example, the basic principles still apply.

The same principles also apply to other biological features. Hair type (straight, wavy, curly), hair color (from blond to black), cheek-bone position (high to low), eye shape (slanted or not), eye color (blue, brown, green, etc.), and so on can disappear or reappear in subsequent generations in short order. In just a few generations, one ethnicity can be transformed into another.

So, who did the Khoisan come from? Who did the Egyptians and Chinese come from? And are modern Egyptians and Chinese the de-scendants of the original? Or have multiple rounds of ethnic change in the intervening years obscured potential links?

****

Back at my Kentucky home, the second of the two window salespeople was a middle-aged African-American man. He said he could trace his relatives back to a plantation during the days of slavery in the United States. Then his history becomes harder to trace.

If you've grown up in the United States, you probably have a ready answer as to why. The ugly history of the Trans-Atlantic slave trade began in the 1500s and mercilessly continued for three centuries. Any American who traces his ancestry back to a slave has a sharp break in his history between the New World and the Old.

The Trans-Atlantic slave trade was one of two major forced African diasporas. While the one in the Americas (the Trans-Atlantic slave trade) might be more familiar, the statistics[2] for it might not. Based on current evidence, around 12 *million* Africans were enslaved, with 10.7 million surviving the journey to the Americas. Fifty percent disembarked in South America. The remaining half were divided between the Caribbean (40%) and the U.S. (10%). Less than 1% ended up in Europe. Based on the few slaves (~100,000) that were rescued from slave ships near the end of the slave trade, about two-thirds of the slaves were men; the rest, women.[3] In terms of geography, slaves were bought almost exclusively on the west coasts of both West and Central Africa. Though the Trans-Atlantic slave trade lasted more than 300 years, the late 1700s and early 1800s saw the peak in this nasty transport of human cargo.

The second major forced African diaspora was the Islamic slave trade. This lesser-known slave trade differed from the Trans-Atlantic on nearly every point — except in sheer numbers.[4] In total, around 11.5 million Africans were taken from their homes and shipped to far-away Muslim lands over the duration of this foul practice. The Islamic slave trade lasted much longer than the Trans-Atlantic. It didn't begin in the A.D. 1500s. Instead, it commenced in the A.D. 600s and lasted into the 1800s. Also, because Middle Eastern Muslim lands lay east and north of Africa, slaves were drawn primarily from the east coast, not the west coast, of Africa. In addition, Muslims were interested in slave girls for their households; hence, the majority of the slaves in the Islamic trade were women, not men.

What happened to them?

For the fate of the Trans-Atlantic slaves, many people in the U.S. think they have a good answer: The African slaves were sold onto U.S. plantations, kept in isolated communities, abused by the plantation owners, eventually emancipated, kept isolated again via segregation, and only within the last 50 years did they begin to be integrated into American society.

What about the slaves from the Islamic slave trade? What happened to those people?

Historically, Islamic kingdoms have been concentrated in the Middle East. It would be reasonable to suspect that the slaves ended

---

2. https://www.slavevoyages.org/assessment/estimates.
3. https://slavevoyages.org/resources/names-database.
4. Segal (2001).

up there. However, some Islamic kingdoms conquered territory in Europe. Might some of the slaves have integrated into European society? In recent years, voluntary immigration to Europe from the Middle East suggests a framework in which to explore this question.[5]

Because of modern events like the civil war in Syria, waves of migrants from the Middle East have flooded into Europe. On the European continent as a whole, Muslims now constitute around 5% of the total population. In Sweden and France, Muslims have reached levels of 8% to 9%.

Even if migration ceases, these percentages will likely continue to rise. Currently among non-Muslim Europeans, the birth rate is below replacement levels. In other words, if we ignore the Muslim population, Europeans are having so few children that the total population of Europe will soon begin to decline. In contrast, Muslim populations have higher birth rates. By 2050, the Muslim population of Europe is projected to reach 7% of the total, and this is without any new immigration.

To understand the significance of this number, compare it to recent figures. For example, in 2010, the Muslim population of Europe was just under 4%. If the Muslim population of Europe exceeds 7% of the total by 2050, this will represent near population *doubling* in just under *two generations*.

Now let's return to the question of the fate of slaves taken during the Islamic slave trade. How many of these African slaves ended up in Europe? Let's rephrase that question: How many would have needed to have arrived in Europe in order to have an appreciable effect on the European population of today?

Let's say that, as a result of the Islamic slave trade, 10 million African slaves made it to Europe. This is unrealistic. But it's a good starting point from which we can run some scenarios, and then we'll reassess with more realistic numbers.

In A.D. 1400, post-Black Death Europe had a total population of 60 million.[6] If, in A.D. 1400, 10 million slaves were added to this total, what happens to the population composition of Europe?

It all depends on the reproductive rates.

In 1975, the population of Europe was 635 million — about a 10-fold increase from A.D. 1400. If 10 million African slaves were added

---

5. https://www.pewforum.org/2017/11/29/europes-growing-muslim-population/.

6. McEvedy and Jones (1975).

to Europe in A.D. 1400, they would have represented about 14% of the 70 million people (60 million + 10 million) in Europe. From A.D. 1400 to A.D. 1975, a total of 575 years passed — or about 23 generations.[7] If Africans had, say, a 13% higher growth rate, how many of the 635 million Europeans in 1975 might have had African ancestry? Be careful answering with intuition. With a 13% higher growth rate, people of African descent would have represented 75%.

A 13% higher growth rate isn't easy to spot. If, in 1400, a European village had 100 European families and 100 African families, a 13% difference would have amounted to the Europeans having 104 children, and the Africans having 118. A casual observer would have had a hard time noticing a difference. Both groups of families would have had many children. The Africans would have had just a few more. Yet this difference would have been enough to dramatically change the demographics of Europe.

"But if this were true, wouldn't Europeans look dark-skinned?" Not necessarily. Dark-skinned Africans would have originally been the minority. If we assume perfect integration of the ethnicities (yes, another unrealistic scenario), then the Africans would have married Europeans. The children of African-European unions would have been middle brown (see the Punnett Squares in previous section for justification). Furthermore, among the A.D. 1400 indigenous Europeans, the vast majority of the marriages would have been European-European — because of the 60 million/10 million split in population numbers in A.D. 1400. In subsequent generations, the middle brown minority in a majority Caucasian population would likely have become completely Caucasian with time. Yet the *ancestry* — the family tree — of this Caucasian-looking population would have been majority (75%) African.

The scenario that I've just described is entirely hypothetical. But this scenario outlines what's plausible and what's not, and it sets the context for what we're about to explore.

Now let's run a more conservative scenario. Let's say that, in A.D. 1400, only 60,000 African slaves had made it into Europe. In a continent of 60 *million* people, these Africans would hardly have been noticed. What would have happened to their descendants?

Just for sake of argument, let's give them a 20% higher reproductive rate. Also, let's assume dispersal and integration into Europe, so that

---

7. Assuming a generation time of 25 years.

most of them ended up as mixed-ethnicity families. Again, only a small fraction of Europe (0.1%) would have ended up as mixed-ethnicity families. The rest (99.9%) would have been Caucasian.

In practical terms, a 20% difference in reproductive rate is low — almost unnoticeable. A group of 100 Caucasians might produce 110 children. At a 20% higher reproductive rate, 100 mixed-ethnicity families would have had 133 children. Again, in a largely Caucasian Europe, this slightly higher rate of offspring would have been difficult to notice.

Yet by A.D. 1975, this slight difference would have resulted in 6% of the European population having African ancestry. Because the overwhelming majority (99.9%) of people in A.D. 1400 were Caucasian, Europe would have remained Caucasian in A.D. 1975. But 6% of them would have been descendants of African slaves.

And all from a slight difference in reproductive rates stemming from an immigrant population.

What if the reproductive difference was higher? Say, instead of 20% higher in Africans, it was 35% higher. What would happen then? Practically, let's again assume dispersal and integration into Europe, so that most of them ended up as mixed-race families. Let's also say that 100 Caucasian families in A.D. 1400 would have produced 108 children. At a 35% higher reproductive rate, 100 mixed-ethnicity families would have had 145 children. Again, this sort of difference would have been hard to notice in a dominant sea (99.9%) of Caucasian Europeans.

But by A.D. 1975, this difference would translate to a surprising proportion of the populace. Over the span of 23 generations (A.D. 1400 to A.D. 1975), a 35% difference in reproductive rate would have meant that *50%* of Europe ended up with African ancestry.

What happened to the slaves from the Islamic slave trade? These calculations make it clear that physical appearances won't give us the answer. Basic genetics and differential reproductive rates can lead to a diversity of outcomes.

Furthermore, we could run these same sorts of calculations for other peoples and other parts of the globe. In each case, the results would be the same. Slight differences in reproductive rates can transform the ancestry of a resident population from indigenous to immigrant. And based on physical appearances, you'd never know any different.

****

In the last few years, it has become commonplace to navigate questions of ethnic ancestry with genetics. AncestryDNA, FamilyTreeD-NA, 23andMe, and other genetic testing companies promise to reveal your true ethnic heritage. Can they?

The biology behind their claims is straightforward. The same biology is also their Achilles' heel.

Biologically, you and I inherit DNA from each of our parents. Half of my DNA comes from my dad, half from my mom. Together, the two versions of DNA give me my unique combination of physical features — a combination that looks like a mix of my two parents. This fact allows us to reconstruct family trees based on the comparison of DNA sequences. The closer the DNA match between two people, the closer the genealogical relationship. The more different the DNA match, the more distant the genealogical relationship.

If you've taken a DNA test from one of the popular genetic testing companies, you're probably already familiar with this principle. And if you've overseen multiple DNA tests, you've probably already encountered its Achilles' heel.

One of my friends doubled up on testing for her parents, sending DNA from each of them to two different companies. Between the two companies, the ethnicity results didn't agree. She also had her own DNA tested. Supposedly, it revealed that she possesses low levels of an ethnicity not found in either of her parents. The levels were low enough (<5%) to avoid awkward questions of paternity. But even low levels raise unsettling questions.

Ultimately, the unsettling questions derive from one of the well-kept secrets of genetic testing. In one sense, it's not really a secret. It arises from principles found in every introductory genetics textbook.

Let's unpack this secret in the context of a common point of curiosity among Caucasian-Americans. I'll use myself as an example.

Can a standard genetic test confirm or refute the existence of a Native American in my family tree? For simplicity, let's say that the rest of my family tree consists, not of Native Americans, but of people of European descent. Let's begin our search by considering the genetics of my hypothetical Native American ancestor and the genetics of his hypothetical offspring. Let's say that he married into my family tree by marrying a woman of European descent. At the genetic level, their children would be only 50% Native American. This conclusion flows from basic biology. Since DNA is inherited from both parents, the child could not have more than 50% paternal (i.e., Native American) contribution; the other 50% would be maternal (i.e., European).

Once these children grew up, who would they marry? Since the rest of the family tree is populated by people of European descent, these children would marry other individuals of European descent. The children of these unions (i.e., the grandchildren of the Native American) would be only 25% Native American. Fifty percent of their DNA would come from a 100% European parent; the other 50% would come from a half-Native American parent. Half of a half is a fourth.

The same principle would play out in subsequent generations. For instance, the great-grandchildren would be the product of the union of the 25% Native American grandchildren and their European-American spouses. These great-grandchildren would be 12.5% Native American. Their children (i.e., the great-great-grandchildren) would be only about 6.25% Native American. The next generation, only 3.125% Native American. As a general rule, the genetic percentage drops by half in each generation.[8]

Already, this complicates my search for a potential Native American relative. In just a few generations, his genetic signal drops to precariously low levels.

The small window of genetic opportunity is made even smaller by the limitations of the commercial tests themselves. For example, the most popular genetic tests do not analyze your entire DNA sequence. They look at only some of the regions of your DNA that tend to vary in the global human population. Then these companies compare your DNA to the DNA from people groups around the globe. But this database has its own shortcomings. Currently, the scientific community possesses the complete DNA sequences from fewer than one million individuals — a far cry from the billions of people that roam earth.

These companies then use proprietary computer methods to determine which of these groups your DNA matches most closely. Even

---

8. While I've stated these numbers with fine mathematical precision, biology isn't this clean. It's messy. Every person's DNA is a mix of ethnicities. The difference may be small, but it's present. This presence is enough to make the percentages vary slightly in each person. In other words, a more accurate way to talk about these percentages is to say that, on average, the percentages represent the genetic signal of one's ancestors.

without access to the details of these methods, the facts that we do possess are not encouraging. Today, many of the same DNA sequences exist among diverse populations around the world — in ways we don't intuitively expect. For example, even though I'm of German descent, some of my DNA will be identical to that of an African. Yet the specific DNA that I share with an African, I might *not* share with another German. Conversely, another German may have some DNA that is identical to that of a Chinese individual. But this specific section of DNA might not be shared with a fellow German. And so on.

These genetic facts are not the result of theoretical calculations or of extrapolations from archaeology. Rather, they're simply empirical findings in genetics. Global DNA sharing makes it hard to find unique genetic signatures for specific ethnicities — and to design specific computer algorithms to detect them.

To summarize, any ethnicity percentage reported at 10% or lower — such as you might find in a readout from one of these companies — is usually not reliable.

Let's apply this fact to my hypothetical Native American ancestor. The theoretical Native American genetic contribution drops below 10% after the great-grandchild generation. So if my hypothetical ancestor is beyond the great-grandparent generation, I might not detect his contribution in my own DNA.

This fact applies across all ethnicities, regardless of whether my hypothetical ancestor is Native American, African, Australian, Chinese, Polish, Finnish, or any other ethnicity. The genetic contribution of each ancestor drops by half each generation. Therefore, the genetic signals of my ancestors become very hard to detect beyond just a few generations.

In short, family trees can be reconstructed from DNA comparisons. However, our ability to do so is severely limited by the fact of *DNA signal dilution*. The DNA signal from my ancestors drops off exponentially each generation.

In terms of determining ethnicity, standard genetic tests are about as useful as physical characteristics. Neither tells you the ethnic history of a person beyond a few generations.

So who were the ancestors of the Khoisan? What happened to the ancient Chinese? From whom do modern Egyptians descend? If we tried to answer any of these questions by relying on the comparison of visible physical characteristics, we'd be grasping at straws. Physical features can change in the generational blink of an eye. Standard genetic tests offer little additional insight.

Again, none of these conclusions follows from anything other than basic biology. The principles of genetics that we all learned in school tell us that ethnic changes can happen much quicker than you or I appreciate.

To find the ancestors and descendants of ancient civilizations, we're going to have to look for clues somewhere else.

Chapter 4 Summary:

- Today, physical features distinguish ethnic groups from one another.

- We naturally assume that these physical features have always defined these ethnic groups, including in the ancient past.

- Simple genetic calculations show that physical features can change in just a few generations — the features of one ethnic group can be transformed into the features of another in the genealogical blink of an eye.

- One ethnic group can blend into another, dominate the second group's family tree, and leave hardly a visible trace. All this is possible via small differences in reproductive rates between the two groups.

- Typical genetic tests do not reveal much about our ethnic histories beyond a few generations.

- Ethnicities could have changed frequently throughout human history, and the typical tools we use to investigate that possibility cannot tell us what happened. We have to look for clues somewhere else.

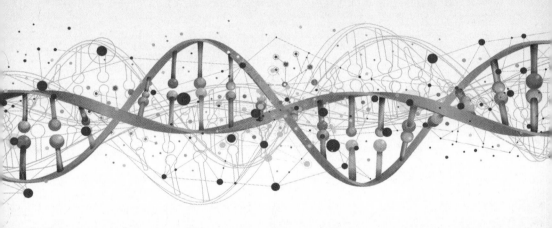

Part II: Finding the Ancients

5

Still African

Sunday, November 26, 1922, Egypt

(From the journal of 48-year-old British archaeologist Howard Carter)

After clearing 9 metres of the descending passage, in about the middle of the afternoon, we came upon a second sealed doorway, which was almost the exact replica of the first. It bore similar seal impressions and had similar traces of successive reopenings and reclosings in the plastering. The seal impressions were of Tut.ankh.Amen and of the Royal Necropolis, but not in any way so clear as those on the first doorway. The entrance and passage both in plan and in style resembled almost to measurement the tomb containing the cache of Akhenaten discovered by Davis in the very near vicinity; which seemed to substantiate our first conjecture that we had found a cache.

Feverishly we cleared away the remaining last scraps of rubbish on the floor of the passage before the doorway, until we had only the clean sealed doorway before us. In which, after making preliminary notes, we made a tiny breach in the top left hand corner to see what was beyond. Darkness and the iron testing rod told us that there was empty space. Perhaps another descending staircase, in accordance to the ordinary royal Theban tomb plan? Or may be a chamber? Candles were procured - the all important tell-tale for foul gases when opening an ancient subterranean excavation - I widened the breach and by means of the candle looked in, while Ld. C., Lady E, and Callender with the Reises waited in anxious expectation.

It was sometime before one could see, the hot air escaping caused the candle to flicker, but as soon as one's eyes became accustomed to the glimmer of light the interior of the chamber gradually loomed before one, with its strange and wonderful medley of extraordinary and beautiful objects heaped upon one another.

There was naturally short suspense for those present who could not see, when Lord Carnarvon said to me 'Can you see anything'. I replied to him Yes, it is wonderful. I then with precaution made the hole sufficiently large for both of us to see. With the light of an electric torch as well as an additional candle we looked in. Our sensations and astonishment are difficult to describe as the better light revealed to us the marvellous collection of treasures: two strange ebony-black effigies of a King, gold sandalled, bearing staff and mace, loomed out from the cloak of darkness; gilded couches in strange forms, lion-headed, Hathor-headed, and beast infernal; exquisitely painted, inlaid, and ornamental caskets; flowers; alabaster vases, some beautifully executed of lotus and papyrus device; strange black shrines with a gilded monster snake appearing from within; quite ordinary looking white chests; finely carved chairs; a golden inlaid throne; a heap of large curious white oviform boxes; beneath our very eyes, on the threshold, a lovely lotiform wishing-cup in translucent alabaster; stools of all shapes and design, of both common and rare materials; and, lastly a confusion of overturned parts of chariots glinting with gold, peering from amongst which was a mannikin. The first impression of which suggested the property-room of an opera of a vanished civilization. Our sensations were bewildering and full of strange emotion. We questioned one another as to the meaning of it all. Was it a tomb or merely a cache? A sealed doorway between the two sentinel statues proved there was more beyond, and with the numerous cartouches bearing the name of Tut.ankh.Amen on most of the objects before us, there was little doubt that there behind was the grave of that Pharaoh.

We closed the hole, locked the wooden-grill which had been placed upon the first doorway, we mounted our donkeys and return home contemplating what we had seen.[1]

Few ancient civilizations evoke as much mystery and fascination as ancient Egypt (**Color Plate 21**). Massive pyramids, glittering tombs, grave robbers, mummies, hidden passages, the Sphinx, an inscrutable language — ancient Egypt has it all. Now, a century after Carter's discovery, we would be hard-pressed to find someone who has *not* heard of King Tut.

Who were the people of the once-glorious power? Who did they come from? What happened to the people of ancient Egypt? Are their descendants still with us today?

Contradictory Clues

Geographically, *Egypt* has always been *African*. The ancient kingdoms of Tut and other Pharaohs anchored their reigns along Africa's longest river, the Nile. The modern state of Egypt exists astride the same African landmark.

From this perspective, it's natural to assume that the peoples of ancient and modern Egypt are part of the same family tree. Surely they are linked in a direct, unbroken genealogical chain. Surely modern Egyptians can claim ancient Egyptians as their ancestors.

The political history of Egypt tells a different story.

Tutankhamun reigned during an era of ancient Egyptian history known as the *New Kingdom* period. During this period, as well as during the prior eras (the *Old Kingdom* and *Middle Kingdom* periods), Egyptian rulers hailed from Africa. Some were from the land of Egypt. Some were Libyans. Others were Kushites. On occasion, Asians (e.g.,

---

1. Tutankhamun: Anatomy of an Excavation. Howard Carter's diaries and journals. The first excavation season in the tomb of Tutankhamun. Part 1: October 28 to December 31, 1922. Griffith Institute, Oxford OX1 2LG. Accessed via http://www.griffith.ox.ac.uk/gri/4sea1not.html, January 15, 2021.

the Hyksos) interrupted these Kingdoms. But, each time, African dynasties reemerged.

In other words, much of what we associate with ancient Egypt has African roots. The mysterious burial site for Tut and many other New Kingdom Pharaohs — the Valley of the Kings — is the product of African people. The Great Pyramid of Giza (Pharaoh Khufu, Dynasty 4, Old Kingdom) is as well. The son of Pharaoh Khufu, Pharaoh Khafre, built the middle-sized Giza pyramid and possibly the Sphinx. Africans inscribed their histories in hieroglyphics. Africans worshipped the pantheon of ancient Egyptian deities.

In the fourth century B.C., the conquests of the Persians brought this long chapter of African history to a permanent close. No African Pharaoh ever rose to rule Egypt again.

Now, thousands of years after the Persian conquest, Egypt looks dramatically different. Contemporary rulers of Egypt no longer build elaborate tombs or pyramids to commemorate their lives and assure their successes in the afterlife. The official language, Arabic, hearkens back to the Arab Muslim conquests. The dominant religion, Islam, reflects over a millennium and a half of Arab and Turkish Muslim rule. Modern Egypt has acquired a strong Asian flavor, not an African one.

From this perspective, we'd be justified in asking our questions anew: What happened to the people of ancient Egypt? After the Persian conquest, where did the builders of this once-glorious civilization go? Do they have any descendants today?

In our pursuit of answers to these questions, geography and political history can take us only so far. Neither directly recorded the full genealogies of ancient and modern Egyptians. To uncover this aspect of Egyptian history, we'll need to turn to something else.

Clues from Elsewhere

Take a look at the family tree[2] in **Color Plate 22**. It depicts the relationships among 600 men from almost every continent, including Africa. Though you can't see the details at this zoomed-out view, each branch tip leads to a single individual — 600 of them. This tree holds the key to unraveling the fate of the ancient Egyptians.

Surprisingly, the tree in **Color Plate 22** is based on DNA. But it's not based on the DNA we inherit from both parents. Recall from

---

2. Based on Bergström et al. (2020). See also supplemental online methods and data.

chapter 4 that this type of DNA takes us back in history only a few generations. Instead, the DNA behind **Color Plate 22** comes from fathers.

Males are the exclusive possessors of a type of DNA known as the *Y chromosome*. When men and women reproduce, fathers are the exclusive sources of the Y chromosome DNA in their male offspring. Mothers have no Y chromosome DNA by which to dilute the genetic signal of the father's Y chromosome DNA.[3]

Notice the color-coded groups of branches in **Color Plate 22**. See how they correspond to clusters of various genealogical depth. Now take a look at the color-coded letter or letter-number combinations associated with these clusters. The most ancient branches in the Y chromosome tree have been assigned letters of the alphabet — *A, B, C,* all the way down to *T*. When an ancient branch subdivides, each sub-branch inherits the letter of the ancient branch to which it belongs. To distinguish these subdivisions, each sub-branch is also assigned a number — e.g., *A1, A2*. When these subdivisions further subdivide themselves, they are assigned another letter of the alphabet — e.g., *A1a, A1b*. This alternating letter-number pattern is repeated until branch divisions cease.

Each letter or letter-number cluster is known as a *haplogroup*. While haplogroup is not a household word, it's the vocabulary of the history embedded in the Y chromosome tree. By the time we're done with this book, this term will become second nature to you.

In Egypt, Y chromosome haplogroups interwove Asian and African history in a way that no one would have predicted.

The Genetic History of Egypt

Today, the Y chromosome haplogroup at the highest levels in Egyptian men is one known as *E1b1b* (see **Color Plate 22** for reference). More than 40% of Egyptian men belong to this branch of the Y chromosome tree.

Could *E1b1b* link modern Egyptians to their ancient African past?

At first pass, *E1b1b* looks rather African. Its highest levels are found in Africa (**Color Plate 23**). (The three-part master reference

---

3. In theory, we could also draw a family tree based on maternally-inherited *mitochondrial DNA* and analyze human history with it. However, in practice, the statistical noise in mitochondrial DNA analyses prevents it from being a useful tool by which to investigate the fine details of human history.

map in **Color Plate A** depicts the identity of each population used in maps throughout this book.[4]) In **Color Plate 23**, the size of the circle represents the abundance of haplogroup *E1b1b*. The bigger the circle, the higher the percentage of the population that carries *E1b1b*. The smaller the circle, the lower the percentage.[5] As you can see in **Color Plate 23**, the biggest circles are found in North and East Africa. Egypt sits between these two African regions.

However, *E1b1b* isn't exclusively African. It spills into Europe, in a roughly south-to-north gradient. *E1b1b* can also be found in Asia among peoples of the Near East. As you travel farther east, *E1b1b* levels decline. In Central Asia and India, *E1b1b* is almost undetectable.

Where did *E1b1b* originate — Africa, Europe, or Asia? Or someplace else? The details of the *E1b1b* branches provided a clue.

Take a look at **Color Plate 24**. Notice how a single *E1b1b* branch split into several in the A.D. 300s to 600s. North African *E1b1b* males fall primarily into one of these early branches. For example, notice where the North African *Mozabite* (Algerian) individuals fall on the tree in **Color Plate 24**. In **Color Plate 24**, they're exclusively on the red branch. East African *E1b1b* individuals (not shown in **Color Plate 24**), such as Somalis, show up in a different branch.

In other words, before the A.D. 300s to 600s, there must have been an original *E1b1b* branch in some location yet to be determined. Then, after the *E1b1b* haplogroup was born, something happened. The branch — the population — divided. One group ended up giving rise to a multitude of North Africans; the other, to East Africans.

Later, some subbranches broke away and entered Europe. For example, in **Color Plate 24**, a *Tuscan* (Italy) individual and a *Druze* (Israel/West Bank) individual had a common ancestor in the A.D. 1700s. This common ancestor then gave rise to lineages that went their separate ways in Europe and in the Middle East.

What historical events could explain these genetic results? Beginning several centuries after Christ, a series of conquests and migrations unfolded in a manner that found a strong cause-effect echo in the *E1b1b* branch of the Y chromosome tree. Unfortunately, they commenced, not in Africa, but in Asia.

---

4. See supplemental online methods and data for details behind the maps.
5. Any population with *E1b1b* levels less than 1% is not depicted with a circle.

Speaking the Language of *E1b1b*

In the early A.D. era, political control of Egypt belonged to Europe — primarily to the Roman Empire. In the middle of the A.D. 600s, control shifted to Asia. On the Arabian Peninsula, Muhammed and his followers unfurled a massive campaign whose eventual rule touched three continents. In the west, Muslim rule in North Africa pushed into Spain (**Color Plate 25**). In the east, Muslims pushed to the borders of India — but never conquered it. To the northeast, Muslims extended into Central Asia.

Today, the political structure of the Middle East does not reflect the unity of the original Arab Muslim empire (see **Color Plate 2**). Instead of flying a single banner, the region is broken up into multiple states of various sizes. In one sense, the history of Arab rule has been lost.

In another sense, the history remains — if you know where to look. And if you learn to see the signature of this history, you'll discover a profound clue to the origin of *E1b1b*.

Embedded in the languages of the Middle East and of Africa is a thread that ties them together. Today, linguists group languages into language *families*. This academic category is more easily understood in the context of familiar languages, like European ones, rather than in the context of the less familiar languages of the Middle East. Let's turn to the familiar first, and then return to the less familiar.

If you compare the languages of Europe, it's readily apparent that some are more similar than others. For instance, let's compare English, German, Spanish, and Italian. Notice the ways in which these languages represent basic vocabulary:

Word	German	Spanish	Italian
Father	Vater	Padre	Padre
Mother	Mutter	Madre	Madre
Born	Geboren	Nacido	Nato
Life	Leben	Vida	Vita

It's clear that English and German look more similar to each other than do English and Spanish, or English and Italian. Conversely, it's also clear that Spanish and Italian look more similar to each other than do Spanish and English, or Spanish and German. It's almost as if English and German were derived from a common ancestral language. Spanish and Italian seem to have been as well. These apparent ancestral links reflect actual relationships, and these relationships influence how we classify languages. English and German are both considered *Germanic* languages, and Spanish and Italian are both classified as *Romance* languages.

These categories can be joined into even larger groupings called language *families*. Though English and Spanish have less in common than English and German, all three languages have more in common with each other than any of them have with, say, Chinese. Hence, the Germanic and Romance languages, together with other languages that share similarities (e.g., Slavic, Iranian languages) together constitute the *Indo-European* language family.

As the name implies, the Indo-European family includes languages ranging from Iceland to India (**Color Plate 26**). All derive from a common ancestral source.

The Middle East and North Africa are united by a different language family: *Afro-Asiatic* (**Color Plate 27**). Geographically, Afro-Asiatic languages are found in many of the same places that the Arab Muslims once ruled (compare **Color Plate 25** to **Color Plate 27**). Afro-Asiatic languages are one of the strongest echoes of Arab Muslim rule.

However, the overlap between the two isn't perfect. Iran and Central Asia seem to have lost this echo of Arab Muslim rule. Why?

A third language family reveals the answer. I grew up thinking that Turkish people have always been in Anatolia, the landmass close to Greece and to the European mainland. The Turkish language tells a different story.

The language of modern Turkey belongs to the *Turkic* family of languages. Of all the Turkic languages still spoken today, Turkish is one of the western-most branches. The rest are spoken in Central Asia, the northwest part of modern China, and even in Siberia (**Color Plate 28**). For example, Kazakhstan (see map in **Color Plate 2** for reference) is one of the former Soviet republics in Central Asia. The Kazak language belongs to the Turkic language family.

Historically, in the early centuries A.D., Turkic-speaking peoples were first documented in Central Asia. Then, in the A.D. 1000s, the

Seljuk Turks moved out of Central Asia and into the Middle East, conquering as they went and taking Turkic languages with them. At its height, the Seljuk empire extended from the Mediterranean through the Middle East and up into Central Asia, almost to the borders of China (**Color Plate 29**).

In the A.D. 1200s, the Mongols pushed the Seljuk Turks nearly out of what is now Turkey (**Color Plate 30**). After the initial Mongol empire split up into four khanates, another Mongol conqueror, Tamerlane, swept through the Middle East and into Turkey in the late A.D. 1300s and early A.D. 1400s (**Color Plate 31**). Only in the A.D. 1500s did the Turks begin to expand out of Turkey and down into Arabia and Egypt (**Color Plate 32**).

These conquests from Central Asia down through the Middle East are the reason Afro-Asiatic languages don't reach as far as the Arab Muslim empire once did. Turkic and other languages displaced them.

Genetics seems to reflect this history. The first branch splits in *E1b1b* (**Color Plate 24**) occurred around the time of the early Arab Muslim conquests. Today, the geographic distribution of *E1b1b* overlaps the distribution of languages (Afro-Asiatic) spread by Arab Muslim conquests (**Color Plate 33**). Haplogroup *E1b1b* is heavy in North Africa, where Arab Muslims reigned uninterrupted by Turkic or Mongol incursions until at least the A.D. 1500s. Where these Central Asian conquerors swept through before the A.D. 1500s (i.e., the Middle East and Turkey), *E1b1b* exists at lower levels. *E1b1b* is also present in Spain, where Muslim rule was eventually pushed out by European conquests. In the Balkans, Ottomans may have brought pre-existing *E1b1b* lineages into Europe during their several centuries of occupation. But where Arab Muslims never conquered — i.e., India, China — *E1b1b* is absent.

Apart from the military conquests, known historical migrations from Arabia to Africa might also explain why *E1b1b* levels are lower in the Middle East as compared to North and East Africa:

> From the tenth to the thirteenth centuries, large numbers of Arab pastoral nomads, known as Bedouin . . . moved gradually out of Arabia and into northern Africa.[6]

---

6. Shillington (2019), p. 205.

In other words, it appears that *E1b1b* was the lineage of the early Arabs. Where they went, *E1b1b* followed. And where later empires overthrew them, *E1b1b* diminished in frequency.

Egypt sits at the crossroads of several of these political changes. Consistent with their geographic position, the Egyptian *E1b1b* lineages include the North African and East African sub-branches. In short, Egypt seems to bear the marks of centuries of Arab Muslim occupation. Which would imply that modern Egypt has become very Asian, not African.

****

Several hundred miles to the south of modern Egypt, the Sahara ends, and sub-Saharan Africa begins. It stretches for thousands of miles further south and west. The Africans in this region of the continent have their own story that, in many respects, transpired independent of Egypt. Yet the beginning of their story did not. It took everything we have learned so far about *E1b1b* and cast it in a different light.

Today, Africans speak more than 2,000 different languages across the entire continent. However, in terms of language families, African languages belong to less than 10. In sub-Saharan Africa, the Niger-Congo language family overwhelms much of the landmass (**Color Plate 34**). A Y chromosome haplogroup, haplogroup *E1b1a*, does as well (**Color Plate 35**). The geographic correlation between Niger-Congo languages and *E1b1a* is strong (**Color Plate 36**).

The details of the Niger-Congo language family make the association even stronger. Within Niger-Congo, one subgroup of languages has become prominent. The *Bantu* language subgroup dominates central and south-central Africa (see **Color Plate 34**). Based on language comparisons within this subgroup, these Bantu languages originated near Cameroon, and then spread out — in a process termed the *Bantu expansion*. Exactly when has been a matter of debate:

> Before the development of radiocarbon dating and the widespread archaeological research that has taken place since the 1950s, it was believed that Bantu speakers spread across eastern, central and southern Africa in the comparatively recent past. The main source of evidence was oral traditions, which seldom traced ruling lineages back more than 500

years. It was assumed, therefore, that to have populated the subcontinent in so short a time there must have been large-scale conquering migrations of whole new peoples.[7]

Today, many haplogroup *E1b1a* lineages have a common ancestor in the A.D. 1200s to 1400s (**Color Plate 37**). The earliest of the *E1b1a* lineages broke away and are now found in far western Africa. For example, take a look at the branches of the *Mandenka* people in **Color Plate 37**. These Mandenka reside in the West African country of Guinea (**Color Plate 38**). In contrast, the lineages that disperse in the 1400s to 1600s are found throughout sub-Saharan Africa. Together, these data suggest that the *E1b1a* dispersal originated in West Africa and then spread out to the rest of sub-Saharan Africa. Alternatively, the *E1b1a* homelands may have been closer to Nigeria/Cameroon. From there, a set of West African branches may have migrated away, and another set of lineages may have dispersed through the rest of sub-Saharan Africa.

Why might the *E1b1a* individuals have dispersed from these lands? A possible answer involves the Trans-Atlantic slave trade. Beginning in the A.D. 1500s, Europeans began enslaving Africans for hard labor in the New World. This plunder of people drew heavily from West Africa and west-central Africa (**Color Plate 39**). Though west-central Africa ended up being the most pillaged for slaves, the earliest captures happened in West Africa — Senegambia and the offshore Atlantic (compare the locations in **Color Plate 40** to the locations in **Color Plate 39**).

It's tempting to invoke a cause-effect relationship among all these factors. Could the early slave trade in West Africa have prompted scores of West Africans to flee east and eventually south, in hopes of escaping capture? Might the Bantu language dispersal be related to this?

Regardless of the answers, *E1b1a* still appears to have arisen in a West/west-central African homeland. And whatever the reasons for its dispersal, it remains the dominant lineage among dark-skinned Africans.

Now let's bring haplogroup *E1b1b* back into the picture. *E1b1b* and *E1b1a* share a common ancestor in the 700s B.C. to 400s B.C. (**Color Plate 41**). The purportedly Asian (Arab Muslim) *E1b1b* branch and the unequivocally sub-Saharan African *E1b1a* branch are *linked*.

---

7. Shillington (2019), p. 69.

The Origin of *E1b1b*

Based on external appearances, no one would likely mistake a Middle-Eastern Arab for a sub-Saharan African. Skin tone, hair type, and other physical features clearly distinguish the two. Still, they share a common ancestor from the first millennium B.C.

From where did the ancestral lineage to *E1b1a* and *E1b1b* spring? We've just seen evidence that the *E1b1a* lineages spread out from a West/west-central African homeland (see **Color Plates 37–38**). Conversely, we've also seen the association of the *E1b1b* lineage with the Arab Muslim expansion (see **Color Plates 25, 33**), which arose in Arabia. It seems natural to put the early *E1b1a* and *E1b1b* peoples in those two regions.

The shortest distance between two points is a straight line. The line connecting Arabia and West Africa resides mostly in Africa, not Asia. The line also happens to pass through northeast Africa — the area near Sudan (**Color Plate 42**).

Could northeast Africa have been the ancestral home of the peoples that split and gave rise to *E1b1a* and *E1b1b*?

Migration from northeast Africa to West Africa is uncomplicated. It's a strictly land-based journey. In contrast, the Red Sea separates northeast Africa from Arabia. However, in pre-Islamic times, these areas were culturally connected. The Ethiopian kingdom of Aksum (**Color Plate 43**) arose around the time of Christ and lasted until around the time of the Muslim conquests several hundred years later. Though based in Ethiopia, Aksum maintained interactions with the southwestern part of the Arabian peninsula — perhaps even ruling it for a time (**Color Plate 43**).

Together, these facts suggest that the early *E1b1* peoples — the ancestors to the *E1b1a* and *E1b1b* lineages — lived in Africa, possibly near Sudan and/or Ethiopia (**Color Plate 44**). These *E1b1* peoples would have also been ancestors to the *E1b1b* that is still present in 40% of modern Egyptian men.

In other words, despite millennia of Asian rule, Egyptians are still dominantly African.

Perhaps the relatives of King Tut are still with us.

Chapter 5 Summary:

- Ancient Egypt was ruled by people of African descent; however, for the last 2,000 years, Europeans and Asians have governed Egypt, implying that the ancient Egyptian lineage may have gone extinct.

- The key to identifying lineages from the ancient past — including from ancient Egypt — is a type of DNA inherited only in males: The *Y chromosome.*

- DNA differences between the Y chromosomes of Egyptians and the Y chromosomes of men from around the globe allow us to reconstruct a family tree of Egypt.

- Major branches in this Y chromosome family tree are called *haplogroups.*

- Haplogroup names follow an alternating letter-number convention.

- The haplogroup *E1b1b* exists in modern Egypt and heavily in North Africa, among other places.

- The branching patterns in the *E1b1b* lineage imply that it was connected to the Muslim Arab conquests of the latter part of the first millennium A.D. — which would suggest that *E1b1b* is Asian in origin.

- *E1b1a* is the dominant sub-Saharan African branch, yet it is connected to the *E1b1b* branch.

- The connection between *E1b1b* and *E1b1a* implies that the ancestor to *E1b1b* may have been African. This means that the dominant Y chromosome lineage in Egypt was African in origin, and could, therefore, have been connected to ancient Egypt.

6

The Corridor

November 17, 1855, deep in sub-Saharan Africa

After twenty minutes' sail from Kalai [which sits on the modern Zambia-Zimbabwe border], we came in sight, for the first time, of the columns of vapour, appropriately called "smoke," rising at a distance of five or six miles, exactly as when large tracts of grass are burned in Africa. Five columns now arose, and bending in the direction of the wind, they seemed placed against a low ridge covered with trees; the tops of the columns at this distance appeared to mingle with the clouds. They were white below, and higher up became dark, so as to simulate smoke very closely. The whole scene was extremely beautiful; the banks and islands dotted over the river are adorned with sylvan vegetation of great variety of colour and form. At the period of our visit several trees were spangled over with blossoms. Trees have each their own physiognomy. There, towering over all, stands the great burly baobab, each of whose enormous arms would form the trunk of a large tree, beside groups of graceful palms, which, with their feathery-shaped leaves depicted on the sky, lend their beauty to the scene. As a hieroglyphic they always mean "far from home," for one can never get over their foreign air in a picture or landscape. The silvery mohonono, which in the tropics is in form like the cedar of Lebanon, stands in pleasing contrast with the dark colour of the motsouri, whose cypress-form is dotted over at present with its pleasant scarlet fruit. Some trees resemble the great spreading oak, others assume the character of our own elms and chestnuts; but no one can imagine the beauty of the view from anything witnessed in England. It had never been seen before by European eyes; but scenes so lovely must have been gazed upon by angels in their flight.[1]

These lines, written by the famous Scottish explorer and missionary, David Livingstone, in a book published in 1857, memorialized his encounter with Victoria Falls (**Color Plate 45**). While he modestly confessed to being the first European to witness the site, his discovery may have been much more far-reaching. It's likely that he was, not just the first European, but the first person outside of sub-Saharan Africa to see the Falls.

Thousands of years earlier and about 3,000 miles to the north, the Pharaohs made no mention of Victoria Falls. In fact, geographic landmarks nearer to Egypt were equally mysterious. The world's longest river, the Nile, provided the basis for the Pharaohs' existence, yet they had no knowledge of its source.

From this perspective, ancient Egypt was isolated from the rest of Africa. In theory, this fact could provide clues to the fate of the ancient Egyptians. Today, we have DNA from peoples all throughout modern Africa. If, among the modern Egyptian lineages, we found one that was isolated from the rest of Africa, this could lead us to the Egyptians of old.

Mainstream science encourages this pursuit. In the context of the mainstream timescale, the separation between Egypt and the rest of Africa has deep roots. Two hundred thousand to three hundred thousand years ago, long before the first Egyptian dynasties, mainstream science indicates that anatomically modern humans arose on

---

1. Livingstone, D. 1857. *Missionary Travels and Researches in South Africa.* London: John Murray, p. 519. https://archive.org/details/missionarytrave00unkngoog/page/n580/mode/1up.

the warm savannahs of sub-Saharan Africa. Then, around 50,000 to 100,000 years ago, a group of Africans split off and left for the colder climates of Europe and Asia. Those who remained in sunny Africa diversified. By 10,000 B.C., Africans were already divided into language families. The Niger-Congo speakers were in West Africa, Nilo-Saharans in modern Sudan, and the Khoisan in modern Tanzania (**Color Plate 46**). Egyptians — Afro-Asiatic speakers — were in the northeast. Then, around 7,000 years later (i.e., 3050 B.C.), Narmer founded the first Egyptian Dynasty along the banks of the Nile.

Thus, according to mainstream science, Egypt may have been the first African civilization, but Egyptians weren't the first African peoples — not by a long shot. The ancient Egyptian civilization that dominates the popular imagination — King Tut and the rest — was born thousands of years after the earliest Egyptian lineages separated from the rest of Africa.

The Y chromosomes of Africa told a very different story — with outsized ramifications for the fate of the ancient Egyptians.

A Geographic Divide

Today across Africa, Y chromosome sequences tend to fall into a few easily identifiable lineages. Initially, the geography of these lineages seemed to lend support to a fundamental divide between Egypt and sub-Saharan Africa. For example, haplogroup *A* occurs infrequently across Africa (**Color Plate 47**). It does so in a manner that overlaps the distribution of two of the major African language families, Nilo-Saharan and Khoisan (**Color Plate 48**). In modern Egypt, a place where primarily Afro-Asiatic languages are spoken, and not Nilo-Saharan or Khoisan, haplogroup *A* exists in just 1% to 2% of the men.

As another example, haplogroup *B* exists all throughout sub-Saharan Africa (**Color Plate 49**). Though it lacks a strong correlation with language families, haplogroup *B* still avoids Egypt. It is undetectable there.

Haplogroup *E* provides a third example of Egyptian isolation. The earliest separation divides *E1* from *E2*. The next separation subdivides *E1* into *E1a* and *E1b*. The geographic distributions of haplogroups *E1a* and *E2* resemble that of haplogroup *B*: They are found across sub-Saharan Africa but are largely absent from North Africa (**Color Plate 50**). Haplogroups *E1a* and *E2* are undetectable in modern Egypt.

All of these results appear to fit the idea of a deep separation between Egypt and the rest of Africa.

However, recent experiments on the Y chromosome have cast all of these conclusions in a new light. In the following section, you might find that the discussion wades, at times, into the technical. Normally, I would move such an explanation to the endnotes or to an appendix. However, because this discussion flows from a sequence of events that are so unusual, and so dramatic in their implications, especially with regard to the timeline of African and Egyptian history, I've left them in the main text.

Contemporaries

For all of African history, the Y chromosome has marked the passage of time in a simple way. When the sperm cells of African men copied their Y chromosome DNA, they did so imperfectly. Think of it like trying to rapidly transcribe a lecture from a fast-talking speaker. Mistakes happen. Within cells, elaborate DNA error correction methods exist, but mistakes still slip through.

These genetic copying errors accumulated with time. The men from one African generation would imperfectly copy their Y chromosomes. Then men from a subsequent generation would repeat the process. As mistakes occurred, they compounded. By analogy, it's like trying to re-type a re-typed document — but with an imperfect spellchecker. And then repeating the re-typing process from the partially corrected version. And then doing it again. The more you copy the copies, the more mistakes get introduced. By the hundredth copy, the document will have hundreds of errors.

The accumulation of DNA mistakes acted like a clock. Every new mistake represented another tick of the clock. After ticking for 200,000 years, the African Y chromosome clock produced DNA that was riddled with copying errors.

Globally, the same process played out with the same result. Y chromosome clocks have been ticking in men outside of Africa for as long as men have been there. The DNA from non-African men has also become riddled with errors.

Well, Y chromosome DNA should have become riddled with errors, if humans have been in existence for hundreds of thousands of years. How does our DNA look? Do our Y chromosomes bear the signature of hundreds of thousands of years of human existence? Or do they tell a different story? The way to find out entailed a two-step process.

The first step involved comparing the DNA from men around the globe. Scientists counted the number of Y chromosome differences that separated one male from another. African men tend to differ from non-African men by 1,000 to 3,000 DNA letters. Non-African men tend to differ from one another by about 700 to 1,000 DNA letters. These results represented the total number of ticks of the Y chromosome clock.

But did these DNA differences represent many ticks? Or a few? The answers to these questions rewrote the temporal context in which we think about ancient Egypt. The answers also arose from the second verification step. In these experiments, the scientific community selected father-son pairs (or other male relatives of known genealogy) and sequenced their Y chromosome DNA. Then they counted the number of differences between the relatives. The number of Y chromosome DNA differences between them revealed how many copying errors occurred each generation. These differences told them how fast the Y chromosome clock ticked.

One of the first studies to measure the error rate was published in 2009. Two Chinese men of a known genealogical relationship going back to the 1800s had their Y chromosome DNA sequences determined. The resultant rate of copying errors was slow. It fit the existence of a "Y chromosome Adam" (the ancestor of all living men) about 200,000 years ago.[2] In 2015, a study of hundreds of Icelandic men produced the same result.[3]

So far, these results would leave the mainstream timescale as is. They would change nothing in our understanding of the relationship between ancient Egypt and the rest of Africa.

However, due to financial and time constraints, these earlier studies were based on low quality DNA sequence. Then, in 2015, another research group compared father and son Y chromosome DNA sequences. This time, they used high quality methods. The result was a copying error rate that was much faster than the previous, lower quality studies: "The number of [father-son Y chromosome] differences was approximately 10-fold higher than the expected

---

2. Xue et al. (2009).
3. Helgason et al. (2015).

number ... considering the range of published [Y chromosome copying mistake] rates."[4]

In fact, the data from this study implied that "Y chromosome Adam" lived just a few thousand years ago.

What was the mainstream scientific community to do? Oddly, they filtered their results, removing data that contradicted the 200,000-year timescale. They did so until the Y chromosome copying error rate matched their expectations. They forced the results from the high-quality methods to fit the results from the lower-quality methods. Why? Because the latter fit their expectations.

These actions represent a form of circular reasoning. They do not constitute an independent, experimental, scientific test of the timescale of human origins.

The clash between experiments and expectations did not stop there. In 2017, researchers compared the DNA sequences between 50 parent-offspring trios — i.e., they obtained DNA from father, mother, and child.[5] Again, they did so by using high quality DNA sequencing methods. Among these 50 trios, several father-son pairs existed. The researchers published detailed analyses of the copying error rate in these people. They discussed the rate that occurs in the DNA that is inherited from both parents. This DNA represents about 98% of our total DNA. But conspicuously absent from their published results was a statement on the father-son Y chromosome copying error rate.[6] Why?

From the raw data that did make it into their published study, a potential answer emerged. From this raw data, the father-son Y chromosome DNA copying error rate could be extracted. The results were consistent with the 2015 high-quality study. The 2017 Y chromosome copying error rate again implied that "Y chromosome Adam" existed about 4,500 years ago.[7]

This "Y chromosome Adam" of 4,500 years ago happens to fall right in line with a unique, ancient, written history. This history has profound implications for the relationship between ancient Egypt and the rest of Africa.

---

4. Karmin et al. (2015), Supplementary Information, p. 4.

5. Maretty et al. (2017).

6. I'm referring specifically to the single nucleotide polymorphism rate, not the insertion-deletion (indel) rate.

7. Jeanson and Holland (2019). See Appendix B for more detailed justification and for additional lines of evidence for the 4,500-year view.

A straightforward reading of the Bible leads to a specific, detailed anthropology for the entire globe. The book of Genesis names Adam and Eve as the ancestors of the entire human race. In combination with other Scriptural passages, Genesis puts the date of their creation by God around 6,000 years ago. Genesis also describes the fate of their descendants. All but Noah, his wife, his three sons (Shem, Ham, and Japheth), and their wives were destroyed in the global Flood. The Flood occurred around 4,500 years ago.

Of the four male survivors of the Flood, three received their Y chromosomes from the same ancestor. Shem, Ham, and Japheth were all direct descendants of Noah. All three inherited their Y chromosomes from him. Naturally, this implies that all males today descend from Noah. Or, to flip the equation around, males today should be able to dial their Y chromosome differences back to zero — to Noah — in just 4,500 years. For the remainder of this book, I'll refer to this point — 4,500 years ago with Noah — as the *beginning*. It's technically the re-beginning after Adam. But just "beginning" makes for simpler shorthand.

Based on these results, "10,000 B.C." and "3050 B.C." must be more recent — at least 2500 B.C. or sooner. However, for technical reasons,[8] these dates are also unlikely to be more recent than 1000 B.C. Long story short, the most plausible scenario at present is one in which these dates are bunched up near 2500 B.C.

In other words, the supposedly separate African peoples (the early speakers of Afro-Asiatic, Niger-Congo, Nilo-Saharan, and Khoisan languages) may have arisen within a few centuries of each other.

Practically, these early African peoples would have been especially conducive to mixing. Despite the continent's large size, Africa hasn't historically harbored large numbers of people. Throughout much of human history, Africa has had only around 15% of the world's population.[9] For example, in 1000 B.C., Africa would have held only 15% of the 50 million people alive, or only 7.5 million total — *in the entire continent*. Thus, when looking for spouses, Egyptians and other Africans would have had fewer options than today.

These factors (small ancestral population sizes and a revised historical timeline) recast the relationship between Egypt and the rest

---

8. See Jeanson (2019) for details on which parts of the mainstream timescale change the most.
9. McEvedy and Jones (1975).

of Africa. These factors suggested that Egypt and sub-Saharan Africa were *not* separated by a deep historical division. Instead, these results hinted that Egyptian lineages might be found all throughout Africa.

In fact, they were found far beyond.

Connected Far and Wide

Geographically, the major African Y chromosome lineages show a clear break between Egypt and sub-Saharan Africa (**Color Plates 47, 49, 50**). Genetically, these African Y chromosome haplogroups are all *connected*. The most recent link joined *E1b1a* and *E1b1b* in the 700s B.C. to 400s B.C. (**Color Plate 51**). Going back in time, two more unions happened almost simultaneously. Haplogroups *E1a* and *E1b* joined in the 1300s B.C. to 900s B.C.; haplogroups *E1* and *E2*, in the 1400s B.C. to 1000s B.C. (**Color Plate 51**). Prior to these events, haplogroups *A* and *B* connected to one another in the 2100s B.C. to 1800s B.C. (**Color Plate 51**). The earliest connection joined haplogroup *A/B* with haplogroup *E*. Their linkage occurred in the 2400s B.C. to 2000s B.C (**Color Plate 51**).

As a side note, you may have noticed that the haplogroup *A* and *B* branches are significantly longer than the haplogroup *E* branches. At first pass, this fact raises a troubling question. What do these branches represent? Events in the future?

Their long length suggests that they represent lineages whose Y chromosome clock ticks faster than the rest — or once ticked faster than the rest. However, no one has yet measured the rate at which copying errors occur in these peoples. The published father-son Y chromosome studies (see previous section) all focus on non-African peoples. Hence, the copying error rate in the people on these longer branches remains a mystery. My suspicion of a faster mutation rate is something that is yet to be determined. In other words, it's a testable *prediction*, the hallmark of a scientific framework.[10]

In light of the genetic connections among haplogroups *A, B,* and *E*, let's revisit the linguistic relationships between Egypt and the rest of Africa. Today, the major African language families (Nilo-Saharan, Khoisan, Niger-Congo, Afro-Asiatic) correlate with the distributions of major Y chromosome haplogroups (*A, E1b1a, E1b1b*) (see **Color**

---

10. One specific testable prediction is that the men in the longest haplogroup *A* individuals on record (e.g., the *Mbo* men in the Karmin et al. (2015) study) have faster mutation rates than the men described earlier in this chapter.

Plates 48, 36, 33). Haplogroups *E1b1a* and *E1b1b* were once a single lineage. So were haplogroups *E* (to which *E1b1a* and *E1b1b* belong) and *A*. Presumably, this means that the language families to which they correlate were also once in close proximity.

Also, the dates for the common ancestors of haplogroups *A* and *E* (and of haplogroups within *E*) all fall contemporaneous with the ancient Egyptian civilization — not thousands of years prior. In other words, the peoples belonging to the four major African language families don't look so deeply divided after all.

Could all four of these groups have originated in Egypt? Might the history of the entire African continent have found its source in northeast Africa? Let's rephrase these questions: Where would the common ancestors of haplogroups *A*, *B*, and *E* have lived? The answer takes us even closer to the ancient civilization astride the Nile.

A Hub of Activity

To uncover this answer, let's follow the geographic clues backwards in time. Let's map the homelands for each Y chromosome haplogroup until we arrive at the most ancient source population.

The most recent genetic split separated *E1b1a* from *E1b1b*. As we saw in chapter 5, the *E1b1a* homeland appears to have been West/west-central Africa. Conversely, the *E1b1b* homeland was, at one point, Arabia. Since these two lineages are linked, the geographic area between the two — the Sudan/Ethiopia region — represents a good candidate for the homeland of peoples ancestral to *E1b1a* and *E1b1b* (see **Color Plates 42, 44**; see also the discussion in chapter 5).

These *E1b1a* and *E1b1b* lineages share a common ancestor with the *E1a* and *E2* lineages. The distributions of *E1a* and *E2* are almost mirrored (**Color Plate 50**). The line dividing the locations of *E1a* from the locations of *E2* (**Color Plate 50**) seems to pass through Cameroon and — similar to the line connecting the *E1b1a* and *E1b1b* homelands (see **Color Plate 42**) — through the Sudan/Ethiopia region. Perhaps *E1a* and *E2* also arose near Sudan/Ethiopia.[11]

In support of this inference, one study of Ethiopian men showed that up to 30% of them contained *E* lineages that were even older than

---

11. Alternatively, the *E1a* and *E2* split might also reflect the timing and direction of the Bantu expansion — the sub-Saharan expansion of peoples speaking the *Bantu* subset of Niger-Congo languages (see chapter 5). But at present, we do not possess enough African Y chromosomes to know.

E1 and *E2*.[12] In another study, the Maasai males of Kenya — neighbor to Ethiopia — had deep *E* lineages at levels around 25%.[13] If haplogroup *E* originated in northeast Africa, this is the type of evidence that you'd expect to find.

This emerging geographic narrative finds an echo in African history. The sequence of African state formation points toward a hub of activity in the northeast. The earliest African state, Egypt, arose there. Contemporary with ancient Egypt, the neighboring Nubian/Kushite kingdom ruled from *Kerma* and *Meroe*, two cities along the Nile in what is now Sudan. Ethiopia existed at a greater distance from Egypt. Ethiopian states arose later in history. The first Ethiopian kingdom, Aksum, didn't flourish until the early A.D. era (see **Color Plate 43**; see also discussion in chapter 5). In faraway sub-Saharan Africa, states formed at even later dates.

It's almost as if African society — and African peoples — were concentrated in Egypt and Sudan early in history. Then, later in history, they spilled over into Ethiopia and beyond. In these early days, other peoples may have existed at great distances from Egypt and Nubia. But their numbers were likely small. The major locus of activity seems to have been northeast Africa.

Consistent with this inference, key events in the history of ancient Egypt/Nubia plausibly explain the splits in the African Y chromosome haplogroups.

The most recent split — the one between *E1b1a* and *E1b1b* — occurred in the 700s to 400s B.C. (see **Color Plate 51**). This overlaps the time when Nubians were ruling Egypt — and when the Assyrian invasion of Egypt brought Cushite rule to an end. Perhaps these events pushed *E1b1a* into sub-Saharan Africa and *E1b1b* down into Ethiopia and eventually into Arabia.

Going backward in time, the next splits span the 1400s to 900s B.C. (see **Color Plate 51**). The ancestral lineage to *E1b1a* and *E1b1b*, namely, *E1b*, split from *E1a*, with *E1a* ending up in West Africa (see **Color Plate 50**). Presumably, *E1b* remained in northeast Africa until *E1b1a* and *E1b1b* split several centuries later (see **Color Plates 52–57** for a visual of the sequence of events that I'm describing). Around the same

---

12. de Filippo, et al. (2011).
13. Haber et al. (2016).

time as the *E1a-E1b* split, haplogroup *E2* split away from *E1* and ended up in central and southern Africa (see **Color Plate 50**).

The upper end of this date range (1400s B.C.) covers the time of a major downfall in Egypt's history. The traditional dates for the Exodus of Israel from Egypt land in the 1400s B.C. According to the Bible, the Ten Plagues that preceded the Exodus devastated the nation of Egypt. It's not hard to imagine that the trauma would send Egyptians fleeing far away from their homes.

The lower end of this date range included the 900s B.C., a century in which the Kush/Ethiopia region saw a major military defeat:

> Zerah the Ethiopian came out against [the kingdom of Judah] with an army of a million men and three hundred chariots, and he came to Mareshah. So Asa [king of Judah] went out against him, and they set the troops in battle array in the Valley of Zephathah at Mareshah. And Asa cried out to the LORD his God, and said, "LORD, it is nothing for You to help, whether with many or with those who have no power; help us, O LORD our God, for we rest on You, and in Your name we go against this multitude. O LORD, You are our God; do not let man prevail against You!"
>
> So the LORD struck the Ethiopians before Asa and Judah, and the Ethiopians fled. And Asa and the people who were with him pursued them to Gerar. So the Ethiopians were overthrown, and they could not recover, for they were broken before the LORD and His army. And they carried away very much spoil (2 Chronicles 14:9–13).

Perhaps this event provoked migration out of northeast Africa and into sub-Saharan Africa.

So far, the only genetic split that we haven't mapped is the one between haplogroups *A/B* and *E* (see **Color Plate 51**). This event takes us back to one of the most ancient time points in the Y chromosome tree. Historically, little is known about this era. It's in the range of mainstream dates that require significant correction in light of recent Y chromosome mutation rate results. At this stage, it's difficult to know from history which events caused this divide.

Nevertheless, where history leaves off, topography takes over. By itself, the topography of Africa implied a narrative for the history of people movements that took us right to the doorstep of ancient Egypt.

Departure

In North Africa, the massive sands of the Sahara strike a sharp contrast to the greenery of West Africa and below (**Color Plate 58**). The divide between the two regions forms an almost perfect horizontal line from west to east. In the east, this line takes us into our region of interest — Sudan and Ethiopia. At least, it does in our current era. In ancient times, this eastern section would have been farther north. Even into the last millennium before Christ, Sudan was more wooded than it is now.[14]

This horizontal line also marks a disincentive to human migration. To get to sub-Saharan Africa from the north, you'd have to brave the desert. Even with the help of the camel, regular crossing of this desert wouldn't have been attractive.

Travel by sea would also have been difficult. From the Mediterranean, your options were limited. The Suez Canal, the connection between the Red Sea and the Mediterranean, wasn't built until A.D. 1869. For the several millennia prior, you would have to go south around the West African coast. Until the European Age of Discovery, this path was effectively closed.

Alternatively, you could sneak up the Nile from its mouth to its source in sub-Saharan Africa. This path takes you into the eastern section of African greenery (**Color Plate 58**).

In other words, the topography of Africa suggests that the Sudan/Ethiopia region acted like a corridor between ancient Egypt and ancient sub-Saharan Africa. People likely arose in Egypt and then migrated into the rest of the African continent. However, it seems they didn't return to Egypt (i.e., see the absence of haplogroups *B*, *E1a*, and *E2* from modern Egypt) — hence, the ignorance of the Pharaohs of Victoria Falls.

These observations make the fate of the ancient Egyptians clearer. Given the small sizes of early African populations, and given the concentration of early Africans in northeast Africa, it's virtually guaranteed that the ancient Egyptian lineages intermingled with those of their African neighbors. It's also likely that we currently possess the

---

14. Phillipson (2005), p. 224.

record of this intermingling.[15] It's hard to believe that haplogroups *E1a, E2, E1b1a, E1b1b*, and perhaps even *A* and *B* were *not* somehow tied to ancient Egypt.

Today, some of these lineages — especially *E1b1b* — exist far beyond the borders of Africa (**Color Plates 23, 35, 47, 49, 50**). Based on these data, it would seem, then, that ancient Egyptian blood has persisted, not just in Africa, but *all the way to Pakistan and Norway.*

Chapter 6 Summary:

- Mainstream science says that major African ethnolinguistic groups were already separate peoples 12,000 years ago. This implies that ancient Egyptian genealogies separated from the rest of Africa a long time ago.

- Several of the major African Y chromosome lineages (*haplogroups*) — A, B, E1a, E1b1a, E2 — are found primarily in sub-Saharan Africa and not in North Africa/Egypt. This would imply that Egypt is disconnected from sub-Saharan Africa, as mainstream science has contended.

- Detailed studies have been performed on the rate at which the Y chromosome undergoes copying errors. These studies imply a revised timescale for human history. The revised timescale makes the ancient Egyptians and other ancient Africans contemporaries.

- The revised timescale also changes the dates for when the major African Y chromosome haplogroups are linked. The timing of their connections is contemporaneous with ancient Egypt.

- The geography of Africa is an additional line of evidence implying that Egypt was an entry point — the corridor — to the rest of Africa.

- Together, these findings imply that much of Africa found its source in ancient Egypt, and that ancient Egyptian lineages eventually spread across three continents.

---

15. A caveat: As more African men have their Y chromosomes sequenced, the number of ancient lineages that we find will increase. What I've just shown is simply the beginning of this quest.

7

Vulnerable

In 753 B.C., along the banks of the Tiber River, the early Romans founded the Italian city that bears their name.[1] For more than four centuries, the early Romans acquired little land beyond central Italy. In 298 B.C., Roman territory extended less than 200 miles on either side of the city. But by the end of the 200s B.C., the Romans were well on their way to ruling the entirety of the Mediterranean world. By the A.D. 100s, they did. From Spain to the Middle East, from England to Egypt, Rome commanded a dominant world empire (**Color Plate 59**).

Three hundred years later, the Roman Empire had split in two. Wave upon wave of Germanic tribes descended from the east onto the western part of the divided Roman Empire (**Color Plate 60**). Rome had no way to keep them out. The western Roman Empire fell permanently.

The eastern Roman Empire (the Byzantine Empire) hung on for another millennium, reconquering some of the lost territory (**Color Plate 61**). But it, too, shrank with time (**Color Plate 61**). In A.D. 1453, it succumbed to the advances of the Ottoman Turks.

What happened to the Roman people? When the Roman Empire fell, did the Roman people disappear with it? Or has Roman blood gone the way of ancient Egypt, intermingling with groups all across the continent and beyond?

In a sense, the fall of the Roman Empire was a natural consequence of its geography. Throughout its history, Europe has been protected

---

1. The traditional date for the founding of Rome is 753 B.C. Modern scholarship disputes this claim.

on three sides by water (**Color Plate 62**). The Mediterranean and the Atlantic have guarded the southern and western borders. The Arctic Ocean has protected the northern border.

On land, other topographical features have discouraged foreign invasion. The Alps, the Pyrenees, and other mountain ranges have protected the south. The bitter cold of the Scandinavian north has kept invading armies looking for other options.

But to the east, Europe has sat exposed. Europe is not an island; it's a peninsula. In the east, no oceans have protected Europe from would-be conquerors. No mountains or deserts have either. If Europe were a house, then this eastern frontier has been an unlocked door swinging in the breeze, sounding an invitation to enter.

In the A.D. 400s, the people to the east received the invitation and invaded. Now, more than 1,500 years after the fact, we're just beginning to uncover the outsized ramifications of the geographic vulnerability for the fate of the ancient Roman people. Roman blood has persisted. But in places we'd never think to look.

The Genetics of Rome

Today, Italian men possess a variety of Y chromosome haplogroups. None of the haplogroups exist in more than a third of Italian men. Most exist at levels below 10%.

Like its ancient neighbor across the Mediterranean, Egypt, modern Italy bears the marks of millennia of immigration and conquest. One of the most recent was the invasion of the Ottoman Turks.

Officially, Italy was never under Ottoman rule. However, just across the Adriatic Sea, the Ottomans occupied European land (see **Color Plate 32**). The genetic effects of this conquest spilled over into Italy. Almost 20% of Italian men belong to haplogroup *J*, the most abundant haplogroup in modern Turkey. Another 10% belong to *E1b1b*, the Arab Muslim lineage that Ottoman Turks likely brought into Europe during their conquests. In other words, the echoes of Ottoman proximity are present in 30% of Italian men.

The remaining 70% — the vast majority — of Italian Y chromosome haplogroups still require explanation. Among these lineages, the ancient Roman heritage might still exist. The most dominant lineage among Italian men today is a haplogroup known as *R1b*. Around 30% belong to *R1b*. Every other haplogroup exists at lower levels.

Outside of Italy, *R1b* is found at high levels in Western Europe (**Color Plate 63**). At lower levels, it is found in Eastern Europe and North Africa. It even spills over into the Near East and can be found as far away as East Asia.

When compared to the geographic extent of the Roman Empire (see **Color Plate 60**), the distribution of *R1b* shows some overlap. *R1b* extends wider than the Roman Empire ever did. But where Rome ruled for centuries — the Mediterranean and Western Europe — *R1b* is found at its highest levels.

Might *R1b* tie modern Italians back to ancient Rome?

For Western Europe, the timing of *R1b* arrival suggests a disconnect from the ancient Europeans. For example, one research study sampled several populations of European men: From Italy ("BergamoItalian", "Sardinian", "Tuscan"), France ("French", "Basque"), the United Kingdom ("Orcadian"), and Russia ("Russian"). Notice how men from each of these places trace their *R1b* lineages back to a common ancestor in the A.D. 1300s to 1600s — not back to the time of Christ (**Color Plate 64**).

In one sense, this result is not surprising. It may not fulfill our hopes for an ancient Roman lineage, but it fits the math we learned in chapter 2. It's the echo of the recent history of human population growth.

Beginning in the A.D. 1400s, the global human population size began exploding. Or, from the reverse perspective, we could say that the human population in the 1400s was 20 times smaller than it is today. Inevitably, the Y chromosome family tree will reflect this fact. Like every other family tree, the branches of the Y chromosome tree replicate population rises and falls.

Upon brief reflection, this fact becomes self-evident. For example, my wife and I have four children. Our family tree has four branches leading from us to them. In other words, the two branches in mine and my wife's generation have expanded to four in our children's generation. Our family size is undergoing population doubling, and the number of branches in our family tree reveals the same conclusion.

This principle applies to the family trees of every person around the globe. Which means it also applies to the *R1b* branches in Europe.

Far fewer people were alive in Europe in A.D. 1400 than today. Far fewer branches of the European family tree existed in A.D. 1400 as compared to today. The branches of *R1b* reflect this mathematical fact.

This branching pattern also implies that modern European nationalities were fluid before the 1500s. Look again at the details of **Color Plate 64**. In the *R1b* branch, men from all four of the sampling locations (Italy, France, UK, and Russia) have a common ancestor in the A.D. 1400s to 1700s. It's as if these nationalities didn't exist back then as separate entities.

Surprisingly, this genetic conclusion finds confirmation in the field of traditional history:

> "The nation-state" and "nationalism" are terms which are frequently applied, or misapplied, to the sixteenth century. They are more appropriate to the nineteenth, when they were invented by historians looking for the origins of the nation-states of their own day. They should certainly not be used to convey premature preoccupations with ethnic identity. What they can properly convey, however, is the strong sense of sovereignty which both monarchs and subjects assumed, as the unity of the Middle Ages disintegrated.[2]

Deeper on the *R1b* lineage, the branches tend *not* to be concentrated in Western Europe. Even in the 1100s to 1500s, some of the Pakistanis in this study (the *Makrani, Balochi*, and *Pathan* peoples) start showing up in *R1b* (**Color Plate 65**). In the A.D. 300s to 800s, lineages link to Afghanistan (the *Hazara* people) (**Color Plate 65**). *R1b* lineages originating in 65 B.C. to the A.D. 400s connect to Central Asia/northwestern China (the *Uygur* people) (**Color Plate 65**).

These early lineages take us geographically far from ancient Rome. But they end up revealing a surprising link with these ancient Italian rulers.

Clues from the Middle Ages

A closer examination of the details of *R1b* allows us to visualize the timing and movement of *R1b* into Europe.[3] For example, one of the early *R1b* branches (*R1b-M73*) that broke away from the main *R1b*

---

2. Davies (1998), p. 520.
3. See supplemental online methods and data for details. Please note: The populations used in this study of *R1b* subgroups are slightly different from the populations used in other studies and maps examined throughout this book. Again, see supplemental online methods and data for details.

lineage tends to be concentrated in Eastern Europe — in Russia near Kazakhstan (**Color Plate 66**). Between the A.D. 700s and 1400s, additional *R1b* branches (*R1b-M269, R1b-L23*) broke away from the main branch. These are found primarily in Eastern and Southeastern Europe, in Turkey, and in the Caucasus region (**Color Plates 67–68**).

After the A.D. 1400s, the *R1b* lineages seem to have undergone a rapid expansion and dispersal. In the span of a century (A.D. 1450s to 1550s), the main *R1b* lineage appears to have left Turkey and the Balkans and migrated into Western Europe. Along the way, it split into several different subgroups. The first split separated it into a central European group (*R1b-U106*) and a southwestern European group (*R1b-S116*). The *R1b-U106* men now dominate the Netherlands, Germany, and Austria (**Color Plate 69**). As you move away from these countries in almost any direction, the frequency of *R1b-U106* drops off. The *R1b-S116* lineage dominates French, Spanish, and Portuguese Y chromosomes (**Color Plate 70**).

The *R1b-S116* group then underwent further subdivision. One branch (*R1b-U152*) seems to have gone primarily into Switzerland and Italy (**Color Plate 71**). The other branch (*R1b-M529*) appears to have crossed the English Channel and concentrated in the British Isles and Ireland (**Color Plate 72**). There, it underwent yet another subdivision into *R1b-M222*, which is found almost exclusively in the British Isles and Ireland (**Color Plate 73**).

Together, these data suggest a migration route (**Color Plate 74**):

- In the A.D. 400s to 700s, the ancestral population of *R1b* men resided somewhere in far Eastern Europe or Central Asia.
- Then, in the A.D. 700s to 1400s, a subgroup of these men started moving westward, leaving the *M73* lineage behind.
- Some of the migrating men settled down in places they crossed, like western Russia, the Caucasus, Turkey, the Balkans, and the former Eastern Bloc European countries. The ones who stayed in these places gave rise to the *M269* and *L23* lineages.

Then, in the A.D. 1400s and 1500s, something happened to push another group in the direction of Central and Western Europe:

- Migration and dispersal appear to have happened rapidly. The sub-lineages that concentrated in central Europe (*U106*), in France and the Iberian Peninsula (*S116*), in Switzerland and Italy (*U152*), and in the British Isles and Ireland (*M529, M222*) all separated within a few decades of each other.

- These lineages that appear suddenly in Central and Western Europe are largely missing from the Balkans, Turkey, and the Caucasus.

This path also happens to follow the natural topography of Europe (**Color Plate 75**). From the east, the easiest route into Europe is around, not over, the Carpathian Mountains. North of the Carpathians takes you into cold Poland. South of the Carpathians takes you into the sunny Balkans.

Once you're in the Balkans, the quickest way out is on flat land through gaps between the Dinaric Alps and Carpathians. Then, once you're in the central European plain, your options are more limited. To get to the British Isles, you have to cross water — the English Channel. To get to Spain or Italy, you have to cross the Pyrenees or Alps, respectively. But these movements involve short distances. Trekking across the Atlantic Ocean or Mediterranean Sea requires more effort. It's almost as if these *R1b* migrants moved out as quickly as they could, and then dispersed as far as they could with minimal effort.

Taken together, these results imply that something happened, perhaps in the Balkan/Turkish region in the A.D. 1400s and 1500s, that prompted a group of *R1b* men to migrate away from and out of this region and into the rest of Europe. But what?

In the latter half of the A.D. 1300s and first half of the A.D. 1400s, the Ottoman empire expanded into Europe (**Color Plate 32**). From A.D. 1451 to A.D. 1566, the Ottomans made their deepest push into Europe, pushing farther north into what is now Hungary, laying waste to the region (**Color Plate 32**). This conquest moved the Ottoman's European territorial border to its farthest extent. Perhaps this Ottoman Turkish advance into southeastern Europe pushed the *R1b* residents out.

None of this links *R1b* to ancient Rome. But it gets us closer.

Migrating In

Why did *R1b* arrive from the east in the first place?

A few centuries after the fall of the western Roman Empire, the *Magyars* arrived from far Eastern Europe/Central Asia (**Color Plate 76**). They spoke languages unlike those of ancient Greece and Rome.

It seems that *R1a* could easily be the signature of the Mongol *political* conquests, in which non-Mongol *ethnicities* dominated.

Who were these ethnicities that gave rise to *R1a*? Let's answer this question by pursuing another: Where was the *R1a* homeland? If *R1a* represents people conquered by the Mongols, it follows then that these people were living in Mongol-conquered lands. These lands spanned the Pacific to Eastern Europe (**Color Plate 30**). We also just observed that some of the early *R1a* branches are found in Europe. This would seem to imply that the conquered *R1a* people lived in the western half, rather than the eastern half, of the Mongol-conquered lands. The western half includes Eastern Europe and Central Asia. It seems natural to put the *R1a* men somewhere there.

Together, the data we have for haplogroups *R1a* and *R1b* are consistent with both of these haplogroups originating in Central Asia, and then overrunning the populations of Western (**Color Plate 63**) and Eastern (**Color Plate 80**) Europe (see **Color Plate 84** for summary).

In other words, it doesn't look like *R1b* arose from the ancient Romans. However, genetic lineages need not arise in ancient Rome to have relevance to these early European peoples. As we've seen in chapters 2 and 3, branches on a family tree have a funny way of becoming tangled over time.

Africa

When the Roman Empire fell to Germanic tribes, some tribes hailed originally from northern Europe and Scandinavia (see **Color Plate 60**). However, the pre-invasion origin of the Germanics is unknown. Their Scandinavian homelands existed near Eastern Europe, which has an open topographical door to Central Asia. From this perspective, it's worth asking if some of them also traced their history farther to the east. The Huns did. Perhaps the Germanics did as well.

Once these invaders arrived in Western Europe, some of them pushed down into North Africa. The Vandals ruled Tunisia and the surrounding area during the A.D. 400s and 500s (see **Color Plate 60**). Reconquest by the eastern Roman Empire in the A.D. 530s dethroned them (see **Color Plate 61**). Arab Muslim conquests in the A.D. 600s and 700s permanently ended European rule in North Africa (see **Color Plate 25**).

Surprisingly, *R1b* — the purportedly Central Asian lineage — is today found among North Africans (see **Color Plate 63**). It also exists deeper in Africa. In some populations in Cameroon, *R1b* exists at high levels. Among the men of the *Ouldeme* people, *R1b* can reach levels of more than 95% (not shown in **Color Plate 63**).[5] This African *R1b* branch broke away from the main *R1b* branch in the A.D. 100s to 600s (e.g., see the North African *Mozabite* individuals in **Color Plate 65**). In other words, somewhere in the A.D. 100s to 600s, it seems that a group of Central Asians split off from their homeland and eventually ended up in North Africa (**Color Plate 85**).

Given the timing, it's natural to associate these events with the influx of Germanic tribes and of the Huns. Historically, the trajectory of their migrations passed through Roman Europe — an empire with whom they eventually intermixed.

Consequently, the *R1b* lineages in North Africa and Cameroon might bear a touch of ancient Roman blood. For now, they might be the closest connection we have to the ancient Roman Empire.

Thus, the geographic vulnerability of Europe gave the ancient Romans a much different historical trajectory than their ancient Egyptian neighbors. Post-Rome, countless Eastern peoples passed through the wide open Eastern European door, overrunning the medieval European civilizations and swamping European family trees with Central Asian branches.

But not completely. The heritage of ancient Rome might still be with us. Just not in the places where we expect to find it.

---

5. Cruciani et al. (2010).

Chapter 7 Summary:

- The ancient Romans were an indigenous European people whose western empire fell more than 1,500 years ago.

- The geography of Europe protects it from invasion on three sides. The fourth side — the eastern frontier — is vulnerable. The ancient Romans fell due to invasions by the Germanic tribes and the Huns, who came from the east.

- The geographic distribution of the major Western European haplogroup, *R1b*, overlaps the geographic distribution of the ancient Roman Empire, suggesting a possible link.

- *R1b* is connected to haplogroups of Central Asian origin, including *R1a*. These links establish the Central Asian — rather than European — origin of *R1b*.

- One of the sub-branches in *R1b* broke away from the main *R1b* lineage around the time of the fall of the western Roman Empire. This suggests a possible genealogical link to the Germanics or the Huns.

- One of the Germanic invaders, the Vandals, eventually ended up in North Africa — just like this *R1b* sub-branch. This strengthens the link between the Germanics and the *R1b* sub-branch.

- Germanics eventually intermixed with the Romans themselves. If the North African *R1b* sub-branch represents one of the Germanics, then this *R1b* sub-branch might be one of the few genealogical links we have to the ancient Romans.

The Middle East

8

Mirror

In 539 B.C., Cyrus, king of the Persians, conquered Babylon and became king of the Middle East. From his homeland in what is now Iran, Cyrus founded an empire that would eventually reach into the Balkans (**Color Plate 86**). If we tried to predict the fate of these ancient Persians from the rules learned in previous chapters, we'd fail miserably.

Topographically, the Middle East begs for foreign invasion. If Europe is like a walled house with a door swinging open in the east, then the Middle East is like a poorly fenced city park. On three sides, Europe has large bodies of water to keep invaders out. On three sides, the Middle East also has bodies of water, but unlike Europe's, these barriers are breached by land bridges that give foreigners easy access (**Color Plate 87**).

If Europeans wanted to march into the Middle East from the west, they could. The Bosporus Strait and the Dardanelles barely separate Asia from Europe. In the 300s B.C., Alexander the Great capitalized on this fact. He crossed at the Dardanelles, a distance of no more than four miles, before conquering Asia (**Color Plate 88**). If conquerors wanted to invade the Middle East from the east, they could. Cyrus the Persian did. Between the Caspian Sea and the Persian Gulf, Iran is a wide causeway (**Color Plate 87**). From the north, the Scythians repeatedly harassed the Persians. They could do so because the Black Sea and Caspian Sea are split by the Caucasus (**Color Plate 87**). To the southwest of the Middle East, the Red Sea and the Mediterranean Sea almost separate Africa from the Middle East, but not quite. The Sinai Peninsula gives Africans a clear path to Middle Eastern conquest (**Color Plate 87**). The Egyptians regularly used it. Because of this topography, for millennia the Middle East has been one of the most volatile, contested tracts of land on earth.

Naturally, this implies that the genetic signal of the ancient Persians quickly disappeared from history.

This conclusion becomes stronger when we compare the Persians to their European contemporaries, the Greeks. For Europe, the ancient Greeks were the fountain of civilization. They existed long before Rome's ascent. In terms of cultural impact, it's difficult to find an ancient European culture with a bigger imprint than the Greeks. From math (Euclidean geometry, Pythagorean theorem) to physics (Archimedes' principle), from medicine (the Hippocratic oath) to biology (Aristotle's classification), from politics (democracy) to the language of the New Testament, Greek influence pervades Western society.

The ancient Persians left no such legacy. They were far from the first to rule the Middle East, and their culture left an impact far smaller than that of the ancient Greeks. Today, the culture of the Middle Eastern world is not dominated by Persian practices. Instead, it's dominated by influences that arose 1,000 years after the Persian Empire collapsed. In the A.D. 600s in Arabia, Mohammed founded the Islamic empire. In the 1,400 years since then, Muslim kingdoms have risen and fallen, and Muslim culture still rules the Middle East, from Syria to Iran to Yemen.

Politically, the post-Persian Middle East remained a hotbed of conflict, one that alternated between two phases. During the reign of the Persians, the Middle East was the seat of power. It was the center of their empire. When Alexander the Great overthrew the Persians, the Middle East became the geographic center of his empire. After Alexander died, the Middle East became the staging area — the fulcrum on which the balance of power tipped.

In the west, the Romans overthrew the Greeks but failed to recover all of Alexander's former lands (**Color Plate 59**). The center of the Middle East marked the limits of the Roman Empire. In the east, the Parthians ruled from the border of India into Iraq (**Color Plate 89**), but no farther. The Middle East thus became the locus of Roman-Parthian conflict.

This type of political situation lasted for more than half a millennium. In Western Europe, half of the Roman Empire fell to invading Germanic tribes while the eastern Byzantine half held on for another thousand years. The Byzantines generally ruled the eastern Mediterranean but saw their dominion progressively shrink with time (**Color Plate 61**). Farther east, the Sasanids took over from the Parthians. Despite the political switch, the geographic reach of the Sasanid domain was almost unchanged from the Parthian one (**Color Plate 90**). The lands between the Byzantines and Sasanids — the Middle East — remained contested land.

In the A.D. 600s, a small band of Arabs flipped the Middle Eastern political script back to pre-Roman times. Beginning in the Arabian Peninsula, Mohammed and his Muslim followers quickly built an empire that touched three continents — from Spain through North Africa into Central Asia (**Color Plate 25**). The Middle East returned to being a seat of power.

In the A.D. 1000s, another group of Muslims entered the Middle East, this time from Central Asia. The Seljuk Turks wrested control from the Arab Muslims, ruling from Kazakhstan to Turkey (**Color Plate 29**). But not for long. In the A.D. 1200s, Genghis Khan and his Mongol hordes conquered half of Asia, including the Middle East (**Color Plate 30**). After the breakup of the Mongol empire into four khanates, the Middle East remained under Mongol rule as the *Il-Khanate* (**Color Plate 78**). In the late A.D. 1300s and 1400s, another Mongol conqueror, Tamerlane, came through (**Color Plate 31**).

And then the Middle East returned to fulcrum mode. After the fall of Tamerlane's empire, the Ottoman Turks resuscitated the Turkish empire (**Color Plate 32**). They eventually controlled lands on three continents. But they could not push back through the Middle East to recover their former Iranian lands. Instead, in Iran, the Safavids took control (**Color Plate 91**). After the Ottomans and Safavids, no other kingdoms created empires that commanded as much of the Middle East as the Ottoman Turks did.

In light of this political history, what can we say about the fate of the ancient Persian peoples? Did perpetual Middle Eastern conflict erase their genealogical signature? Or did they defy expectations and, somehow, leave descendants to this day? What happened to the people of the ancient Persian Empire?

In Europe, we found that the lineages from the ancient Roman era were eventually swamped by lineages from subsequent migrants (chapter 7). These later arrivals (haplogroups *R1b* and *R1a*) came from Central Asia during the Middle Ages. In the Middle East, we've just observed that one of the last dominant Middle Eastern empires also traced its beginnings to Central Asia. The Ottoman Turks ruled from the area that is now modern Turkey, but their ancestors came from Central Asia. The earlier Turks arrived in the Middle East at the same time as their Central Asian counterparts arrived in Europe: During the Middle Ages.

From this perspective, it makes sense for us to begin our search for the ancient Persian lineage by identifying the Ottoman Turkish lineage. Then we can work backward toward the ancient genetic signals. If we can untangle all the recent lineages from the Middle East, then the ancient Persian branch of the Middle Eastern family tree might emerge.

It did emerge. But not in a way anyone would have guessed.

"Turkic"

Today, among Turkish men, the most abundant Y chromosome haplogroup is haplogroup *J2*. Consistent with centuries of Ottoman Turkish rule in Europe, Europe also harbors *J2* (**Color Plate 92**). Haplogroup *J2* also exists in parts of North Africa, another region once under Ottoman sway. Fittingly, *J2* is also found across much of the Middle East and into Central Asia, following nearly the same path as the Seljuk Turks (**Color Plate 92**).

So far, we'd be justified in calling *J2* a Turkish lineage.

But India also has men with *J2* (**Color Plate 92**). India was never under Ottoman or Seljuk rule. How did *J2* arrive there?

The details of the *J2* branching patterns held a critical clue. Within *J2*, branches tended to form regional subclusters. For example, in one study, four European populations (British, Spanish, Toscani in Italy, and Finnish) and five South Asian populations (Punjabi from Pakistan; Bengali from Bangladesh; Indian Gujarati who were living in Houston, Texas; Sri Lankans who were living in the UK; and Indian Telugus who were living in the UK) were sampled. In this study, the European *J2* branches formed clusters that were distinct from the South Asian ones (**Color Plate 93**). These clusters joined at various points in what roughly corresponds to the era known as the Middle Ages.

In theory, this genetic pattern might have arisen in one of three scenarios. In the first scenario, beginning in the Middle Ages, a European migrated over to India and never returned to Europe. This would show up as a permanent split between European and South Asian branches in *J2*. Under the second scenario, the reverse may have occurred. Beginning in the Middle Ages, an Indian may have migrated over to Europe and never returned to India. This would also result in a permanent split between European and South Asian branches in *J2*. In the third scenario, a population in between Europe and India existed, and then split into two camps. One camp headed into India; the other, into Europe.

In the A.D. 1200s, the *Ghurids*, another Central Asian people, entered northern India and founded the Muslim Delhi Sultanate (**Color Plate 94**). The Ghurids were a *Tajik* people whose language was likely in the Iranian branch of the Indo-European language family. But the Ghurid armies made heavy use of Turkish soldiers who were also from Central Asia — so much so that this period has been labeled "The Coming of Turkish Rule."[1]

Around the same time, the Mongols came from northeast Asia and cut down through the Middle East. As mentioned earlier, they never conquered India (**Color Plates 30, 31**). But their victories effectively cut off the Indian subcontinent from the rest of Asia. In the west, the survivors of the Mongol conquests were the Seljuk Turks (**Color Plate 29**) whose Turkic successors, the Ottomans, created an empire that eventually reached into Europe (**Color Plate 32**).

If *J2* was originally Turkic, then Turkic history readily explains the *J2* branching patterns. Seljuks and Ottomans didn't take *J2* into India. The Turkish soldiers in the Ghurid armies did. Their relatives, the Seljuks and Ottomans, took *J2* west into Turkey and eventually into Europe. Mongol conquests kept the western Turks from rejoining their relatives in India.

If this were the whole story of *J2*, we could move on from *J2* and look for a better candidate for the ancient Persian lineage. However, as we've already discovered, the genetic history of mankind is rarely simple. Haplogroup *J2* is no exception. In the context of other haplogroups, the origin of *J2* — and its seeming irrelevance to the ancient Persians — aren't quite what they appear.

---

1. Thapar (2004), p. 434.

Mixture

Haplogroup *J2* isn't the only Y chromosome lineage to echo the history of Turkish rule. Haplogroup *G* (**Color Plate 95**) shows a geographic distribution remarkably similar to that of *J2*. Both are spread from Central Asia to Europe. Both have a presence all across Europe. Both reach into the far eastern/northeastern parts of Asia. Both can be detected in India. Both exist at higher levels in Turkey as compared to the Arabian Peninsula. Superimposed, the distribution of *G* and *J2* show a strong overlap (**Color Plate 96**).

However, the overlap between the two is not perfect. One of the few points of difference between *G* and *J2* is in the absolute concentration of each. When haplogroups *G* and *J2* are found together, *G* tends to exist at lower levels. Consistent with this pattern, the overall geographic distribution of *J2* is slightly wider than that of *G*. It's as if *G* and *J2* migrated together, but *J2* was more abundant in this initial migratory population.

On the Y chromosome tree, the similarities between *G* and *J2* increase. In the branches of *G*, we can find splits between European and Indian/South Asian lineages. These seem to occur around the same time in both *G* (**Color Plate 97**) and *J2* (**Color Plate 93**).

Together, these data suggest that the Turkic migrations from Central Asia involved men in both *J2* and in *G*.

If you reflect on this conclusion, the mix of both *J2* and *G* makes sense. Why wouldn't the Turkish peoples have had a mix of ethnicities and lineages? Modern populations certainly do. Modern Egyptians have a mix of Y chromosome haplogroups (see chapters 5 and 6), as do modern Italians (see chapter 7). In fact, most modern African and European populations are mixtures of lineages.[2] Surely the peoples of the past also harbored a diversity of lineages.

If *J2* and *G* did migrate together, then from whom did *J2* first arise? Was *J2* originally Turkic? Or was it something else? Perhaps Persian?

As the *J2* name implies, the *J* lineage has at least two branches. Haplogroup *J2* is the second of these branches. The first *J* branch uncovered another sequence of post-Persia events which take us

---

2. For visual proof, just compare the maps of the Y chromosome haplogroup distributions in this chapter and in previous chapters. The populations that were examined were consistent across these studies. Pick one (e.g., German or Moroccan or Nigerian) and count the number of haplogroup maps in which it appears.

closer to the answers to these questions — and closer to the ancient Persian past.

"Arab"

In the southern half of the Middle East's Arabian Peninsula, the dominant haplogroup is neither *J2* nor *G*. It's *J1* (**Color Plate 98**).

Haplogroup *J1* seems to tell a story that's different from that of either *J2* or, by extension, *G*. Yet, we'll soon discover that the *J1* story complements the stories of *J2* and *G*, and in a manner that provides subtle clues to the fate of the ancient Persians.

The differences between the narratives implied by *J1* and *J2/G* may not be so obvious on the surface. Geographically, the overall distribution of haplogroup *J1* overlaps that of haplogroup *J2* (**Color Plate 99**). Both run through the Middle East. Both reach into North Africa. Both are found in Europe and Central Asia. But, upon close inspection, the discrepancies emerge. Unlike *J2*, *J1* doesn't seem to quite make it into India. Also, we already observed that *J1* exists at much higher levels than *J2* in the Arabian Peninsula. In terms of its European and North African concentrations, *J1* shows a pattern that mirrors, rather than replicates, the distribution of *J2*. Compared to its concentration in North Africa, *J2* exists at higher levels in Europe. The reverse is true in *J1*; *J1* exists at higher levels in North Africa than in Europe.

In one sense, the geography of *J1* is familiar. It echoes the distribution of a haplogroup that we encountered in chapter 5. *E1b1b* is also found in the Middle East, North Africa, and Europe. Like *J1*, *E1b1b* fails to make it into India. *E1b1b* also exists at higher levels in North Africa as compared to Europe (**Color Plate 100**). Though the overlap between *E1b1b* and *J1* isn't perfect,[3] the similarities between the two haplogroups are noticeable.

In chapter 5, we concluded that *E1b1b* had something to do with the expansion of the Arab Muslim empires in the A.D. 600s to 700s, and the migration of Arab tribes into North Africa around the 900s to 1200s. Might *J1* as well? A detailed look at the history of Arabia suggests that *J1* did indeed.

In the Arabian Peninsula, the conquests of Mohammed and his followers arose out of more than religious zeal: They also sprang from unusual population growth.

---

3. For example, overall, *E1b1b* is more abundant that *J1*, and its geographic reach is wider than that of *J1*.

As a general rule in the Middle East and in Iran, population growth has followed a predictable trajectory. Like the rest of the world, population growth has lagged for a millennia or two; then, in the last few centuries, it has spiked (**Color Plate 101**).[4] (In **Color Plate 101**, the dashed lines represent the actual history of population growth. The solid lines represent the effective history — where the only population rises that matter are those that are *not* wiped out by later population declines). At this 30,000-foot view, the unique place of the Arabian Peninsula might not be so obvious.

If we zoom in on the pre-spike era, the differences become clearer (**Color Plate 102**). All around the Middle East and Iran, populations have risen and declined. (Again, in **Color Plate 102**, the dashed lines represent the actual history of population growth. The solid lines represent the effective history — where the only population rises that matter are those that are *not* wiped out by later population declines.) But in the Arabian Peninsula, the declines have not been as dramatic. The people there were able to avoid the depredations of the Mongol armies (**Color Plates 30, 31**). Consequently, their population declines have not been as dramatic as in the rest of the Muslim world.

Prior to the Arab Muslim conquests, the Arabian Peninsula underwent a significant and permanent population rise. Later population rises were erased by subsequent declines. But the initial rise from 200 B.C. to around A.D. 450 persisted (**Color Plate 102**).

The same scenario did not play out in the rest of the Middle East and in Iran. In these locations all the way into the recent era, population rises were completely cancelled by declines. Effectively, population growth was flat from 200 B.C. until the A.D. 1400s (**Color Plate 102**).

Recall that family trees record changes in population size. When populations grow, the number of branches on the tree grows. When populations decline, the number of branches on the family tree declines.

This same principle applies to the Y chromosome tree but with a slight modification. The Y chromosome tree that we're using is based on DNA from the *survivors* of history.

Trees of survivors don't have branches that lead to peoples who went extinct. They also don't reveal every instance of population growth. Periods of growth that were wiped out by declines are invisible in these trees. In other words, these trees record *effective* population sizes. If their

---

4. McEvedy and Jones (1975).

ancestors underwent population growth, this shows up in their family trees only if the growth was *not* cancelled by later population declines.

From the *J1* branches of the Y chromosome family tree, a consistent population history emerges (see **Color Plate 103** for an example from one of the trees). Across multiple studies, earlier *J1* individuals underwent population growth in the A.D. 50s to 400s. Then, the population curve goes almost flat. Growth resumes around the A.D. 1400s.

This early population growth history in *J1* is reminiscent of the known history of population growth in the Arabian Peninsula.

Later in history, the *J1* and historical growth curves diverge. But this divergence is explicable. The branches that multiply around the A.D. 1400s don't lead to men living in the Arabian Peninsula. Instead, they lead to men, for example, from Europe ("Sardinian" in **Color Plate 104**) where population growth began to spike in the A.D. 1400s (**Color Plate 105**). The population spike in Middle Eastern *J1* men occurs later (see the "Bedouin" men of Israel/West Bank in **Color Plate 104**), consistent with the known population history of the Israel/West Bank region (see **Color Plates 101–102**).

When you consider that the population growth curve in **Color Plate 103** is based on the DNA from fewer than 30 men in total, this result is quite spectacular. The current male population of the Middle East is in the millions, yet the DNA from thirty men can roughly approximate 2,000 years of Arabian population history.

In other words, taken together, the *E1b1b* and *J1* branches look like they were *both* part of the Arab Muslim expansion. This implies that the Arab Muslims were a population of mixed lineages.

And why wouldn't they be? Again, modern populations are almost always a mix of different Y chromosome lineages. Surely historical populations followed the same pattern.

So far in our journey, we've connected *J1* to the Arab Muslim expansions and *J2* to the Turkic migrations. Both of these movements occurred 1,000 years or more after the fall of Cyrus' empire. In exploring the histories implied by *J2* and *J1*, we're still a long way from ancient Persia. Yet both of these haplogroups reveal historical narratives that run through the geographic domains of ancient Persia. Though they might be 1,000 years removed from Cyrus and his people, they're still geographically close. We seem to be on the right path. We just need to dive deeper into the past.

To do so, we'll need a more ancient genealogical link. Surprisingly, this link arises, not in Asia, but in Europe. A fuller understanding of the ancient history of Europe takes us back to pre-Roman times and connects us — via haplogroups *J1* and *J2* — to the ancient Persians.

Indo-European

Today, in Western and Eastern Europe, males are dominated by lineages from Central Asia (see chapter 7). Across Spain, France, Great Britain, Norway, Germany, Italy, Denmark, and Hungary, *R1b* is the top haplogroup (see **Color Plate 63** and online Supplemental Table 1). Across Poland, western Russia, and Ukraine, *R1a* is the top haplogroup (i.e., see **Color Plate 80** and online Supplemental Table 1). Both *R1a* and *R1b* arose from Central Asia and migrated into Europe in the Middle Ages.

Neither of these lineages seems to tell the history of the indigenous Europeans.

However, across Europe, another haplogroup exists at generally lower levels than either *R1a* or *R1b*: Haplogroup *I*. This lineage also stands out as an ideal candidate for a historically European lineage, and one which could connect us to ancient Persia.

Haplogroup *I* is found almost exclusively in Europe (**Color Plate 106**). Among Africans — even North Africans — haplogroup *I* is undetectable. In Asia, it shows up in Turkey, the Caucasus, Afghanistan, Tajikistan, and Siberia, but only at frequencies less than 7%. The rest of Asia is free of *I*. It's like historical members of *I* roamed Europe — and almost nowhere else.

This type of lineage may not seem like a natural candidate to uncover the origin and fate of the ancient Persians, but its deeper history holds the critical clues.

In terms of its origin, the branches in haplogroup *I* run all the way back to the 2200s B.C. to 1800s B.C. (**Color Plate 107**). It's like these men arose in Europe around that time and then stayed there. This inference is consistent with the political history of Europe. Recall that as a result of Alexander the Great's conquests, Greeks once lived as far east as the border of India (**Color Plate 88**). But after Alexander's death, almost two millennia would pass before a European empire reached as far into Asia again. After Alexander, the Romans pushed into the Middle East but never went as far east as he did (**Color Plate 59**). After the western Roman Empire fell, the kingdoms of the Germanic tribes traded borders, but all were within the confines of Europe. Only in the A.D. 1500s and 1600s, during the Russian expansion, would Europe penetrate as far east as Alexander did (**Color Plate 82**).

The reverse was also true. The enemies of Europe tended to stay out of Europe. After the time of Alexander, Asian empires never went much farther west than Ukraine. Asian ethnic groups migrated into Europe (see chapter 7), but European politics stayed mostly free of Asian lordship.

In light of this history, could haplogroup *I* be the lineage of the ancient Greeks? Perhaps of the ancient Romans? The geography of *I* fits the geographic restriction of the post-Greek European kingdoms. Whoever *I* individuals were originally, it appears that they stayed mostly in Europe for thousands of years. This fits both post-Roman and post-Greek histories. Perhaps haplogroup *I* represents the lineages of *both* the ancient Greeks and ancient Romans.

However, the first division in haplogroup *I* post-dates the historical split between the Greeks and Romans. Rome was founded in the 700s B.C., and the Mycenaean Greeks existed even earlier. In haplogroup *I*, the first major division occurred in the 800s B.C. to 500s B.C. (**Color Plate 107**). From this perspective, it seems that *I* could be only one or the other — or neither. But the Romans conquered the Greeks. In the Byzantine Empire, which ruled from the Balkans, the Greek language remained an official language. We also know that genealogies naturally intermingle, unless a stubborn barrier to migration separates them (see chapters 2 and 3).

From this perspective, it's likely that members of haplogroup *I* have both Greek and Roman blood in their veins.

So far, nothing about this history suggests any connection to ancient Persia. But the pre-Roman and pre-Greek history — the pre-haplogroup-*I* history — does. The clues to this historical bridge between Europe and Asia arise first in the realm of languages.

Ancient Greek and ancient Latin both belong to the Indo-European language family, a family whose modern members exist from Iceland to India (**Color Plate 26**). Current linguistic scholarship put the first Indo-European speakers near central Russia. From there, these Indo-Europeans moved near the Black Sea/Caucasus region. Then the European (e.g., Greek, Roman) and Asian (e.g., Iranian/

Persian) branches went their separate ways.[5] From this perspective, Europe and Asia have an ancient connection.

The Y chromosome haplogroups seem to reflect this connection. When haplogroup *I* arose in the 2200s B.C. to 1800s B.C., it broke away from another haplogroup — one that we've already discussed at length, but as separate sub-lineages. Haplogroups *J1* and *J2* were originally one lineage, haplogroup *J*. They were joined as one somewhere in the 1200s B.C. to the 700s B.C. (**Color Plate 108**). Before the 2200s B.C. to 1800s B.C., haplogroup *J* was one lineage with haplogroup *I* (**Color Plate 108**).

In other words, it looks like a modern, strongly European lineage (haplogroup *I*) was once joined to a modern, strongly Asian lineage (haplogroup *J*, which now exists as haplogroups *J1* and *J2*) — just like modern, strongly European languages (e.g., Germanic, Romance) were once joined to modern, strongly Asian languages (e.g., Indo-Iranian) as part of the Indo-European language family (**Color Plate 26**).

The language of the ancient Persians was a member of the Indo-European family of languages. Since Indo-European languages seem to be linked to haplogroups *I*, *J1*, and *J2*, perhaps the ancient Persian lineage might be found among haplogroups *I*, *J1*, and *J2*.

To explore this possibility, let's start with the Asian branches of these lineages and work backward in time to the distant past.

By the A.D. 600s, *J1* seems to have been in Arabia (**Color Plate 109**). To take part in the Arab conquests, it had to have been present. In contrast, *J2* seems to have been residing in Central Asia for some time prior to the A.D. 1000s (**Color Plate 109**). You'd think that participation in the Seljuk Turk expansion from Central Asia would imply residence in Central Asia for some time. Yet, at some point prior to this, these two lineages must have been part of a single population. And this single population would have been located . . . where?

Centuries before the Persians ruled the Middle East, another Indo-European people dominated. The Hittite Empire (**Color Plate 110**) lasted until a major Near Eastern downturn affected the region. In the mainstream timescale, the Late Bronze Age collapse (1190 B.C. for Hittite fall) just precedes the dates for the split in *J1* and *J2* (**Color Plate 108**). Perhaps the collapse sent the survivors south into Arabia and east into Iran (**Color Plate 111**).

---

5. Beckwith (2009), p. 32.

In Iran, the *J2* individuals would have given rise to the ancient Persians. Their empire (**Color Plate 86**) lasted until the conquests of Alexander the Great (**Color Plate 88**). Alexander pursued the Persians into Central Asia where Darius III died at the hands of the Bactrians, a resident Central Asian people. But then Alexander stopped. If you were a fleeing Persian, Central Asia could easily have been the conclusion of your journey.

The empires of subsequent Iranians — Parthians and Sassanids — would have kept *J2* in the Central Asian/Iranian region (**Color Plates 89–90**). Then the Turks, whose ancestral lineage may have been *G*, would have arrived in Central Asia. After intermingling with the descendants of the *J2* Persians, the Turks would have moved *G* and *J2* back across the Middle East to Turkey (**Color Plate 111**).

From this perspective, haplogroup *J2* looks like the best candidate for the ancient Persian lineage.

Thus, the fate of the ancient Persians followed a trajectory that mirrored, rather than followed, that of their ancient European foes. The early Europeans were eventually overrun by Central Asians despite topographical protection on three sides. The early European lineage (haplogroup *I*) survived, but it failed to dominate Europe. In contrast, the topographically vulnerable Persians arrived in the Middle East in the millennium before Christ. Then they experienced invasion after invasion from multiple sides. Yet, one of the dominant haplogroups (*J2*) among Near East countries is still Persian in origin.

Who would have guessed?

Chapter 8 Summary:

- Geographically, the Middle East is one of the most vulnerable places on earth. It lacks natural barriers to invasion on all sides.

- The ancient Persians were but one of a long list of ruling powers in the Middle East, suggesting that the ancient Persian lineage has been lost.

- Among Middle Eastern lineages still in existence today, haplogroup *J2* is one of the most prominent. Haplogroup *J2* shows signs of being a Turkish lineage, not a Persian one.

- Haplogroup *G* also fits a Turkish origin, raising the possibility that *J2* might correspond to a different ancestral people.

- Haplogroup *J1* is a relative of haplogroup *J2*; *J1* fits the history of the Muslim Arabs, suggesting that, like *J2*, it originated in Asia, specifically in the Arabian Peninsula.

- Haplogroup *I* is also connected to haplogroups *J2* and *J1*, yet it looks like an indigenous European lineage. Haplogroups *I*, *J1*, and *J2* look like they might have arisen from the first Indo-European peoples — from whom the ancient Persians descended.

- By the time of the Persians, haplogroup *J* was likely already in the Middle East and would have split into *J1* and *J2*. The original *J* lineage may have been the Hittites, who would have given rise to peoples of the Arabian Peninsula and Iran.

- Together, the evidence is consistent with haplogroup *J2* being a lineage of the ancient Persians.

South Asia

9

Relative Mystery

In A.D. 1631, the empress of what is now India was pregnant with her thirteenth child. Empress *Mahal* was the third wife of the Mughal ruler, Emperor *Shah Jahan*. She was his favorite. Betrothed to Jahan when she was 14, she married him when she was 19. Over the next nineteen years, she would bear him twelve children. The birth of the thirteenth ended in tragedy.

Mahal was born *Arjumand Banu Begum*. But the emperor was so taken by her that he named her "beloved ornament of the palace," or *Mumtaz Mahal*. When she died in A.D. 1631 at age 38, the emperor was so distraught that he disappeared to mourn for an entire year. Reportedly, when the 40-year-old emperor returned to public life, his hair had turned white.

Twenty-two years later, Emperor Jahan's labor force completed the gardens and buildings for the mausoleum to his deceased wife. The place bore her name. You'll probably recognize it: The Taj *Mahal* (**Color Plate 112**).[1]

To many in the West, the term *India* conjures up little more than images of the Taj Mahal. Just a few years ago, I would have belonged to this group of people. I didn't know the names of any of India's historical leaders. The name *Ghandi* rang a bell, but beyond that, I had no idea who the past heads of state were. I knew the names of none of

---

1. Source for Taj Mahal narrative: https://www.tajmahal.gov.in/, accessed January 12, 2021.

the major kingdoms, except maybe the British Raj — the last empire to rule India before it achieved independence in 1947. Even the Taj Mahal was little more than a pretty structure. I didn't know when it was constructed or who built it.

What's the story of this mysterious subcontinent? Before Europeans arrived, who roamed this land? What were they doing?

Surprisingly, for Europeans, the answers to these questions have never been far off or hard to find. The story of Europe is, in many respects, the story of India itself — in more ways than meet the eye.

I Heard This Before

The history of India began when, like Europe, the Indian subcontinent hosted one of the cradles of civilization (**Color Plate 3**). From the outset, the early people of the Indus Valley faced a future that recalled the one faced by early Europeans. Like Europe, India was geographically insulated on three sides. It was a peninsula (**Color Plate 113**). The Arabian Sea and the Bay of Bengal (**Color Plate 113**) guarded the southwest and southeast borders. The breathless heights of the Himalayas discouraged invasion from the northeast. But the northwest provided minimal security.

At first glance, this geographic vulnerability might not be obvious. Mountains, not plains, separate India from Central Asia and from the Middle East. But these mountains are passable. They act as a weak barricade — one that's as effective as a split rail fence in the face of a tank.

For the last 2,000 years, Indian history has been replete with foreign invasions. Primarily, these came from Central Asia, through the open door in the northwest. Before the British Raj commenced, the Mughals (Mongols) from Central Asia descended upon India and conquered it (**Color Plate 83**). In the A.D. 1200s, the Delhi Sultanate (**Color Plate 94**) controlled northern India. The Delhi Sultanate was founded by Ghurids, who manned their armies with Turkish soldiers from Central Asia. In the A.D. 400s, another Central Asia group, the *Hephthalites*, invaded. Centuries prior to the Hephthalites, the Central Asian *Yuezhis* came from the north and ruled parts of India through the *Kushan* kingdom (**Color Plate 114**).

Almost all of these empires have left a genetic signature among modern Indian males. Around 25% belong to the Mughal Y chromosome haplogroup, *R1a*. Another 5% to 10% have the echo of the Ghurid invasions, haplogroup *J2*. And the Y chromosomes from another 10% to 20% of Indian men harken back to the Yuezhi people in that they belong to haplogroup *R2*, a lineage with a significant South Asian and Central Asian presence (**Color Plate 115**).[2]

Together, foreign invaders have given rise to around half of India's male population.

This number might be even higher. Another 10% of India's men belong to haplogroup *L*, a lineage linked back to the Middle East, not aboriginal India (see chapter 13 for details). Altogether, about 60% of India's males do not look like they arose in India.

In other words, the genetic history of India sounds just like the genetic history of Europe. In both places, the indigenous populations have been overrun by invaders from Central Asia. And in both places, the reason for these invasions has been the same: Geographic vulnerability.

Furthermore, *the same ancestral peoples* have given rise to modern Europeans and modern Indians. For haplogroup *R1a*, the common ancestor to European *R1a* men and South Asian *R1a* lived just a few centuries ago (**Color Plate 81**). The common ancestors to European *J2* and South Asian *J2* go back a little further, but still within the A.D. era (**Color Plate 93**). Even South Asian *R2* is linked indirectly to Europeans. Though *R2* is not detectable in modern Europe, the *R2* lineage was joined to the *R1* lineage (i.e., the ancestor to *R1a* and *R1b*) in the 800s B.C. to 200s B.C. (**Color Plate 116**).

Europeans and South Asian peoples share links throughout their respective histories.

What about the indigenous Indians? Do they exist? Are the remaining 40% of India's males the descendants of the founders of the Indus Valley civilization? Stated succinctly, the answer seems to be *yes*. India does possess a population that looks disconnected from Central Asia, the Middle East, and Europe.

But when examined in detail, even this part of India's story is difficult to separate from the European stories that we've told in previous chapters.

---

2. As discussed in subsequent paragraphs, the haplogroup *R1-R2* split is earlier than the migration of the Yuezhis from northwestern China into Central Asia and northern India. But the split between the precursors to the Yuezhis and those who remained in Central Asia may have preceded the Yuezhi migration. Regardless of who specifically *R2* ends up being, it seems likely to have been resident in Central Asia before entering India, making it a foreign lineage to India, not an indigenous one.

Aboriginal Connections

Linguistically, India has a good candidate for an early Indian population. It's not in northern India. The languages of the north belong to the Indo-European family (**Color Plate 26**). These languages were brought into India from the outside — from central Russia. In contrast, in southern India, the dominant language family is *Dravidian* (**Color Plate 117**).

The geography of the Dravidian languages suggests an indigenous origin. It's not just because they're found in modern India. It's because their distribution fits the political history of indigenous Indian kingdoms.

Historically, Indian polities rarely expanded their domains *outward*. The two largest Indian empires — that of the Mauryans (**Color Plate 118**) and of the Guptas (**Color Plate 119**) — reached into modern Pakistan. But no farther. Dravidian languages have a similar spread.

More importantly, these languages have no connection to Central Asia, the Middle East, or Europe.

Genetically, the Dravidian languages appear to have an echo. In southeast India and in Sri Lanka, the top Y chromosome haplogroup is one that we haven't encountered before. Haplogroup *H* exists there at levels between 25% and 30%. Going eastward to Bangladesh, more than 35% of males belong to haplogroup *H*.

On the Y chromosome tree, the branches of haplogroup *H* run deep. They arose in the 2600s B.C. to 2200s B.C. — near the beginning of human history (**Color Plate 120**). This fits the profile of a lineage that birthed a cradle of civilization.

Geographically, haplogroup *H* (**Color Plate 121**) is reminiscent of the political history of indigenous India. These kingdoms rarely ventured outside of India. Haplogroup *H* looks like it arose in India and rarely left.

In other words, haplogroup *H* makes a good candidate for an indigenous, if not the first, Indian lineage.

Ironically, these early Indians would have been genealogically close to their early European counterparts. In fact, these two would have been closer to each other than are many Europeans and Indians today.

Take a look for yourself on the Y chromosome tree. Recall that haplogroup *I* represents our best candidate for an early indigenous European population. Recall as well that these Europeans have an Asian relative: Haplogroup *J*. Haplogroup *J2* exists in modern India. Consequently, haplogroup *I* Europeans and haplogroup *J2* Indians are kin.

But their kinship lies deep in the ancient past. In **Color Plate 122**, the modern European and Indian branches of the *I-J* lineage have been separated for at least 130 generations.[3] Since the 2200s B.C. to 1800s B.C., *I* and *J* have gone different ways.

By contrast, when the Indus Valley civilization was in full swing, haplogroups *H* and *I-J* were just distant cousins. Only a few generational steps separated the early segments of *H* from *I-J* (**Color Plate 123**).[4] For that matter, only a few generational steps separate early *H* from most of the non-African branches.

It's just what happens when the global family tree is shallow. Human history is only a few thousand years long, which constrains how deep the branches can go. Early branches are connected. They must be.

In other words, despite appearances to the contrary, the people of India and Europe haven't always been foreigners. They began as close relatives. Millennia of isolation have produced unfamiliarity and mystery between these two regions. But genealogically, Europe and South Asia have never been far apart.

---

3. To calculate the generations separating them, I took the DNA differences from separation to tip, and divided this by 3 mutations per generation.
4. To calculate the generations separating them, I took the DNA differences from separation to tip, and divided this by 3 mutations per generation.

Chapter 9 Summary:

- Today, the peoples of South Asia (India) remain mysterious to peoples of European descent.

- Genealogically, over the last 2,500 years, many Y chromosome connections have existed between Europe and South Asia.

- Prior to this, Europe and South Asia shared another genealogical connection. This connection linked the indigenous South Asian lineage (haplogroup *H*) with what gave rise to the indigenous European lineage (i.e., haplogroup *I-J*, which gave rise to haplogroup *I*).

- The branches connecting early haplogroup *H* and early haplogroup *I-J* are very short. This implies that these early, geographically-distant peoples were close relatives.

- Thus, the peoples of Europe and South Asia have never been genealogically far apart.

The Far East

10

The Great Divide

Today, the name *China* is synonymous with a large Far Eastern country under oppressive Communist rule. The Chinese Communist Party demands ideological and political purity, and it is actively striving to make China an ethnically homogeneous state. It has been so successful in clamping down on internal disunity that it is now looking outside of China to extend its influence on the far corners of the globe.

Over two and half millennia ago, China was a very different place. In the 600s B.C., the Chinese landmass was broken into a multitude of small kingdoms. These Chinese polities fought against each other and built barricades to defend their local homelands. A unified China didn't exist back then.

By the 200s B.C. the internecine conflict ceased, and China unified. The defensive structures were repurposed. Fortifications between previously competing states were demolished, and in the north, fortifications were erected to defend against foreign incursions.

This new purpose held for the next two millennia. The northern defense was intermittently improved. The result? Five thousand five hundred miles of barriers that we know today as *The Great Wall of China* (**Color Plate 124**).

Aside from the Great Wall and the Communist party, much of China remains unfamiliar to the West. With respect to Europe and the Americas, China sits on the opposite side of the world. As a label, the *Far* East is apropos.

Linguistically, the tonal Chinese language is among the most difficult for Westerners to master. For English-speakers, a tonal language is easy to grasp as a concept. We all understand that voice inflection communicates meaning. However, in practice, tonal languages exist on another plane entirely. In Chinese, the same word, spoken in four different tones, can have four completely different meanings.

Written Chinese presents additional challenges. The Chinese script consists, not of letters, but of characters. You don't master Chinese by understanding the rules by which letters can be combined into words. Instead, you have to memorize thousands of characters — words — in order to be fluent in the written language.

Several other factors maintain the cultural gap between China and the West. Chinese food is famously exotic. Chinese-American cuisine is slowly familiarizing West and East, but strongly indigenous dishes still produce strongly negative reactions. Chinese religions — Buddhism, Taoism, Atheism — stand in stark contrast to the nominally Christian United States. Chinese people have a physical appearance (dark hair, olive skin, generally shorter stature) that sets them apart from the typical person of European or African descent. Art and architecture (**Color Plate 125**), social practices (reserved, respectful of elders), together with many other traditional elements of Chinese society keep China enigmatic.

From a historical perspective, China is unlike the other civilizations that we've encountered thus far. In the previous chapters, each civilization had some sort of tie to the West. Rome itself was a Western power. The land of Egypt was, at various points in its history, under Western (Greek, Roman) control. Three of the peoples — Romans, Persians, and Indians — were linked to one another via the Indo-European language family. None of this was true in Chinese history. Western powers never conquered China. Western languages belong to families with no relationship to Chinese. Aside from long-distance trade routes via the Silk Road, Chinese civilization has had no connection to the West. In a sense, the Great Wall wasn't just a military barricade. It was also a symbol, a physical representation of the divide between East and West.

Who are the Chinese people? What is their story? Who did they come from? What happened to them throughout the millennia of their isolation from the West?

Ironically, the same Wall that divided West from East also marked the borders, not of an insular and cloistered community, but of a vibrant Far Eastern sphere of humanity that expanded, multiplied, and diversified in ways that no one would have anticipated.

Diversity

Today, East Asia[1] is one of the most diverse places on earth. Simply listing the sheer number of nations calls to mind the wealth of varied peoples that call East Asia home: China, Mongolia, Korea, Japan, Taiwan, Vietnam, Laos, Cambodia, Thailand, Burma, Malaysia, Indonesia, the Philippines, and the list goes on.

As compared to previous regions we've explored, East Asia harbors some of the greatest linguistic complexity on earth. Today in Europe, only two language families dominate: Indo-European and Finno-Ugric (**Color Plates 26, 77**). If we include pockets of other families (Turkic, *Mongolic, North Caucasian*),[2] the number totals only five. In mainland Africa, only four language families have a significant footprint: Afro-Asiatic, Niger-Congo, Nilo-Saharan, and Khoisan (**Color Plate 34**), with a fifth (Indo-European) stemming from the effects of recent European colonialism. The Middle East and Central Asia have three major families: Indo-European, Turkic, and Afro-Asiatic (**Color Plates 26-28**). Again, the number increases to just five if we include pockets of other families (*Kartvelian, North Caucasian*).[3] South Asia has just two notable language families: Indo-European and Dravidian (**Color Plates 26, 117**). If we include families that spill over from Central and East Asia, we could bump the total to six. In contrast, East Asia has at least eight major language families or language isolates: Sino-Tibetan (which includes Chinese), Mongolic, Korean, Japanese, Hmong-Mien, Austroasiatic, Tai-Kadai, and Austronesian (**Color Plate 126**). If we include the language families of far northwestern China (Turkic) and far northeastern Siberia (Chukotko-Kamchatkan), then total rises to ten (**Color Plate 126**).[4]

---

1. For reasons that will shortly become clear, I'm including Southeast Asia under the banner of East Asia.
2. Found in Russian lands and in the region of the Caucasus Mountains.
3. Found in the region of the Caucasus Mountains.
4. The total could be even higher if we included smaller pockets of language families (e.g., *Tungusic*) as well as the languages found on islands that belong in part to Indonesia (e.g., *Irian Jaya*, the western half of the island of New Guinea).

Many East Asian language areas have their own ancient history. China birthed a cradle of civilization (**Color Plate 3**). Next door, Mongolia was the homeland of the northern "barbarians" who were in continual conflict with the Chinese going back to the B.C. era. These "barbarians" even ruled parts of China from time to time. Korean kingdoms began in the B.C. era, and Japanese kingdoms commenced in the early A.D. period.[5] The first Vietnamese kingdoms also trace to the B.C. era.

Where did these numerous ancient states come from? What's their story? If we didn't know any better, we'd be tempted to go looking for as many stories as there are language families and states in the Far East today. And if we did so, we'd eventually arrive at an unexpected but unavoidable conclusion: The complexity of East Asia arises from a common source.

Unity

From a geographical perspective, the Far East resembles Europe and India more than it does Africa or the Middle East. It's naturally protected on three sides against invasion. On its western borders, the vast Tibetan Plateau and the Himalayas hold invading armies at bay (**Color Plate 127**). The high elevation continues east and south until it meets the sea. Beyond the mountains, dense jungles separate Southeast Asia from India. Beyond the jungles to the south, the Bay of Bengal and the Indian Ocean guard the borders. Past the limits of land to the east, the Pacific Ocean keeps potential invaders from the Americas thousands of miles away. Only in the north has the Far East been vulnerable.

But unlike Europe and India, the people of the Far East explicitly addressed their geographic vulnerability: The Chinese built the Great Wall (**Color Plate 128**). In fact, the Great Wall formed the northern border of at least one Chinese dynasty (the *Han* Dynasty) (**Color Plate 129**).

Within these natural and man-made fortifications that have defined East Asia, the peoples have freely moved — and intermixed. Some have even breached the Wall. I've already mentioned the fact that the northern "barbarians" ruled China from time to time, intermingling with the Chinese people. The Koreans may have had an even closer link with China, arising out of what are now Chinese lands. Around the time of transition between two ancient Chinese dynasties,

---

5. Based on written Chinese records.

A refugee named Wiman from an unstable peripheral Han[6] client kingdom (called Yan) located in southeastern Manchuria fled to northern Korea and established a small kingdom there in 195 [B.C.]. Wiman's new kingdom was called Chosŏn, and he ruled over a mixed population of natives and refugees. . . . In 108 [B.C..], Emperor Wu of the Han Dynasty invaded and conquered Chosŏn. . . . If the native populations under Han Dynasty rule in Korea remained culturally distinct from the Chinese imperial metropolitan elite, they also did not yet constitute a single unified and homogeneous Korean people either. Internally, there remained a surprising variety of different ethnic groups. . . . A third-century Chinese history (the *Sanguo zhi*, or *Chronicles of the Three Kingdoms*) describes several different peoples occupying the general area that we now call Korea. The Puyŏ lived well north of the peninsula, in central Manchuria, and might not seem relevant, except that according to Korean legend the Puyŏ were directly ancestral to other more obviously Korean peoples such as Koguryŏ.[7]

This Chinese-Korean link may have ultimately extended to Japan:

Archaeologists speak of an old tomb (*kofun*) period in Japan, covering roughly the years 250–552 [A.D.]. . . . It is interesting that the exact same term, *old tomb*, is also used for the tumuli of roughly contemporary Three Kingdoms Korea. Though the word is pronounced *kofun* in Japanese and *kobun* in Korean, both are written with the same two Chinese characters. . . . Fairly frequent contact between the islands and the peninsula in these centuries is beyond doubt. . . .

Fierce modern nationalistic debates over whether Japan conquered Korea or Korea conquered Japan in this period are largely misguided and anachronistic, if only because neither Japan nor Korea really existed yet as a coherent identity. However, people from the Japanese islands apparently did have some presence on the Korean peninsula in these

---

6. Han was one of the ancient Chinese dynasties.
7. Holcombe (2017), p. 82–83.

early centuries, and the Japanese islands clearly did absorb a number of highly critical influences from the peninsula. . . . There were also a significant number of actual immigrant persons from the continent. In early historical Japan, this was still openly acknowledged. In a record of 1,059 prominent families living in the capital region that was compiled in 815, for example, some 30 percent were explicitly said to be of foreign descent. In these critical centuries, at the dawn of Japanese history, immigrants played a vital role in shaping the emerging Japanese state.[8]

Other neighbors of China have histories that also hint of connections to the ancient Chinese. We've just explored the neighbors to the east/ northeast of China: Japan and Korea. To the south of modern China sits Southeast Asia. These people also came from modern Chinese lands:

> What today is southeast China, as far north as roughly the line of the Yangzi River, was, late in prehistory, culturally and linguistically more aligned with what is now Southeast Asia than with China. The word Viet (pronounced Yue in modern Mandarin) seems to have originated as the name of a mid-Zhou[9] era Warring States[10] kingdom (circa seventh century to 333 [B.C.]) located in the vicinity of modern Zhejiang, on what was then the southern margins of the Chinese cultural horizon. Yue (Vietnamese: Viet) subsequently became a generic Chinese name for all of the various prehistoric non-Chinese peoples of the southeast, extending from Zhejiang (in what is now China) to the Red River (in what is now Vietnam). Independent non-Chinese kingdoms in what is today Fujian Province (across the straits from the island of Taiwan) were not conquered by the Chinese Han Dynasty until 110 [B.C.], and Fujian was not extensively settled by the Chinese people until as late as the mid-eighth century [A.D.].[11]

---

8. Holcombe (2017), p. 89–90.
9. *Zhou* was another Chinese dynasty.
10. *Warring States* is the name for an era of early Chinese history.
11. Holcombe (2017), p. 200–201.

Perhaps the biggest hint of an underlying East Asian unity comes from external appearances. The diverse peoples of East Asia all resemble one another (**Color Plate 130**). It's almost as if they all had a common ancestor in the ancient past, and then slowly went their separate ways over the millennia, gradually developing minor differences in their physical features.

Is this the actual history of these peoples? What story does their DNA tell? Let's ask an even better question: What story *could* their DNA tell? Like every narrative based on genetics, the genetic history of East Asia was, in part, a product of its population history.

For millennia, the greatest concentration of East Asian people has been in China.[12] From the A.D. 400s to the A.D. 1900s, Chinese people have outnumbered the peoples of Southeast Asia, of Korea, and of Japan by a factor of five or more. Around the time of Christ, the difference was at least 10-fold. This mathematical discrepancy has constrained and informed the genetic history of East Asia — in a manner that complemented, rather than contradicted, the geographic, historical, and physical clues we've just observed.

Genetic Diversity

In many respects, the genetic history of the Far East recalls a history that we've already witnessed — the history of Africa. In Africa, we saw that language families and Y chromosome haplogroups overlapped (**Color Plates 33, 36, 48**). The genetic history of East Asia tells a similar story.

For example, in East Asia, haplogroup *O1b2* is concentrated in Korea and Japan (**Color Plate 131**). Korea and Japan both possess languages that are classified as isolates (**Color Plate 132**). The overlap between these languages and *O1b2* is almost perfect (**Color Plate 133**).

Haplogroup *O1b2* is part of a larger *O1b* haplogroup, and the rest of the *O1b* branches (i.e., excluding the *O1b2* branches) are found on the southern side of China, in or near Southeast Asia (**Color Plate 134**). Like *O1b2*, *O1b* finds an echo in linguistics. The Southeast Asian peninsula harbors speakers from at least three different language families — *Austroasiatic, Hmong-Mien*, and *Tai-Kadai* (**Color Plate 135**). The distribution of *O1b* overlaps the distribution of these language families (**Color Plate 136**).

---

12. Data in this paragraph based on McEvedy and Jones (1975).

However, the match between genetics and linguistics is not perfect. The reach of *O1b* extends beyond the reach of these language families (**Color Plate 136**). Among the Indonesian islands and Madagascar, *O1b* looks more like an Austronesian lineage (see **Color Plate 137**) than anything else. Perhaps it's because the peninsular Southeast Asian *O1b* peoples intermixed with Austronesian speakers — and then went wherever Austronesian peoples migrated.

The original Austronesian speakers may have been part of another haplogroup. Taiwan is thought to be the ancestral homeland of the Austronesian speakers, and haplogroup *O1a* is found in around 85% of the aboriginal mountain tribes of Taiwan (**Color Plate 138**). Haplogroup *O1a* does not reach all the places where Austronesian speakers reside. But where *O1a* is detected, Austronesian speakers tend to be found, such as the Philippines, Indonesia, and Madagascar (compare **Color Plate 137** and **Color Plate 138**).

If any haplogroup represents the early Chinese peoples, then the last of the major sub-lineages in haplogroup *O*, haplogroup *O2*, is the best candidate. In northern China, over half of *Han*[13] Chinese men belong to *O2*. In southern Han Chinese men haplogroup *O2* exists at levels above 75% (**Color Plate 139**).

Yet haplogroup *O2* also goes far beyond the bounds of China, even beyond the borders of what were the two largest Chinese kingdoms (**Color Plate 140**). It even exceeds the reach of the language family (Sino-Tibetan) to which the Chinese language belongs (compare **Color Plate 139** to **Color Plate 126**). Siberia, Central Asia, Southeast Asia, and the Pacific all have men in *O2*. Why?

Chinese migrations independent of politics might be the explanation. For the Pacific islands, recent history has seen the influx of mainland Chinese. These recent arrivals are known to have intermixed with the locals. In Southeast Asia, mainland Chinese are known to have been present for generations. In light of this recent history, it still seems plausible to associate haplogroup *O2* with the Sino-Tibetan peoples.

So far, the genetic data we've explored suggest diverse and disparate histories for the peoples of East Asia.

---

13. The vast majority of Chinese today identify as *Han* Chinese, in reference to the ancient Chinese dynasty by the same name.

Genetic Unity

However, if you've been paying attention to the names of these haplogroups, then you know I've told you only half of the genetic story. Haplogroups *O1b2, O1b, O1a,* and *O2* are all subdivisions within haplogroup *O* — which means that these haplogroups are connected.

Each of these haplogroups connected around the same time — roughly, the beginning of the last millennium B.C. (**Color Plate 141**). *Connecting* and *separating* are two sides of the same coin. Thus, you could say that these dates also represent the time when these haplogroups *broke away* from one another. Perhaps it represents a time when they *migrated away* from one another.

The timing of these links/separations finds an echo in Chinese history: The time of transition between the critical first[14] Chinese Dynasty (the *Shang* Dynasty) and the second Chinese Dynasty (the *Zhou* Dynasty). This early era of history is especially material to our discussion because of its relevance to the question of East Asian ethnic identity:

> Although the Zhou and Shang were different peoples, both. . . . fed into a Chinese identity that was still in the process of formation. Over the course of the eight centuries of the Zhou Dynasty [including the Western Zhou (1045 B.C. to 771 B.C.) and Eastern Zhou (770 B.C. to 256 B.C.) periods[15]], a conscious sense of identity as *Huaxia* (Chinese) apparently did coalesce, especially in contrast to the clearly alien semi-nomadic cultures to the north. However, many of the peoples living in what we think of today as China, including virtually the entire south, still lay outside this *Huaxia* world in Zhou times.[16]

How fitting that the diverse peoples of East Asia might have been joined to a "Chinese" lineage around the time that "a Chinese identity . . . was still in the process of formation."

Process is an apt description, given the tumult in Chinese history that followed the ascension of the Zhou. The *Spring and Autumn Period* (770 B.C. to 481 B.C.) and the *Warring States Period* (480 B.C. to 221

14. I'm treating the existence of the Xia Dynasty as questionable.
15. Dates from Holcombe (2017).
16. Holcombe (2017), p. 33.

B.C.)[17] produced an especially divided Chinese nation (e.g., see **Color Plate 142**). The fighting was heavy:

> Statistical research identifies a total of 358 inter-state wars in the period of 535 to 286 B.C., yielding a frequency of 1.37 wars per year.[18]

Is it any surprise that genetic separation among East Asian peoples fell just before this era? Perhaps constant fighting pushed these breakaway groups of people even farther from the core landmass of modern China and into other parts of East Asia.

If we were to stop our discussion here, we'd have a fairly comprehensive narrative for the origin of the peoples of East Asia. But it wouldn't be complete. Thus far in our discussion we have left out the story of the "barbarians," the long-standing northern enemies of China. Their history completes our journey — and gives the origin of the Chinese people a new twist.

"Chinese"

Today, in the lands to the north and far northwest of China, haplogroup *N* is abundant (**Color Plate 143**). It spans the entire length of modern Russia. It even spills over into Scandinavia. Across Asia, it tends to decrease in a north to south direction. And it can still be found among the modern Chinese.

On the Y chromosome tree, the haplogroup *N* branches leading to Chinese ("NorthernHan" in **Color Plate 144**) appear at different times. One set of Chinese branches split off in the A.D. 1200s to 1400s (**Color Plate 144**). A deeper branch split occurred in the A.D. 100s to 400s.

Both of these time periods correspond to times of foreign rule in China. The Mongols (*Yuan* Dynasty) began conquering China in the early A.D. 1200s. They were overthrown by the Ming Dynasty in A.D. 1368. About a millennium earlier, another northern "barbarian" tribe, the *Xianbei*, ruled as the Northern Wei Dynasty (A.D. 386 to A.D. 534) during China's Age of Division.[19]

Could *N* be the echo of Mongol and Xianbei rule? It fits the profile of a people who ruled China in the early A.D. era, intermingled

---

17. Dates from Feng (2013).
18. Feng (2013), p. 187–188.
19. Term from Holcombe (2017), p. 58.

with the Chinese, then were pushed back out to the north, then intermingled again. When the Mongols ruled China in the A.D. 1300s, they could easily have brought descendants of the Xianbei with them. Mongol armies regularly employed the soldiers of conquered peoples.

Haplogroup *N* doesn't look like an indigenous Chinese lineage. Instead, it looks like a group outside of China that came in from time to time.

Deep in human history, haplogroups *N* (the candidate "barbarian" lineage) and *O* (the candidate early Chinese lineage) were linked (**Color Plate 145**). This Chinese-barbarian linkage also fits Chinese history. Of the two earliest Chinese dynasties (Shang Dynasty, Zhou Dynasty), one may not have been indigenous to China. In terms of the timing, Shang dynastic rule (roughly 1500s B.C. to 1045 B.C.)[20] preceded the Zhou Dynasty (1045 B.C. to 256 B.C.[21]). The Shang may have also preceded the Zhou in Chinese space.

When the Zhou arrived in the Shang capital in 1045 B.C., they concluded a journey that had begun farther to the west. Zhou homelands were technically within the purview of modern Chinese borders (**Color Plate 146**). But ancient Chinese empires were smaller than modern ones. Centuries later, the *Qin* Dynasty ruled a Chinese domain whose size was bigger than any preceding kingdom (**Color Plate 147**). Prior to the Qin, the Warring States Period saw Chinese states compete over a smaller plot of land (**Color Plate 142**). Before the Warring States Period and after they had conquered the Shang, the Zhou ruled over even less (**Color Plate 148**). Before conquering the Shang, the pre-dynastic Zhou would have roamed the frontier between China and the "barbarians" (**Color Plate 146**).

Were the Zhou originally Chinese? Or were they part of the "barbarian" peoples? History suggests some ambiguity. Genetics underscores this ambiguity (**Color Plate 145**).

Thus, the Great Wall of China didn't quite mark the boundary of East Asia. Peoples on both sides of the Wall were kin. Together, these relatives created a thriving, complex, diverse, and ultimately unified world.

They also created a world that was harder to divide into *East* and *West*. Unlike haplogroup *O*, haplogroup *N* eventually spilled over into the West (**Color Plate 143**). And in the beginning, the peoples of the

---

20. Dates from Holcombe (2017), p. xix.
21. I'm lumping the Western and Eastern Zhou together.

Far East and the peoples of the West were just like the early Europeans and early South Asians: They were distant cousins (**Color Plate 149**).[22] Only a few generations separated them.

Culturally, a great divide still exists between East and West. But genetically, all great divides eventually disappear.

Chapter 10 Summary:

- To people in the West, East Asia is one of the most alien places on earth.

- East Asia is also one of the most diverse, harboring the largest number of language families of any region we have explored so far.

- Natural and man-made barriers (i.e., the Great Wall of China) keep East Asia isolated from the rest of the world — and also keep it free and open to mixing within these boundaries.

- Historical and physical comparisons among the diverse peoples of East Asia suggest an underlying unity.

- Several Y chromosome lineages reveal the diversity of East Asia:
    * Haplogroup *O1b2* looks like a Korean/Japanese lineage.
    * Haplogroup *O1b* (*sans O1b2*) looks like a heavily Southeast Asian lineage — one that overlaps with major Southeast Asian language families.
    * Haplogroup *O1a* looks like it may have originally been an Austronesian lineage.
    * Haplogroup *O2* looks like the best candidate for an ancient Chinese lineage.
    * Haplogroup *N* looks like a candidate lineage for the "barbarians" north of China.

---

22. To calculate the generations separating them, I took the DNA differences from separation to tip, and divided this by 3 mutations per generation.

- These five haplogroups all join around the beginning of the last millennium B.C. — and plausibly could have originated in the landmass that is now China.

- In other words, these five haplogroups reveal a history of East Asia that is largely isolated from the histories in the other places of the world that we've explored thus far, but is dynamic and complex within itself.

- Nevertheless, the alien peoples of East and West have a common beginning and overlapping fates. The earliest *N-O* lineage was just a few generations away from the earliest European lineages, and the Siberian haplogroup *N* spills over into Europe.

The Pacific

11

From West to East

On August 21, 1959, Hawaii became an official U.S. state — the last of the 50 states to join the Union. Almost two centuries had passed since the 13 British colonies had declared independence from Britain to become the United States. In the intervening years, the nation had expanded relentlessly westward. During that time, the Civil War had come and gone, as had World War I. Yet the islands of Hawaii had remained largely out of the picture. When the Japanese had attacked Pearl Harbor in 1941, they had bombed a naval base located on a U.S. territory, not a U.S. state. Even the Korean War had transpired before Hawaii added the last star to the flag of the United States. For much of U.S. history, Hawaii has been, well, an afterthought.

Today, the islands of the Pacific remain in the category of *afterthought* for much of the West. Say the names *Tahiti, Fiji*, and *Bora Bora*, and the Western mind immediately visualizes sandy beaches, warm breezes, bright sunshine, palm trees, and relaxation. But that's it. The islands are vacation destinations, not daily players on the world political stage. Their culture and food are rare sights in the West, except for the occasional attempt at cheap imitation, such as a "Polynesian" sauce that you might find in a restaurant. Even Chinese food is much more prevalent than Pacific Island fare. Pacific languages are unknown. In the Western mind, Pacific history is almost non-existent.

From a Western perspective, this neglect of Pacific history has long been the rule. When Columbus landed in the New World in 1492, he thought he had reached India. Never mind that the world's largest body of water — the Pacific — still stood between him and his goal. Two decades later, Vasco Nuñez de Balboa navigated across Panama and arrived on the shores of the Indian Ocean . . . or so he thought. In fact, about 9,000 miles still separated him from China. In between lay the vast Pacific Ocean.

Ferdinand Magellan penetrated this vast and deep blue unknown in November of A.D. 1520. His fleet had set sail from Spain one year prior. Rounding the southern tip of South America, they sailed west and north, landing less than 2,000 miles from the Chinese coast in March of A.D. 1521. Guam was one of the western-most islands of the Pacific (**Color Plate 150**).

The eastern extent of the Pacific islands wouldn't be realized for another two centuries. In 1722, Dutch commander Jacob Roggeveen and his crew arrived on an unknown Pacific island, *Rapa Nui*. They landed on Easter Day; hence, Rapa Nui is more commonly known as *Easter Island* (**Color Plate 150**). On Rapa Nui, Commander Roggeveen and his colleagues encountered a culture that was puzzling, if not fantastic. The indigenous people were exotic in their appearance and dress. Their statues were colossal (**Color Plate 151**). Most baffling of all, here was a people who existed at least 2,000 miles from any known major landmass. Yet somehow, they had managed to successfully navigate long stretches of open ocean with pre-modern technology.

Surely the people of Rapa Nui — and the peoples all across the Pacific, from Hawaii to Guam — had a story. But what? Europeans hadn't known about the existence of the New World, let alone the Pacific islands, until late in history. Western chronicles provided no clues. The history of the Far East was equally blank for this region of the world.

Over time, a narrative for the people of Rapa Nui — and of the wider Pacific — has trickled in, piece by piece. Linguistics, archaeology, and physical appearances have contributed to their growing story. Despite languishing for millennia in neglect, a coherent history for the Pacific Islanders is emerging.

Clues Far and Wide

One of the first clues to the history of the people of Rapa Nui has come from their language. Their native tongue belongs to the wider Austronesian language family, the family that connects the natives along a chain of islands back to East Asia (**Color Plate 137**). This link suggests the Easter Islanders — and Pacific Islanders in general — arose from East Asia, perhaps Taiwan.

Culturally, Easter Islanders have been classified as Polynesians (**Color Plate 152**). Physically, Polynesians bear a strong resemblance to East Asians (**Color Plate 153**). Again, these connections suggest an origin in East Asia.

However, the wider geographic scope of the Easter Islanders' home has made their story more complex. Easter Island, and Polynesia in general, belong to the Pacific sphere known as *Oceania* (**Color Plate 154**). Melanesia and Australia also belong to Oceania, yet both Melanesia and Australia harbor native peoples who look different from Polynesians. In terms of outward appearances, the Aborigines of Australia and the natives of New Guinea and Melanesia have much more in common with Africans than with East Asians (**Color Plate 155**). This makes Oceania one of the most physically complex and diverse places on earth.

How did this sort of physical diversity arise? Why do African-looking and Asian-looking peoples both exist in Oceania? From whom did they originate? For the entire Pacific region, archaeology — and specifically radiometric dating — has uncovered a critical insight.

The earliest evidence for occupation anywhere in the Pacific comes from Australia and New Guinea. People seem to have settled there first (**Color Plate 156**). In Polynesia, human settlements date later. Archaeologically, Polynesia was colonized in at least two phases. By 900 B.C. to 700 B.C., Samoa was inhabited. At this point in history, further migration seems to have paused. Then about two thousand years later, in the A.D. 1000s to 1100s, Polynesians left their base in Samoa and settled the Society Islands. By the A.D. 1100s to 1200s, they reached as far as New Zealand, Hawaii, and Rapa Nui (**Color Plate 156**).

Perhaps the first Pacific settlers arrived in Australia and Melanesia, and then continued migrating east and north to the other Pacific islands. Or maybe the Polynesians originated separately from the Australians and Melanesians. This latter sequence would fit the physical differences between Polynesia and Australia/Melanesia.

Linguistics lends support to this latter view. Austronesian languages, the primary languages of Polynesia, skirt Melanesia and avoid Australia (**Color Plate 137**). Conversely, the Aborigines of Australia speak languages that belong to their own indigenous language family (**Color Plate 157**). On New Guinea, linguistic complexity is so great that the languages are broken into twenty-three separate language *families* (**Color Plate 157**).

In other words, on three counts (physical appearance, archaeology, linguistics), the history of Polynesia appears to be different from that of Australia and Melanesia. So far, we'd be justified in tracing the history of the Polynesians to East Asia, and the history of the Australians and Melanesians to someplace else. Perhaps even to Africa.

Genetics has taken this story and turned it upside down.

The First Settlers

Initially, genetics seemed to support the conclusions derived from archaeology, linguistics, and physical appearances. In the Y chromosome family tree, three of the deepest haplogroups are *K, M,* and *S* (**Color Plate 158**). The origin of *K/M/S* is near the beginning of human history (**Color Plate 158**).

The highest levels of *K/M/S* are found among dark-skinned Pacific peoples (**Color Plate 159**). More than 85% of the Papuans on New Guinea belong to one or more of these three. These haplogroups also abound among the Aborigines of Australia. In the Philippines, *K/M/S* distinguishes between peoples of typically Asian and typically African appearance. The majority of Filipinos look Asian. Among this majority, *K/M/S* are found on average in less than 7% of the males. By comparison, among dark-skinned Filipinos such as the *Aeta* and *Agta* (i.e., "Negrito") people groups (see image in **Color Plate 159**), *K/M/S* levels reflect those found in New Guinea — more than 85% (**Color Plate 159**).

Outside of dark-skinned Pacific populations, *K/M/S* are almost nonexistent (**Color Plate 159**). Some spillover reaches the islands surrounding Australia and Melanesia, but levels there are low. Among these locations, the highest levels are found on Samoa. Even there, the combined levels of *K/M/S* are only 15%.

It's worth noting that the distribution of *K/M/S* haplogroups does *not* resemble the distribution of Austronesian languages. Yes, *K/M/S* can be found on some of the Indonesian and eastern Pacific islands. But they are absent from Madagascar (**Color Plate 159**) — the most distant westward location of Austronesian speakers (see **Color Plate 137**).

So far, these results fit an ancient origin of *K/M/S* among non-Austronesian (i.e., Australian, Melanesian) peoples, followed by slight intermixing with later Austronesian arrivals. These late arrivals skirted Melanesia and may have taken some *K/M/S* with them as they went east.

From where did the *K/M/S* haplogroups arise? Given the physical appearance of Melanesians and Australians, we'd be justified in asking whether they have any genealogical connections to Africa.

In short, the answer is no. The branches for dark-skinned African and dark-skinned Pacific peoples exist on opposite sides of the Y chromosome tree (**Color Plate 160**). The *A*, *B*, and *E* branches that constitute modern sub-Saharan Africa show no intermingling of their branches with the *K/M/S* branches of the Pacific. The separation between these two groups of lineages goes back to ancient times — to the time of Noah. Africans are not descendants of Melanesians, and *K/M/S* Melanesians are not descendants of Africans.

But what about the deep genealogical history of the Polynesians? Might they have some connection to Australians and Melanesians? If the latter are genetically distinct from Africans, is it possible that all Pacific peoples are connected?

The answers to these questions turned out so shocking and so counterintuitive that you'd have to see it to believe it.

Polynesians

Among Polynesians, one haplogroup dominates, and it's not *K/M/S*. On Samoa and Tahiti and among the *Maori* people of New Zealand, around 50% to 70% of the males belong to haplogroup *C*. On Rapa Nui, it's haplogroup *C* that exists in all the males that have been sampled (see **Color Plate 161** for Old World distribution of *C*; I cover the New World relevance of *C* in chapter 12).

However, haplogroup *C* is not restricted to Polynesians (**Color Plate 161**). Among the Aborigines of Australia, it's one of the most abundant haplogroups. In the south, around 40% are in the *C* lineage. In the north, it's around 70%.

Was haplogroup *C* originally a Melanesian/Australian lineage? Did the lighter-skinned Polynesians come from dark-skinned Australians? The deeper history of haplogroup *C* indicated otherwise.

Consistent with the physical appearance of Polynesians (**Color Plate 162**), haplogroup *C* ties Polynesia back to East/Northeast Asia.

Siberia appears to have been the homeland for *C*. The highest Asian levels of *C* are found in Mongolia and Siberia. Among these northerly peoples (*Mongols, Buryats*, and *Evenks*), around 60% to 70% of the males belong to *C*.

Siberia also appears to have been the launch pad for migrations elsewhere. Within the *C* lineage, the first branches to form are found in Siberia (**Color Plates 163–164**). The next split left people in Japan (**Color Plates 163–164**). From Japan, *C* lineages seem to have migrated south, perhaps to Indonesia. Once there, one group went west to India; the other, east (**Color Plates 163–164**). Of the eastern migrants, a subset departed for Australia; the rest eventually landed on New Guinea or the islands beyond (**Color Plates 163–164**).

This migration seems to have happened quickly. On the Y chromosome tree, the length of the branches separating the Siberian, Japanese, Indian, and Pacific lineages is small (**Color Plate 163**; compare the horizontal distances between branches when they separate to the horizontal distances before and after the split).

In terms of timing, this migration occurred in the distant past. Intriguingly, the timing of the separation — 1200s B.C. to 700s B.C.— matches almost exactly the time of the separation among the haplogroup *O* sublineages (*O1a, O1b, O1b2, O2*) (compare dates in **Color Plate 163** to dates in **Color Plate 141**). It's as if something happened in Siberia/East Asia that spurred a massive migration event to the far reaches of the East/Pacific.

Together, these results suggest that the *C* migration occurred after the initial settling of Australia and Melanesia.

It also suggests an explanation for what happened when Polynesians and Melanesians encountered one another. Today, haplogroup *C* exists among both dark-skinned and light-skinned peoples of the Pacific. However, it seems to have arisen in a lighter-skinned Asian people. Presumably, as compared to the peoples of Australia and Melanesia, these migrants were few in number. Thus, when they arrived among dark-skinned peoples, they were the minority. Consequently, the skin tones of the majority population dominated, and dark-skinned haplogroup *C* individuals arose in Australia and Melanesia. Where haplogroup *C* individuals did not encounter dark-skinned persons, such as the islands to the east beyond Samoa, they retained an Asian appearance.

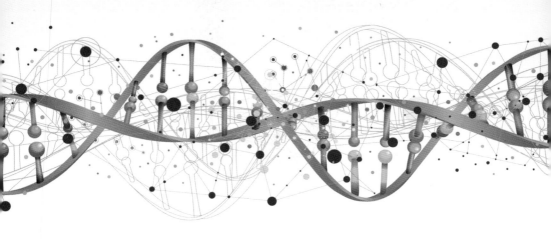

Color Plate Section

Color Plate A:
Human populations
analyzed for various Y
chromosome lineages
throughout this book.

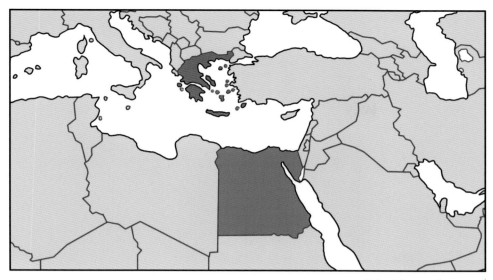

Color Plate 1: Greece (red) and Egypt (blue) exist in close geographical proximity.

Color Plate 2: Political map of the modern world.

Color Plate 3: Sites for the cradles of civilization (blue).

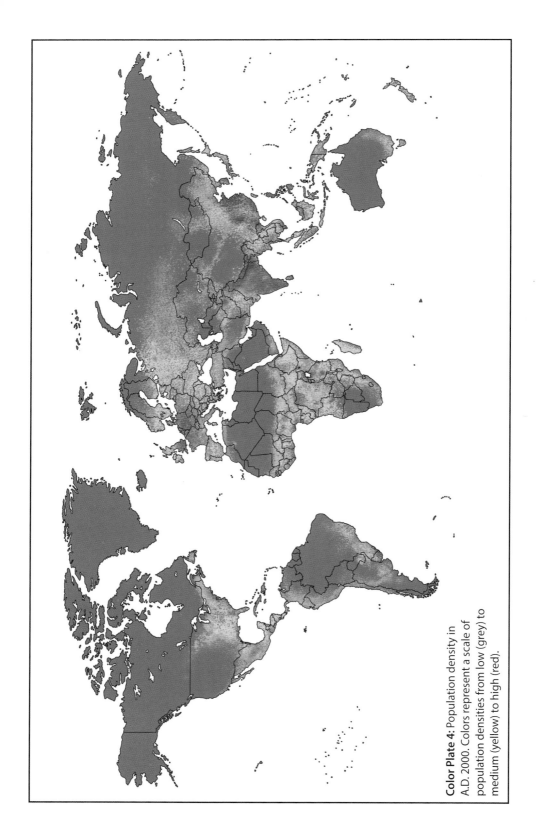

Color Plate 4: Population density in A.D. 2000. Colors represent a scale of population densities from low (grey) to medium (yellow) to high (red).

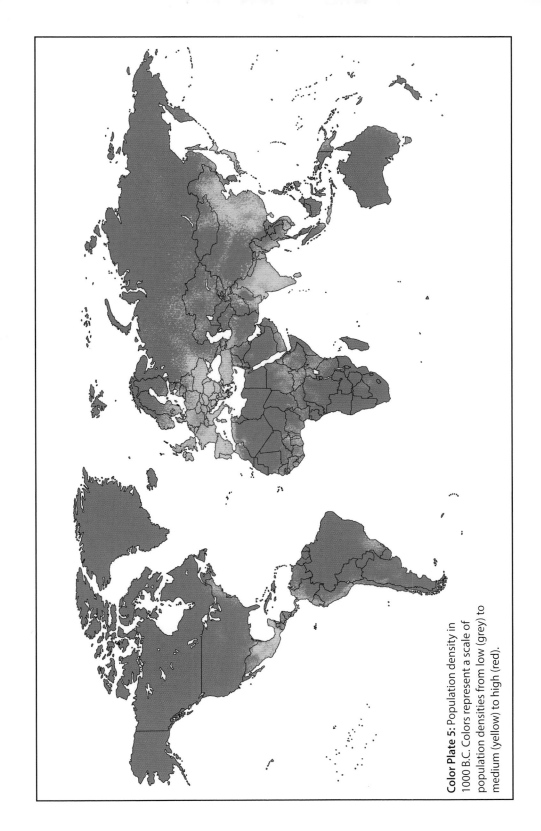

Color Plate 5: Population density in 1000 B.C. Colors represent a scale of population densities from low (grey) to medium (yellow) to high (red).

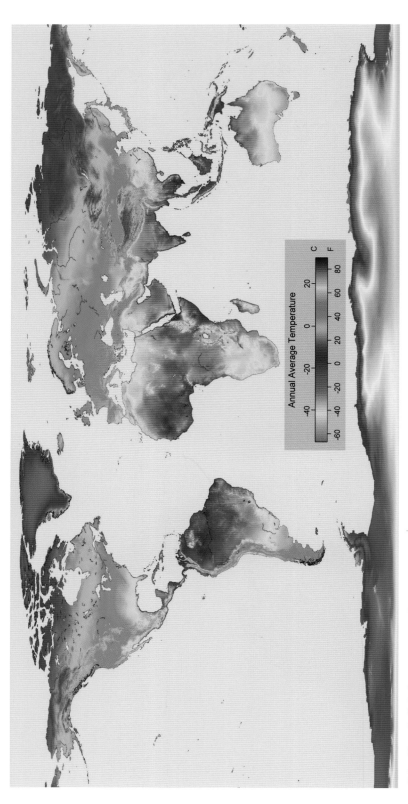

Color Plate 6: Global average annual temperatures.

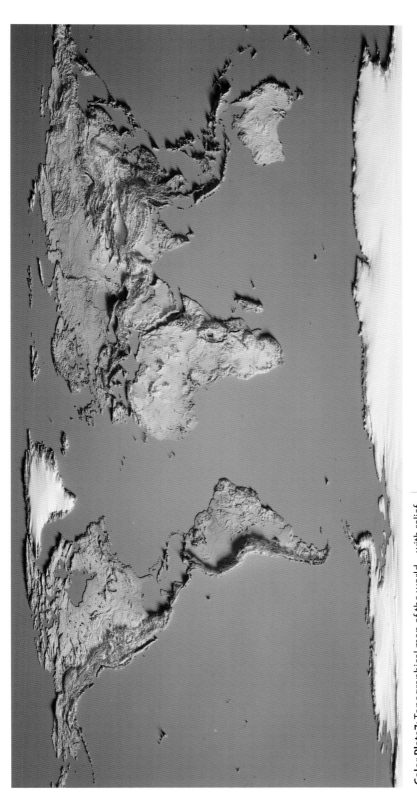

Color Plate7: Topographical map of the world—with relief exaggerated to highlight topographical features.

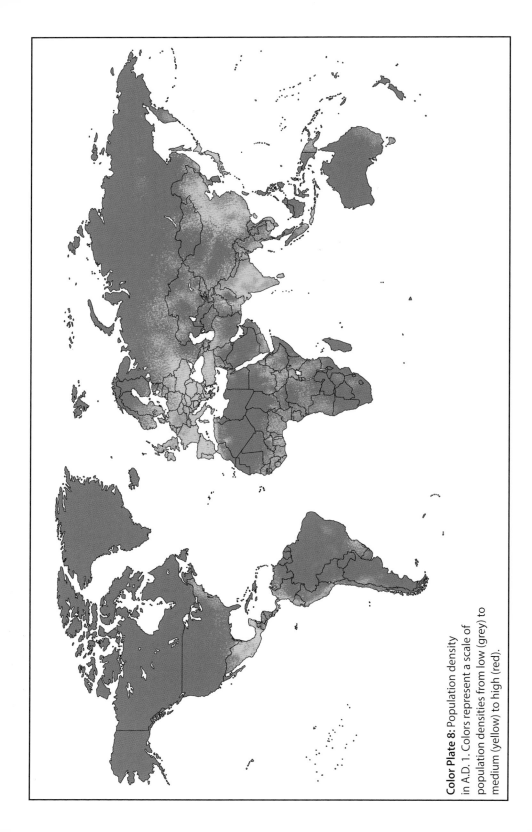

Color Plate 8: Population density in A.D. 1. Colors represent a scale of population densities from low (grey) to medium (yellow) to high (red).

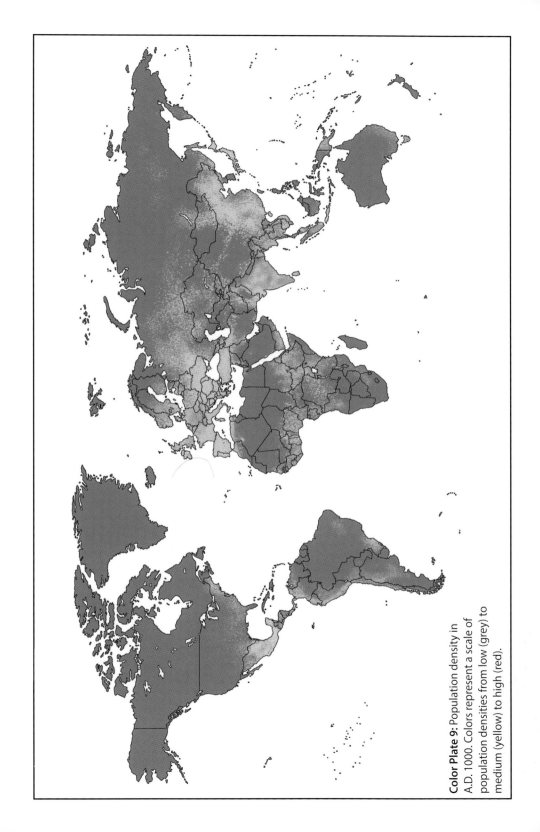

Color Plate 9: Population density in A.D. 1000. Colors represent a scale of population densities from low (grey) to medium (yellow) to high (red).

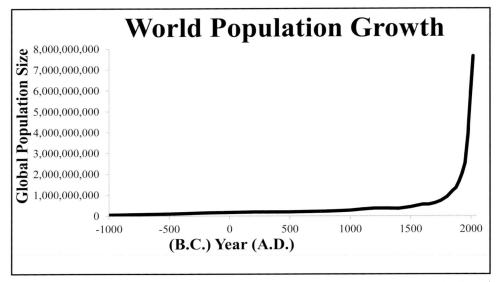

Color Plate 10: History of world population growth from 1000 B.C. to the present. Years in the B.C. era are shown as negative numbers.

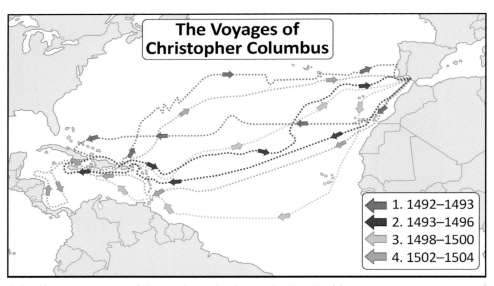

Color Plate 11: Voyages of Christopher Columbus to the New World.

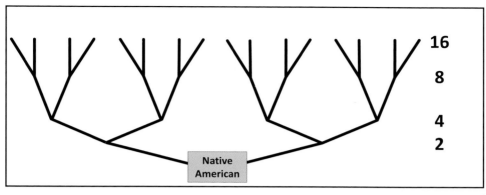

16

8

4

2

Color Plate 12: Hypothetical family tree for a Native American. Time moves from bottom to top: Lowest position is the most recent generation; top position is the oldest generation. Branches double each generation because each person has two parents.

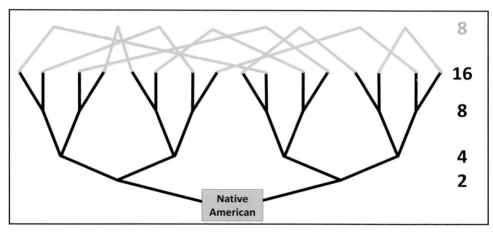

8

16

8

4

2

Color Plate 13: Hypothetical family tree for a Native American, now depicted with inevitable branch connections (i.e., light grey lines) in earlier generations. Time moves from bottom to top: Lowest position is the most recent generation; top position is the oldest generation.

Color Plate 14: Excavated terracotta army of third century B.C. Chinese emperor, Qin Shihuangdi.

Color Plate 15: Warrior from terracotta army of third century B.C. Chinese emperor, Qin Shihuangdi.

Color Plate 16: Khoisan woman showing typically Asian eye features.

Color Plate 17: Mixed-ethnicity family. Skin tone of child is intermediate between that of the parents.

Color Plate 18: Punnett Square for hypothetical dark-skinned parent *(AABB)* and hypothetical light-skinned parent *(aabb)*.

A A B B

		AB	AB	AB	AB
a	ab	AaBb	AaBb	AaBb	AaBb
a	ab	AaBb	AaBb	AaBb	AaBb
b	ab	AaBb	AaBb	AaBb	AaBb
b	ab	AaBb	AaBb	AaBb	AaBb

Color Plate 19: Punnett Square for hypothetical dark-skinned parent *(AABB)* and hypothetical parent with intermediate skin tone *(AaBb)*.

A A B B

		AB	AB	AB	AB
A	AB	AABB	AABB	AABB	AABB
a	Ab	AABb	AABb	AABb	AABb
B	aB	AaBB	AaBB	AaBB	AaBB
b	ab	AaBb	AaBb	AaBb	AaBb

Color Plate 20: Punnett Square for hypothetical parent with intermediate skin tone *(AaBb)* and hypothetical parent with light skin tone *(aabb)*.

A b B b

		AB	Ab	aB	ab
a	ab	AaBb	Aabb	aaBb	aabb
a	ab	AaBb	Aabb	aaBb	aabb
b	ab	AaBb	Aabb	aaBb	aabb
b	ab	AaBb	Aabb	aaBb	aabb

Color Plate 21: Famous landmarks from ancient Egypt—pyramid of Khafre and the Sphinx.

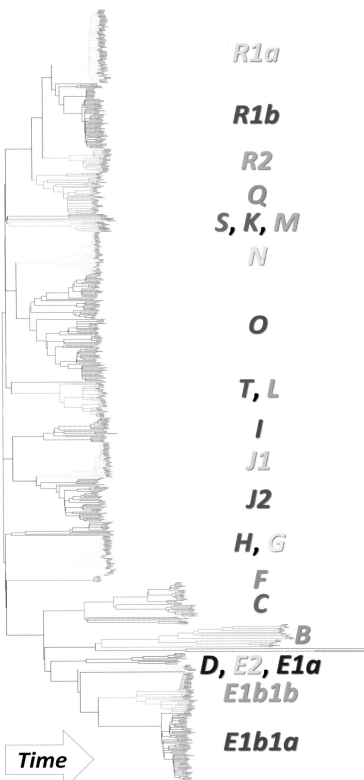

R1a

R1b

R2

Q

S, K, M

N

O

T, L

I

J1

J2

H, G

F

C

B

A

D, E2, E1a

E1b1b

E1b1a

Time

Color Plate 22: Representative global family tree based on male-inherited DNA, the Y chromosome, from around 600 men. Labels for individual men are not visible at this zoomed-out level of viewing. Branches connecting the men correspond to actual genealogical relationships. Letters correspond to branch groupings known as *haplogroups*. Subsequent illustrations zoom in on groups of individuals in these *haplogroups*.

Haplogroup *E1b1b*

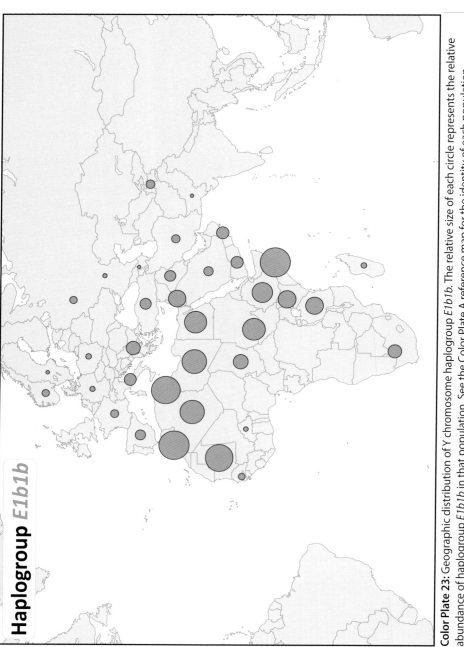

Color Plate 23: Geographic distribution of Y chromosome haplogroup *E1b1b*. The relative size of each circle represents the relative abundance of haplogroup *E1b1b* in that population. See the Color Plate A reference map for the identity of each population. Populations with undetectable levels of haplogroup *E1b1b* or with haplogroup *E1b1b* levels below 1% are omitted from this map.

Haplogroup *E1b1b*

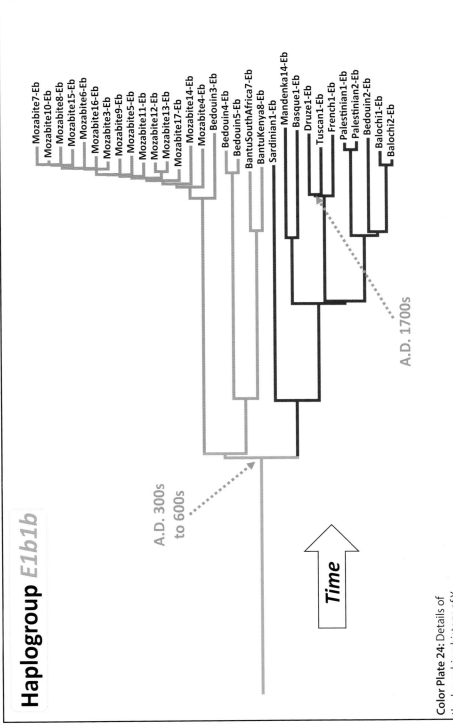

Color Plate 24: Details of the branching history of Y chromosome haplogroup *E1b1b*.

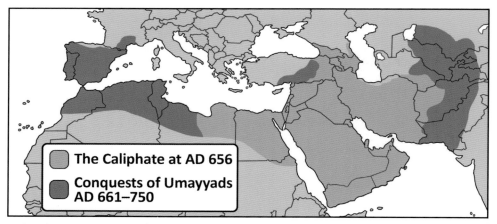

Color Plate 25: History of the expansion of the Arab Muslim empire. For reference, modern geographic boundaries are shown.

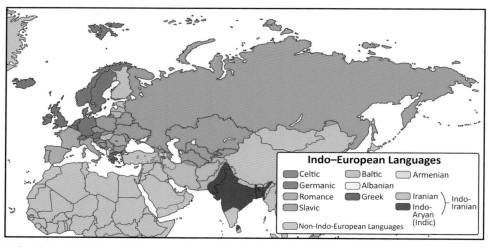

Color Plate 26: Global distribution of languages in the Indo-European language family. Subcategories within Indo-European are shaded various colors.

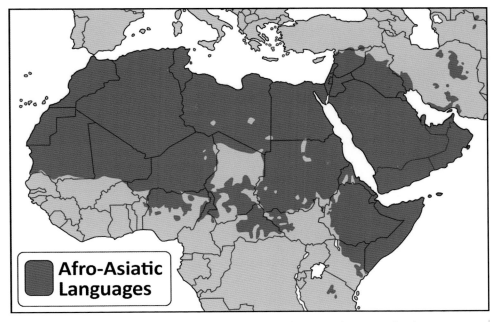

Color Plate 27: Global distribution of languages in the Afro-Asiatic language family.

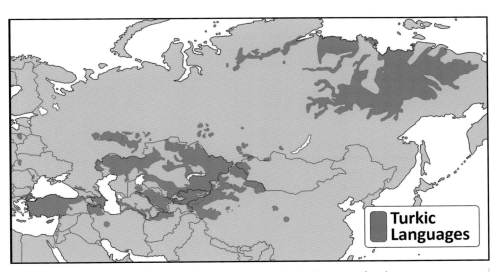

Color Plate 28: Global distribution of languages in the Turkic language family.

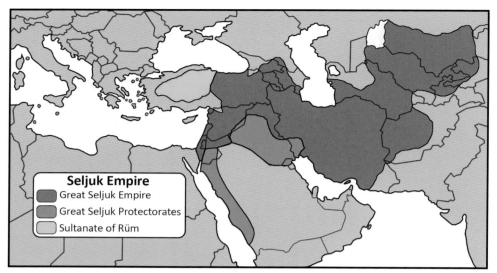

Color Plate 29: Geographic extent of the Turkic Seljuk empire. For reference, modern geographic boundaries are shown.

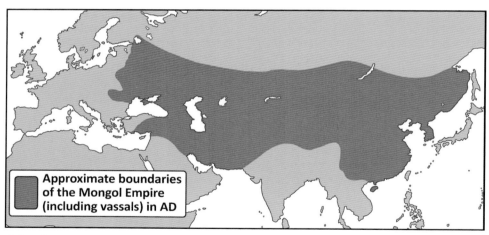

Color Plate 30: Geographic extent of the Mongol empire.

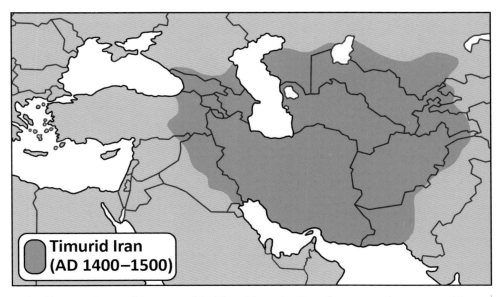

Color Plate 31: Geographic extent of the Timurid empire. For reference, modern geographic boundaries are shown.

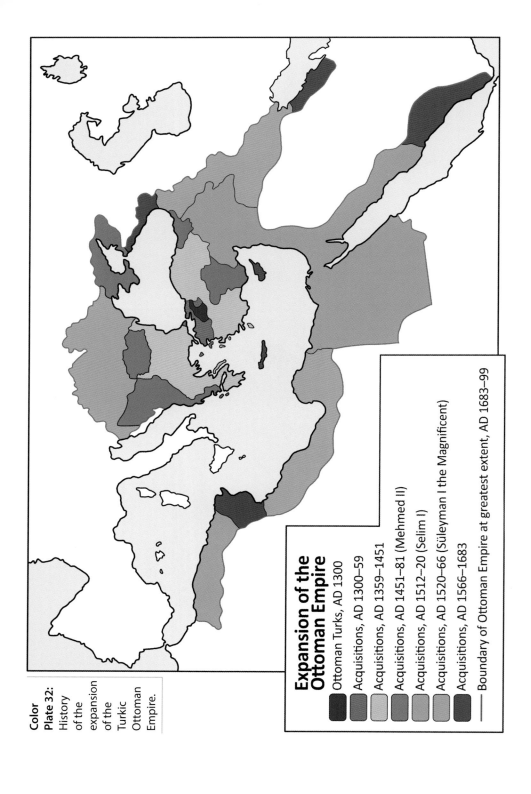

Color Plate 32: History of the expansion of the Turkic Ottoman Empire.

Expansion of the Ottoman Empire

- Ottoman Turks, AD 1300
- Acquisitions, AD 1300–59
- Acquisitions, AD 1359–1451
- Acquisitions, AD 1451–81 (Mehmed II)
- Acquisitions, AD 1512–20 (Selim I)
- Acquisitions, AD 1520–66 (Süleyman I the Magnificent)
- Acquisitions, AD 1566–1683
- Boundary of Ottoman Empire at greatest extent, AD 1683–99

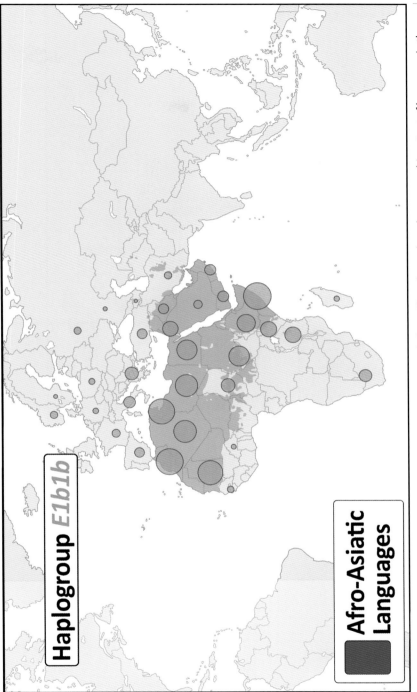

Color Plate 33: The geographic extent of Y chromosome haplogroup *E1b1b* significantly overlaps the geographic extent of languages in the Afro-Asiatic language family.

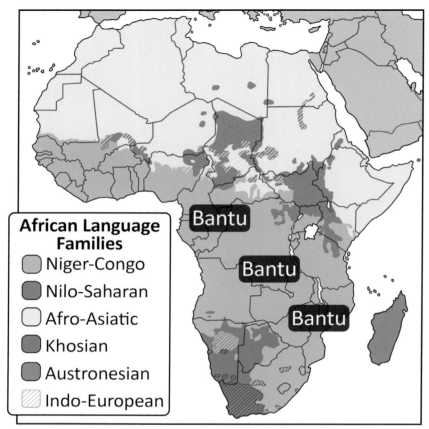

Color Plate 34: Distribution of language families within Africa.

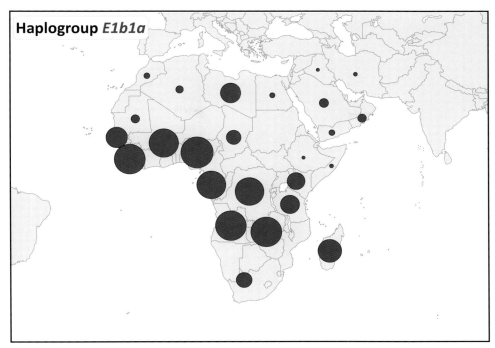

Color Plate 35: Geographic distribution of Y chromosome haplogroup *E1b1a*. The relative size of each circle represents the relative abundance of haplogroup *E1b1a* in that population. See the Color Plate A reference map for the identity of each population. Populations with undetectable levels of haplogroup *E1b1a* or with haplogroup *E1b1a* levels below 1% are omitted from this map.

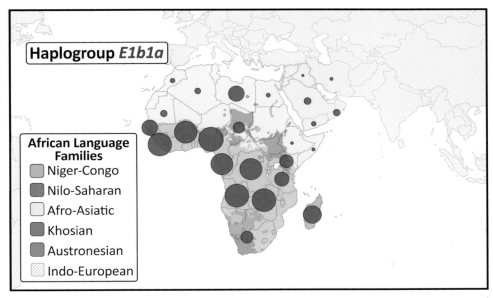

Color Plate 36: The geographic extent of Y chromosome haplogroup *E1b1a* significantly overlaps the geographic extent of languages in the Niger-Congo language family.

Haplogroup *E1b1a*

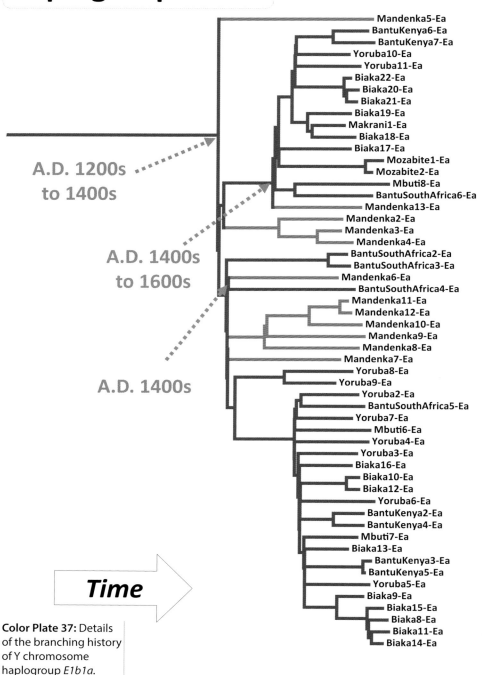

Color Plate 37: Details of the branching history of Y chromosome haplogroup *E1b1a*.

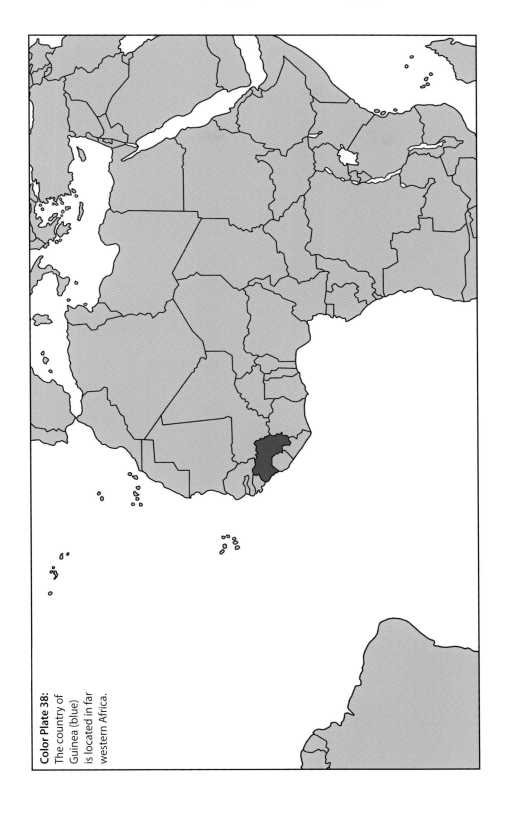

Color Plate 38:
The country of Guinea (blue) is located in far western Africa.

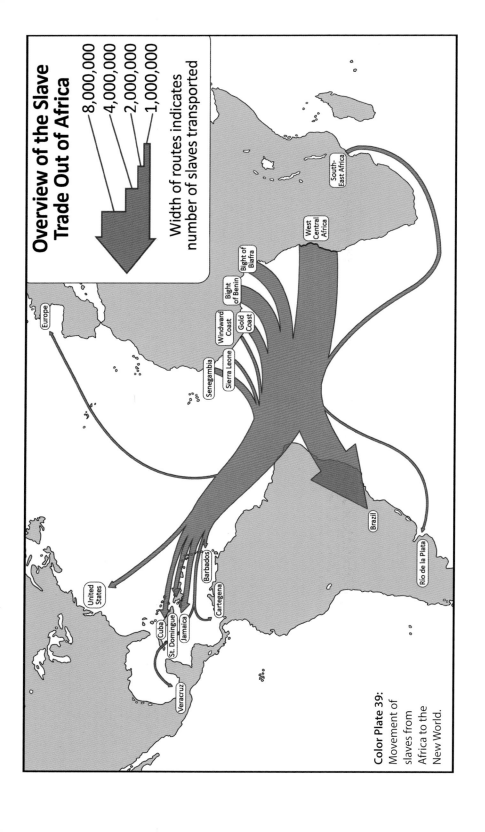

Overview of the Slave Trade Out of Africa

8,000,000
4,000,000
2,000,000
1,000,000

Width of routes indicates number of slaves transported

Color Plate 39: Movement of slaves from Africa to the New World.

Europe

Senegambia
Sierra Leone
Windward Coast
Gold Coast
Bight of Benin
Bight of Biafra
West Central Africa
South-East Africa

United States
Veracruz
Cuba
St. Domingue
Jamaica
Cartegena
Barbados
Brazil
Rio de la Plata

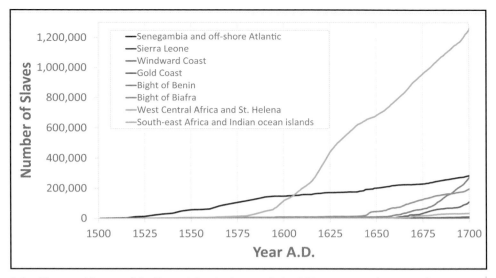

Color Plate 40: History of the Trans-Atlantic slave trade by African region. The vertical axis represents the cumulative number of embarking slaves. The specific African geographic locations are depicted on the map in **Color Plate 39.**

Haplogroup *E1b*

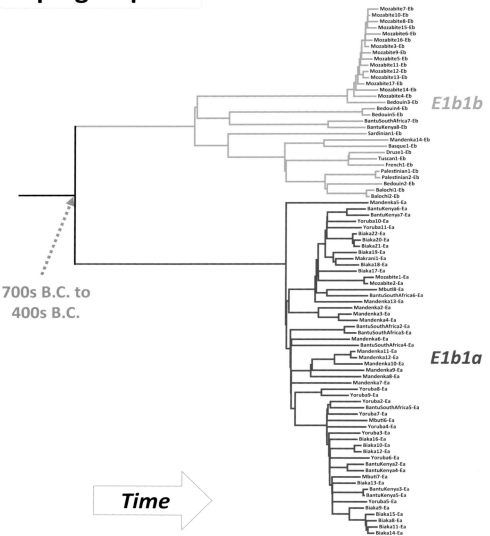

700s B.C. to 400s B.C.

Time

Color Plate 41:
Details of the branching history of Y chromosome haplogroups *E1b1a* and *E1b1b*.

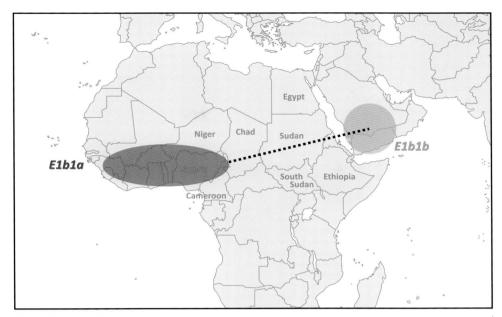

Color Plate 42: African homelands of the ancestors to haplogroups *E1b1a* and *E1b1b*. The recent expansion of *E1b1a* appears to have begun in West Africa. The recent expansion and migration of *E1b1b* appears to have begun on the Arabian Peninsula. The earlier ancestors to both of these groups probably lived somewhere between them. Most of the land between them is African.

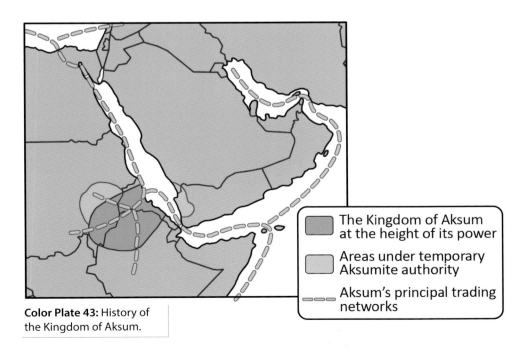

The Kingdom of Aksum at the height of its power

Areas under temporary Aksumite authority

Aksum's principal trading networks

Color Plate 43: History of the Kingdom of Aksum.

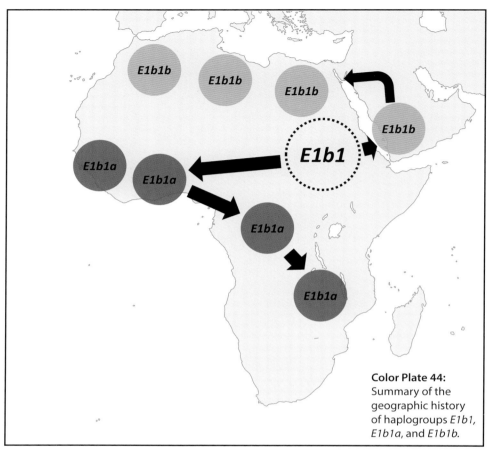

Color Plate 44:
Summary of the geographic history of haplogroups *E1b1*, *E1b1a*, and *E1b1b*.

Color Plate 45:
Victoria Falls.

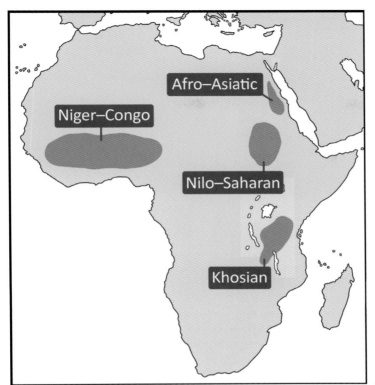

Color Plate 46: Geographic locations of major African language families in the ancient past, according to mainstream science.

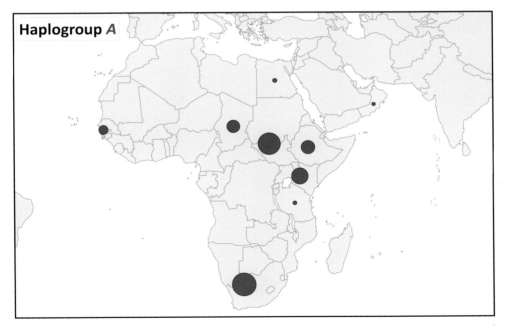

Color Plate 47: Geographic distribution of Y chromosome haplogroup *A*. The relative size of each circle represents the relative abundance of haplogroup *A* in that population. See the Color Plate A reference map for the identity of each population. Populations with undetectable levels of haplogroup *A* or with haplogroup *A* levels below 1% are omitted from this map.

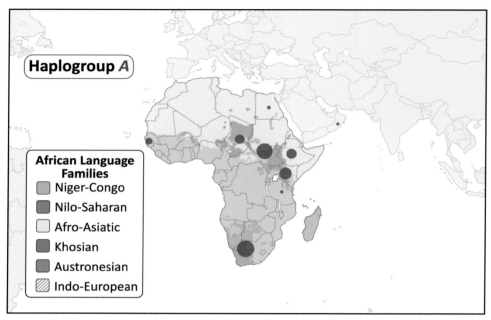

Color Plate 48: Geographic overlap between languages and Y chromosome haplogroup *A*. Haplogroup *A* tends to be found where Nilo-Saharan and Khoisan languages are spoken.

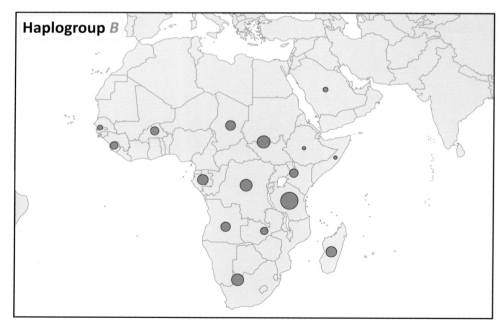

Color Plate 49: Geographic distribution of Y chromosome haplogroup *B*. The relative size of each circle represents the relative abundance of haplogroup *B* in that population. See the Color Plate A reference map for the identity of each population. Populations with undetectable levels of haplogroup *B* or with haplogroup *B* levels below 1% are omitted from this map.

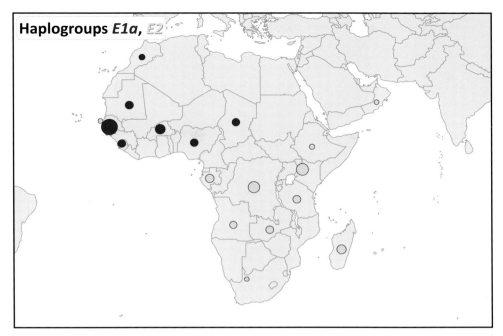

Color Plate 50: Geographic distribution of Y chromosome haplogroups *E1a* and *E2*. The relative size of each circle represents the relative abundance of haplogroup *E1a* (dark color) or haplogroup *E2* (light pink color) in that population. See the Color Plate A reference map for the identity of each population. Populations with undetectable levels of haplogroups *E1a* or *E2*, or with haplogroup *E1a* or *E2* levels below 1% are omitted from this map.

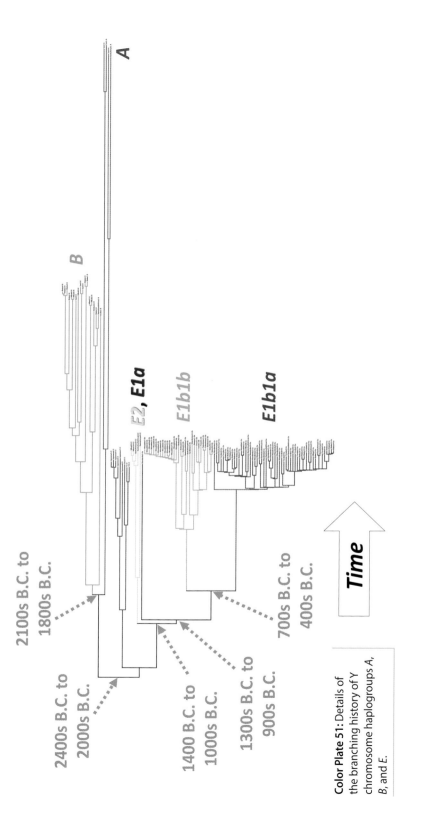

Color Plate 51: Details of the branching history of Y chromosome haplogroups *A*, *B*, and *E*.

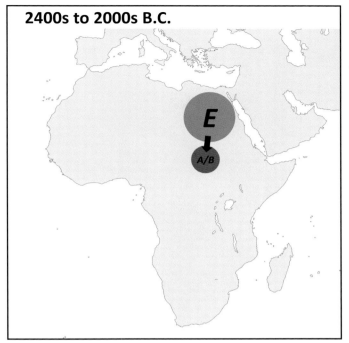

2400s to 2000s B.C.

Color Plate 52: Genetic history of Africa — ancient genetic splits and migrations.

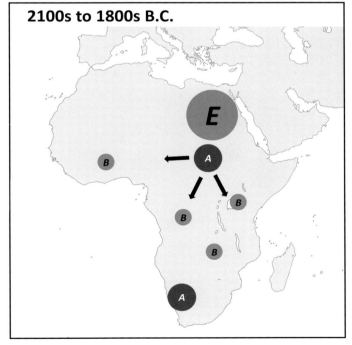

2100s to 1800s B.C.

Color Plate 53: Genetic history of Africa — early genetic splits and migrations.

Color Plate 54:
Genetic history of
Africa — mid-B.C.-era
genetic splits and
migrations.

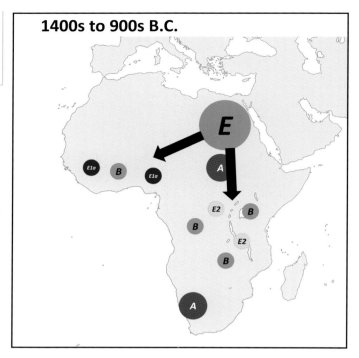

1400s to 900s B.C.

Color Plate 55:
Genetic history of
Africa — late B.C.-era
genetic splits and
migrations.

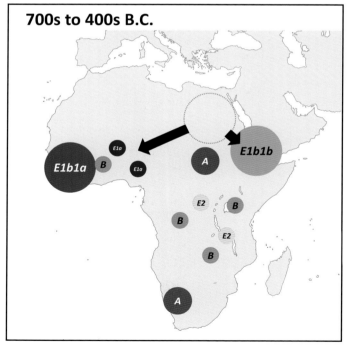

700s to 400s B.C.

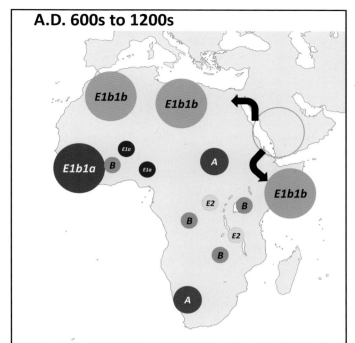

A.D. 600s to 1200s

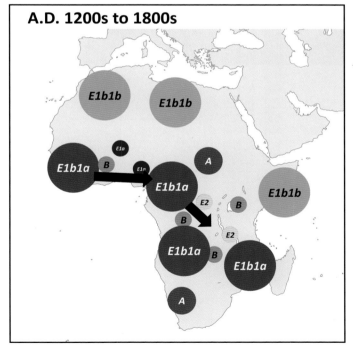

A.D. 1200s to 1800s

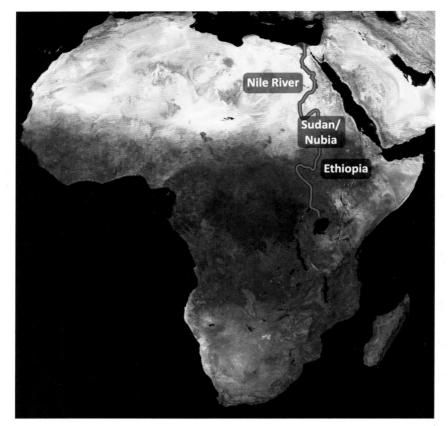

Color Plate 58: Satellite map of Africa, with blue line highlighting the Nile River.

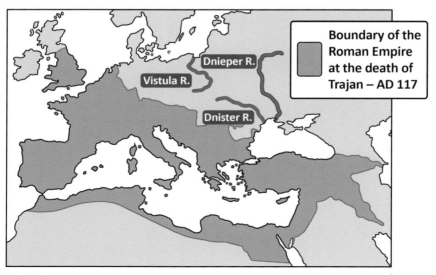

Color Plate 59: Geographic extent of the ancient Roman Empire.

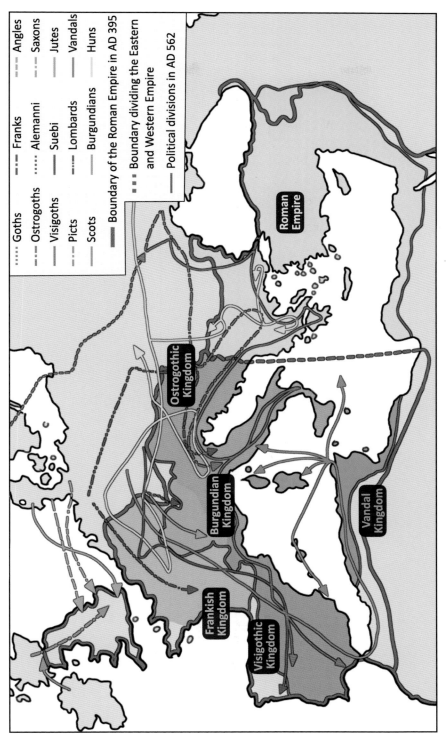

Color Plate 60: History of the overthrow of the western Roman Empire by invaders from the east.

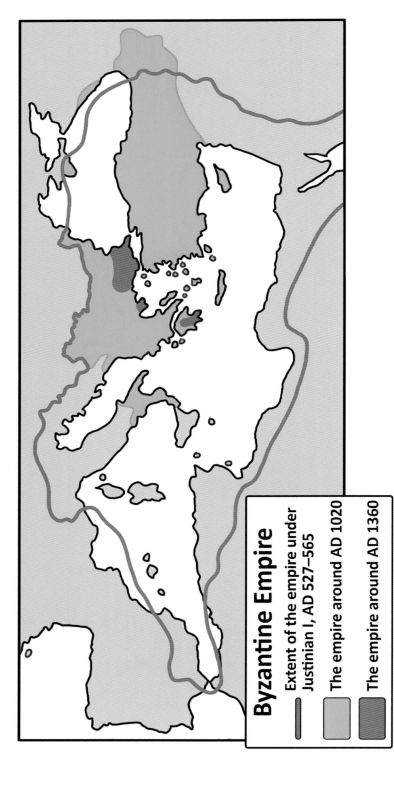

Byzantine Empire

— Extent of the empire under Justinian I, AD 527–565

The empire around AD 1020

The empire around AD 1360

Color Plate 61: History of the decline of the eastern Roman (Byzantine) Empire.

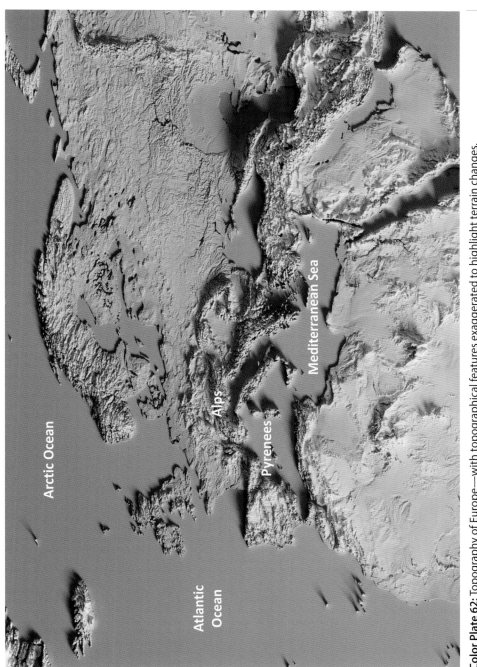

Color Plate 62: Topography of Europe—with topographical features exaggerated to highlight terrain changes.

Haplogroup R1b

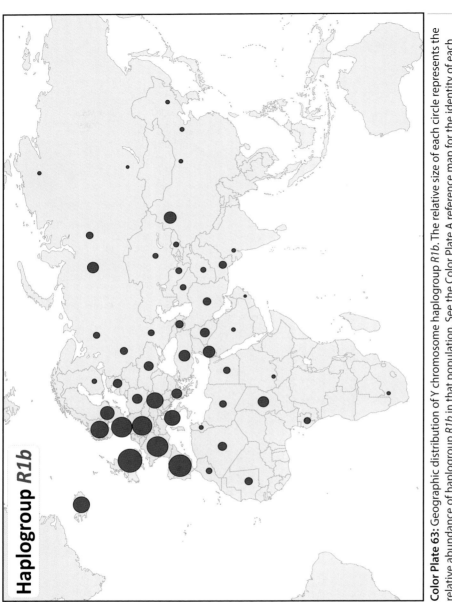

Color Plate 63: Geographic distribution of Y chromosome haplogroup *R1b*. The relative size of each circle represents the relative abundance of haplogroup *R1b* in that population. See the Color Plate A reference map for the identity of each population. Populations with undetectable levels of haplogroup *R1b* or with haplogroup *R1b* levels below 1% are omitted from this map.

Haplogroup *R1b*

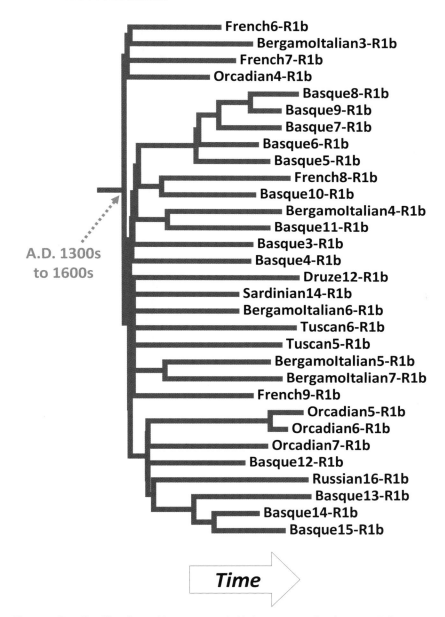

Color Plate 64: Details of late branching patterns in Y chromosome haplogroup *R1b*.

Haplogroup *R1b*

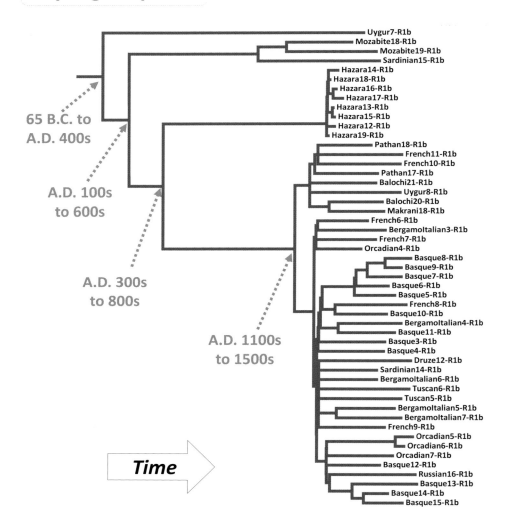

Color Plate 65: Details of early and late branching patterns in Y chromosome haplogroup *R1b*.

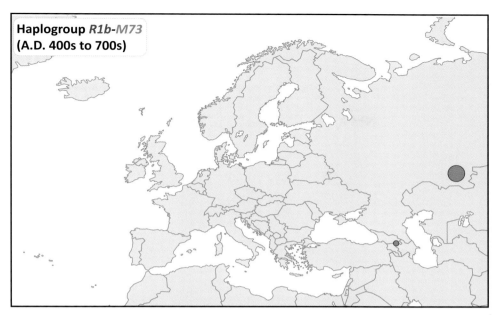

Color Plate 66: Geographic distribution of the *M73* subgroup within Y chromosome haplogroup *R1b*. The relative size of each circle represents the relative abundance of *M73* in that population. These populations are different from those in the reference map of Color Plate A (see supplemental online data for details). Populations with undetectable levels of *M73* or with *M73* levels below 1% are omitted from this map.

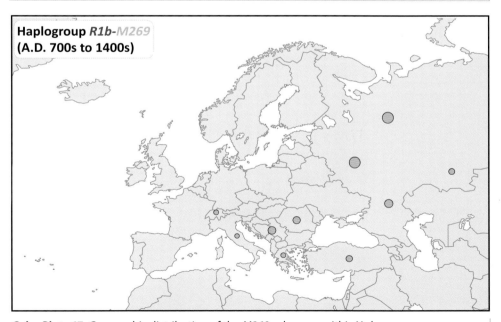

Color Plate 67: Geographic distribution of the *M269* subgroup within Y chromosome haplogroup *R1b*. The relative size of each circle represents the relative abundance of *M269* in that population. These populations are different from those in the reference map of Color Plate A (see supplemental online data for details). Populations with undetectable levels of *M269* or with *M269* levels below 1% are omitted from this map.

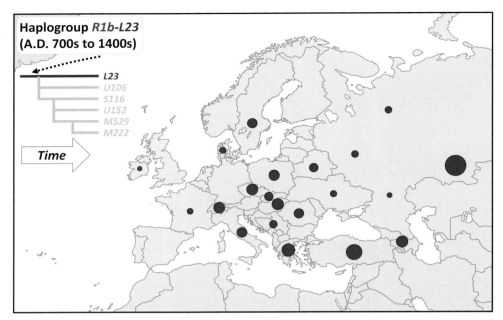

Color Plate 68: Geographic distribution of the *L23* subgroup within Y chromosome haplogroup *R1b*. The relative size of each circle represents the relative abundance of *L23* in that population. These populations are different from those in the reference map of Color Plate A (see supplemental online data for details). Populations with undetectable levels of *L23* or with *L23* levels below 1% are omitted from this map.

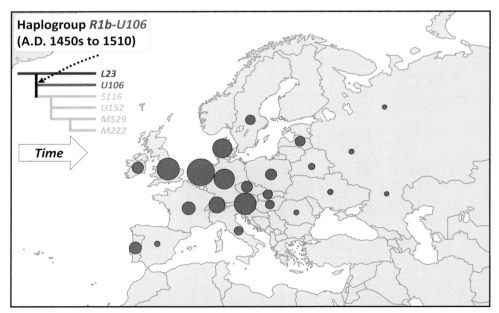

Color Plate 69: Geographic distribution of the *U106* subgroup within Y chromosome haplogroup *R1b*. The relative size of each circle represents the relative abundance of *U106* in that population. These populations are different from those in the reference map of Color Plate A (see supplemental online data for details). Populations with undetectable levels of *U106* or with *U106* levels below 1% are omitted from this map.

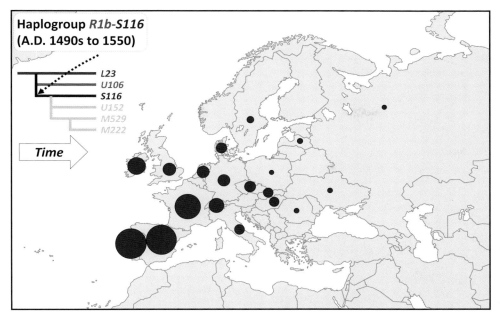

Color Plate 70: Geographic distribution of the *S116* subgroup within Y chromosome haplogroup *R1b*. The relative size of each circle represents the relative abundance of *S116* in that population. These populations are different from those in the reference map of Color Plate A (see supplemental online data for details). Populations with undetectable levels of *S116* or with *S116* levels below 1% are omitted from this map.

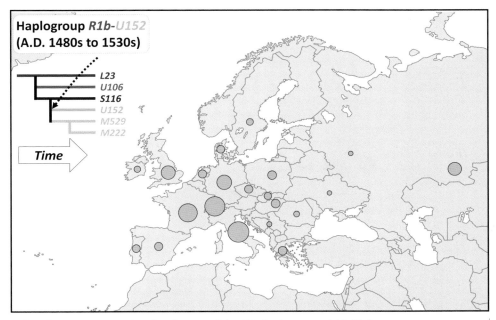

Color Plate 71: Geographic distribution of the *U152* subgroup within Y chromosome haplogroup R1b. The relative size of each circle represents the relative abundance of *U152* in that population. These populations are different from those in the reference map of Color Plate A (see supplemental online data for details). Populations with undetectable levels of *U152* or with *U152* levels below 1% are omitted from this map.

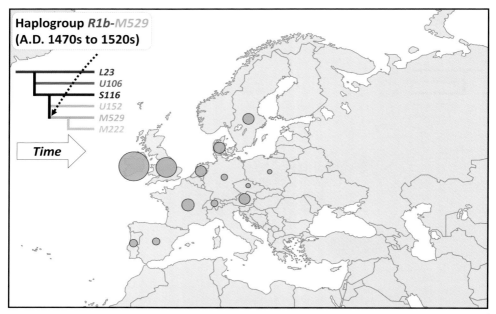

Color Plate 72: Geographic distribution of the *M529* subgroup within Y chromosome haplogroup *R1b*. The relative size of each circle represents the relative abundance of *M529* in that population. These populations are different from those in the reference map of Color Plate A (see supplemental online data for details). Populations with undetectable levels of *M529* or with *M529* levels below 1% are omitted from this map.

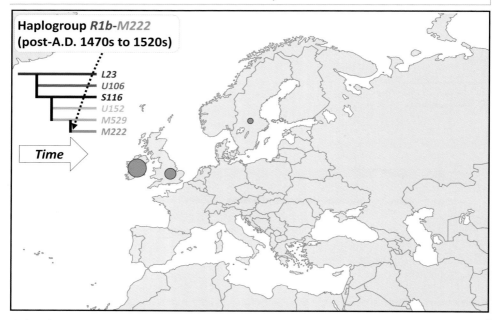

Color Plate 73: Geographic distribution of the *M222* subgroup within Y chromosome haplogroup *R1b*. The relative size of each circle represents the relative abundance of *M222* in that population. These populations are different from those in the reference map of Color Plate A (see supplemental online data for details). Populations with undetectable levels of *M222* or with *M222* levels below 1% are omitted from this map.

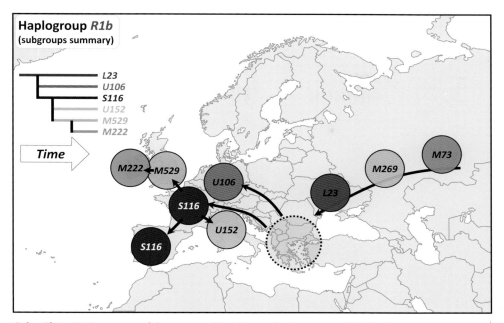

Color Plate 74: Summary of the geographic history of subgroups within Y chromosome haplogroup *R1b*.

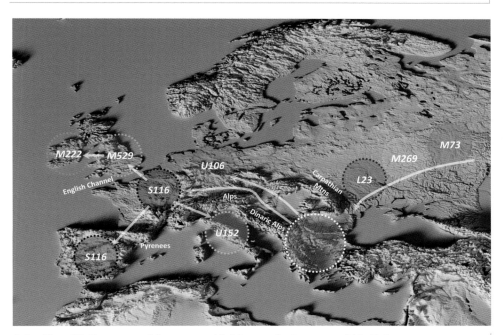

Color Plate 75: Summary of the geographic history of subgroups within Y chromosome haplogroup *R1b*—with underlying European topographical features exaggerated to highlight terrain changes.

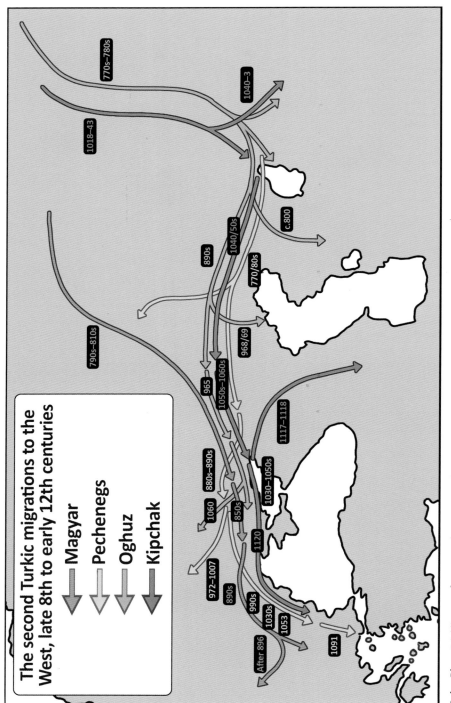

The second Turkic migrations to the West, late 8th to early 12th centuries

→ Magyar
→ Pechenegs
→ Oghuz
→ Kipchak

770s–780s
1018–43
1040–3
890s
1040/50s
c.800
770/80s
968/69
790s–810s
965
1050s–1060s
1117–1118
880s–890s
1030–1050s
1060
850s
1120
972–1007
890s
990s
1030s
After 896
1053
1091

Color Plate 76: History of westward migrations from Central Asia during the European Middle Ages.

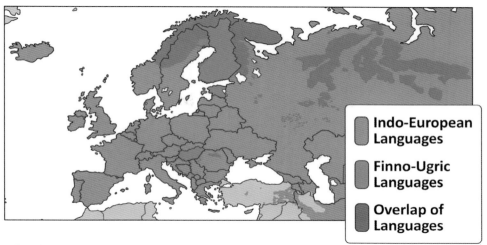

Color Plate 77: Geographic distribution of Finno-Ugric languages. The distribution of Indo-European languages is shown for reference.

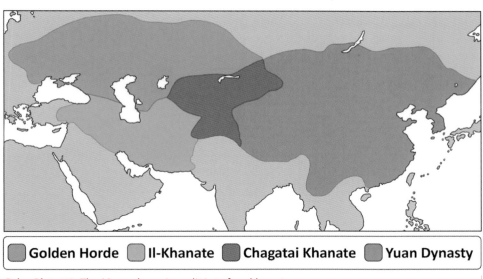

Golden Horde   Il-Khanate   Chagatai Khanate   Yuan Dynasty

Color Plate 78: The Mongol empire split into four khanates.

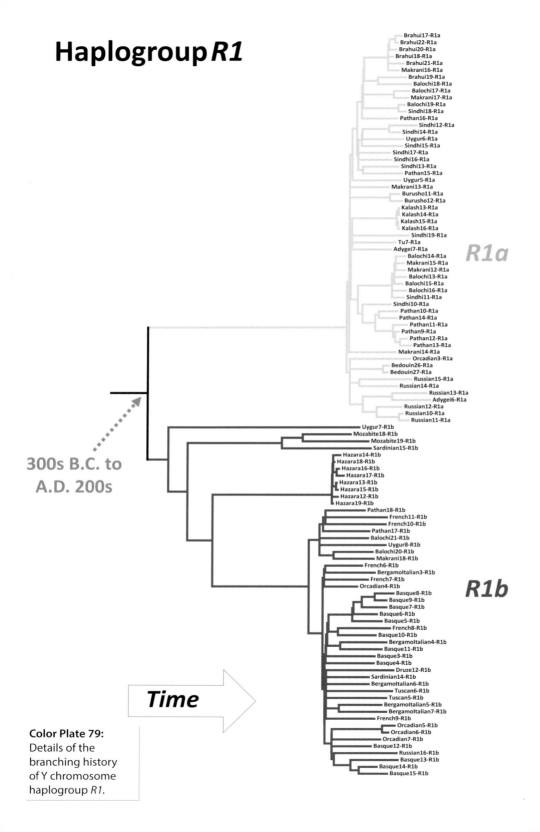

Haplogroup *R1*

R1a

300s B.C. to A.D. 200s

R1b

Time

Color Plate 79:
Details of the branching history of Y chromosome haplogroup *R1*.

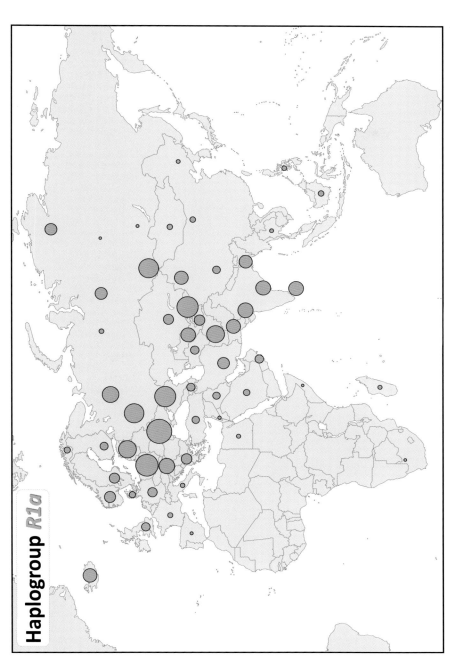

Haplogroup R1a

Color Plate 80: Geographic distribution of Y chromosome haplogroup *R1a*. The relative size of each circle represents the relative abundance of haplogroup *R1a* in that population. See the Color Plate A reference map for the identity of each population. Populations with undetectable levels of haplogroup *R1a* or with haplogroup *R1a* levels below 1% are omitted from this map.

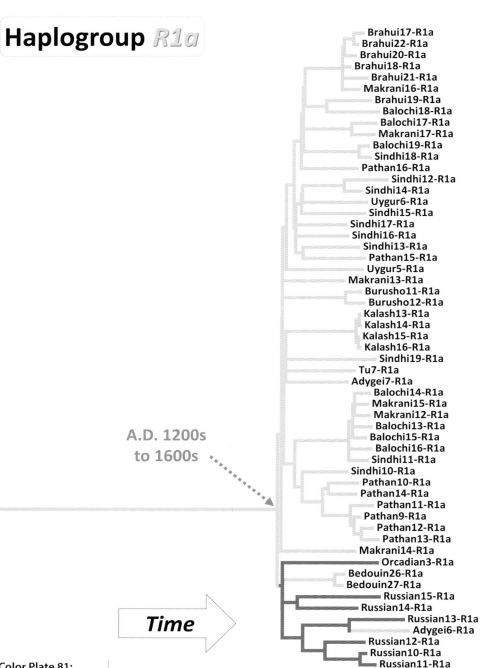

Haplogroup *R1a*

Brahui17-R1a
Brahui22-R1a
Brahui20-R1a
Brahui18-R1a
Brahui21-R1a
Makrani16-R1a
Brahui19-R1a
Balochi18-R1a
Balochi17-R1a
Makrani17-R1a
Balochi19-R1a
Sindhi18-R1a
Pathan16-R1a
Sindhi12-R1a
Sindhi14-R1a
Uygur6-R1a
Sindhi15-R1a
Sindhi17-R1a
Sindhi16-R1a
Sindhi13-R1a
Pathan15-R1a
Uygur5-R1a
Makrani13-R1a
Burusho11-R1a
Burusho12-R1a
Kalash13-R1a
Kalash14-R1a
Kalash15-R1a
Kalash16-R1a
Sindhi19-R1a
Tu7-R1a
Adygei7-R1a
Balochi14-R1a
Makrani15-R1a
Makrani12-R1a
Balochi13-R1a
Balochi15-R1a
Balochi16-R1a
Sindhi11-R1a
Sindhi10-R1a
Pathan10-R1a
Pathan14-R1a
Pathan11-R1a
Pathan9-R1a
Pathan12-R1a
Pathan13-R1a
Makrani14-R1a
Orcadian3-R1a
Bedouin26-R1a
Bedouin27-R1a
Russian15-R1a
Russian14-R1a
Russian13-R1a
Adygei6-R1a
Russian12-R1a
Russian10-R1a
Russian11-R1a

A.D. 1200s
to 1600s

Time

Color Plate 81:
Details of the
branching history
of Y chromosome
haplogroup *R1a*.
European branches
are highlighted in
pink.

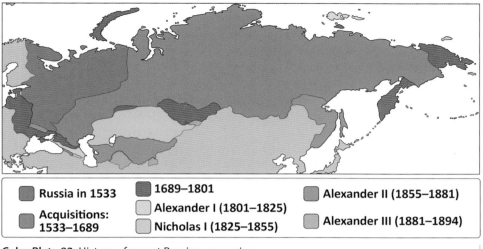

Russia in 1533	1689–1801	Alexander II (1855–1881)
Acquisitions: 1533–1689	Alexander I (1801–1825)	Alexander III (1881–1894)
	Nicholas I (1825–1855)	

Color Plate 82: History of recent Russian expansion.

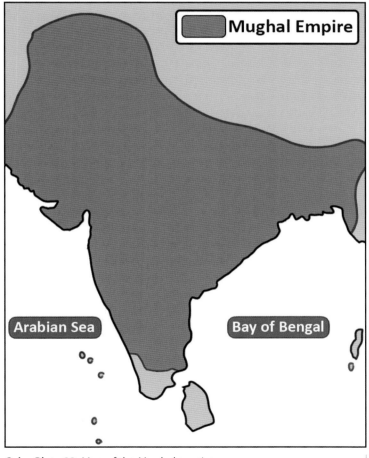

Color Plate 83: Map of the Mughal empire.

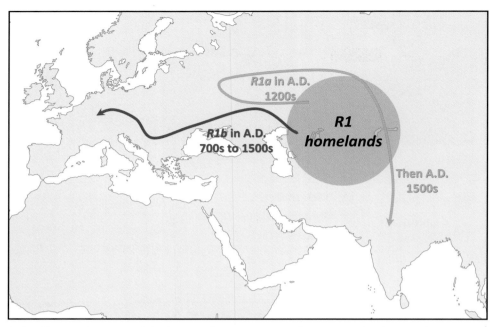

Color Plate 84: Summary of the history of migrations in Y chromosome haplogroup *R1*.

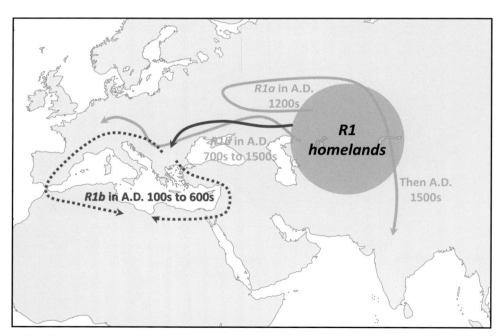

Color Plate 85: Summary of the migrations of one subgroup within Y chromosome haplogroup *R1b* that may have relevance to the ancient Roman Empire.

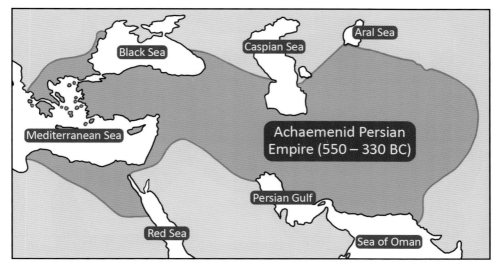

Color Plate 86: Geographic extent of the ancient Persian Empire.

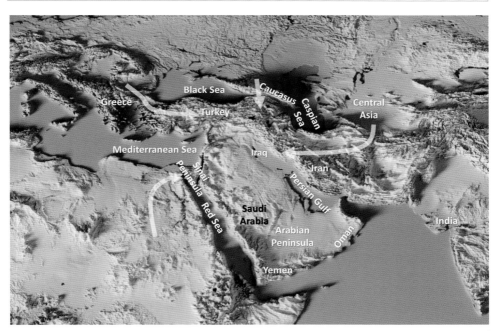

Color Plate 87: Topography of the Middle East—with topographical features exaggerated to highlight terrain changes.

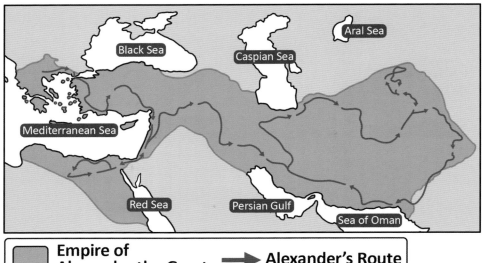

Color Plate 88: Map of the conquests and empire of Alexander the Great.

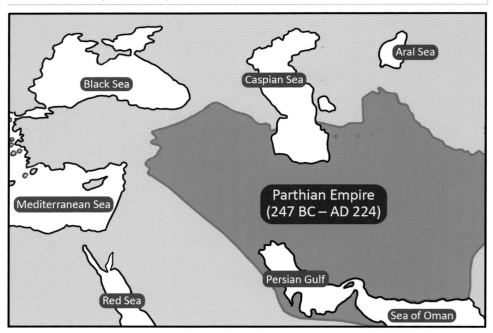

Color Plate 89: Geographic extent of the Parthian empire.

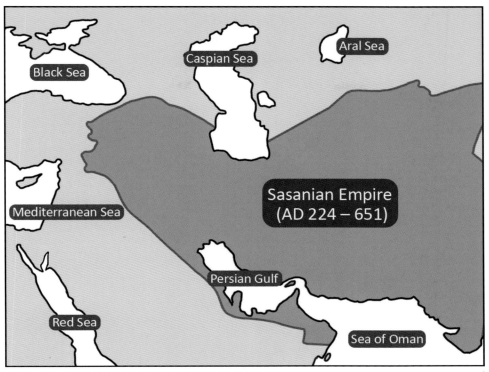

Color Plate 90: Geographic extent of the Sasanid (Sasanian) empire.

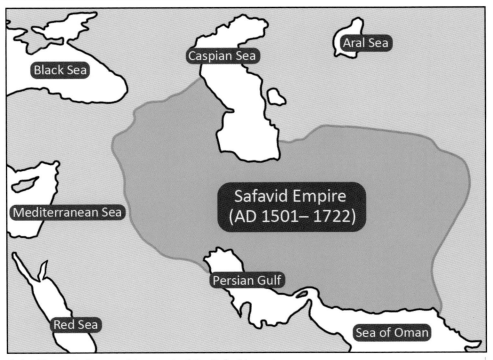

Color Plate 91: Geographic extent of the Safavid empire.

Haplogroup *J2*

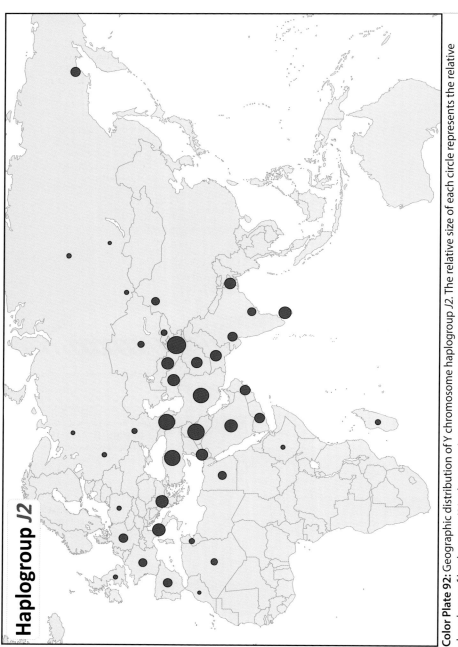

Color Plate 92: Geographic distribution of Y chromosome haplogroup *J2*. The relative size of each circle represents the relative abundance of haplogroup *J2* in that population. See the Color Plate A reference map for the identity of each population. Populations with undetectable levels of haplogroup *J2* or with haplogroup *J2* levels below 1% are omitted from this map.

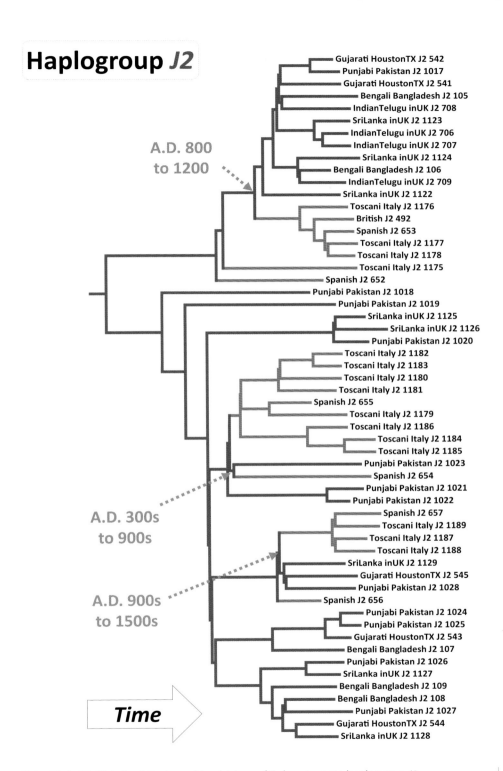

Haplogroup *J2*

A.D. 800 to 1200

A.D. 300s to 900s

A.D. 900s to 1500s

Time

Gujarati HoustonTX J2 542
Punjabi Pakistan J2 1017
Gujarati HoustonTX J2 541
Bengali Bangladesh J2 105
IndianTelugu inUK J2 708
SriLanka inUK J2 1123
IndianTelugu inUK J2 706
IndianTelugu inUK J2 707
SriLanka inUK J2 1124
Bengali Bangladesh J2 106
IndianTelugu inUK J2 709
SriLanka inUK J2 1122
Toscani Italy J2 1176
British J2 492
Spanish J2 653
Toscani Italy J2 1177
Toscani Italy J2 1178
Toscani Italy J2 1175
Spanish J2 652
Punjabi Pakistan J2 1018
Punjabi Pakistan J2 1019
SriLanka inUK J2 1125
SriLanka inUK J2 1126
Punjabi Pakistan J2 1020
Toscani Italy J2 1182
Toscani Italy J2 1183
Toscani Italy J2 1180
Toscani Italy J2 1181
Spanish J2 655
Toscani Italy J2 1179
Toscani Italy J2 1186
Toscani Italy J2 1184
Toscani Italy J2 1185
Punjabi Pakistan J2 1023
Spanish J2 654
Punjabi Pakistan J2 1021
Punjabi Pakistan J2 1022
Spanish J2 657
Toscani Italy J2 1189
Toscani Italy J2 1187
Toscani Italy J2 1188
SriLanka inUK J2 1129
Gujarati HoustonTX J2 545
Punjabi Pakistan J2 1028
Spanish J2 656
Punjabi Pakistan J2 1024
Punjabi Pakistan J2 1025
Gujarati HoustonTX J2 543
Bengali Bangladesh J2 107
Punjabi Pakistan J2 1026
SriLanka inUK J2 1127
Bengali Bangladesh J2 109
Bengali Bangladesh J2 108
Punjabi Pakistan J2 1027
Gujarati HoustonTX J2 544
SriLanka inUK J2 1128

Color Plate 93: Details of the branching history of Y chromosome haplogroup *J2*.

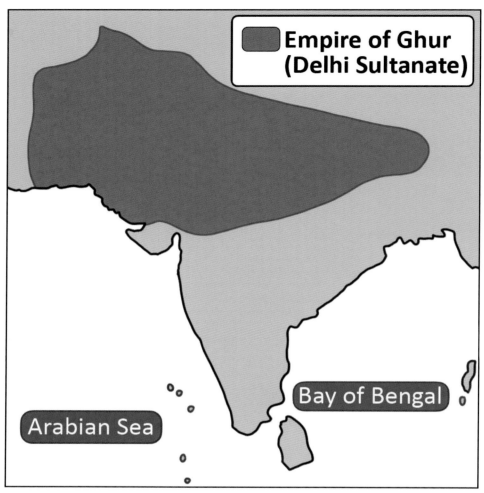

Color Plate 94: Geographic extent of the Ghurid empire (the Delhi Sultanate).

Haplogroup G

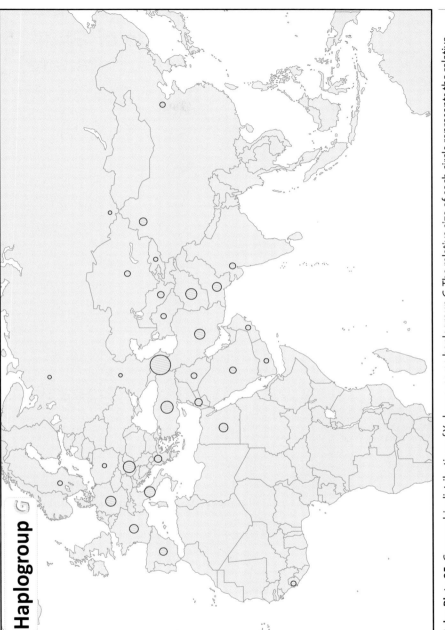

Color Plate 95: Geographic distribution of Y chromosome haplogroup G. The relative size of each circle represents the relative abundance of haplogroup G in that population. See the Color Plate A reference map for the identity of each population. Populations with undetectable levels of haplogroup G or with haplogroup G levels below 1% are omitted from this map.

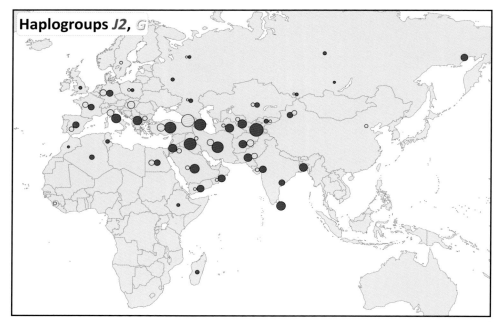

Color Plate 96: Geographic overlap between the distributions of Y chromosome haplogroups *J2* (dark green) and *G* (light pink). The relative size of each circle represents the relative abundance of the haplogroup *J2* or *G* in that population. See the Color Plate A reference map for the identity of each population. Populations with undetectable levels of haplogroup *J2* or *G*, or with haplogroup *J2* or *G* levels below 1% are omitted from this map.

Haplogroup G

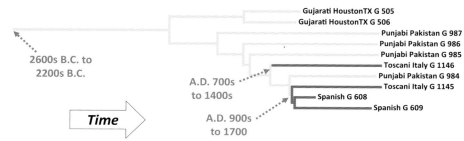

Color Plate 97: Details of the branching history of Y chromosome haplogroup *G*.

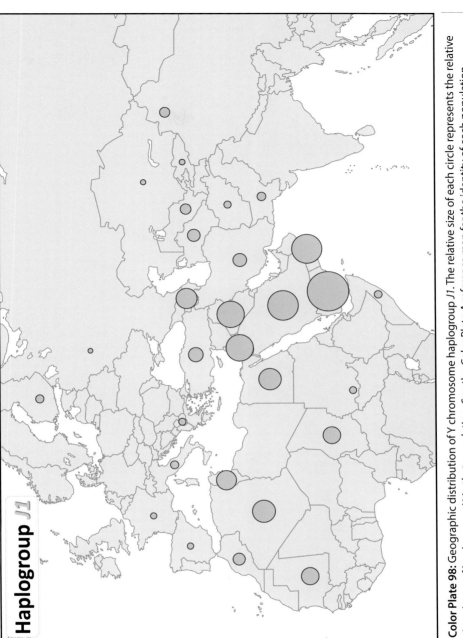

Color Plate 98: Geographic distribution of Y chromosome haplogroup *J1*. The relative size of each circle represents the relative abundance of haplogroup *J1* in that population. See the Color Plate A reference map for the identity of each population. Populations with undetectable levels of haplogroup *J1* or with haplogroup *J1* levels below 1% are omitted from this map.

Haplogroup *J1*

Haplogroups *J1*, *J2*

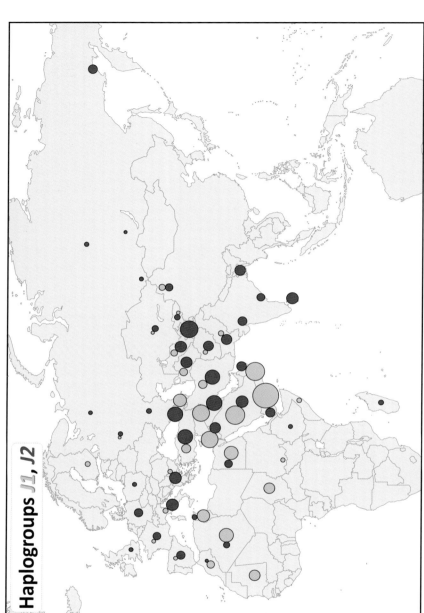

Color Plate 99: Geographic overlap between the distributions of Y chromosome haplogroups *J1* (light blue) and *J2* (dark green). The relative size of each circle represents the relative abundance of the haplogroup *J1* or *J2* in that population. See the Color Plate A reference map for the identity of each population. Populations with undetectable levels of haplogroup *J1* or *J2*, or with haplogroup *J1* or *J2* levels below 1% are omitted from this map.

Haplogroups *J1*, *E1b1b*

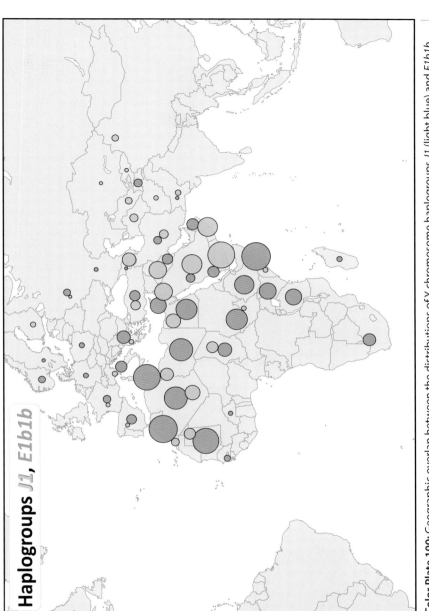

Color Plate 100: Geographic overlap between the distributions of Y chromosome haplogroups *J1* (light blue) and *E1b1b* (tan). The relative size of each circle represents the relative abundance of the haplogroup *J1* or *E1b1b* in that population. See the Color Plate A reference map for the identity of each population. Populations with undetectable levels of haplogroup *J1* or *E1b1b*, or with haplogroup *J1* or *E1b1b* levels below 1% are omitted from this map.

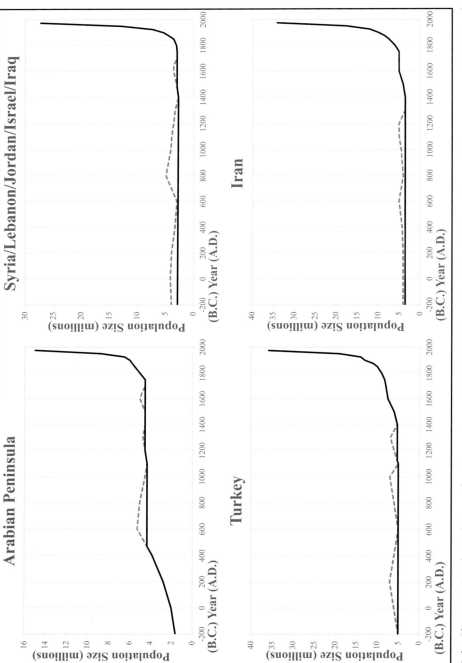

Color Plate 101: Population history of various regions of the Middle East and Iran. The actual growth curve is shown as a grey dashed line, and the minimum growth curve is shown as a solid black line.

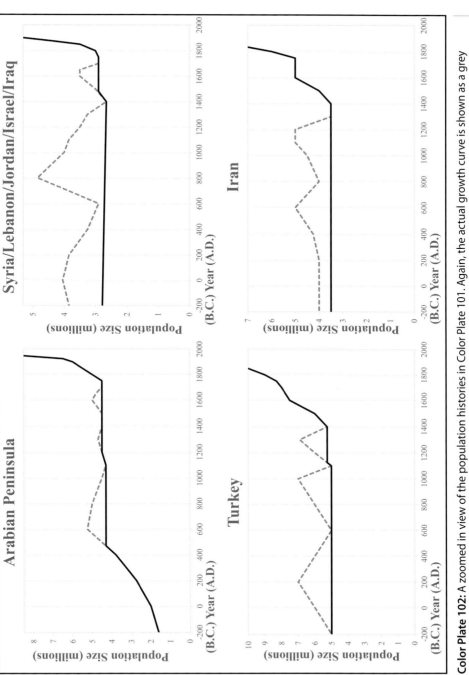

Color Plate 102: A zoomed in view of the population histories in Color Plate 101. Again, the actual growth curve is shown as a grey dashed line, and the minimum growth curve is shown as a solid black line.

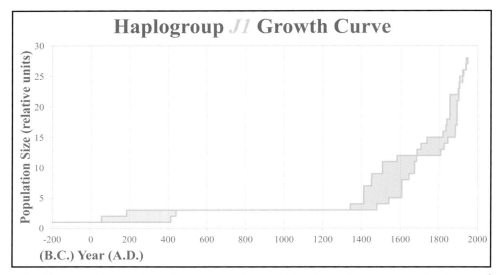

Color Plate 103: History of population growth in men belonging to Y chromosome haplogroup *J1*. Shaded area represents the full statistical range of the growth curve.

Haplogroup *J1*

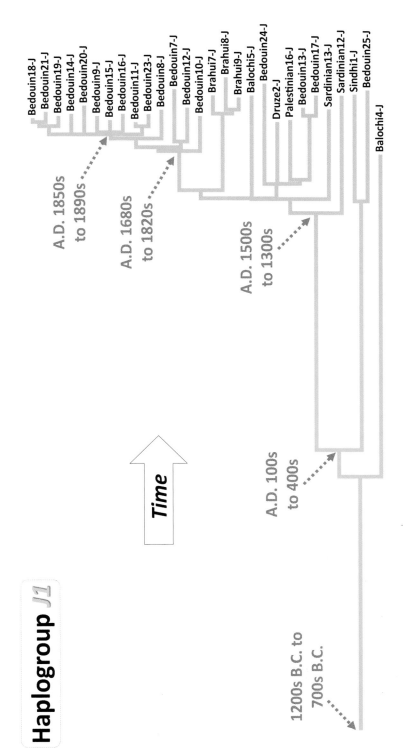

Color Plate 104: Details of the branching history of Y chromosome haplogroup *J1*.

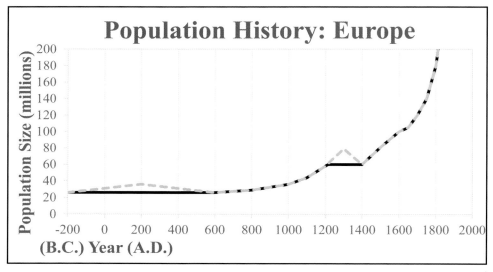

Color Plate 105: History of population growth in Europe from 200 B.C. (shown as a negative number) to the present. This graph obscures the full height of the recent population spike in order to zoom in on the details of the Middle Ages. The actual growth curve is shown as a gray dashed line, and the minimum growth curve is shown as a solid black line.

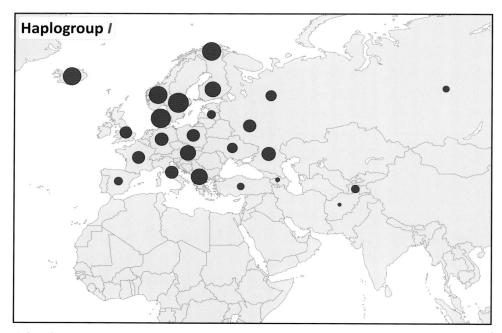

Color Plate 106: Geographic distribution of Y chromosome haplogroup *I*. The relative size of each circle represents the relative abundance of haplogroup *I* in that population. See the Color Plate A reference map for the identity of each population. Populations with undetectable levels of haplogroup *I* or with haplogroup *I* levels below 1% are omitted from this map.

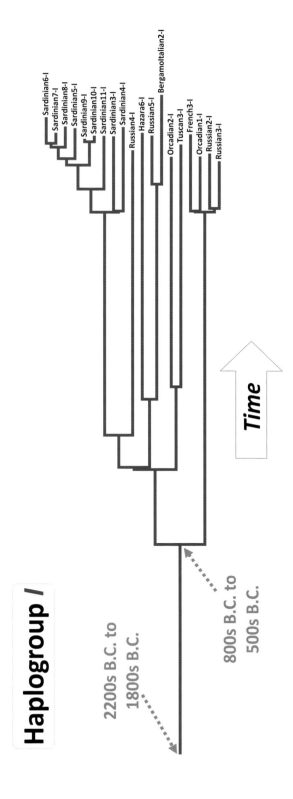

Color Plate 107: Details of the branching history of Y chromosome haplogroup *I*.

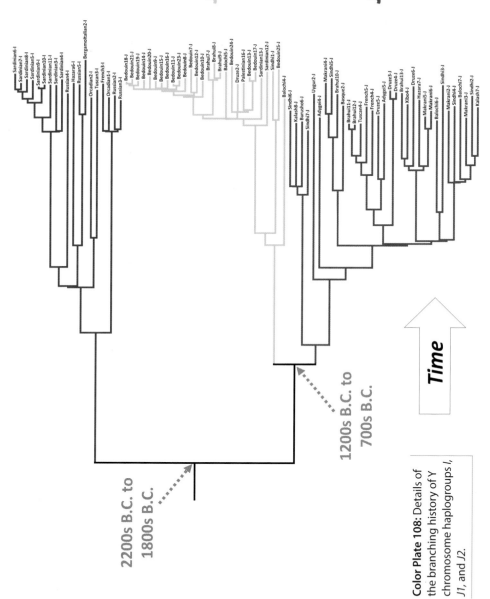

Color Plate 108: Details of the branching history of Y chromosome haplogroups *I*, *J1*, and *J2*.

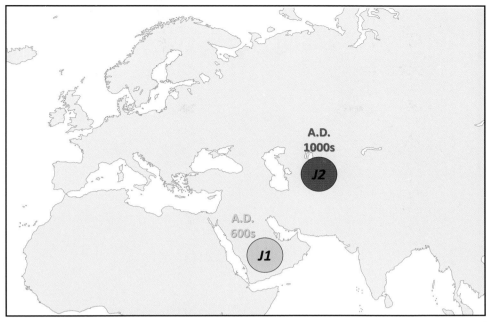

Color Plate 109: Summary of the geographic fates of Y chromosome haplogroups *J1* and *J2*.

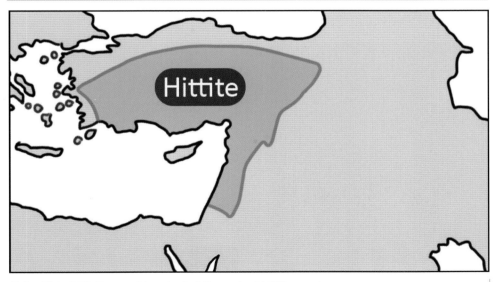

Color Plate 110: Geographic extent of the ancient Hittite empire.

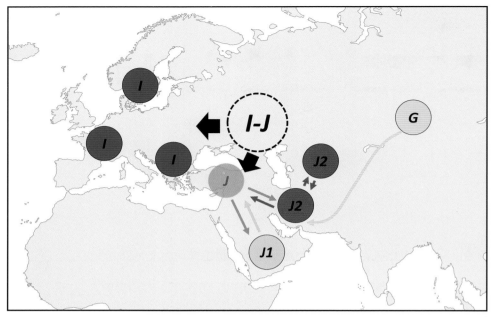

Color Plate 111: Summary of the geographic fates of Y chromosome haplogroups *G, I, J1,* and *J2.*

Color Plate 112: Taj Mahal.

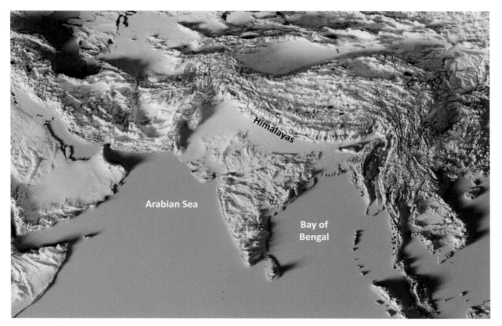

Color Plate 113: Topography of South Asia—with topographical features exaggerated to highlight terrain changes.

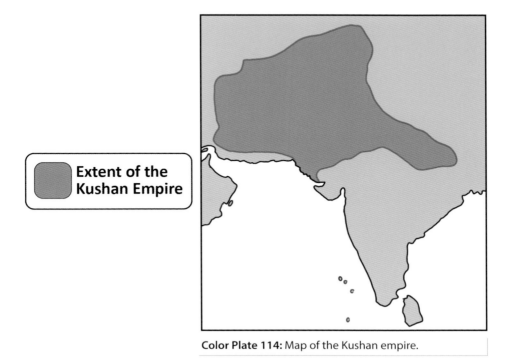

Color Plate 114: Map of the Kushan empire.

Haplogroup *R2*

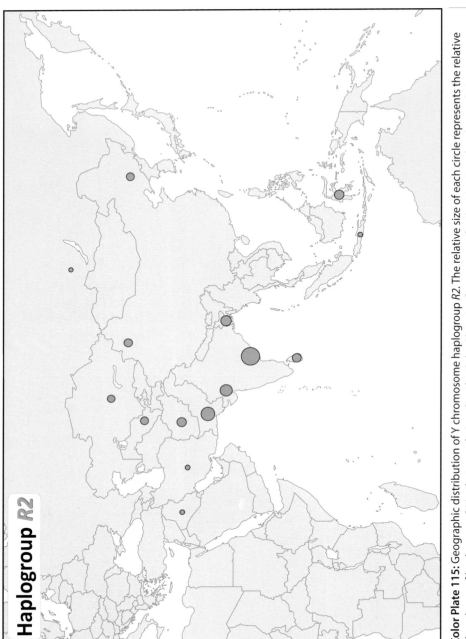

Color Plate 115: Geographic distribution of Y chromosome haplogroup *R2*. The relative size of each circle represents the relative abundance of haplogroup *R2* in that population. See the Color Plate A reference map for the identity of each population. Populations with undetectable levels of haplogroup *R2* or with haplogroup *R2* levels below 1% are omitted from this map.

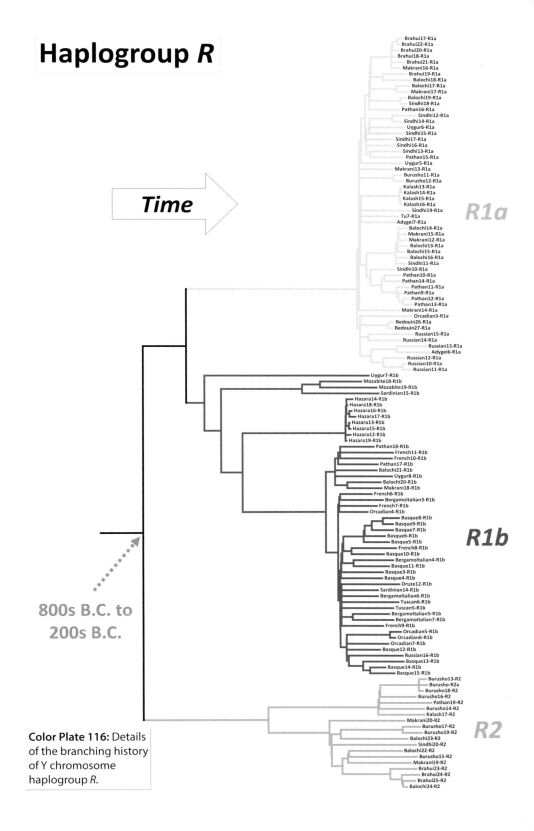

Haplogroup *R*

Time

R1a

R1b

R2

800s B.C. to
200s B.C.

Color Plate 116: Details
of the branching history
of Y chromosome
haplogroup *R*.

Color Plate 117:
Geographic extent
of languages in the
Dravidian language
family.

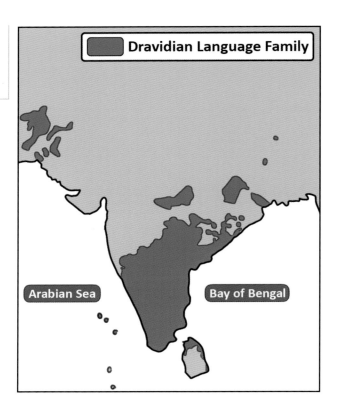

Color Plate 118:
Geographic extent of
the Mauryan empire.

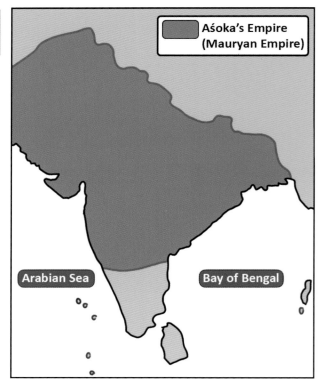

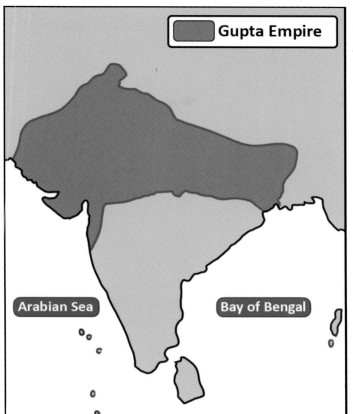

Color Plate 119: Geographic extent of the Gupta empire.

Haplogroup *H*

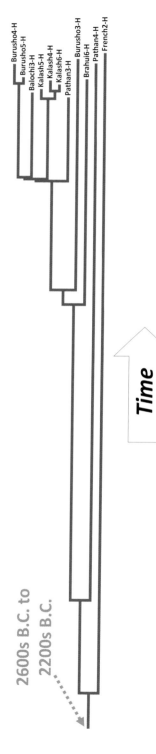

2600s B.C. to
2200s B.C.

Time

Burusho4-H
Burusho5-H
Balochi3-H
Kalash5-H
Kalash4-H
Kalash6-H
Pathan3-H
Burusho3-H
Brahui6-H
Pathan4-H
French2-H

Color Plate 120: Details of the branching history of Y chromosome haplogroup *H*.

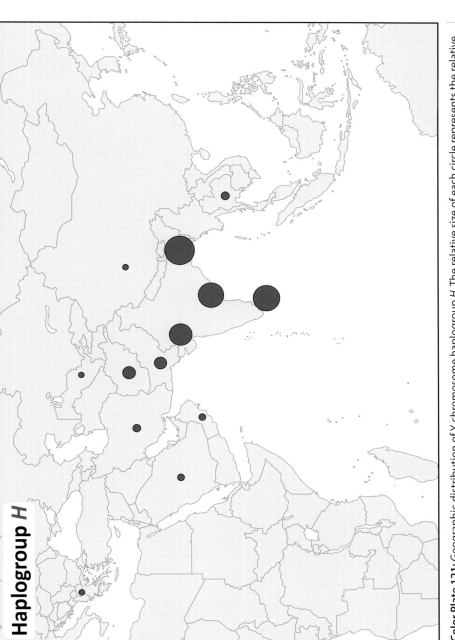

Color Plate 121: Geographic distribution of Y chromosome haplogroup *H*. The relative size of each circle represents the relative abundance of haplogroup *H* in that population. See the Color Plate A reference map for the identity of each population. Populations with undetectable levels of haplogroup *H* or with haplogroup *H* levels below 1% are omitted from this map.

133 generations of separation

(between modern *I* and modern *J*)

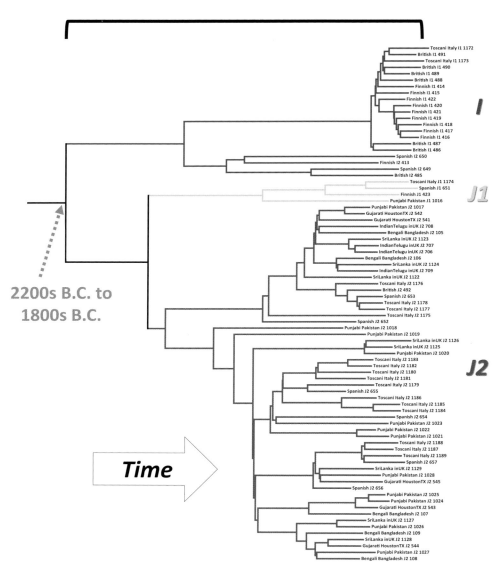

Color Plate 122: Details on the length of time (i.e., as represented by branch lengths) separating European individuals (i.e., those belonging to Y chromosome haplogroup *I*) from Asian individuals (i.e., those belonging to haplogroups *J1*, *J2*).

12 generations of separation
(between ancient *H* and ancient *I-J*)

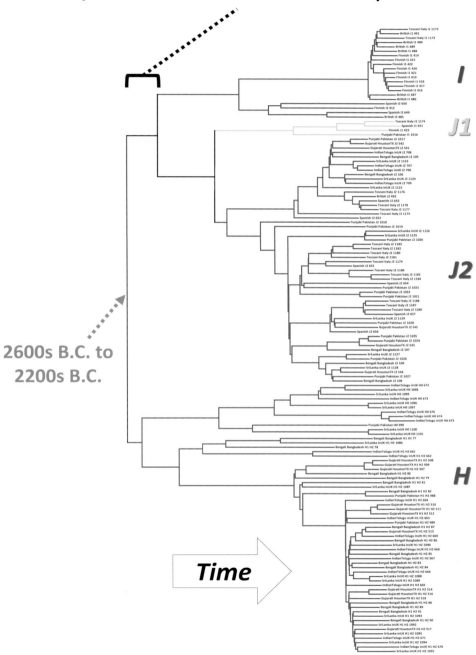

Color Plate 123: Details on the length of time (i.e., as represented by branch lengths) separating Y chromosome haplogroup *I-J* individuals from haplogroup *H* individuals.

Color Plate 124: The Great Wall of China.

Color Plate 125: Chinese art and architecture in the Forbidden City (Beijing, China).

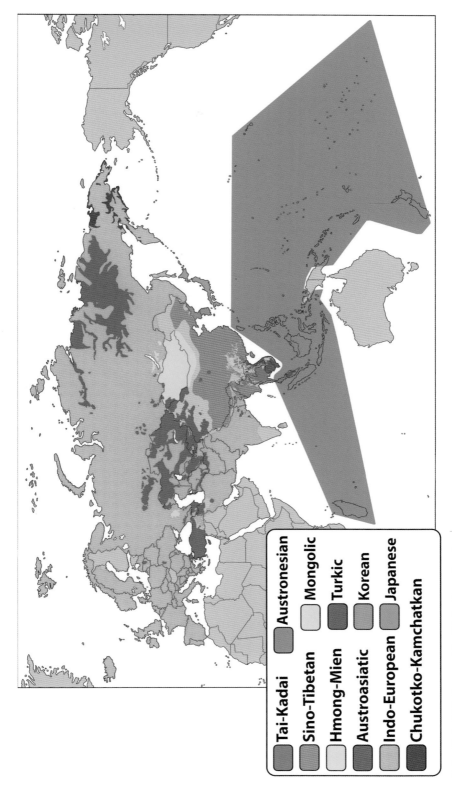

Color Plate 126: Geographic distribution of major language families and isolates in or near East Asia.

Tai-Kadai	Austronesian
Sino-Tibetan	Mongolic
Hmong-Mien	Turkic
Austroasiatic	Korean
Indo-European	Japanese
Chukotko-Kamchatkan	

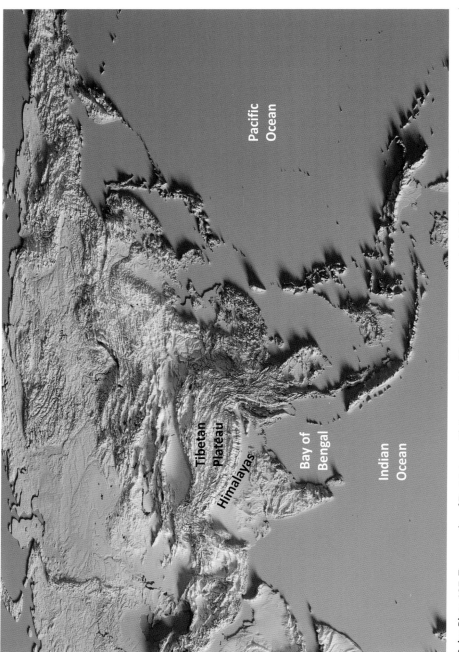

Color Plate 127: Topography of East Asia—with topographical features exaggerated to highlight terrain changes.

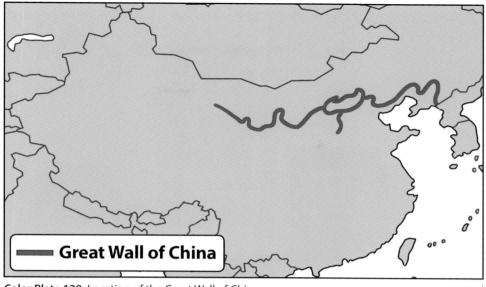

Color Plate 128: Location of the Great Wall of China.

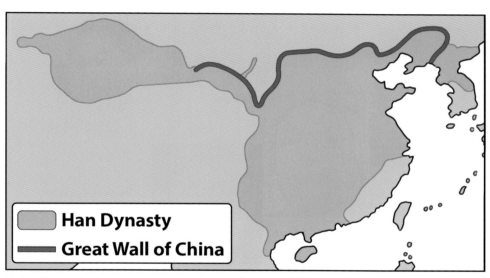

Color Plate 129: Geographic extent of the Han Dynasty of China, with its borders defined in part by the Great Wall of China.

Color Plate 130: Similar ethnic features across diverse East Asian ethnicities.

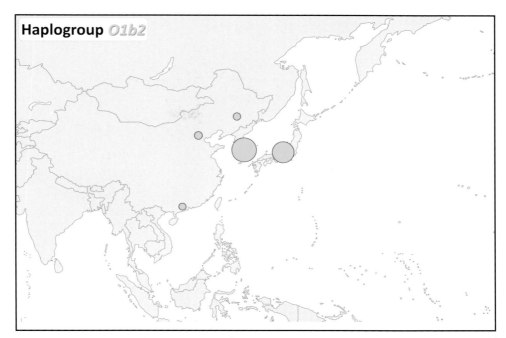

Color Plate 131: Geographic distribution of Y chromosome haplogroup *O1b2*. The relative size of each circle represents the relative abundance of haplogroup *O1b2* in that population. See the Color Plate A reference map for the identity of each population. Populations with undetectable levels of haplogroup *O1b2* or with haplogroup *O1b2* levels below 1% are omitted from this map.

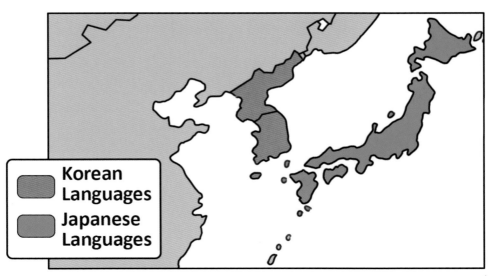

Color Plate 132: Geographic distribution of the Korean and Japanese language isolates.

Color Plate 133: Geographic overlap between the distribution of haplogroup *O1b2* and of the Korean and Japanese languages.

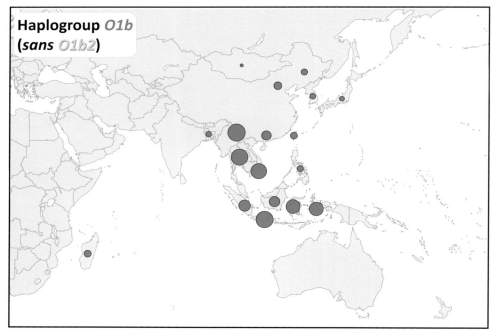

Color Plate 134: Geographic distribution of Y chromosome haplogroup *O1b* (excluding the *O1b2* branches within *O1b*). The relative size of each circle represents the relative abundance of haplogroup *O1b* in that population. See the Color Plate A reference map for the identity of each population. Populations with undetectable levels of haplogroup *O1b* or with haplogroup *O1b* levels below 1% are omitted from this map.

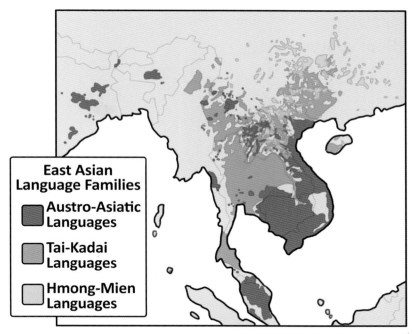

Color Plate 135: Geographic distribution of languages within the Austro-Asiatic, Tai-Kadai, and Hmong-Mien language families.

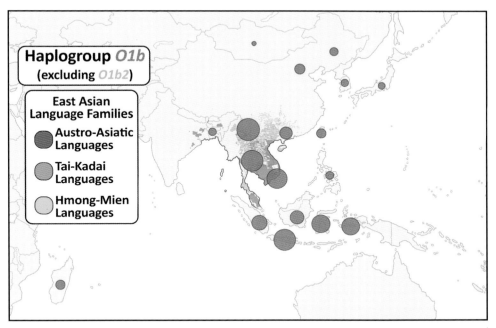

Color Plate 136: Geographic overlap between the distribution of haplogroup *O1b* and of the languages within the major Southeast Asian language families (Austro-Asiatic, Tai-Kadai, and Hmong-Mien).

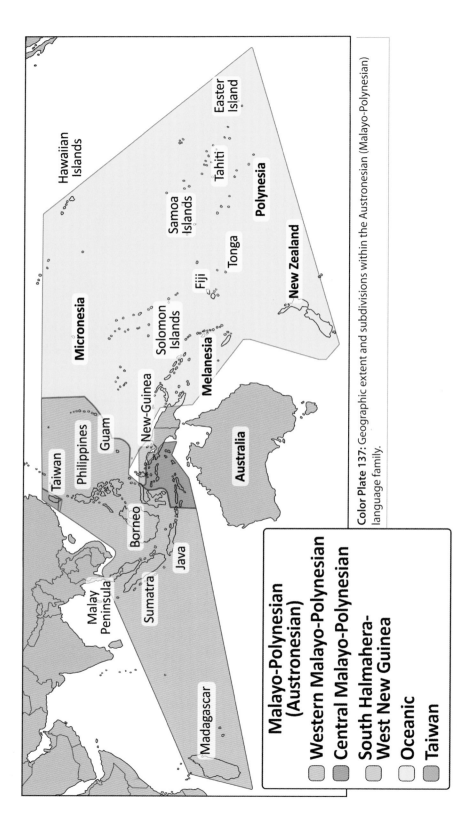

Color Plate 137: Geographic extent and subdivisions within the Austronesian (Malayo-Polynesian) language family.

Haplogroup *O1a*

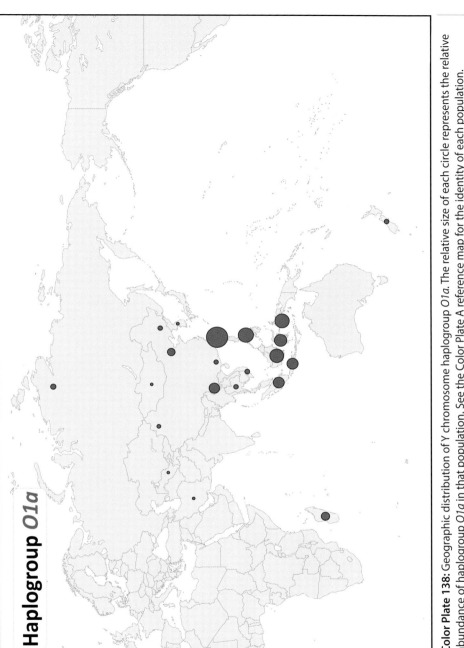

Color Plate 138: Geographic distribution of Y chromosome haplogroup *O1a*. The relative size of each circle represents the relative abundance of haplogroup *O1a* in that population. See the Color Plate A reference map for the identity of each population. Populations with undetectable levels of haplogroup *O1a* or with haplogroup *O1a* levels below 1% are omitted from this map.

Haplogroup O2

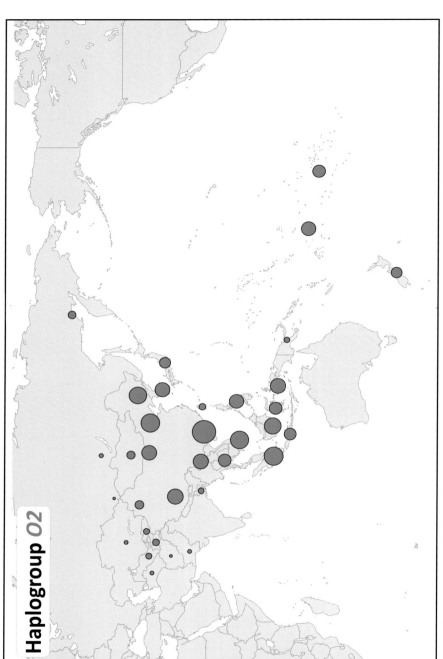

Color Plate 139: Geographic distribution of Y chromosome haplogroup O2. The relative size of each circle represents the relative abundance of haplogroup O2 in that population. See the Color Plate A reference map for the identity of each population. Populations with undetectable levels of haplogroup O2 or with haplogroup O2 levels below 1% are omitted from this map.

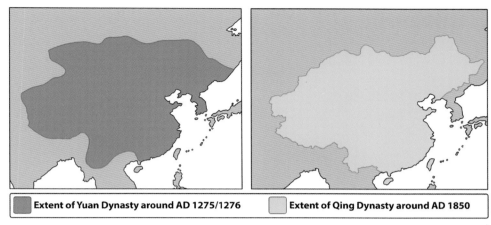

| **Extent of Yuan Dynasty around AD 1275/1276** | **Extent of Qing Dynasty around AD 1850** |

Color Plate 140: Geographic extent of the two largest Chinese empires.

Haplogroup *O*

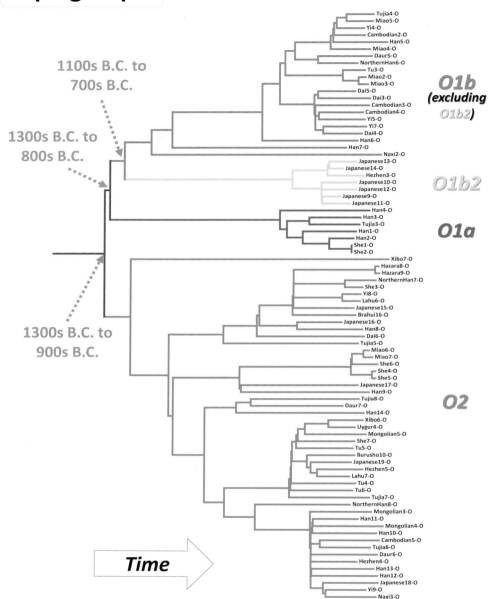

Color Plate 141: Details of the branching history of Y chromosome haplogroup *O*.

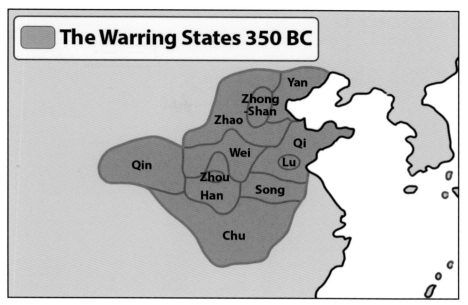

Color Plate 142: Geographic details of kingdoms during the Warring States Period.

Haplogroup N

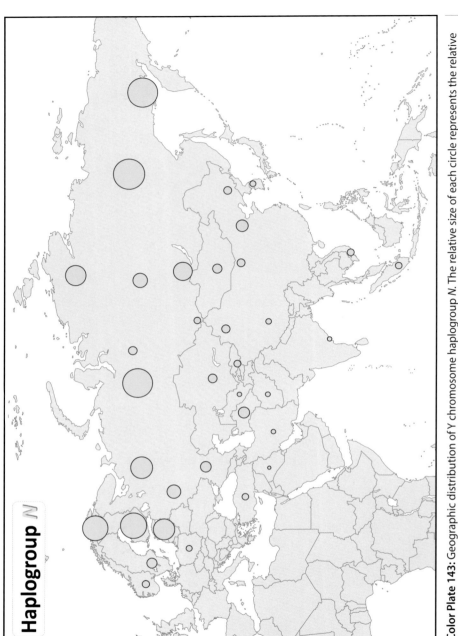

Color Plate 143: Geographic distribution of Y chromosome haplogroup N. The relative size of each circle represents the relative abundance of haplogroup N in that population. See the Color Plate A reference map for the identity of each population. Populations with undetectable levels of haplogroup N or with haplogroup N levels below 1% are omitted from this map.

Haplogroup N

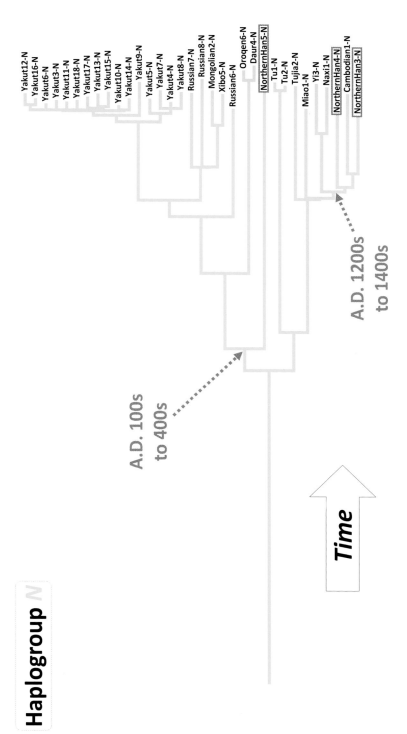

Color Plate 144: Details of the branching history of Y chromosome haplogroup N.

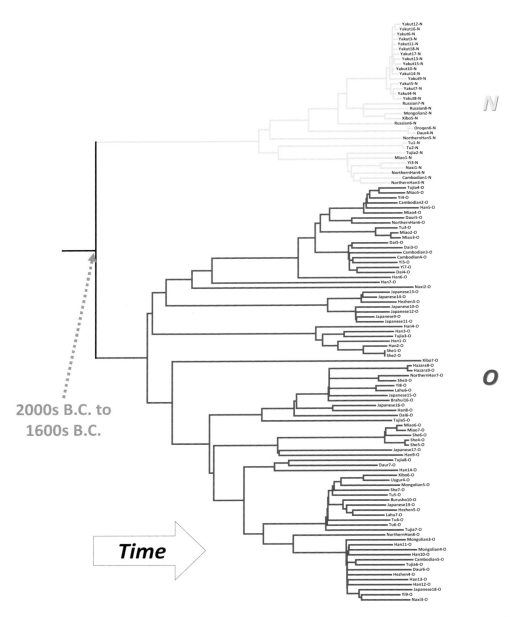

Color Plate 145: Details of the branching history of Y chromosome haplogroups *N* and *O*.

Color Plate 146: Conquests in early Chinese history. In 1045 B.C., the Shang Dynasty was overthrown by invaders from the west who set up the Zhou Dynasty.

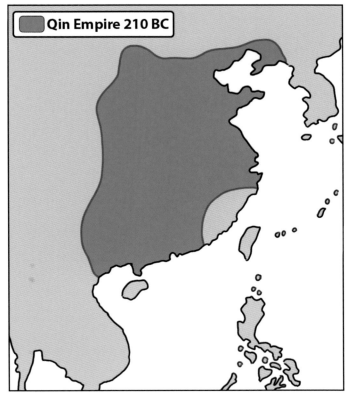

Color Plate 147: Geographic extent of the Qin empire.

Color Plate 148: Estimated geographic extent of the Western Zhou empire.

20 generations of separation
(among ancient *H*, *I-J*, *L-T*, *N-O*)

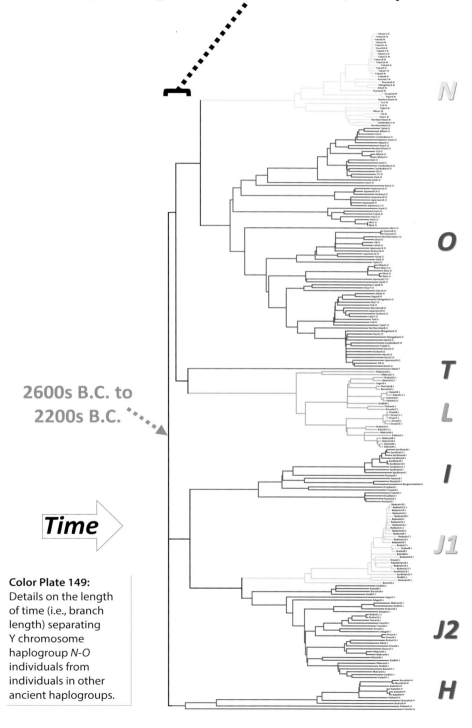

2600s B.C. to 2200s B.C.

Time

Color Plate 149:
Details on the length of time (i.e., branch length) separating Y chromosome haplogroup *N-O* individuals from individuals in other ancient haplogroups.

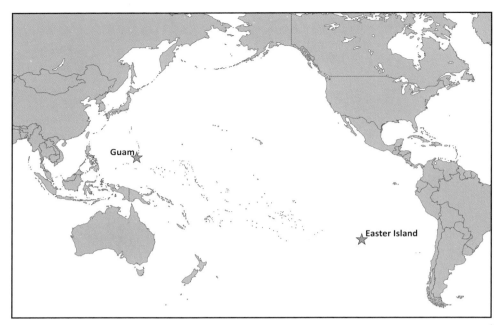

Color Plate 150: Geographic location of significant islands mentioned in the text.

Color Plate 151: Large sculpted heads (moai) of Rapa Nui (Easter Island).

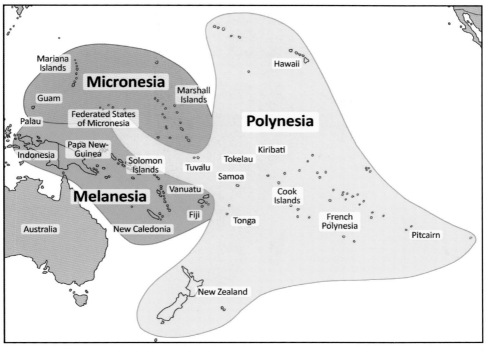

Color Plate 152: Major cultural areas of the Pacific.

Maori

Tahitian

Chinese

Korean

Color Plate 153: Polynesians and East Asians have similar ethnic features.

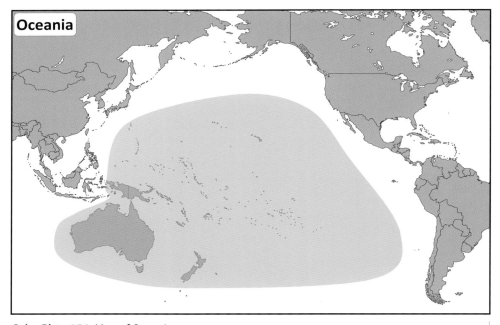

Color Plate 154: Map of Oceania.

Australian Aborigine

Papuan

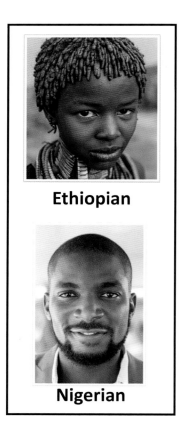

Ethiopian

Nigerian

Color Plate 155: Australian Aborigines and Melanesians have ethnic features similar to sub-Saharan Africans.

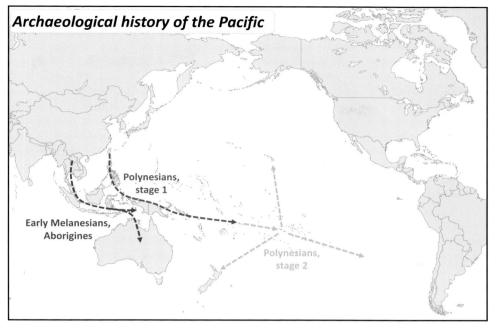

Color Plate 156: Archaeological history of the Pacific. Settlement occurred in at least three phases—a Melanesian/Australian phase, an initial Polynesian phase, and a late Polynesian phase.

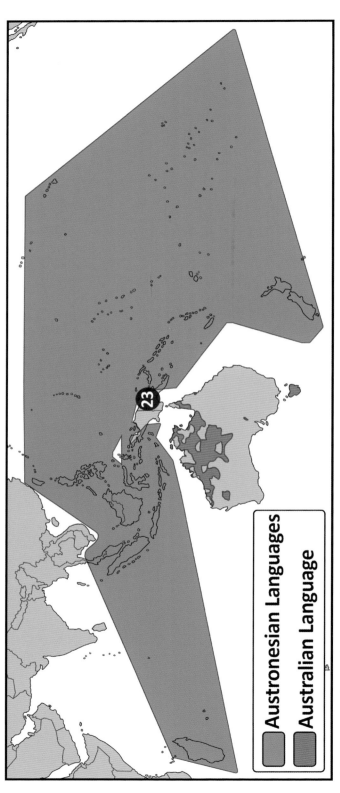

Color Plate 157: Geographic extent of the language families of the Pacific. On New Guinea, around 23 language families exist in addition to Austronesian. For simplicity, these 23 are represented by a numeral instead of by 23 different shaded areas.

Austronesian Languages

Australian Language

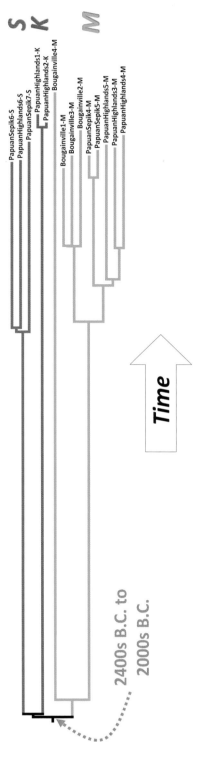

Color Plate 158: Details of the branching history of Y chromosome haplogroups *K*, *M*, and *S*.

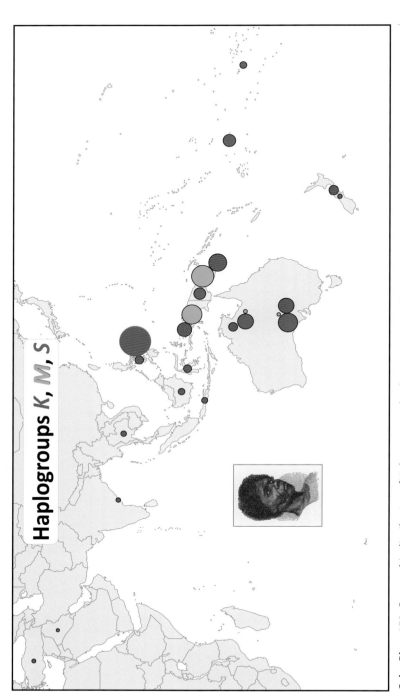

Haplogroups *K, M, S*

Color Plate 159: Geographic distribution of Y chromosome haplogroups *K, M,* and *S.* The relative size of each circle represents the relative abundance of haplogroup *K* (muted red color), *M* (teal color), or *S* (green color) in that population. See the Color Plate A reference map for the identity of each population. The two circles shown on/near the Philippines represent two different Filipino populations. The smaller circle with the black border represents the average level across several islands of the Philippines. The larger circle with the red border represents the level found in the population of Filipino Negritos, one of whom is depicted in the small portrait. Populations with undetectable levels of haplogroup *K, M, or S,* or with haplogroup *K, M, or S* levels below 1% are omitted from this map.

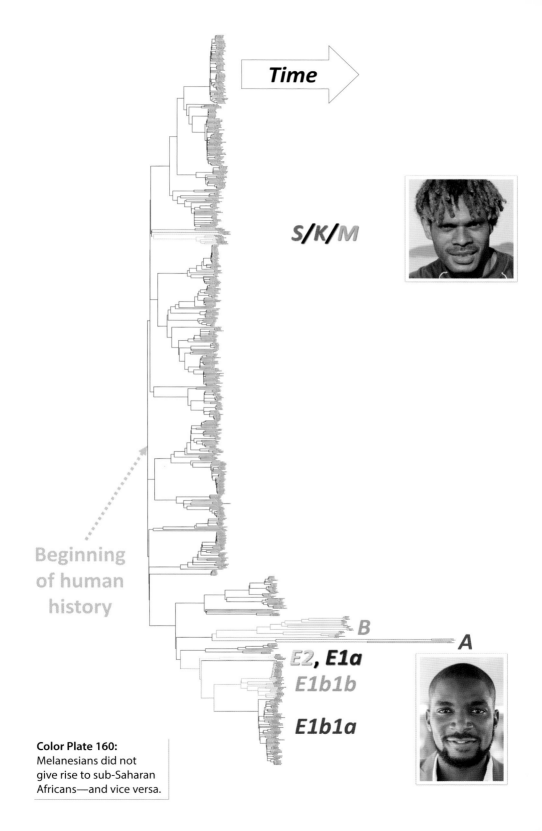

Time

S/K/M

Beginning
of human
history

B

A

E2, E1a
E1b1b

E1b1a

Color Plate 160:
Melanesians did not
give rise to sub-Saharan
Africans—and vice versa.

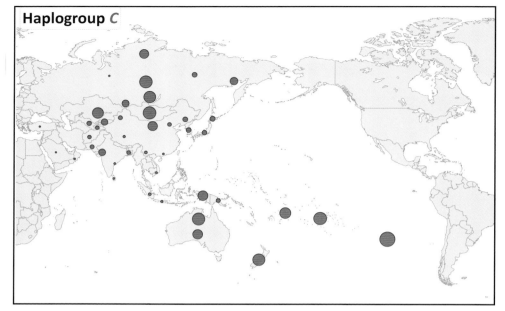

Color Plate 161: Old World geographic distribution of Y chromosome haplogroup *C*. The relative size of each circle represents the relative abundance of haplogroup *C* in that population. See the Color Plate A reference map for the identity of each population. Populations with undetectable levels of haplogroup *C* or with haplogroup *C* levels below 1% are omitted from this map.

Color Plate 162: Polynesians have ethnic features that are similar to both East Asians and Northeast Asians/Siberians.

Haplogroup C

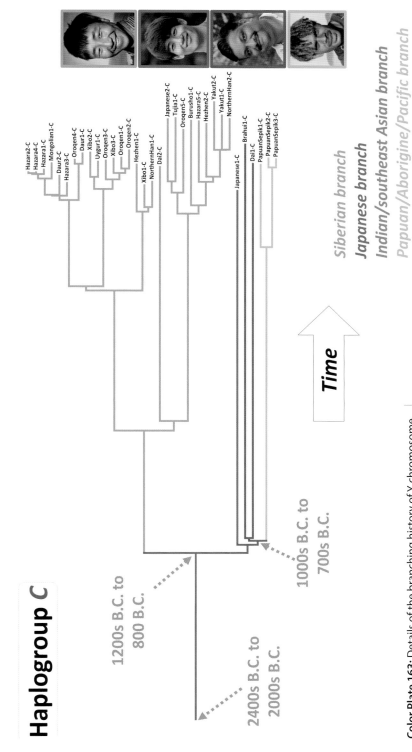

Color Plate 163: Details of the branching history of Y chromosome haplogroup C. This haplogroup has given rise to diverse ethnicities.

Haplogroup C
(sub-lineages)

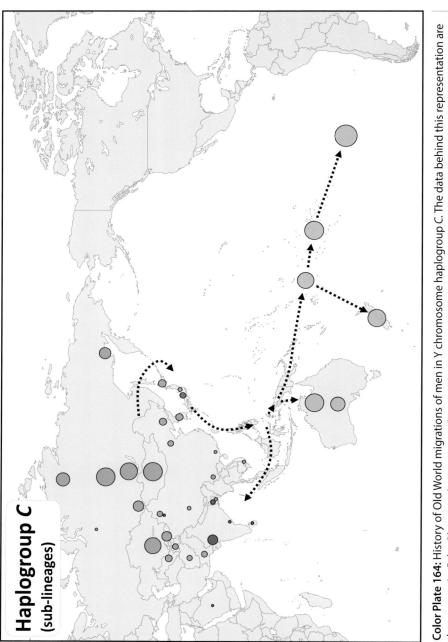

Color Plate 164: History of Old World migrations of men in Y chromosome haplogroup C. The data behind this representation are the same as in Color Plate 161, but now specifying sublineages within Y chromosome haplogroup C. The various colors correspond to the various sublineages shown in Color Plate 163. Some populations lacked subgroup information, and these were omitted from the display.

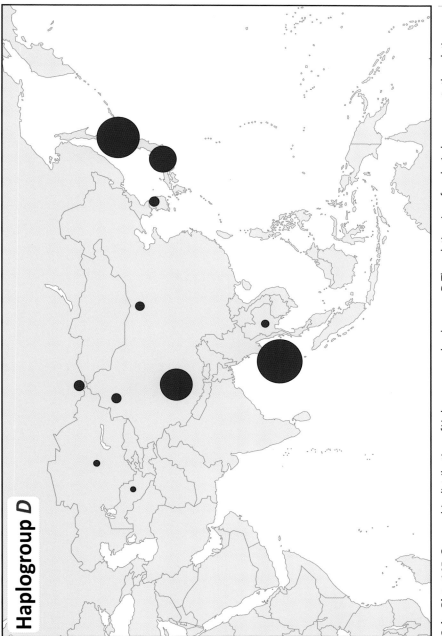

Color Plate 165: Geographic distribution of Y chromosome haplogroup *D*. The relative size of each circle represents the relative abundance of haplogroup *D* in that population. See the Color Plate A reference map for the identity of each population. Populations with undetectable levels of haplogroup *D* or with haplogroup *D* levels below 1% are omitted from this map.

Haplogroup *D*

Haplogroup *D*

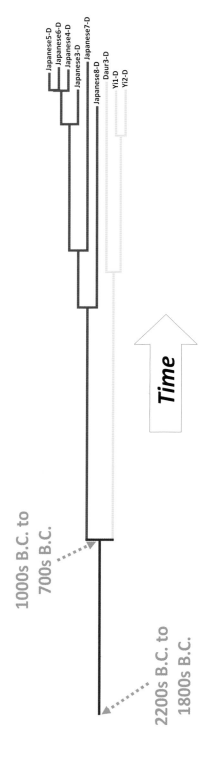

1000s B.C. to 700s B.C.

2200s B.C. to 1800s B.C.

Japanese5-D
Japanese6-D
Japanese4-D
Japanese3-D
Japanese7-D
Japanese8-D
Daur3-D
Yi1-D
Yi2-D

Time

Color Plate 166: Details of the branching history of Y chromosome haplogroup *D*.

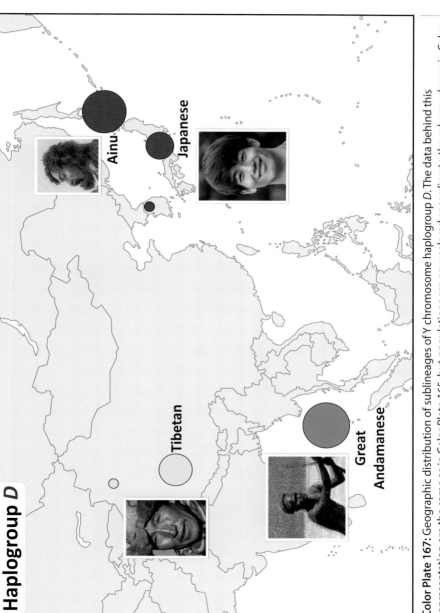

Haplogroup D

Ainu

Japanese

Tibetan

Great Andamanese

Color Plate 167: Geographic distribution of sublineages of Y chromosome haplogroup *D*. The data behind this representation are the same as in Color Plate 165, but populations are now colored according to the schema shown in Color Plate 166 (Tibetan, Japanese) or according to other data that show early sublineage separation (the people of the Great Andamanese islands). Some populations lacked subgroup information, and these were omitted from the display.

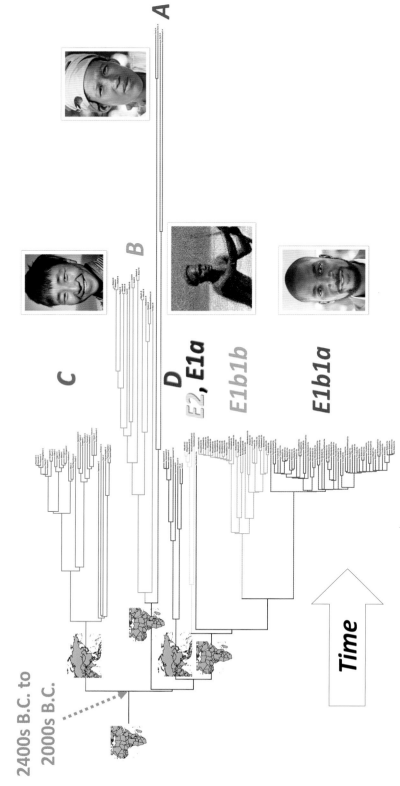

Color Plate 168: The Asian haplogroup C and D branches are nested among the major haplogroup branches of sub-Saharan Africa.

Color Plate 169: Ethnic features do not reveal the whole story of Oceania. Genetics links peoples who do not look similar (Polynesians with sub-Saharan Africans) and separates those who do (Melanesians and Australian Aborigines from sub-Saharan Africans).

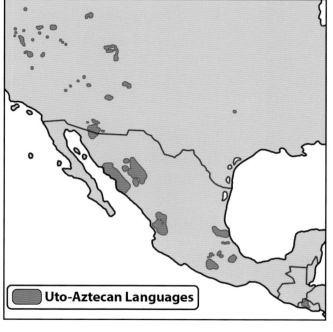

Uto-Aztecan Languages

Color Plate 170: Geographic distribution of languages in the Uto-Aztecan language family.

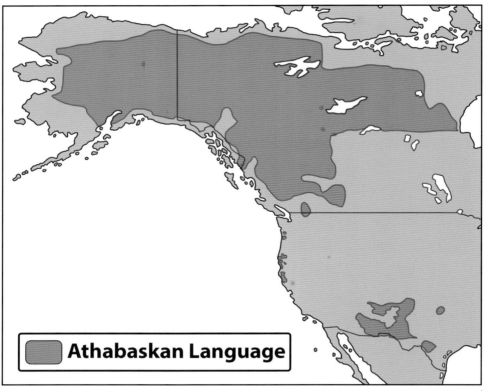

Athabaskan Language

Color Plate 171: Geographic distribution of languages in the Athabaskan language family.

George Armstrong Custer

Sitting Bull

Color Plate 172: Military leaders of the battle of Little Bighorn.

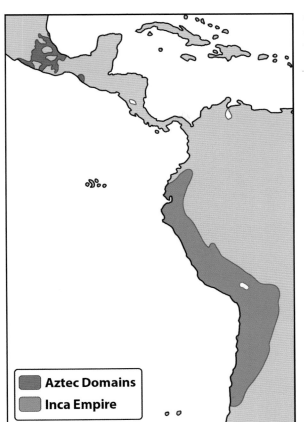

Color Plate 173:
Geographic extent of the pre-European Aztec and Incan empires.

Aztec Domains
Inca Empire

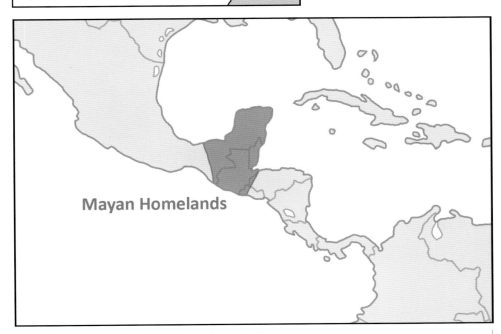

Color Plate 174: Location of the Mayan homelands.

Mayan Homelands

Color Plate 175: Mayan ruins at *Chichen Itza*. Castillo.

Color Plate 176: Mayan ruins at *Tikal*. Temple I is in the center.

Color Plate 177: Mayan ruins at *Palenque*. Temple of the Inscriptions.

Color Plate 178: Mayan ruins at *Tulum*. Tallest building is the Castillo.

Color Plate 179: Mayan ruins at *Uxmal*. Governor's palace.

Color Plate 180: Mayan ruins at *Chichen Itza*. Caracol observatory.

Color Plate 181: Mayan ruins at *Palenque*. Tower.

Color Plate 182: Mayan ruins at *Palenque*. Temple of the Sun.

Color Plate 183: Mayan ruins at *Uxmal*. House of the Magician is the pyramid on the right.

Color Plate 184: Pyramid of the moon at *Teotihuacan*.

Color Plate 185: Pyramid of the sun at *Teotihuacan*.

Color Plate 186: Sculpted Olmec head.

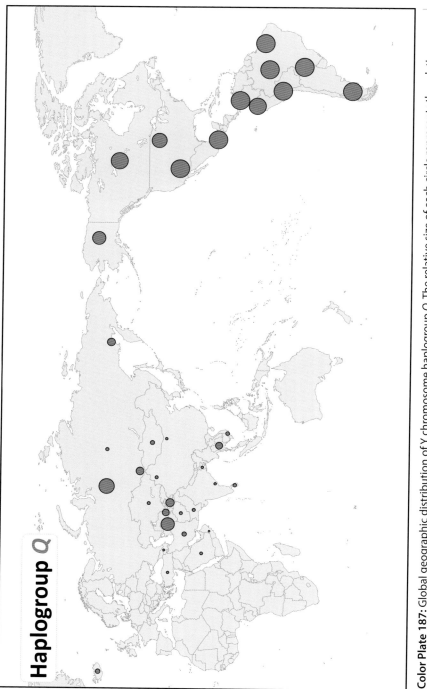

Haplogroup Q

Color Plate 187: Global geographic distribution of Y chromosome haplogroup Q. The relative size of each circle represents the relative abundance of haplogroup Q in that population. See the Color Plate A reference map for the identity of each population. Populations with undetectable levels of haplogroup Q or with haplogroup Q levels below 1% are omitted from this map.

Haplogroup C
(sub-lineages)

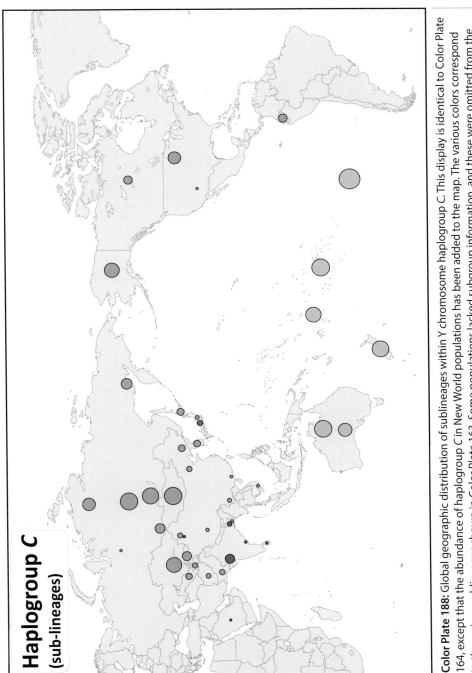

Color Plate 188: Global geographic distribution of sublineages within Y chromosome haplogroup C. This display is identical to Color Plate 164, except that the abundance of haplogroup C in New World populations has been added to the map. The various colors correspond to the various sublineages shown in Color Plate 163. Some populations lacked subgroup information, and these were omitted from the display. The sublineage of haplogroup C in the New World traced back to Siberian populations.

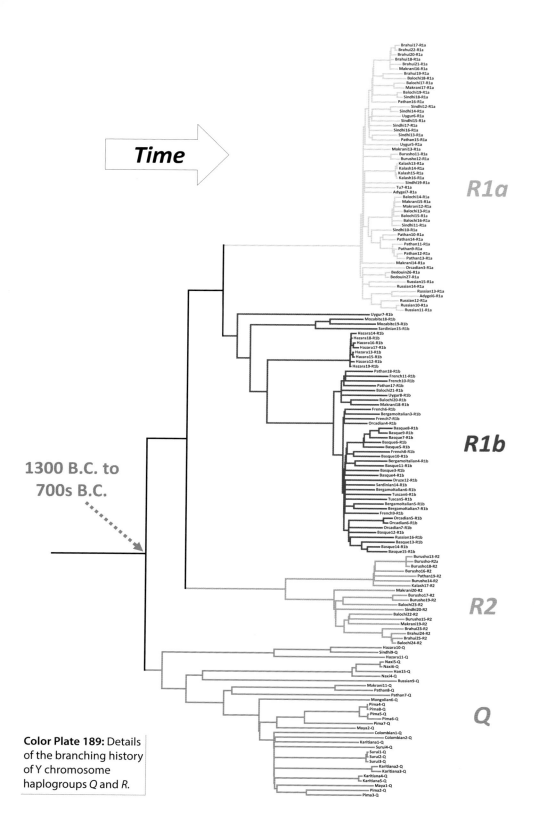

Color Plate 189: Details of the branching history of Y chromosome haplogroups *Q* and *R*.

Population collapse and recovery

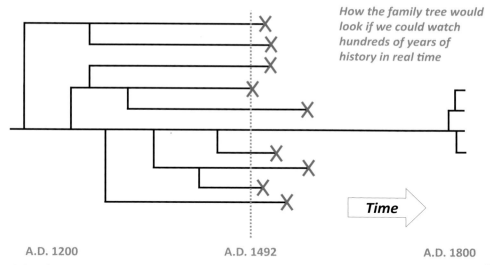

How the family tree would look if we could watch hundreds of years of history in real time

Time

A.D. 1200   A.D. 1492   A.D. 1800

Color Plate 190: Hypothetical family tree that illustrates a real-time view of a population collapse. Red x's represent deaths. Survivors are those individuals whose branches do not terminate in a red x.

Population collapse and recovery

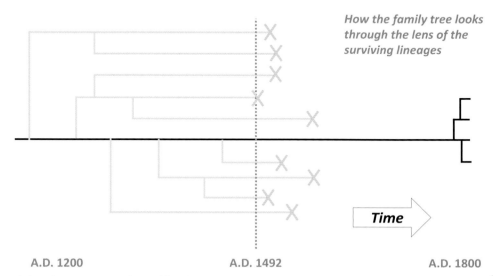

How the family tree looks through the lens of the surviving lineages

Time

A.D. 1200   A.D. 1492   A.D. 1800

Color Plate 191: Hypothetical family tree that illustrates a population collapse through the lens of the family tree of the survivors. Red x's represent deaths. Survivors are those individuals whose branches do not terminate in a red x. Because branches that terminate in a red x do not leave descendants, these extinct branches are invisible in the family tree of the survivors.

Haplogroup *Q*

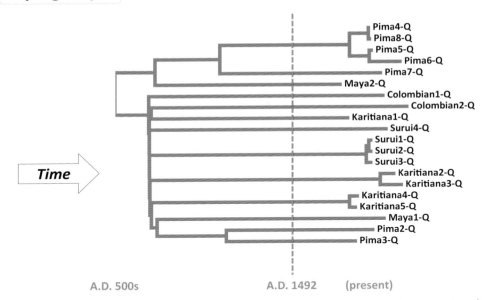

Pima4-Q
Pima8-Q
Pima5-Q
Pima6-Q
Pima7-Q
Maya2-Q
Colombian1-Q
Colombian2-Q
Karitiana1-Q
Surui4-Q
Surui1-Q
Surui2-Q
Surui3-Q
Karitiana2-Q
Karitiana3-Q
Karitiana4-Q
Karitiana5-Q
Maya1-Q
Pima2-Q
Pima3-Q

Time

A.D. 500s   A.D. 1492   (present)

Color Plate 192: Details of the branching history of New World Y chromosome haplogroup *Q*.

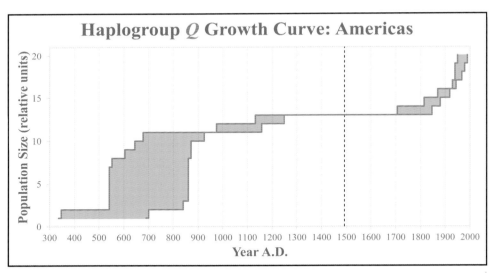

Color Plate 193: History of population growth in New World men belonging to Y chromosome haplogroup *Q*. Shaded area represents the full statistical range of the growth curve.

Haplogroup Q

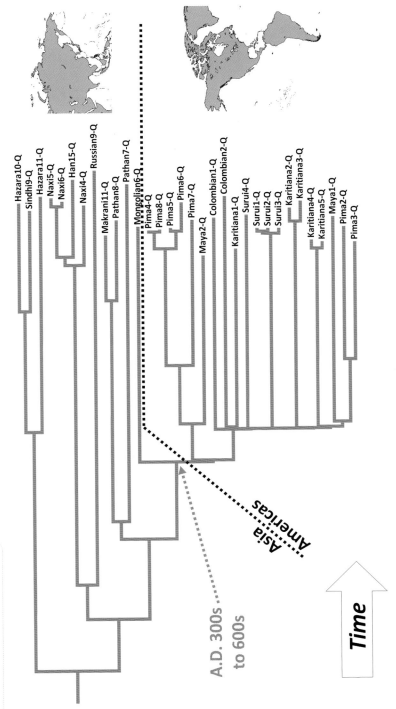

Color Plate 194: Details of the branching history of Old World and New World Y chromosome haplogroup Q. Populations in the Old World show a clear break in the tree from populations in the New World.

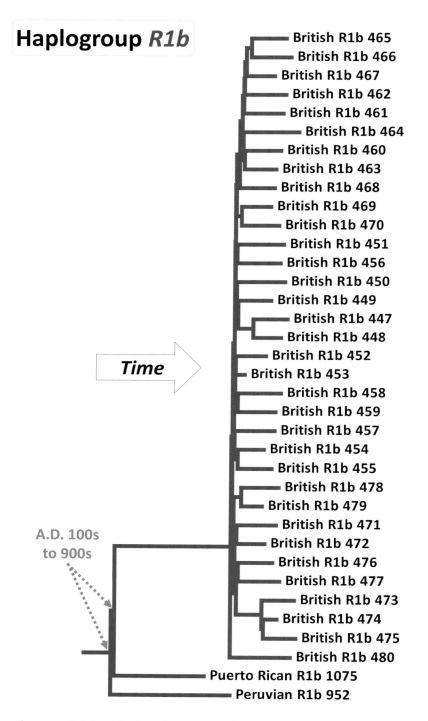

Haplogroup *R1b*

Time

A.D. 100s to 900s

British R1b 465
British R1b 466
British R1b 467
British R1b 462
British R1b 461
British R1b 464
British R1b 460
British R1b 463
British R1b 468
British R1b 469
British R1b 470
British R1b 451
British R1b 456
British R1b 450
British R1b 449
British R1b 447
British R1b 448
British R1b 452
British R1b 453
British R1b 458
British R1b 459
British R1b 457
British R1b 454
British R1b 455
British R1b 478
British R1b 479
British R1b 471
British R1b 472
British R1b 476
British R1b 477
British R1b 473
British R1b 474
British R1b 475
British R1b 480
Puerto Rican R1b 1075
Peruvian R1b 952

Color Plate 195: Details of the branching history of *R1b*, this time showing rare early branches found in the Americas. These branches might not be due to European immigration to the New World in the A.D. 1700s and 1800s, but to the same migration event that brought *Q* to the New World from Central Asia in the early A.D. era.

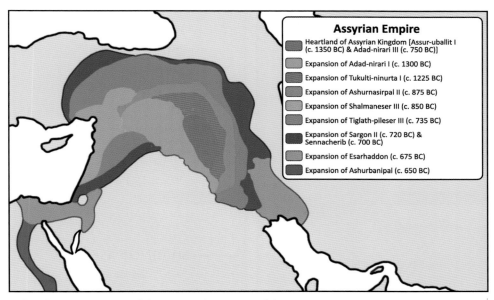

Color Plate 196: History of the geographic extent of the ancient Assyrian Empire.

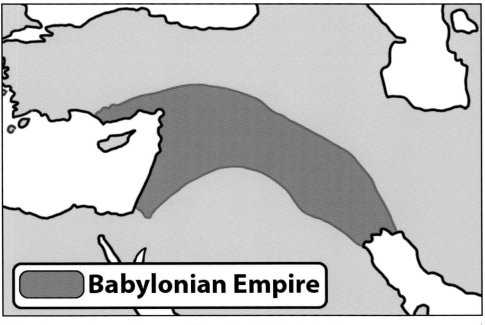

Color Plate 197: Geographic extent of the ancient Babylonian Empire.

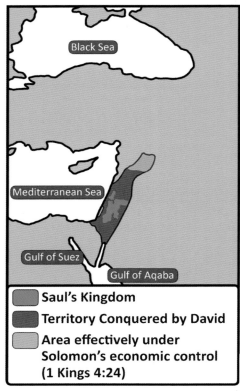

Color Plate 198: Geographic history of the ancient Israelite empire.

Legend:
- Saul's Kingdom
- Territory Conquered by David
- Area effectively under Solomon's economic control (1 Kings 4:24)

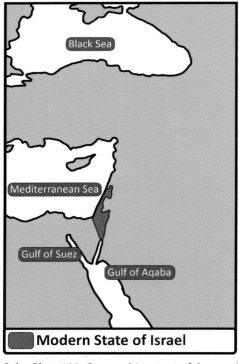

Color Plate 199: Geographic extent of the modern state of Israel.

Legend:
- Modern State of Israel

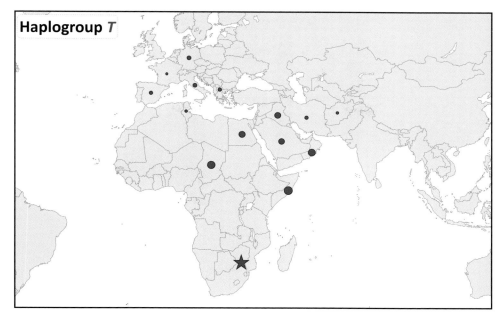

Color Plate 200: Geographic distribution of Y chromosome haplogroup *T*. The relative size of each circle represents the relative abundance of haplogroup *T* in that population. See the Color Plate A reference map for the identity of each population. Populations with undetectable levels of haplogroup *T* or with haplogroup *T* levels below 1% are omitted from this map. The star represents the location of the African Lemba men who belong to haplogroup *T*.

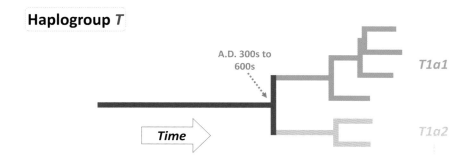

Color Plate 201: Details of the branching history of Y chromosome haplogroup *T*.

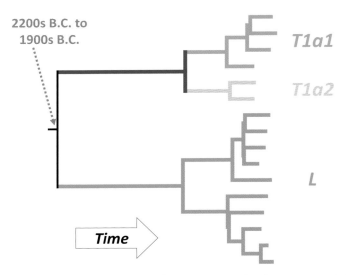

Color Plate 202: Details of the branching history of Y chromosome haplogroups *L* and *T*.

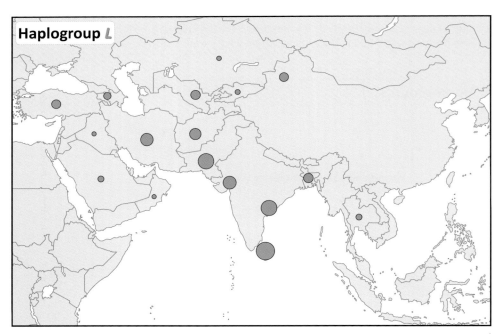

Color Plate 203: Geographic distribution of Y chromosome haplogroup *L*. The relative size of each circle represents the relative abundance of haplogroup *L* in that population. See the Color Plate A reference map for the identity of each population. Populations with undetectable levels of haplogroup *L* or with haplogroup *L* levels below 1% are omitted from this map.

Haplogroups *L*, *T*

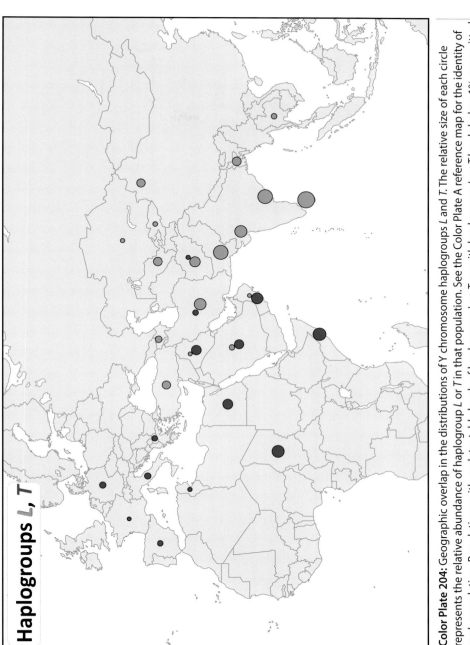

Color Plate 204: Geographic overlap in the distributions of Y chromosome haplogroups *L* and *T*. The relative size of each circle represents the relative abundance of haplogroup *L* or *T* in that population. See the Color Plate A reference map for the identity of each population. Populations with undetectable levels of haplogroup *L* or *T*, or with haplogroup *L* or *T* levels below 1% are omitted from this map.

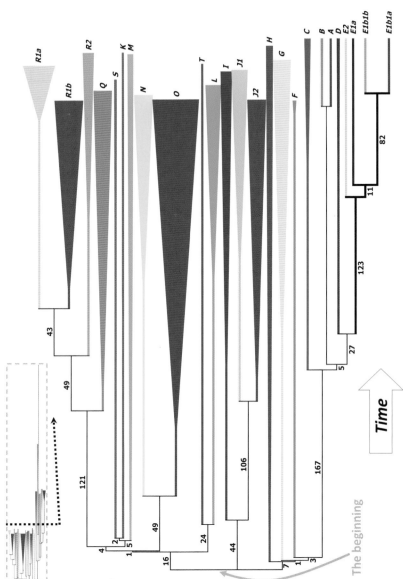

Color Plate 205: Family tree based on Y chromosome DNA from 600 men. Same tree as shown in Color Plate 22, except that individual branches are collapsed into triangles whose size is proportional to the number of men in each group. Full tree is shown in the upper left corner. The long branches in haplogroups *C, B, A, D, E2, E1a, E1b1b,* and *E1b1a* have been truncated to allow zooming in on the details of the tree. Numbers with each branch represent branch lengths as measured in units of DNA differences.

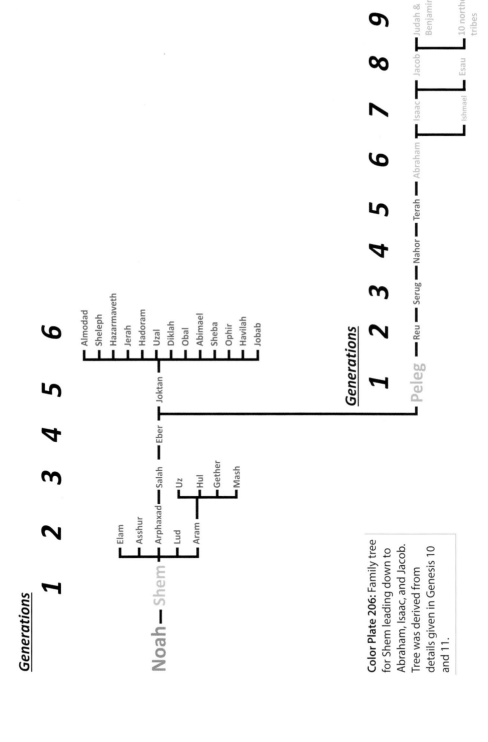

Color Plate 206: Family tree for Shem leading down to Abraham, Isaac, and Jacob. Tree was derived from details given in Genesis 10 and 11.

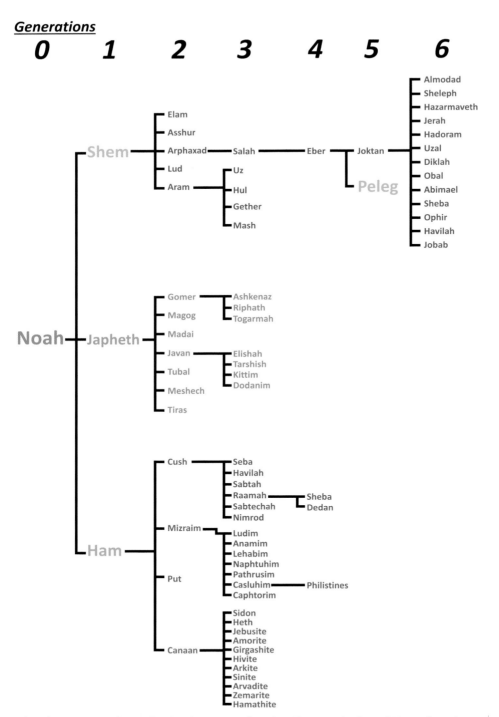

Generations

0　1　2　3　4　5　6

Noah

Shem
- Elam
- Asshur
- Arphaxad — Salah — Eber — Joktan
  - Almodad
  - Sheleph
  - Hazarmaveth
  - Jerah
  - Hadoram
  - Uzal
  - Diklah
  - Obal
  - Abimael
  - Sheba
  - Ophir
  - Havilah
  - Jobab
  - Peleg
- Lud
- Aram
  - Uz
  - Hul
  - Gether
  - Mash

Japheth
- Gomer
  - Ashkenaz
  - Riphath
  - Togarmah
- Magog
- Madai
- Javan
  - Elishah
  - Tarshish
  - Kittim
  - Dodanim
- Tubal
- Meshech
- Tiras

Ham
- Cush
  - Seba
  - Havilah
  - Sabtah
  - Raamah
    - Sheba
    - Dedan
  - Sabtechah
  - Nimrod
- Mizraim
  - Ludim
  - Anamim
  - Lehabim
  - Naphtuhim
  - Pathrusim
  - Casluhim — Philistines
  - Caphtorim
- Put
- Canaan
  - Sidon
  - Heth
  - Jebusite
  - Amorite
  - Girgashite
  - Hivite
  - Arkite
  - Sinite
  - Arvadite
  - Zemarite
  - Hamathite

Color Plate 207: Family tree for the three sons of Noah—Shem, Japheth, and Ham—based on the details given in Genesis 10.

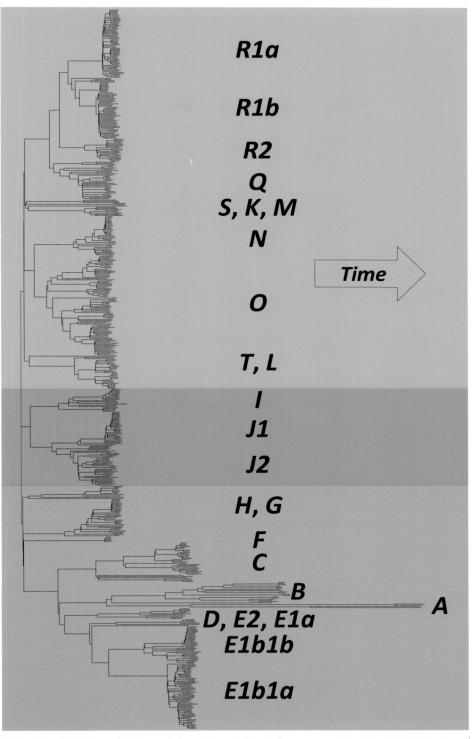

Color Plate 208: Three fundamental partitions in the Y chromosome tree. Tree is identical to the one in Color Plate 22, except that branch colors have been converted to black.

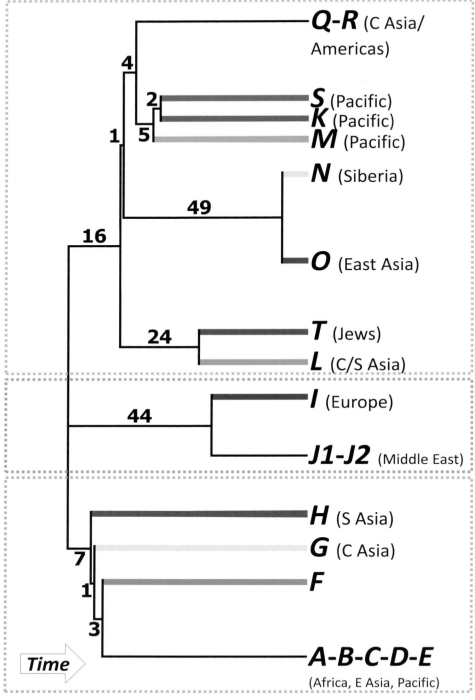

Color Plate 209: Three fundamental partitions in the Y chromosome tree. This image represents a zoomed-in version of the deepest parts of the tree in Color Plate 205.

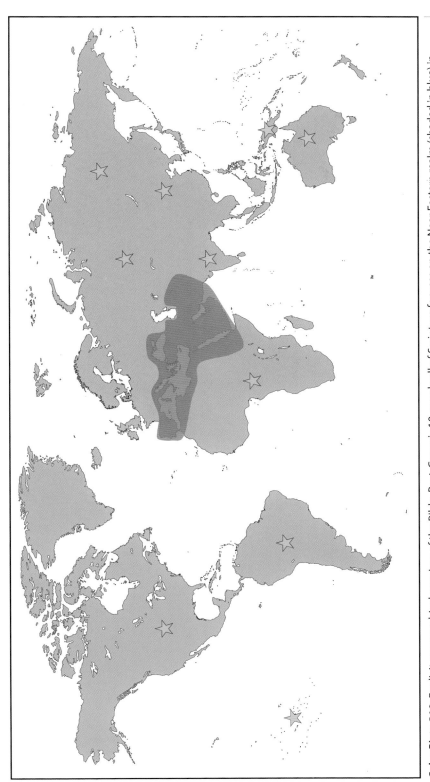

Color Plate 210: Explicit geographical purview of the Bible. Post-Genesis 10, nearly all of Scripture focuses on the Near Eastern realm (shaded in blue) in geographic and economic proximity to ancient Israel. Stars identify regions at a distance from this sphere which receive little to no explicit mention.

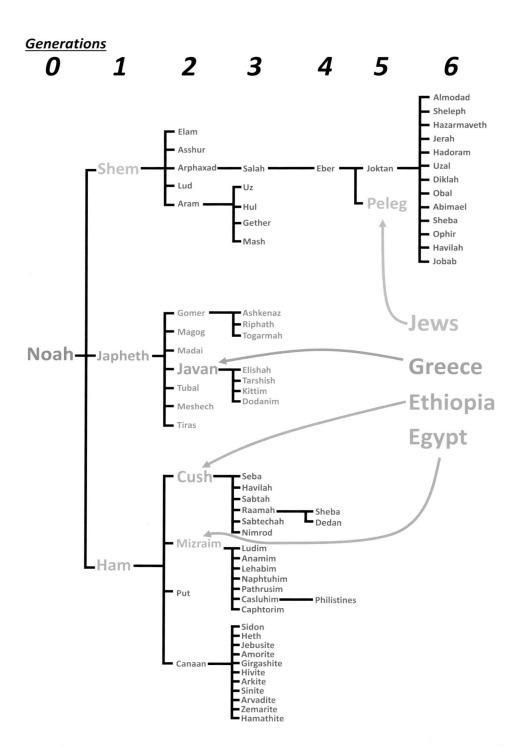

Generations

0   1   2   3   4   5   6

Shem
- Elam
- Asshur
- Arphaxad — Salah — Eber — Joktan
  - Almodad
  - Sheleph
  - Hazarmaveth
  - Jerah
  - Hadoram
  - Uzal
  - Diklah
  - Obal
  - Abimael
  - Sheba
  - Ophir
  - Havilah
  - Jobab
  - Peleg
- Lud
- Aram
  - Uz
  - Hul
  - Gether
  - Mash

Jews

Japheth
- Gomer
  - Ashkenaz
  - Riphath
  - Togarmah
- Magog
- Madai
- Javan
  - Elishah
  - Tarshish
  - Kittim
  - Dodanim
- Tubal
- Meshech
- Tiras

Greece

Noah

Ham
- Cush
  - Seba
  - Havilah
  - Sabtah
  - Raamah
    - Sheba
    - Dedan
  - Sabtechah
  - Nimrod
- Mizraim
  - Ludim
  - Anamim
  - Lehabim
  - Naphtuhim
  - Pathrusim
  - Casluhim — Philistines
  - Caphtorim
- Put
- Canaan
  - Sidon
  - Heth
  - Jebusite
  - Amorite
  - Girgashite
  - Hivite
  - Arkite
  - Sinite
  - Arvadite
  - Zemarite
  - Hamathite

Ethiopia

Egypt

Color Plate 211: Key nations which Scripture identifies with people in Genesis 10.

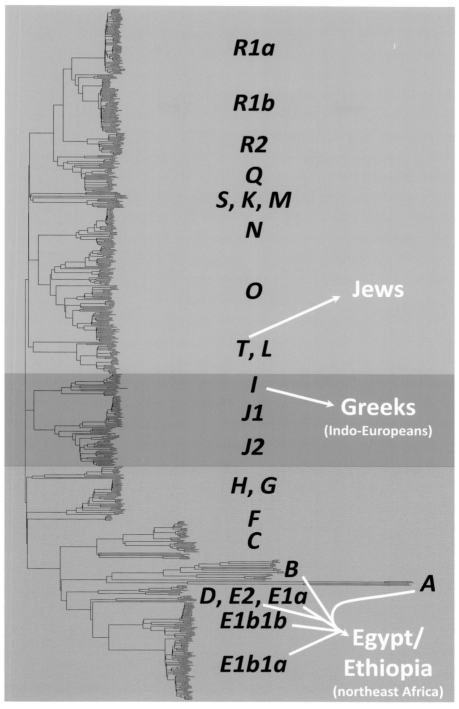

Color Plate 212: The three fundamental partitions in the Y chromosome tree have haplogroups associated with the peoples whose history can be biblically traced to Genesis 10. Background color shading identifies candidate partitions corresponding to Shem's lineage (blue), Japheth's lineage (green), and Ham's lineage (pink).

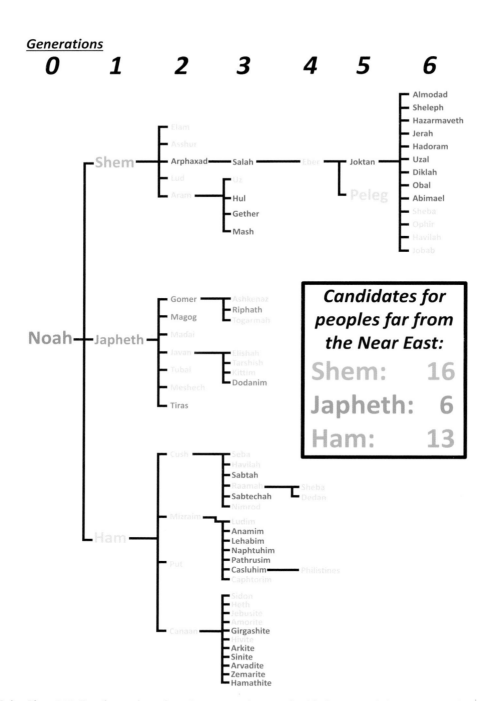

Color Plate 213: Family tree based on Genesis 10, this time highlighting candidate ancestors for peoples at a distance from the Near East. Names in grey are people explicitly identified later in Scripture with specific nations, or are peoples who remained in proximity to the Near Eastern realm of ancient Israelite interactions (i.e., the geographic region shaded in blue in Color Plate 210). Names in color are peoples who have no biblical association with this Near Eastern sphere and whose fate Scripture does not specify. In essence, the names in color are candidates for explaining the origins of people at the stars in Color Plate 210.

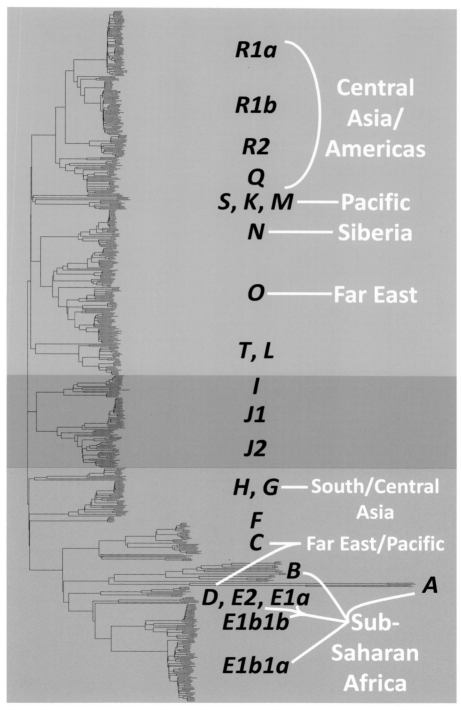

Color Plate 214: The three fundamental partitions in the Y chromosome tree differ in how many distant peoples they produced. The candidate lines of Shem (blue) and Ham (pink) produced several independent peoples who lived far from the Near Eastern realm of ancient Israelite interactions. The candidate line of Japheth (green) produced none.

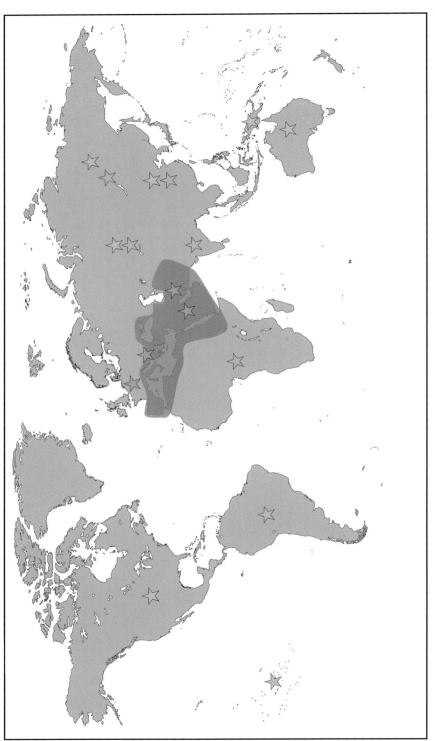

Color Plate 215: Geographic depiction of the information in Color Plate 214. The candidate lines of Shem (blue stars) and Ham (pink stars) produced several independent peoples who lived far from the Near Eastern realm (blue shaded region) of ancient Israelite interactions. The candidate line of Japheth (green stars) produced none.

Expectations from Genesis 10 and 11

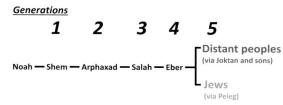

Generations

1 **2** **3** **4** **5**

Noah — Shem — Arphaxad — Salah — Eber ┐

Distant peoples
(via Joktan and sons)

Jews
(via Peleg)

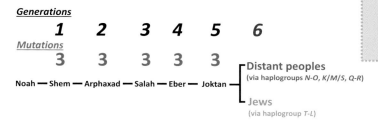

Implications of Y chromosome tree

Generations

1 **2** **3** **4** **5** **6**

Mutations

3 **3** **3** **3** **3**

Noah — Shem — Arphaxad — Salah — Eber — Joktan ┐

Distant peoples
(via haplogroups *N-O, K/M/S, Q-R*)

Jews
(via haplogroup *T-L*)

Tree labels: *Q-R* (C Asia/Americas); *S* (Pacific); *K* (Pacific); *M* (Pacific); *N* (Siberia); *O* (East Asia); *T* (Jews); *L* (C/S Asia); 4, 2, 1, 51, 16, 49, 24

Color Plate 216: Comparison of biblical expectations for the early genealogy of the Jews to the genealogy implied by the Y chromosome tree. Initial results suggested a discrepancy of one generation between them.

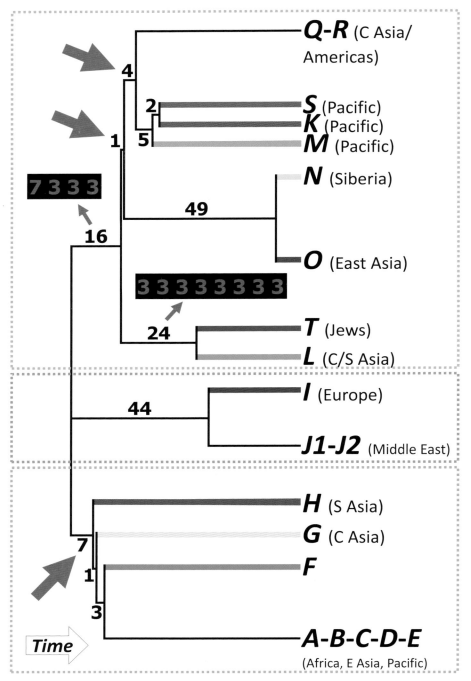

Color Plate 217: Key DNA differences in the early branches of the Y chromosome tree. The three fundamental partitions remain the same as in previous color plates, with the blue box representing the candidate lineage of Shem, the green box the candidate lineage of Japheth, and the pink box the candidate lineage of Ham. The DNA differences leading to the putative Jewish haplogroup (*T*) have been decomposed in the black boxes into candidate generation steps. Large red arrows highlight important DNA differences discussed in the main text.

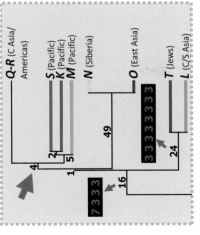

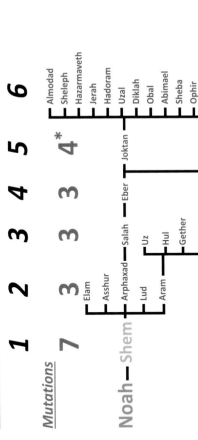

Color Plate 218: Tight agreement between biblical genealogical expectations in the line of Shem and specific genealogical steps implied by DNA differences in the Y chromosome tree. Asterisks by numbers in red denote mutational steps whose value differs in other studies of the Y chromosome tree.

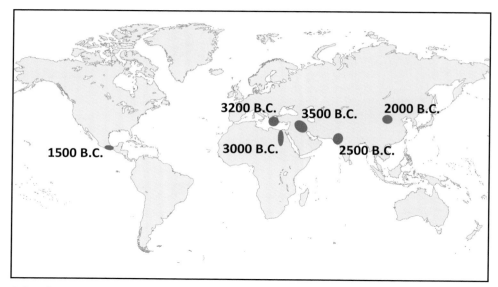

Color Plate 219: Mainstream science dates for the cradles of civilization.

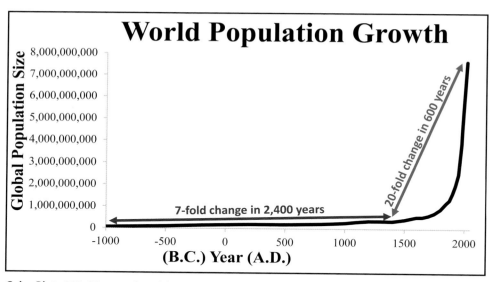

Color Plate 220: History of world population growth from 1000 B.C. to the present, this time with multiplicative changes highlighted. Years in the B.C. era are shown as negative numbers.

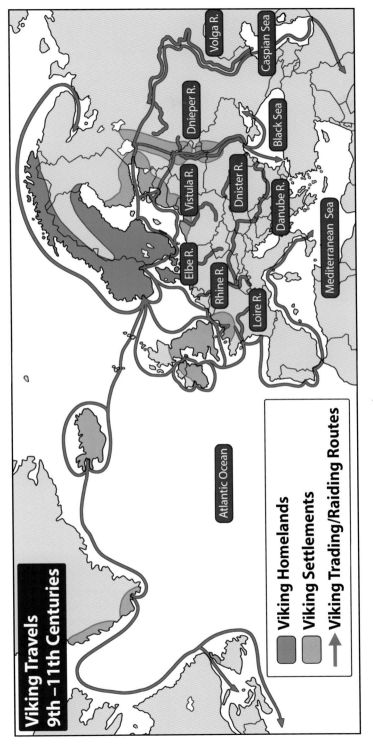

Color Plate 221: Geographic extent and history of the migrations of the Vikings.

	Africa	Middle East	Central Asia	South Asia	Siberia
	Khoesan	Iraq	Kazak	Gujarati (India)	Mongol
A	44				
B	11				
C			53	21	71
D			2		
E1a					
E1b1a	23	1			
E1b1b	16	11	1		
E2	2				
G		2	3	3	
H				21	
I					
J1		31	1		
J2		27	5	9	
K		1			
L		1	1	9	
M					
N		1	7		8
O1a					1
O1b					1
O2			2		9
Q			3		5
R1a	1	7	13	28	4
R1b	2	11	3	2	
R2			3	9	
S					
T		6			
Sum	**99**	**99**	**98**	**100**	**100**

Color Plate 222: Summary of Y chromosome haplogroup levels in representative human populations. Each row shows the percent of each haplogroup (left-most column) in each population (rest of the columns). Blanks represent undetectable levels of the haplogroup or levels below 1%. The sum total of the haplogroup percentages in a column are shown in the bottom row. Numbers in each box have been heat mapped for ease of viewing: The more intense the blue, the lower the value; the more intense the red, the higher the value. White represents a 50% value.

East Asia	Southeast Asia	Oceania	Americas	Europe
Japanese	Indonesian Sumatra	South Australian Aborigine	Navajo	British (England, Scotland)
11	4	43	1	
36				
				15
				2
		23		
		1		
	4			
	23			
36	19			
18	50			
			99	
				9
				74
		34		
100	**100**	**100**	**100**	**100**

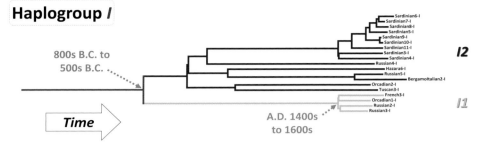

Color Plate 223: Details of the branching history of Y chromosome haplogroup *I* and of sublineages therein.

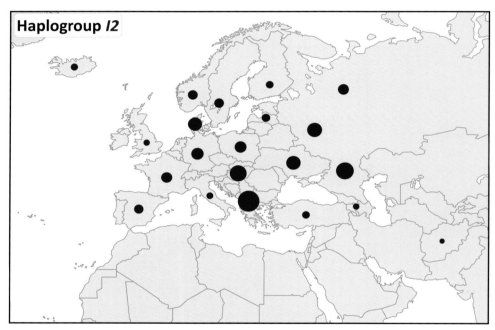

Color Plate 224: Geographic distribution of Y chromosome haplogroup *I2*. The relative size of each circle represents the relative abundance of haplogroup *I2* in that population. See the Color Plate A reference map for the identity of each population. Populations with undetectable levels of haplogroup *I2* or with haplogroup *I2* levels below 1% are omitted from this map.

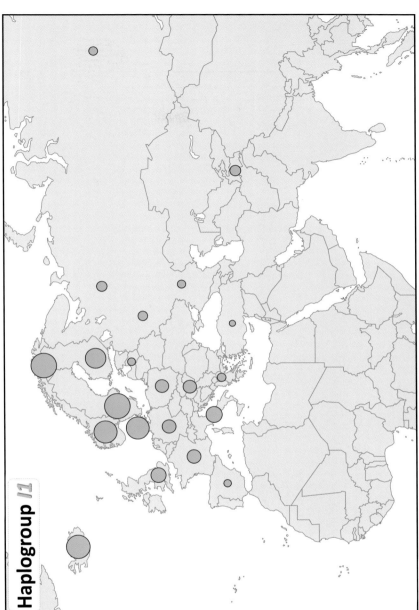

Haplogroup *I1*

Color Plate 225: Geographic distribution of Y chromosome haplogroup *I1*. The relative size of each circle represents the relative abundance of haplogroup *I1* in that population. See the Color Plate A reference map for the identity of each population. Populations with undetectable levels of haplogroup *I1* or with haplogroup *I1* levels below 1% are omitted from this map.

Haplogroup *F*

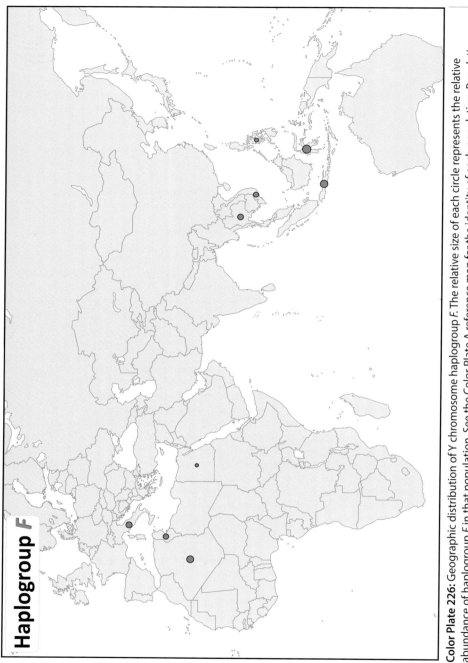

Color Plate 226: Geographic distribution of Y chromosome haplogroup *F*. The relative size of each circle represents the relative abundance of haplogroup *F* in that population. See the Color Plate A reference map for the identity of each population. Populations with undetectable levels of haplogroup *F* or with haplogroup *F* levels below 1% are omitted from this map.

Haplogroup *F*

2600s B.C. to
2200s B.C.

Time

A.D. 1800s

Color Plate 227: Details of the branching history of Y chromosome haplogroup *F*.

Haplogroup *H*

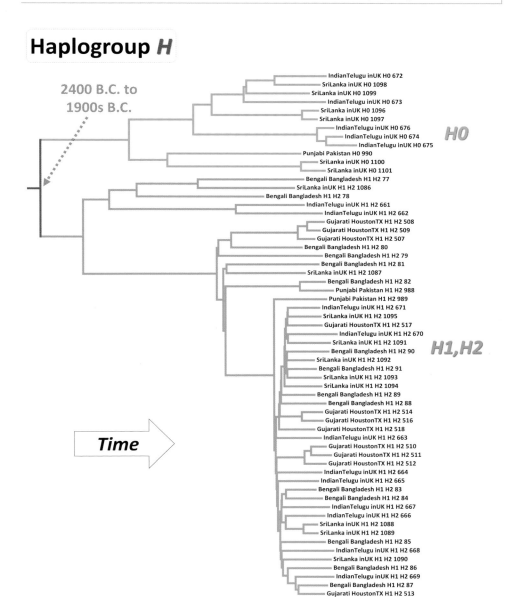

Color Plate 228: Details of the branching history of Y chromosome haplogroups *H0* and *H1/H2*.

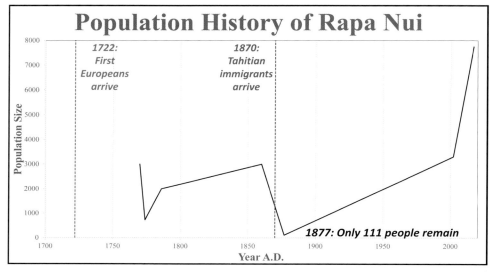

Color Plate 229: Population rises and falls on Rapa Nui (Easter Island), with key historical events noted.

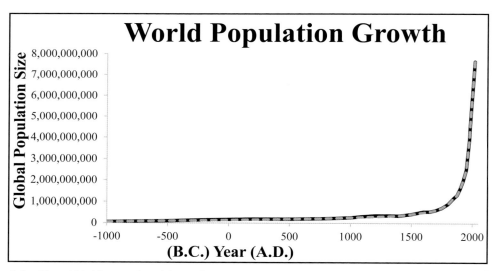

Color Plate 230: History of world population growth from 1000 B.C. to the present—but with the minimum growth curve shown as a grey dashed line. Years in the B.C. era are shown as negative numbers.

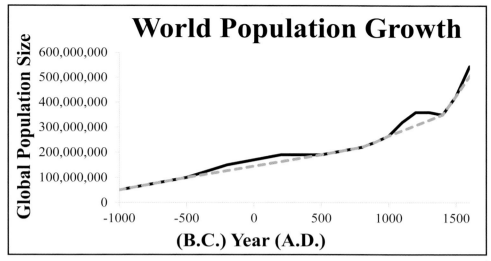

Color Plate 231: History of world population growth from 1000 B.C. to A.D. 1600. The minimum growth curve is shown as a grey dashed line. This is a zoomed-in version of Color Plate 230 to see the details of key population declines in human history. Years in the B.C. era are shown as negative numbers.

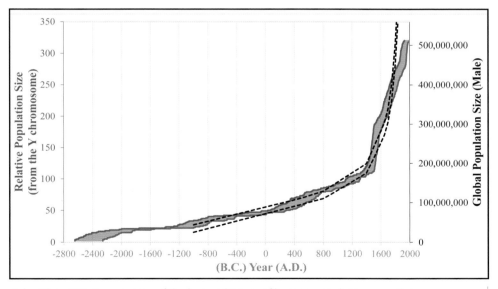

Color Plate 232: Comparison of the known history of human population growth to a reconstruction based on the Y chromosome tree. The two dashed black lines represent the known history of human population growth. The vertical axis on the right corresponds to this dashed line. The solid blue curve represents the statistical range of the reconstruction based on the Y chromosome. The vertical axis on the left corresponds to this solid curve. Both the dashed line and solid curve shared the same horizontal axis.

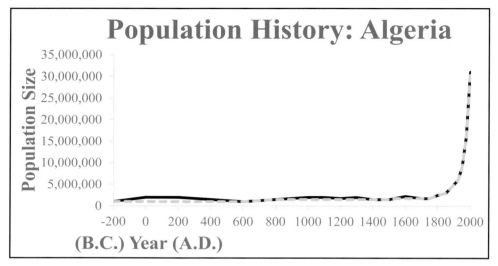

Color Plate 233: History of population growth in Algeria from 1000 B.C. to the present. The minimum growth curve is shown as a grey dashed line. Years in the B.C. era are shown as negative numbers.

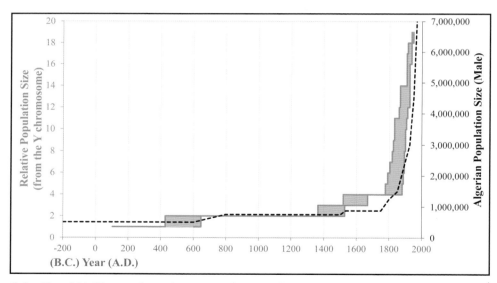

Color Plate 234: History of population growth in Mozabite men. The dashed black line is the same as the dashed grey line in Color Plate 233. The solid tan curve represents the statistical range of the reconstruction based on the Y chromosome. Years in the B.C. era are shown as negative numbers.

Y chromosome haplogroup	Biblical lineage	Early geographic location	History	More detail:
A	Ham	Northeast Africa	Likely the original Nilo-Saharan and Khoisan speakers	Chapters 5 and 6
B	Ham	Northeast Africa	Likely the original Nilo-Saharan and Khoisan speakers	Chapters 5 and 6
C	Ham	Africa	Originally Siberian, then migrated through Japan, to Southeast Asia, India, and the Pacific; some also migrated independently to the Americas	Chapter 11
D	Ham	Africa	Became Japanese and Tibetan	Chapter 11
E1a	Ham	Northeast Africa	Possibly an early Egyptian lineage; then migrated into sub-Saharan Africa	Chapters 5 and 6
E1b1a	Ham	Northeast Africa	Possibly an early Egyptian lineage; candidate for later Bantu expansion	Chapters 5 and 6
E1b1b	Ham	Northeast Africa	Possibly an early Egyptian lineage; then became an Arab Muslim lineage; likely the Afro-Asiatic lineage	Chapters 5 and 6
E2	Ham	Northeast Africa	Early migrant into sub-Saharan Africa	Chapters 5 and 6

Color Plate 235: Summary of the history of Y chromosome haplogroups as presented in this book.

Y chromosome haplogroup	Biblical lineage	Early geographic location	History	More detail:
F	Ham	Unknown	Unknown	Chapter 14
G	Ham	Central Asia	Likely an originally Turkic lineage; unknown heritage in B.C. era	Chapter 8
H	Ham	South Asia	Possibly the lineage of the Indus valley civilization; likely the early Dravidian speakers	Chapter 9
I1	Japheth	Europe	Indigenous European lineage; might be connected to the Vikings	Chapters 8 and 14
I2	Japheth	Europe	Indigenous European lineage	Chapter 8 and 14
J1	Japheth	Middle East	Possible early Hittite lineage which became a later Arab Muslim lineage	Chapter 8
J2	Japheth	Middle East	Possibly ancient Persian lineage, which joined with Turkic migrations in later A.D. era	Chapter 8
K	Shem	New Guinea/ Australia	Early settlers of New Guinea/ Australia	Chapter 11
L	Shem	Middle East	Might be the Edomites or Lost Tribes of Israel	Chapter 13

Y chromosome haplogroup	Biblical lineage	Early geographic location	History	More detail:
M	Shem	New Guinea/ Australia	Early settlers of New Guinea/ Australia	Chapter 11
N	Shem	Siberia	Early settlers of Siberia/"barbarian" lineage to the north of ancient China	Chapter 10
O1a	Shem	East Asia/ China	Likely the lineage of the early Austronesian speakers	Chapter 10
O1b	Shem	East Asia/ China	Likely the lineage of the early Southeast Asian settlers	Chapter 10
O1b2	Shem	East Asia/ China	Likely the lineage of the early Korean and Japanese	Chapter 10
O2	Shem	East Asia/ China	Likely the early Chinese lineage	Chapter 10
Q	Shem	Central Asia	Originally Central Asian; candidate for ancient Scythians; gave rise to indigenous Americans in A.D. era	Chapter 12
R1a	Shem	Central Asia	Originally Central Asian; then more widely distributed as a result of Mongol, Russian, and Mughal conquests	Chapter 7

Y chromosome haplogroup	Biblical lineage	Early geographic location	History	More detail:
R1b	Shem	Central Asia	Originally Central Asian; migrated into Europe during Middle Ages; spread to western Europe possibly as a result of Ottoman expansion in Europe	Chapters 7 and 12
R2	Shem	Central Asia	Originally Central Asian; may have been Yuezhi migrants/Kushan kingdom in northern India	Chapter 9
S	Shem	New Guinea/ Australia	Early settlers of New Guinea/ Australia	Chapter 11
T	Shem	Middle East	Likely lineage of Abraham, Isaac, Jacob, and the Jews	Chapter 13

Nothing about this narrative so far reveals anything counterintuitive. Yes, ethnic blending and mixing may have occurred, but the evidence still supports distinct narratives for Polynesians vis-à-vis Australians and Melanesians.

Additional clues from East Asia took this story in a different direction.

A Twist

Haplogroup *C* wasn't the only East/Northeast Asian lineage to separate in the last millennium B.C. Today, haplogroup *D* is found primarily in East Asia: Japan and Tibet (**Color Plate 165**). The Japanese and Tibetan lineages separated around the same time that the *C* sub-lineages and haplogroup *O* sublineages separated (compare **Color Plate 166** to **Color Plates 163, 141**). The date overlap is strong enough to suggest that all of these separations may have been part of the same event.

Again, from a historical perspective, the early part of the last millennium B.C. in East and Northeast Asia was a time of upheaval. In China, the *Spring and Autumn Period* and the *Warring States Period* (see chapter 10) wreaked havoc on Chinese political unity. Prior to these periods, the Shang and Zhou Dynasties represented an era in which Chinese identity was still being formed. If ethnic identity was not yet established in the oldest and most numerous Far Eastern people, then perhaps it was also in flux among the younger and smaller ones.

So far, the results for haplogroups *C* and *D* might suggest that they both arose in East or Northeast Asia. After all, both lineages reach deep into the past (**Color Plates 163, 166**). Both are still found among East and Northeast Asian peoples (**Color Plates 161, 165**). And one (haplogroup *C*) has a specific migration pattern that traces back to Siberia (**Color Plates 163–164**).

However, one population of exclusively *D* individuals fails to fit this East/Northeast Asian profile (**Color Plate 167**). The people of the Great Andamanese Islands reside in what is technically considered Asia. Yet, based on physical appearances, they resemble dark-skinned sub-Saharan Africans. Their *D* sub-lineage (not shown in **Color Plate 166**) formed contemporaneous with, or prior to, the split in the Tibetan and Japanese *D* branches.

In other words, deep in the history of *D* exists a dark-skinned people, the Andamanese. Yet the ancestors to the Andamanese gave rise to both dark-skinned (Andamanese) and light-skinned (Tibetan, Japanese) people.

Going even deeper into the past, the picture grows more complex. On the Y chromosome tree, the nearest relatives to both the *C* and *D* lineages are the lineages of Africa — *A, B,* and *E* (**Color Plate 168**). The position of *D*, and perhaps *C*, intimate the possibility of a dark-skinned African origin.

Intriguingly, the closest lineage to haplogroup *C* is haplogroup *A/B*. Today, haplogroup *A* is found in almost half of the *Khoisan* men of southwestern Africa (**Color Plate 47**; see also supplemental online data). The Khoisan have a physical appearance that seems to combine the physical features of African (curly hair, darker skin tone) and Asian (eye shape) ethnicities (**Color Plate 16**). Perhaps this stems from early Asian-African intermixing on the continent of Africa. When haplogroup *C* individuals first left Africa, perhaps they looked like the Khoisan. Then, later in their history, they would have lived in close proximity to peoples of a more typically Asian appearance, such as the Chinese. Perhaps their features then changed to a more typically Asian look.

For haplogroup *D*, the case for a dark-skinned origin is stronger. The origin of haplogroup *D* is later than the origin of haplogroup *C* (see horizontal sequence of branching events in **Color Plate 168**). Haplogroup *D* doesn't make as clean of a break from the African haplogroups as haplogroup *C* does. Instead, peoples of unambiguous African origin arise and break away (haplogroup *A/B*), leaving another lineage (haplogroup *D/E*) which itself gives rise to more African peoples (haplogroup *E*) (**Color Plate 168**). Haplogroup *D* is found amid all this African activity (**Color Plate 168**). It's hard to imagine a scenario in which the early history of *D* did *not* involve people with dark skin.

In light of this possibility, the dark-skinned appearance of the *D* individuals on the Great Andamanese Islands makes sense. Their history traces to dark-skinned Africa.

Today, dark-skinned Australian Aborigines and light-skinned Easter Islanders both reside in the Pacific. Both may have been originally dark-skinned. But based on the Y chromosome tree, only one could have been originally African. And it's not the one that you'd expect (**Color Plate 169**).

Chapter 11 Summary:

- Much of the history of the Pacific — and of Easter Island — has been shrouded in mystery.

- Archaeological and linguistic clues suggest a sequence of events for the settling of the Pacific:

   * Melanesia and Australia were the earliest places to be settled.

   * Far eastern Polynesia was one of the last places to be settled.

- Physical clues suggest that Melanesians and Australians may have arisen from Africa; Polynesians, from East/Northeast Asia.

- Genetically, haplogroups *K, M,* and *S* appear to be the lineages of the early Melanesians and Australians. But these haplogroups do not connect to Africa.

- Haplogroup *C* is one of the dominant lineages of Polynesia, and it traces back to Siberia.

- In its earliest stages, haplogroup *C* appears to have been located in Africa.

- Thus, the people of African appearance — Melanesians/Australians — look genetically like they arose outside of Africa. Yet the people of East Asian appearance — Polynesians/Easter Islanders — look genetically like they might have arisen from within Africa.

The Americas

12

A New World

Fifteen thousand years ago in the bitterly cold north that separates the Americas from Asia, a group of Central Asians crossed the Bering Strait to an uninhabited wilderness. Stone Age in their technology, these early Americans lived in isolation, cut off from technological advances in the rest of the world. Free from the influence of European narratives and styles of thought, they invented elaborate, poetic myths to explain their own existence. Primitive, yet resourceful, these small bands learned to respect their environment, taming the wilds without destroying them.

When Columbus arrived in the Americas in A.D. 1492, the 15,000-year divide was finally bridged. But the bridge was more of a one-way street. Europeans disrupted the ancient way of life, exposed the fallacy of the received myths, overran the territories of the Native Americans, and eventually confined the Native Americans to reservations.

Compared to the rest of the globe, the genetic history of the Americas is the most predictable. We can convert the 15,000-year date from mainstream science to one consistent with the Y chromosome timeline, but the story changes little. Practically, the only difference is the length of the isolation, not the fact of it. The Americas were still settled in ancient times, and then were never bothered by anyone until Europeans arrived in the last few centuries. To ask what happened to the early Americans is to answer the question. They're still here. In one sense, the history of the Natives is, well, boring.

Geographically, we'd be tempted to reach the same conclusion. Being completely surrounded by water, the Americas are an island unto themselves, cut off from the Old World. This makes the Americas the polar opposite of places like the Middle East and Central Asia. They don't invite invaders from every side or, really, from any side. Instead, the Pacific, Arctic, and Atlantic Oceans discourage conquerors from even considering an exploratory trip.

But appearances can deceive. We've discovered this conclusion time and time again in our exploration of the Y chromosome tree. The Americas are no exception. In fact, they're the most striking example.

Nearly every aspect of the history I described above has turned out to be wrong.

Dynamic

Growing up in Wisconsin, I learned about Native American (Indian) history only as it related to the newly arrived Europeans. In school, we talked about the Indian tribes that European settlers encountered as they moved from east to west. I was taught about the Iroquois and their longhouses in the eastern woodlands. We discussed the buffalo-dependent, migratory lifestyles of the Sioux and other tribes of the Great Plains. We touched on the sedentary ways of the Navajos and peoples of the Southwest. But the discussion was almost entirely static. The only action in these stories involved encounters between settlers moving west and Native Americans that had been there for, well, time immemorial, I presumed. I knew nothing about the pre-Columbian Americas. It remained a puzzle until I moved to Texas in 2009.

Because my parents still called Wisconsin home, they would take trips to visit me. We'd do the usual site-seeing things in the Dallas-Fort Worth metroplex, including the historical Texas sites, like the Fort Worth Stockyards. For me, the most memorable part was not the monuments to past cowboy life. It was a map in one of the many gift shops.

I'm still disappointed that I never took a picture. The map stood high on a wall and showed the area of the United States before Europeans moved through. The whole map was full — replete with individual Native American domains bumped up one against another. Just like European kingdoms had been for centuries.

Here, finally, was a handle, my first grip on the mystery of the pre-Columbian world.

European history was familiar. European kingdoms were bunched together because they reflected a long sequence of political and migratory events. Surely the pre-Columbian world also reflected a long sequence of political and migratory events. I didn't know what those events were. But I finally had a framework in which to understand whatever else I might discover.

This mental step might seem small. "Of course they had a long history of political and migratory events!" Yes, of course. But if you grow up not knowing any of these events, they almost fade into non-existence. When I saw the map in the Fort Worth Stockyards gift shop, the pre-Columbian world came to life again.

While in Texas, I came across a book on the most prominent Native American tribe in Texas — the Comanches. *Empire of the Summer Moon: Quanah Parker and the rise and fall of the Comanches, the most powerful Indian tribe in American history*, by S.C. Gwynne, was a riveting read. But what struck me most was not the violent back and forth between the settlers and the Comanches. It was an almost throw-away sentence at the beginning of the book.

Gwynne described the backstory to the settler-Indian conflict by narrating the pre-settler history of the Comanches. "They came from the high country, in the place we now call Wyoming, above the headwaters of the Arkansas River."[1] This sentence was the first pre-European action that I had encountered, my first insights into the black box of the pre-Columbian world. Here, finally, was something *dynamic*.

Since moving from Texas to Kentucky, I've discovered a clue as to why Comanche history traces to the Rockies. It's their language. The Rockies were the home of the Shoshone people. The Shoshone and Comanche languages belong to the same language family — Uto-Aztecan.

If you've ever engaged the pre-Columbian history of Mexico, then the latter half of that language family name probably rings a bell. On the eve of European arrival in the A.D. 1500s, the Aztecs were the most powerful confederation in Central America. They spoke *Nahuatl*. Nahuatl is also part of the Uto-Aztecan language family, which means that the tribes in what is now the U.S. were linked to peoples south of the Rio Grande (**Color Plate 170**).

I've also discovered that language links U.S. tribes in the other direction. In the American Southwest, the Navajos and Apaches are two

---

1. Gwynne (2010), p. 27.

of the most famous tribes. Their languages belong to the same language family — *Eyak-Athabaskan*. Languages in this same family are
also found in Canada (**Color Plate 171**).

Historically, the Navajos and Apaches arrived late in history to the
American Southwest. The Pueblo peoples preceded them, and they
speak of the intrusion of the Navajos and Apaches. From a homeland
in Canada, the Eyak-Athabaskan members landed in the Southwest
perhaps as late as the A.D. 1500s.[2]

The pre-Columbian world was much more dynamic than I had
been taught. Once I moved to Kentucky, I learned why. Again, the discovery was more accidental than deliberate.

I live in a town of around 20,000 people.[3] Despite its small size,
it has an excellent library. In browsing the history section one day, I
came across a book that caught my eye: *1491: New Revelations of the
Americas before Columbus*. The author, Charles Mann, was a science
writer with an impressive pedigree. But it was his personal backstory
that hooked me in:

> My interest in the peoples who walked the Americas be-
> fore Columbus only snapped into anything resembling focus
> in the fall of 1992. By chance one Sunday afternoon I came
> across a display in a college library of the special Columbian
> quincentenary issue of the *Annals of the Association of Amer-
> ican Geographers*. Curious, I picked up the journal, sank into
> an armchair, and began to read an article by William Dene-
> van, a geographer at the University of Wisconsin. The article
> opened with the question, "What was the New World like
> at the time of Columbus?" Yes, I thought, what *was* it like?
> Who lived here and what could have passed through their
> minds when Europeans sails first appeared on the horizon?
> I finished Denevan's article and went on to others and didn't
> stop reading until the librarian flicked the lights to signify
> closing time.
>
> I didn't know it then, but Denevan and a host of fellow
> researchers had spent their careers trying to answer these
> questions. The picture they have emerged with is quite

---

2. Sturtevant (1978–2004), vol. 9 (Southwest), p. 162.
3. https://data.census.gov/cedsci/all?q=burlington,%20kentucky.

different from what most Americans and Europeans think, and still little known outside specialist circles.

A year or two after I read Denevan's article, I attended a panel discussion at the annual meeting of the American Association for the Advancement of Science. Called something like "New Perspectives on the Amazon," the session featured William Balée of Tulane University. . . . Gee, someone ought to put all this stuff together, I thought. It would make a fascinating book.

I kept waiting for that book to appear. The wait grew more frustrating when my son entered school and was taught the same things I had been taught, beliefs I knew had long been sharply questioned. Since nobody else appeared to be writing the book, I finally decided to try it myself. Besides, I was curious to learn more. The book [*1491*] is the result. . . .

[*1491*] is not a systematic, chronological account of the Western Hemisphere's cultural and social development before 1492. Such a book, its scope vast in space and time, could not be written — by the time the author approached the end, new findings would have been made and the beginning would be outdated. Among those who assured me of this were the very researchers who have spent much of the last few decades wrestling with the staggering diversity of pre-Columbian societies.[4]

This was why I had learned so little about the pre-Columbian Americas. There's so much more than meets the eye, and it's changing too quickly for educators to keep up with.

These changes involve more than filling in a blank historical slate with new information. The revolution in pre-Columbian history is also changing our perspectives on previously documented events — ones that Americans (like myself) have taken for granted.

Riding Into the Sunset

In 1876, the U.S. was recovering from the Civil War and pushing its boundaries west. To provide safe passage for settlers and fortune-seekers, the U.S. Army was rounding up Indians and consigning them

---

4. Mann (2005), p. ix–x.

to reservations. On June 25, 1876, the 7th U.S. Cavalry fought and lost a now infamous battle.

On that day, George Armstrong Custer (**Color Plate 172**) led his troops in pursuit of a group of Sioux and Cheyenne. Custer tried to surprise the Indian camp — but ended up surprised himself. Led by Sitting Bull (**Color Plate 172**), the Indian band — numbering around 2,000 warriors, not the 800 that Custer estimated — routed the U.S. Army. In Custer's last stand, he and five of the twelve companies of the 7th Cavalry lost their lives.

Nearly fifteen years later, on December 29, 1890, a fight broke out near Wounded Knee Creek between U.S. Army soldiers and some of the last remnants of the Lakota Sioux tribe. When it was all over, several hundred Indians lay dead, buried in a mass grave. The era of the wild Indian west was over.

If you're like me, you've viewed these events through the lens of popular assumptions. We think the Indians lost, ultimately, because they had bows and arrows, while the Europeans had guns. Though some Indians had firearms, they were dependent on Europeans for them. It was an unwinnable technological mismatch.

I've since learned that the seeds of the Indian's ultimate fall were sown centuries prior.

Collapse

When Custer fell at Little Bighorn, nearly 400 years had elapsed since Europeans first set permanent foot in the New World. This time gap concealed one of the most important secrets about the fate of Native Americans. The secret was hidden in the baptism and death records of the Spanish churches in the New World. In the A.D. 1950s, researchers began to examine the numbers in these records, and they discovered a troubling discrepancy between births (baptisms) and deaths. You've probably heard about Native deaths due to smallpox and other European-borne diseases. You've probably not heard about the magnitude of them.

The exact number of Indians who lived in the pre-Columbian Americas remains a contentious subject. Estimates range from 8 million to 113 million. The exact number is significant because it affects the degree to which the population collapsed. By the 1800s, only around 8 million Native Americans were left.

Middle-of-the-road estimates (i.e., William Denevan's,[5] referenced by Charles Mann above) put the total around 54 million. About 4 million lived north of the Rio Grande. Another 24 million called Central America and the Caribbean home. In South America, 26 million resided.

By 1800, more than 85% of the combined total were gone. In other words, when Custer and his men engaged the Sioux and Cheyenne, the Indians were already a dying people. Overwhelming numerical disadvantage all but ensured the outcome.

For comparison, the total population of Europe in A.D. 1400 was only 60 million. (The Black Death had culled anywhere from 25% to 33% of the earlier European population.) On the eve of European arrival in the New World, the Americas held nearly as many people. And then almost 90% of the Indians would disappear.

Lost in the Jungle

Where were all these pre-Columbian people living? What were they doing? This time, it wasn't Spanish baptism and death records that held the answer. It was the dense jungles of South and Central America.

In 2018 a team of investigators published an unusual study on the pre-Columbian Amazon.[6] Well, it was unusual by the standards of popular expectations. Measured against the trajectory of results coming from the pre-Columbian Americas research community, it was simply another piece of the emerging puzzle.

From an agricultural perspective, the Amazon rainforest holds little potential — at first glance. The soil is poor and nutrient deficient. Clearing the trees and brush exposes it to leaching. A region this uninviting would seem to offer little support to a population that is trying to grow.

However, the Amazon also harbors a diversity of trees that produce fruits useful for human consumption. Treat the Amazon as a potential orchard instead of a potential wheat field, and you've just transformed the scope of possibility. Add in deliberate fertilizing, and the Amazon takes on a whole new look. Charles Mann in his book *1491* summarized the emerging evidence for this new perspective: Up to 12% looked "anthropogenic"[7] — as if it was the result of deliberate human activity.

---

5. Denevan (1992).
6. de Souza et al. (2018).
7. Mann (2005), p. 305.

Evidence was accumulating that the supposedly pristine, untouched rainforests of South America were deliberately designed orchards. The 2018 study of the Amazon added to this body of evidence.

The focus of the research team was human-created earthworks in the Amazon region. From the archaeological evidence of human activity, they estimated the population size of the people responsible for the earthworks:

> We infer a regional population between ~500,000 and 1 million for the SRA [South Rim of the Amazon] during Late Pre-Columbian times, based on a bottom-up approach using empirical archaeological data. This figure calls for a re-evaluation of models solely based on carrying capacity or projections of recent ethnographic data, which often presuppose that most of the Amazonian Pre-Columbian population was settled along riverbank settings, with low densities and limited environmental impact in *terra firme* areas. Moreover, the fact that the predicted area of earthworks along the SRA, an area comprising merely 7% of the Amazon, could have sustained a population in the hundreds of thousands (even if one accepts the lower threshold of our estimate), definitively discredits early low estimates of 1.5–2 million inhabitants for the whole basin.[8]

If the wider Amazon region were explored in similar detail, what would happen to these estimates? What if, not 7%, but 100% of the Amazon were subject to in-depth archaeological surveys? What if they showed similar archaeological evidence for human occupation? We can estimate an answer by extrapolating from the researchers' conclusions.

Let's say that the whole region was once settled at similar density. To estimate the total population size, we would just have to take their ratio and multiply it up to 100%. In other words, if 7% held 500,000 to 1 million people, then 100% could have held 7 to 14 million people.

The pre-Columbian world was populous — especially in regions thought to have been otherwise untouched wilderness, such as the Amazon.

---

8. de Souza et al. (2018), p. 7–8.

Part of the reason we've missed these conclusions is the speed with which the evidence has disappeared. In 2018, another group of scientists reported their examination of the history of an Ecuadorian cloud forest.[9] Again, widely held stereotypes inform our expectations: *Once a cloud forest, always a cloud forest*, right? These researchers answered this question by sampling the history of the cloud forest through sediments in a nearby lake. With radiocarbon dating, they established the chronology of the layers. They also analyzed the plant contents within these layers. The plant remnants indicated what sort of flora dominated the surrounding landscape.

In the uppermost layers, the plant material was consistent with the surrounding cloud forest ecosystem. In deeper layers, which they dated to the A.D. 1600s and early 1700s, the plant material suggested the area was an open grassland, not a cloud forest. Even deeper, prior to European arrival in this region in A.D. 1588, the sediments revealed a shock. *The pre-European layers showed that the now-cloud forest was once farmland — fields of maize.* In just a few centuries, farmland went to open grassland, which then turned into a cloud forest, burying the evidence of prior human activity.

Jungles in the Americas have also buried the evidence of earlier political activity. On the eve of European arrival, power in the Americas was concentrated in two large empires. In Central America, the Aztecs reigned supreme (**Color Plate 173**). On the west coast of South America, the Incas controlled more than 2,000 miles of land, from modern Ecuador to Chile (**Color Plate 173**).

Centuries prior, the dominant empire resided in Central America and belonged to the Mayans (**Color Plate 174**). But the European newcomers wouldn't have known any different. By the time the Conquistador Hernán Cortés marched into Mexico and then through Central America, the ruins of the Classic-era Mayan civilization were unrecognizable.

Today, radar scans of the jungle are revealing just how extensive the pyramid, temple, and city complexes of the ancient Mayans were — beyond what we've already uncovered (**Color Plates 175–183**). In 2018, a team reported the results of radar scans of the Guatemalan landscape, part of the ancient homeland of the Maya.[10] From the

9. Loughlin et al. (2018).
10. Canuto et al. (2018).

structures the scans uncovered, the team estimated population densities. From these densities, they calculated the Mayan population size for the Late Classic (A.D. 650 to 800) era: 7 to 11 million people.

By comparison, modern Germany is more than three times the size of modern Guatemala. In A.D. 800, Germany held just over 3 million people. Yet the Mayan population was two to four times larger.

In these early years, the Mayans weren't the only builders of magnificent structures. To the northwest in what is now Mexico, the city of *Teotihuacan* boasted large pyramids (e.g., **Color Plates 184–185**) and an estimated population of 200,000 people.

Why were the Mayan remains so hard to detect? What happened to them that their magnificent civilization would disappear so quickly? By the A.D. 900s, the cities in the Mayan lowlands were depopulated. The construction of the massive temples ceased, and Classic Mayan civilization was gone. To the north, Mayan culture persisted in the Yucatán. But the defining features of the Classic Mayans were swallowed by the jungle, lost to history for the next millennium. No one knows why.[11]

For years, Europeans have viewed the Native American way of life as *primitive*. When early European settlers encountered Iroquois, Sioux, Cheyenne, and other tribes, these Europeans saw a people with technology that was inferior to their own. To this day, the uncontacted tribes who emerge from the Amazon jungle look like they came from another era. They dress in little or no clothing. They hunt with bows and arrows. They show little evidence of the material progress that defines the modern era.

But the Native Americans haven't always been this way. Their post-Columbian societal collapse reduced them to a shadow of their former glory. As Charles Mann put it, the label *primitive* is uninformed by historical fact. It's as if we came "across refugees from a Nazi concentration camp, and concluded that they belonged to a culture that had always been barefoot and starving."[12]

In light of this newly discovered history, we'd do well to step back and ask some basic questions of the indigenous peoples of the Americas. Who are the Native Americans? Who did these mislabeled peoples come from? What's their story?

---

11. Within the mainstream scientific community, the collapse of the Classic-era Mayans remains a subject of intense academic debate.
12. Mann (2005), p. 9.

Ironically, Native Americans have been telling their stories for centuries. These narratives have typically been dismissed as mythical, devoid of useful historical information.

This attitude is now changing — with stunning implications for the history of the Americas.

In Their Own Words

The Osage tribe were once rulers of the North American Great Plains. They and the Omaha, Ponca, Kaw, and Quapaw tribes formed the *Dhegiha* Siouan grouping. The Osage themselves claimed that "all five Dhegiha tribes were once one nation that lived east of the Mississippi River in the vicinity of the Ohio River."[13] Initially, this narrative didn't fly with the academic community.

These winds are now shifting:

> In the early 1990s, Susan Vehik (1993) and Dale Henning (1993), separately undertook critical, thorough reassessments of Dhegiha origins studies. In light of more current archaeological data and critical scrutiny of all lines of evidence presented to determine Dhegiha origins, in 1993 Vehik concluded that even though so many anthropologists have discounted oral histories, the archaeologists have failed to offer a more plausible account for the area of Dhegiha tribal origins. . . .
>
> Likewise in 1993, Henning came to a similar interpretation. Henning, like Vehik (1993), believed that the logical course of analysis should be to let the Dhegiha tribes speak for themselves by means of the recorded legends and ethnohistoric records (Henning 1993:253). He offered clear words of advice to archaeologists that adhere to a direct historical approach that relies primarily on archaeological materials and on material culture retention. Henning (1993:262) warns that archaeologists may misinterpret history by not considering all lines of evidence available. The Dhegiha Sioux offer a prime case in point due to the adaptive patterning exhibited by these tribes. By relying on the tribes' own migration

---

13. https://www.osagenation-nsn.gov/who-we-are/historic-preservation/osage-cultural-history.

legends, linguistic analyses, their history, and ethnohistory, Henning (1993:260–262) concluded that an ancestral Dhegiha locus is most likely in the Ohio River valley with the tribes migrating west of the Mississippi River and splitting into their tribes just prior to European contact.[14]

This insight into pre-Columbian history may not seem like a bombshell. But it's an account that presents a much more dynamic picture of the pre-European Americas than the one I grew up with.

Another North American tribe, the Chickasaw, once resided in the southeastern part of what is now the United States. They say that they arose first in the west, and then migrated to the east. Their own history even mentions crossing the Mississippi River.[15]

Back then, once they had crossed the Mississippi, the Chickasaw account says that the band of migrants split into two groups. Two brothers — *Chiksa'* and *Chahta* — had been leading the group. After crossing the river, they disagreed on how to interpret the direction of the sacred pole that had been guiding their journey. Chahta decided to stay. Chiksa decided to continue east. Each had a following:

> From that day on, the people that followed Minko' Chiksa', who were relatively few compared to the significant number who remained in camp, were referred to as Chickasaws, and those who stayed with Minko' Chahta were called Choctaws.[16]

Again, this migration account puts much more activity in pre-European North America than I had assumed took place.

A third North American tribe, the Delaware, or *Lenni Lenape*, documented an extensive migration journey, complete with geographic detail and list of tribal rulers (*sachems*).[17] The Lenape origins account contained the most revolutionary insights into pre-Columbian history.

Apparently, the original homeland of the Lenape was Central Asia or Siberia:

---

14. https://www.osagenation-nsn.gov/who-we-are/historic-preservation/osage-cultural-history.
15. https://www.chickasaw.net/Our-Nation/History/Prehistoric.aspx.
16. https://www.chickasaw.net/Our-Nation/History/Prehistoric.aspx.
17. McCutchen (1993).

After the Flood, the Lenape, the True Men, the Turtle People, were crowded together, living there in cave shelters.

Their home was icy. Their home was snowy. Their home was windy. Their home was freezing.

To the north slope, to have less cold, many big-game herds went.

To be strong, to be rich; the travelers the builders; the Hunters broke away.

Strongest of all, best of all, holiest of all, the Hunters are.

Northern, eastern, southern, western; the Hunters, the Explorers.

In the old land, the winter land, the Turtle land, the great land, were the Turtle Men, the Lenape.[18]

Before the Lenape traveled to the Americas, another group seems to have preceded them:

All the enemy Snake Lodge fires were troubled; the Snake priest said to them all, "Let us go."

The Snakes there in the east all went forth, going away, grim, grieving.

Fleeing, tired and shivering, through the wasteland; torn and broken, to Akomen, the Wilderness.[19]

Later, the Lenape followed across what seems to be the Bering Strait:

Beaver Head and Great Bird, they said "Let us go!" "To Akomen!" they said.

The allies all declared, "All our enemies will be destroyed."

The northerners agreed, the easterners agreed, across the icy ocean was a better place to be.

On a wondrous sheet of ice all crossed the frozen sea at low tide in the narrows of the ocean.

Ten times a thousand they crossed; all went forth in a night; they crossed to Akomen, the East Land, crossing, marching, marching, everyone together. . . .

18. McCutchen (1993), p. 68, 72.
19. McCutchen (1993), p. 72.

All came to settle in the evergreen land. The western people reluctantly came there, for they loved it best in the old Turtle country.[20]

Once in "Akomen" (the Americas), the Lenape migrated from the cold northwestern part of North America to the area around modern Delaware.

The description of this journey is found in the history of their sachems. In the New World, the Lenape were ruled by a sequence of around 95 sachems. For each, the Lenape account gives something significant about them, or about events contemporary with them.

Based on the descriptions in this list of sachems, about three calendar dates can be associated with individual leaders. From these three dates, a rough average of the time of each sachem's rule can be calculated. With this number in hand, we can calculate backwards to determine the date for when the first Lenape arrived in the Americas (Akomen). The lower bound for these estimates puts the crossing in the A.D. 200s to 300s. The upper bound puts it in the A.D. 800s to 900s.

If these dates are accurate, they imply that the Lenape were not the first in the Americas. Archaeologically, Mayan history traces back to the first few centuries before Christ.

And about a millennium prior to the Mayans, a people called the *Olmecs* lived in what is now modern Mexico. The Olmecs left us a unique, tangible reminder of their civilization: gigantic, sculpted heads (**Color Plate 186**). The beginning of both the Olmec and Mayan civilizations seems to predate the Lenape arrival in the Americas.

Perhaps the Olmecs and Mayans did precede the Lenape in the Americas. The Lenape narrative makes it clear that others — the "Snake" people — were already in "Akomen" before the Lenape arrived.

Were they? Was the pre-Columbian history of the Americas so dynamic that it involved at least two independent settling events from Asia — one that gave rise to the Olmecs and Mayans, and one that gave rise to the civilizations that followed them?

On this question, the Y chromosome held one of the biggest secrets of all.

---

20. McCutchen (1993), p. 76.

Pre-Columbian Asian-Americans

In mainstream science, two Y chromosome haplogroups dominate the discussion of Native American history: Haplogroup *Q* occupies the main focus, and haplogroup *C* a lesser focus. Other haplogroups also exist in the Americas. Because of European colonialism and the Trans-Atlantic slave trade, haplogroups from Europe (e.g., haplogroups *I, R1b*) and Africa (e.g., haplogroup *E1b1a*) abound in the Americas, spilling over even into Native American populations. The mainstream science community subtracts these European and African haplogroups from analyses of Native American DNA. Then they explore the haplogroups that remain. Overwhelmingly, what's left is haplogroup *Q* (**Color Plate 187**). To a lesser extent, it's also haplogroup *C* (**Color Plate 188**).

Haplogroup *Q* belongs to a lineage that includes *R1a, R1b*, and *R2*. The *R1* lineages have played a large role in European history, linking modern Europeans to Central Asians (chapter 7). Haplogroup *R2* links the history of India with the history of Central Asia (chapter 9). Haplogroup *Q* is the earliest of these four branches, splitting off from haplogroup *R* in the 1300s to 700s B.C. (**Color Plate 189**). Haplogroup *C* may have originally arisen in Africa, but more recently, it underwent a dispersal from Siberia (see chapter 11).

How does this genetic history align with the pre-Columbian history of the Americas? In short, it rewrites it.

As we observed at the beginning of this chapter, mainstream science starts the story of the Americas 15,000 years ago. Mainstream scientists invoke this date based on radiometric dating of the earliest archaeological remains in the Americas. Mainstream genetics has followed suit. In fact, mainstream genetics is so dependent on the archaeological narrative that mainstream geneticists use archaeological dates as a literal "sanity check."[21] When mainstream scientists run analyses of the Y chromosome, they check to make sure that the Native American branches break away from Central Asian branches around 15,000 years ago. If not, they consider the analyses to be off.

Effectively, in the Americas, mainstream genetics plays second fiddle to mainstream archaeology. Mainstream science doesn't use

---

21. Poznik et al. (2016), Supplementary Information, p. 87. (Special thanks to Rob Carter for pointing this out to me.)

genetics as an independent check on archaeology. Instead, it assumes the archaeology-based chronology to be correct, and then stretches a sequence of genetic events over it.

As we saw in chapter 6, measurements of the Y chromosome clock contradict the mainstream timescale.

Embedded in the Y chromosome tree is an independent way to evaluate this chronological dispute. In chapter 8, we derived the history of Arab population growth. We did so from the haplogroup *J1* branching patterns that we observed in the Y chromosome tree. A similar derivation can be performed for Native American population history. This time, we'll use the haplogroup Q branching patterns. (We have more data for Q than for C.)

If Q represents the Native American lineage in A.D. 1491, then it should bear the stamp of the post-Columbian population collapse.

Haplogroup Q should also bear the stamp of a second post-Columbian population event. Beginning in the 1800s and 1900s, the Native American population decline abated, and the Native peoples began to recover. As an example,[22] in 1868, only 9,000 Navajos still existed. By 1898, the number had risen to 20,000. By A.D. 2000, the population had grown to around 175,000. Thus, haplogroup Q should show a European-migration-induced population collapse, followed by an 1800s/1900s-era population recovery.

Today, we do not possess reliable Y chromosome DNA from the pre-Columbian peoples who died out in the population collapse. Instead, we possess the Y chromosome DNA from the *survivors* of this collapse. From the family tree based on their DNA, we can reconstruct the history of their population growth and decline. The theory behind this statement is not common knowledge, but it's easy to understand, once you see it.

Let's examine the hypothetical family trees in **Color Plates 190–191**. They show how a family tree changes after a population catastrophe occurs. They also show a later population recovery. **Color Plate 190** shows you what you would see if you could watch several centuries of population history like a movie. **Color Plate 191** shows you what you would see if all you had were a family tree based on the DNA of the survivors.

---

22. Navajo population data were obtained from http://www.navajobusiness.com/pdf/ FstFctspdf/Tbl3GrwthRate.pdf.

The primary evidence for a population catastrophe resides in specific branches of the tree — those that were present around the time the catastrophe occurred. When a massive population collapse occurs, at that point in history the branches of the survivors are nearly empty or flat. They don't show regular splitting and multiplication (**Color Plates 190–191**).

Once population growth resumes, the branches on the family tree resume multiplying (**Color Plates 190–191**).

Now apply this theory to the question of Native American population history. In the several centuries after Columbus' arrival in the Americas, 80% to 90% of the indigenous people died. Practically, the loss of so many people would have killed off massive numbers of branches. For this period of history, the branches of the family tree from the survivors would be empty or flat. At a minimum, you'd expect to find flatlining from around A.D. 1492 to around the A.D. 1800s.

However, you'd also expect this flatlining to extent backward in time *prior* to A.D. 1492. An 80% to 90% decrease in population size would kill off Natives whose ancestors lived *before* European arrival. The genetic signature of these early peoples would disappear because their descendants vanished. For an illustration of this principle, see **Color Plates 190–191**. In these simulations, I've killed off 90% of the branches in the original population. Notice how these extinct branches had their origin prior to A.D. 1492.

Now take a look at **Color Plate 192**. This diagram shows the haplogroup Q branches from Native Americans who hail from northwest Mexico ("Pima"), the Yucatán ("Maya"), Colombia, and Brazil ("Karitiana" and "Surui"). These men are the *survivors* of the Native American population collapse. Notice how, on either side of the date of Columbus' arrival (A.D. 1492), their branches are mostly flat. Almost no branch multiplication occurs. Closer to the present, branch multiplication resumes (**Color Plate 192**).

Another way to display this same result is with a population growth curve. You can see examples of this in **Color Plate 193**. In the century/centuries before and after A.D. 1492, the population growth curve from the Q survivors is flat (**Color Plate 193**). Then around the A.D. 1700s and 1800s, population growth resumes (**Color Plate 193**).

Mainstream science does not show this recovery curve. It can detect the evidence for a population collapse, but it does not capture the resumption of population growth. This fact makes the mainstream chronology inferior to the one based on the Y chromosome.

You may have noticed that, going backward in time, the growth curve stops between A.D. 330 and 700 (**Color Plate 193**). The reason is hidden in the branches of the Y chromosome tree. After these dates, one side of the Q branches in the tree is populated by Native Americans (**Color Plate 194**). Before these dates, the tree is populated by individuals in the Old World (**Color Plate 194**). For example, these latter branches lead to people occasionally from Europe (e.g., Russia) but mainly from Asia, including Afghanistan (*Hazara*), Pakistan (*Sindhi, Makrani,* and *Pathan*), China (*Naxi, Han*), and Mongolia.

In other words, these stopping points on the Native American growth curve (**Color Plates 194**) reflect a critical juncture in Native American history. They represent the time when the genealogies of the Old World and the New went their separate ways — the point at which haplogroup Q individuals migrated over to the Americas, just like the Lenape origins account described.

Apparently, the arrival of haplogroup Q individuals in the Americas was followed by a time of rapid population growth. Notice the sharp spike upward in the growth curves in **Color Plate 193**. The spike occurred in the A.D. 500s to A.D. 800s (**Color Plate 193**).

This time of growth also seems to have functioned as a time of geographic dispersal. Take a look at **Color Plate 192** and find the spots where Native American branches bunch together. You could also call this spot the place where many Native American branches break away from one another. Notice the individuals to which these branches lead. They represent peoples from northwest Mexico (*Pima*) all the way down into Brazil (*Karitiana* and *Surui*).

Now take an even closer look at the spot where a whole bunch of Native American branches separate from one another. Notice that the splitting happens with little space between the branches. They're clustered tightly together. This means that the geographic dispersal happened between close relatives and in a narrow window of time — just like the Chickasaw origin narrative described.

If you look at **Color Plate 193**, you may notice something intriguing about the period of rapid population growth. It overlaps the time of another collapse. In the A.D. 600s, the city of Teotihuacan (**Color Plates 184–185**) was violently overthrown. Perhaps a cause-effect relationship exists between the arrival of the Q individuals and the collapse of the earlier American civilizations.

Indigenous American haplogroup C shows a break from Central Asia that is similar to the one I described for haplogroup Q — but it occurs at a later date. Instead of leaving the Old World in the A.D. 300s to 600s, the haplogroup C men left around A.D. 1000 (data not shown).[23]

Who were these new arrivals from Asia? From which people did the American haplogroup Q and C individuals spring? Because these migrations occurred during the period of recorded history, we already have some good candidates. In fact, the Y chromosome history of Europe provided the biggest clue to the story of Q.

Old World Sources

Recall from chapter 7 that the western Roman Empire fell at the hands of invaders from the east in the A.D. 400s. Germanic tribes and Huns swept through, with some eventually ending up in North Africa as part of the Vandal kingdom. We saw the genetic echo of this event in some of the early *R1b* branches (see **Color Plates 65, 85**).

Ancient Rome wasn't the only empire to fall around this time. The Han Dynasty fell in the A.D. 200s at the hands of Central Asians/northern "barbarians" who ushered in several centuries of foreign rule. Central Asian *Hephthalites* harassed northern India in the A.D. 400s and 500s. So great was the activity of the Central Asians during the early centuries A.D. that this era is known as the *Völkerwanderung* — the *Great Wandering of Peoples.*

The arrival of Central Asians in the Americas falls right in line with the *Völkerwanderung*. Whatever prompted Central Asians to overrun much of Eurasia seems to have also prompted them to overrun the Americas.

The evidence for this link isn't simply temporal correlation. The *R1b* branches themselves suggest that the invaders of the Americas were part of the same people group who overran the western Roman Empire. In chapter 7, we connected the latter to an *R1b* branch that broke away from the main trunk in the A.D. 100s to 600s (**Color Plate 65, 85**). Native Americans are occasionally found in a similar branch.

---

23. I'm basing these conclusions for the haplogroup C branching pattern on those reported for the Chipewyan individual in Pinotti et al. (2019) figure 2. I converted the dates via methods similar to the ones I used in the supplemental online tables.

This fact has been overlooked, due to the massive influx of Europeans to the Americas within the last two centuries. Today, if Native Americans are found in the *R1b* branch, they usually reside in the later branches — the ones that gave rise to Western Europeans (i.e., those branches in **Color Plates 64, 69–73**). However, on rare occasions, Native Americans also can be found on *R1b* branches that arose at the same time as those that ended up in North Africa (compare the dates for the origin of the *Puerto Rican* and *Peruvian* individuals in **Color Plate 195** to the dates for the North African *Mozabite* individuals in **Color Plate 65**).

The narrative embedded in Native American Y chromosomes firmly anchors the origin of the pre-Columbian Americans within recorded history.

It also leaves major questions unanswered.

A New pre-Columbian History

Given the archaeological history of the Americas, the new *Q* and *C* arrivals from Asia must not have been the first peoples in the Americas. Recall that Mayan history goes back to the B.C. era. Olmec history traces to the 1500s B.C. The entrance of haplogroups *Q* and *C* to the Americas post-dates the origin of both of these civilizations.

Once the haplogroup *Q* and *C* individuals grew and dispersed in the Americas, they seem to have been wildly successful. Today, haplogroups *Q* and *C* are the most dominant among Native Americans. That is, once you remove the obvious European (i.e., due to post-Columbian immigration) and African (i.e., due to the Trans-Atlantic slave trade) branches from consideration, what's left is almost exclusively *Q* and *C*. This implies that the *Q* and *C* immigrants replaced whoever was here first. Perhaps *Q* and *C* wiped them out. Whatever the specific events that transpired, the first Native American Y chromosome lineages seem to have disappeared.

Consider how this conclusion puts the history of the Americas at odds with the history in the other regions of the globe we've explored. In Africa (chapters 5 and 6), we identified several candidate lineages (*A, B, E*) for the earliest peoples, including the Egyptians. In Europe (chapter 7), we saw that Central Asian lineages (*R1b, R1a*) have overwhelmed the indigenous ones. But in chapter 8, we identified a candidate (the *I-J* lineage) for the early Indo-European speakers, from whom early peoples like the Romans and Greeks likely descended. The *I-J* lineage is also a good candidate for an ancestor to early Middle Eastern peoples, like the ancient Persians (chapter 8). In South Asia (chapter 9), haplogroup *H* looks like the early Indian/Pakistani peoples. To the east, haplogroups *N* and *O* stand at the fountainhead of several ancient East Asian peoples (chapter 10). Haplogroups *C* and *D* are ancient lineages that infiltrated early Asia and spread to the Pacific. Haplogroups *K, M,* and *S* stand at the dawn of the history of Oceania (chapter 11). Only in the Americas is the earliest lineage missing.

You could say for now that the history of the first peoples of the Americas remains hidden.

Where Do We Go from Here?

As a researcher, I don't find this situation troubling. I find it exciting.

Part of my enthusiasm stems from my love of mystery. I relish being drawn in by well-written detective stories.

In a sense, science is a sophisticated form of a *whodunit*. For the first Americans, *whodunit* is a succinct summary of where we are. Nobody knows who first settled the Americas. We know something about these early people from their archaeological remains. But we don't know their genealogical heritage.

Classic detective novels eventually reveal the answer to the mystery. All you have to do is keep reading. On the question of the identity of the first Americans, we don't have such luxuries — at least, none that I know of yet. But we do have a potential avenue by which to explore the question further.

If you're reading this book and you're an American Indian, perhaps you'd like to join the search. Perhaps the oral or written history of your own tribe or nation already contains the answer. Perhaps that answer has been neglected. I'd like it to be neglected no more.

Or maybe you're an American Indian student with aspirations toward genetics. Perhaps you'd like to one day work on solving this mystery. The members of the American Indian communities hold the key to the answer. Somewhere in the Americas, a group of males might still be walking around whose genealogy traces to the earliest Americans. If we sequence their Y chromosomes, we might discover the ancestry of these early peoples.

I hope this chapter fires your aspirations. And I hope it leads to the uncovering of the answer. The revelation of it would be a generous gift from the American Indian nations, not just to the academic community, but to the rest of the world.

Chapter 12 Summary:

- Mainstream science puts the origin of the Native Americans 15,000 years ago, and it describes their existence as isolated from the rest of the world until the arrival of Europeans in the A.D. 1400s.

- Traditional understandings of Native American history have viewed the pre-Columbian era as one in which primitive Indians were few in number and in which they lived in harmony with nature.

- Recent scientific findings are casting the pre-Columbian history of the Americas in a new light.

  * Historical records show that massive numbers of people existed here on the eve of Columbus' arrival.

  * New archaeological investigations are revealing the pre-Columbian Americas to have been a highly developed landscape, not an untouched wilderness.

  * Native American accounts of their own origins suggest a dynamic pre-Columbian world.

  * The Y chromosome-based family tree shows that today's Native Americans were not the first arrivals in the New World. In the A.D. era, invaders from Central Asia appear to have wiped out whoever was here first — including the Olmecs and possibly the Mayans. This genetic history is consistent with the origin account of the Lenape (Delaware Indians).

- The identity of the first American Y chromosome lineage is an unsolved scientific mystery. Thus, the earliest history of the Americas remains hidden.

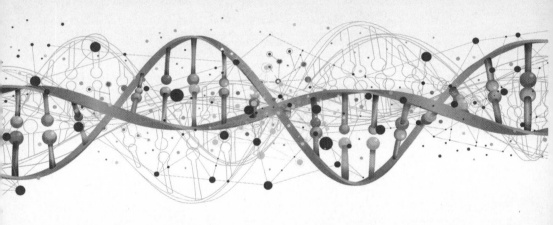

Part III: Past, Present, and Future

13

Breaking at the Dawn

Imagine waking up to the first light of the warm summer sun in A.D. 1400 in Central Europe. Outside your farmhouse, the surrounding fields and pastureland stretch in all four directions. Farmhands are hard at work, following horse or oxen teams and herding sheep.

Breakfast requires your attendance at the hearth. Thanks to your elbow grease yesterday at the wash basin and the warm air flowing through garments suspended from the clothesline, you have a clean set of clothes for the day. Dressed and fed, you make a pit stop at the outhouse. The smell of human waste combined with manure lend an unmistakable aroma to your everyday rural life.

A castle on the distant hilltop provides mental reassurance that salvation is near, should marauders march through your family lands. Armed with swords, crossbows, and maybe a primitive *harquebus*, castle soldiers train to engage invaders at close range — not miles and miles away. Life far beyond the castle is of little relevance to you.

Travel is a rare privilege. Horse and wagon take you slowly over the countryside. Should you reach the sea, a sailing ship could take you beyond Europe toward one of the other known continents — Africa or Asia. (No one in Europe is aware of the existence of Australia or of the Americas.)

Life in 15th-century Europe was, well, rather primitive.

Fast forward several hundred years. If today you were to live in Central Europe, you would wake up in a climate-controlled room to the roar of jet engines and the scent of car exhaust. You'd throw your clothes in the washer and hop in the shower. An hour car ride would take you miles from your home to a modern office building or skyscraper.

Over the weekend, you might take the same car to meander along country roads to a remote, but well-supplied, seaside resort. Along the way, you might see tractors and combines crawling through the fields. Or you might not notice their existence. With fast food available in every city, no one needs to worry about the success of the summer crops or to pay attention to the operations of a modern farm. If all else fails, food can be imported from around the world.

Over the holidays, you might set your sights on a more distant location. Flights to Cancún, Cairo, Mumbai, Beijing, and Honolulu are all feasible destinations for a week-long escape. The main question guiding your vacation choice is not whether the trip is possible but whether you can afford it.

At night, if the sky is clear, you might gaze upward and catch a glimpse of the International Space Station. If the night is cloudy, you might surf television channels in search of a livestream or maybe look for a live feed over the internet. For an even more immersive experience, you might purchase a virtual reality device and live life in space for a few minutes, all within the confines of your room.

At the end of the day, you can relax — physically and mentally. No need to remember where the nearest walled city is. You can rest in peace, knowing that your country is protected by drones, tanks, jet fighters, aircraft carriers, and ballistic missiles. Your government has people dedicated to monitoring the political and military situations on all six inhabited continents — yes, six, not the three known continents of the A.D. 1400s.

Life in the 21st century is worlds apart from life in the 15th.

The Inevitable March

The recent progress of human civilization has been so dramatic that we now take it for granted. Each year, we don't ask whether any technological breakthroughs will occur. Instead, we ask which of the technological breakthroughs we'll incorporate into our daily routines. Should I stick with the old iPhone or get the new? Is my laptop outdated? What's the latest video streaming technology?

A fundamental driver of this relentless march of human progress is a primal quest: The survival of the fittest. You don't want to be the VHS video rental store owner when Netflix and Disney+ arrive. No one pities the loss of the wagon-maker's occupation or of the blacksmith's trade. Good riddance to the bow and arrow manufacturers. Keep up, or get swallowed up by progress. It's inescapable.

Earlier human history bears out this same rule. The sudden rise of the massive Mongol empire was facilitated by the Mongols' military skill on horseback. Eastern Europeans, Middle Easterners, and Central Asians were unprepared to defend themselves against a highly mobile force of mounted archers. The eventual fall of the Mongols stemmed in part from the obsolescence of their technology. Horses can't outrun a hail of rifle bullets.

More than a millennium before the Mongols, the ancient Romans overthrew their Mediterranean and European neighbors. They did so through their mastery of military discipline and tactical skill. Before the Romans, civilizations with iron weapons replaced those with bronze. Early bronze civilizations overran those relying on stone technology.

Mainstream science applies the same principle to the beginning of civilization. From whom did the ancient Egyptians, Romans, Persians, Indians, Chinese, Pacific Islanders, and Native Americans arise? Mainstream science says that each arose from more primitive hunter-gatherers indigenous to their locations.

From whom did the primitive hunter-gatherers arise? Mainstream science says that they evolved over long periods of time — hundreds of thousands to millions of years — from even more primitive species. Before anatomically modern humans arose, primitive Neanderthals had evolved from even simpler life forms. Before the Neanderthals, *Homo erectus* had evolved from an ape-like ancestor. This ancestor came from an even more primitive predecessor — one that also fathered the genealogical lineage leading to modern chimpanzees.

It's simple-to-complex all the way back to the deepest parts of the human family tree. In each case, the strongest and fittest survived; the weakest receded and went extinct. Life progresses.

It's a single, simple explanation for all of human history and pre-history.

The trouble with this explanation is that *the overall timeframe doesn't fit genetics*. The rate at which copying errors are introduced into the Y chromosome is much too fast to support a narrative spanning hundreds of thousands of years, let alone millions of years. We observed this fact in chapter 6.[1]

But where does this result leave the simple-to-complex narrative? If humans didn't have long periods of time in which to evolve into higher and more advanced states of existence, how did human history begin? If not through slow and gradual survival of the fittest, how did humanity arise?

We've already uncovered a clue to these questions in the previous chapter. In chapter 12, we saw that the simple-to-complex narrative fails to explain the history of the Native Americans. When Europeans first encountered the "primitive" lifestyles of the Natives, they wrongly concluded that the Natives had always been simple peoples. In fact, the Natives had achieved a high level of sophistication in centuries past, but new diseases and other factors decimated their numbers, rendering them a shell of their former glory.

In short, the history of the Native Americans demonstrates that progress *isn't* inevitable. It can be shattered in a heartbeat. Going backward is just as plausible as going forward. *Primitive appearances can belie complex histories.*

In light of these facts, let's reframe our questions: If appearances can deceive, how do we uncover the beginning of the human race? How do we figure out what the "primitive" appearance of early humans signified? Was their "primitive" state simply due to temporal factors — to being alive at an early stage of a simple-to-complex evolution? Or did it arise through a backward step from an earlier, more advanced state?

The biggest challenge in finding the answers to these questions appeared in preceding chapters. For each ancient civilization we examined, subsequent history clouded the ancient picture. In many cases, the ancient lineage was still recoverable (e.g., Egypt, Persia). In other cases, it was diminished in frequency or lost entirely (e.g., Rome, the earliest Americans). In all cases, we found that the way to pursue ancient genetic signals was to first peel back the layers of later history.

By definition, the beginning has been covered by the most layers of subsequent events. The beginning is the time point from which the rest of human history follows. It's the period most shrouded in mystery.

---

1. For more discussion of evolution and of its relationship to human history, see Appendix B.

In previous chapters, we peeled back many layers of subsequent history. In this chapter, we're going to peel back even more. We'll do so primarily by following the history of a small, ancient Near Eastern kingdom.

We'll begin by attempting to find the fate of the ancient Israelites.

Few ancient peoples have had an existence as unpredictable and turbulent as the Israelites have had. The fate of the Jewish people has been difficult to track down, and it will take us some time to find it. In essence, for a good chunk of this chapter we're going to pause our exploration of the beginning of humanity. However, despite the length of this diversion, our hard work will be richly rewarded. Of all the ancient Near Eastern kingdoms, the Israelites kept some of the most detailed genealogical records of their origins. These records will allow us to trace their genetic lineage backward in time to uncover their roots.

Once we do, we'll discover that the genetic history of Israel leads us to more than the beginning of their story. It also takes us to the dawn of the whole world.

An Unexpected Fate

By 570 B.C., the Middle Eastern sphere of ancient Israel had already seen millennia of political upheaval and change. Several major Mesopotamian powers had already come and gone. The major power at the time was just three decades away from realizing the same fate. None would last into the modern era. Except one — the Israelites, one of the most politically resilient peoples the world has ever seen.

Of the large, ancient Mesopotamian powers, the first arose in the land we now know as modern Turkey. The Hittites (**Color Plate 110**) carved out their share of the crossroads of civilization. After their fall, the Assyrians created a kingdom from Egypt to Iran (**Color Plate 196**). By 570 B.C., the Assyrian kingdom had been swallowed up by the Babylonians (**Color Plate 197**). In 539 B.C., the Persians (**Color Plate 86**) dispatched the Babylonians. And then in the 300s B.C., Europeans marched through the Middle East and toppled the last of the great ancient Mesopotamian powers (**Color Plate 88**).

In much of the Middle East, the ancient states, cultures, and religions are gone. Today, the Hittites do not rule modern Turkey, nor do the Assyrians. The Babylonians don't hold it. None of these ancient peoples persist as kingdoms in Iraq, Syria, or Jordan. Instead, the Arab

Muslim conquests of the first millennium A.D. ushered in a new empire, a new religion, and a new language.

In modern Iran, a case could be made that the ancient Persians have persisted. We saw the evidence for their genealogical endurance in chapter 8. Linguistically, Persian continues as the official language of modern Iran: *Farsī*, a descendant of Old Persian. But even Iran has not escaped the impact of the Arab conquests. More than 99% of Iranians are professing Muslims.

A very different fate awaited the ancient Israelites.

At its height (**Color Plate 198**), the Israelite political realm never achieved the same geographic domination as the Hittites, Assyrians, Babylonians, and Persians. Israelite rule lasted several centuries but most of that time as a divided kingdom. The northern half persisted only into the 700s B.C. when it fell to Assyrian invaders (compare **Color Plate 198** to **Color Plate 196**). The southern kingdom of Judah held on longer — but weakly. Under King Hezekiah, the Assyrians were repulsed, but Judah remained a tiny island in a sea of Assyrian rule (**Color Plate 196**). Finally, in 587/586 B.C., the Babylonians conquered Judah (**Color Plate 197**). The period of Israelite rule closed. But not permanently.

Today, the nation of Israel (**Color Plate 199**) overlaps a significant chunk of its ancestral lands (**Color Plate 198**). Based on religious profession, three-fourths of the Israeli population is Jewish. Hebrew is one of the official languages. And Jewish ancestry is a requirement for citizenship.[2]

From a historical perspective, it shouldn't have turned out this way. Hittites, Assyrians, Babylonians, and Persians were not the targets of Hitler's murderous obsessions during the Second World War. The Jews were. Millions of Jewish deaths later, the Third Reich ended, and the Jewish people began to rise again. In 1948, the modern state of Israel was born. It's a remarkable, if tumultuous, persistence.

Has the same story played out in the Y chromosome?

From a strictly Old Testament perspective, you'd expect the answer to be yes. According to the book of Genesis, *Israel* was the name given to the patriarch Jacob (Genesis 32:28), the son of Isaac, the son of Abraham. Israelites are called *Hebrews* because Abraham was the great-great-great-great-grandson of *Eber* (Genesis 11:16–26).

---

2. https://www.israeltoday.co.il/read/how-to-obtain-citizenship-in-israel/.

And the Hebrews are known as a *Semitic* people because Eber was the great-grandson of Shem, one of Noah's three sons (Genesis 11:10–14). Shem was on the Ark with Noah. Going the other direction from Jacob (Israel), the twelve tribes of Israel trace their ancestry to Jacob's twelve sons.[3] They entered Egypt in Joseph's day, then multiplied for hundreds of years, and then escaped in the 1400s B.C. In the Exodus, Moses, a descendant of Jacob's third son, Levi, led them out of Egypt through the Red Sea. Moses' brother Aaron was the first high priest, the leader of Israel's elaborate sacrificial religious system.

Males play an enormous role in Jewish history and in defining Jewish identity.

Furthermore, for thousands of years, Jews have maintained tight-knit religious communities wherever they have lived. To this day, a group of Jewish men — the *Cohanim* — claim descent from the priestly line of Israel. Surely a people as resilient as the Jews would have a clear Y chromosome signature. In 1997, the scientific community announced that they had discovered one.[4]

Twelve years later, they added to the evidence.[5] Michael Hammer and his colleagues found haplogroup *J-P58* in nearly half of the Cohanim. Among non-priestly Israelites, it occurred at a frequency of 14%.

So far, so good.

In retrospect, however, several aspects of this study should have given pause. If a Jewish priestly lineage exists, then it should trace back to one man: Aaron, the brother of Moses. The authors acknowledged this, yet they also said that their data indicated "several founding lineages within the Cohanim."[6] In other words, their "Jewish priestly Y chromosome lineage" did *not* arise from one male.

In terms of timing, the authors concluded that this lineage had arisen roughly 2,000 to 4,000 years ago — right around the time of the origin of the Jewish nation. However, their conclusions rested on the larger framework of the mainstream timescale — a timescale that is contradicted by the Y chromosome data itself (see chapter 6). When converted to a time of origin that is compatible with the Y chromosome-based chronology, the origin of *J-P58* moves up into the A.D. era.

---

3. Manasseh and Ephraim were sons of Jacob's son Joseph.
4. Skorecki et al. (1997).
5. Hammer et al. (2009).
6. Hammer et al. (2009), p. 715.

Finally, their "priestly" *J-P58* lineage is itself a subset of haplogroup *J1*. As we observed in chapter 8, haplogroup *J1* looks like it's connected to the ancient Hittite lineage, which is a branch of the Indo-European haplogroup *I-J*. The Jewish language, Hebrew, does not belong to the Indo-European language family.

Perhaps this attempt-and-miss at finding a Jewish lineage is to be expected. Historically, Jewish Y chromosome ancestry became harder to measure in the early A.D. era. Since then, mainstream Judaism has defined Jewish ancestry in terms of *maternal* inheritance rather than *paternal* inheritance.[7] It's worth asking if a distinctly Jewish Y chromosome lineage should exist.

In light of what we discussed in chapters 5 through 12, it's probably not even worth attempting to predict an answer. Instead, it's better to stubbornly investigate until an answer emerges.

The questions we need to ask are straightforward: Do males exist today who can trace an unbroken line of descent — via their Y chromosome — back to Abraham? Like the Jewish people as a whole, has the Jewish male genetic lineage persisted in the face of seemingly impossible odds? Finding the answers to these questions has turned out to be much harder than it looks.

Same Song, Another Verse?

Among living Jewish males, the Y chromosome data present a complicated picture. Even among the Cohanim, haplogroup *J-P58* (i.e., *J1*) is one of at least twelve haplogroups that exist (see the following table).[8] In other words, Jewish populations — even Jewish priestly populations — are just like the rest of the groups we've observed: They have a mixed paternal heritage.

In light of Jewish history, this mixture is unsurprising. During the Exodus from Egypt, the Israelite nation was joined by a "mixed multitude" (Exodus 12:38). In other words, the nation of Israel began ethnically heterogeneous. Once in the land of Canaan, they failed to drive out the indigenous inhabitants, so much so that some Israelites even ended up intermarrying with the Canaanites.[9] Later in Israelite history, the Assyrians conquered the northern tribes and resettled them

---

7. Cohen (2000), p. 263.
8. Raw data from Hammer et al. (2009).
9. See the Book of Judges.

Haplogroup	% of Cohanim	% of Israelites
E1b1b	7.0	18.7
C	0.0	0.4
F	0.0	0.5
G	3.3	9.8
H	1.9	0.3
I	0.5	3.0
J	0.0	0.1
J1	46.0	14.9
J2	29.3	21.0
N	0.0	1.2
L	0.5	0.3
Q	0.9	4.7
R1a	2.3	4.7
R1b	6.0	11.5
R2	0.9	6.1
T	1.4	2.7

far away from their Israelite homelands. In the southern kingdom of Judah, the Babylonians marched Jewish captives off to Babylon. Other Jews fled to Egypt.

Intermingling has been a regular part of Israelite history.

The Diaspora also suggests an explanation for the abundance of *J1* and *J2* among modern Jews. After the Babylonian conquest, some Jews remained in the Middle East. Over a millennium later, in the A.D. 600s, they would have been contemporaries of the growing religious community of Arab Muslims. By that time, haplogroup *J1* was likely in the Arabian Peninsula (see chapter 8). Is it any surprise, then, that modern Jews show up strongly in *J1*?

Later in the A.D. era, Jews were also found in Europe. Some fled persecution and landed in the Ottoman Empire. The migrations of Turkish peoples from Central Asia in the A.D. 1000s would have brought haplogroup *J2* from Persian lands into the Ottoman domains (see chapter 8). Is it any surprise, then, that modern Jews also have significant levels of *J2*?

Among the rest of the haplogroups that exist in modern Jewish men, few stand out as good candidates for an ancient Israelite lineage. After *J1* and *J2*, the next most abundant lineage is *E1b1b* (see table above). Like *J1, E1b1b* seems to reflect the history of Arab activity (see chapter 5). Before that, it seems to have been in northeast Africa. At the beginning of their history as a nation, the Israelites were in northeast Africa — in Egypt. Their sojourn ended at the Exodus centuries before *E1b1b* split from *E1b1a* (see **Color Plate 41**). After the Babylonian conquest in the 500s B.C., some Israelites returned to Egypt. Perhaps during the latter stay the Jews picked up *E1b1b* in Egypt. Or they may have acquired it later in Arabia, at the same time they were incorporated into *J1* lineages.

After *E1b1b*, haplogroups *R1b* and *G* have the next highest levels in the Cohanim (see table above). Haplogroup *R1b* is strongly Western European — but originally Central Asian (see chapter 7). Haplogroup *G* also seems to be Central Asian in origin, but more specifically Turkish. None of those associations bring us back to Abraham, Isaac, and Jacob.

Several haplogroups exist in Jews at even lower frequencies (see table above). Among these, none immediately suggest an Israelite heritage. Like *R1b*, the low frequency *R1a*, *R2*, and *Q* lineages arose in Central Asia (see chapters 7, 9, 12). Conversely, haplogroup *I* shares an ancestor with *J* and appears to be European — and ultimately Indo-European — in origin (see chapter 8). Again, this doesn't connect us back to Moses and Aaron.

Of the haplogroups that remain (*C, F, H, N, L, T*), only two are enriched in the Cohanim — *H* and *L*. The latter is almost non-existent in both Cohanim and non-priestly Israelites. The former is found heavily in or near India (see chapter 9). Consistent with this pattern, Cohanim belonging to *H* in this study happened to be residents of India or Iran. In other words, these individuals appear to have acquired *H* locally, not from an ancient Semitic source.

Subtracting *H* and *L* from our list leaves only haplogroups *C, F, N*, and *T*. Haplogroups *C, F*, and *N* exist in non-priestly Israelites but are undetectable in this sample of Cohanim. This leaves only *T* as a candidate.

Is haplogroup T originally Jewish? It's not enriched in Cohanim. And in this study, it exists in less than 3% of non-priestly Jews. Not exactly encouraging statistics.

Globally, T exists on three continents — Europe, Africa, and Asia (**Color Plate 200**). On each continent, it shows up in few countries. And where it does show up, it exists at low levels. The Jewish T frequencies reflect this low abundance pattern.

So far, nothing terribly promising in these results.

However, both North/north-central Africa and the Middle East show higher levels of T than does Europe. North/north-central Africa and the Middle East are both tied to Jewish history.

In addition, when we shift our focus away from the frequency of T at a national level to the frequency of T at ethnic and religious levels, the picture becomes more intriguing. Among populations in the Middle East, Iran, and Africa, haplogroup T tends to be significantly enriched in Jews. In some cases (Iraq, Iran), the level of haplogroup T in the resident Jewish population reaches 10% to 20% (see table on following page).[10] This is far higher than any of the national levels in **Color Plate 200**.

The most intriguing levels of T are found in a sub-Saharan African group. The *Lemba* people reside in South Africa and Zimbabwe (see the star in **Color Plate 200**), yet they claim Jewish ancestry. They also might not be indigenous to southern Africa:

> According to oral traditions of origin, the Lemba claim to come from a place in the north called Sena (sometimes Sena One). The Lemba habitually refer to themselves as "the white men who came from Sena."[11]

Today, the Lemba have the physical characteristics of dark-skinned sub-Saharan Africans.[12]

In terms of Y chromosome haplogroups, one study found that almost a fifth of the Lemba belonged to haplogroup T (see following table). Direct comparisons to national levels of T in Zimbabwe and

---

10. Raw data from Mendez et al. (2011).
11. https://www.jewishvirtuallibrary.org/lemba.
12. https://www.jewishvirtuallibrary.org/zimbabwe-s-quot-black-jews-quot-the-lemba-people.

Traced

Region	Population	National % Haplogroup T	Jewish % Haplogroup T	Fold-enrichement for Jewish T
Near Eastern	Turks	1.1	5.9	5
Near Eastern	Iraqis	5.6	21.9	4
Near Eastern	Iranians	1.4	13.6	10
Near Eastern	Yemenis	0.0	6.8	7
North African	Ethiopians	6.9	4.8	0.7
South African	Lemba	(none)	17.6	18

South Africa are not currently available. But *T* is generally absent from sub-Saharan Africa. If true, then the Lemba are more enriched for *T* than are the Middle Eastern and Iranian Jewish groups.

These Lemba *T* individuals are not found scattered throughout the *T* branches. Around the A.D. 300s to 600s, haplogroup *T* split into *T1a1* and *T1a2* branches (**Color Plate 201**). Jews from Iraq and Iran reside exclusively in *T1a1*; Lemba are found exclusively in *T1a2*.

Why?

If the Lemba did indeed come from the north; and if they are indeed of Jewish heritage; and if they are linked on haplogroup *T* to Jews in the northern/northeast part of the Middle East (Iraq, Iran), then it's plausible that they originated from lands between Iraq/Iran and South Africa. That's a lot of *ifs*. But these *ifs* suggest that one of the potential Lemba homelands is the Arabian Peninsula — a region known to have harbored Jews in the early centuries A.D.

It's also an area that, in the A.D. 600s, would have been threatening to Jewish existence. Mohammad began his Islamic conquests from Arabia. His antipathy toward Jews who refused to convert to Islam is well-known. It's not hard to imagine that, in the face of Muslim opposition, Jews would flee in all directions. Some could have gone north/northeast. Others, across the Red Sea to Africa, and then south.

Together, these lines of evidence suggested that a link may indeed exist between Abraham and haplogroup *T*.

The deeper history of *T* added to this evidence.

An Ancient Separation

Before *T* became its own haplogroup, it was joined to another haplogroup deep in human history. In the 2200s B.C. to 1900s B.C., haplogroup *T* joined haplogroup *L* (**Color Plate 202**). This date range overlaps the time of the early Israelite patriarchs: Abraham, Isaac, and Jacob.

Could *L* also be a descendant of Abraham?

Initially, geography seemed to suggest that the answer was *no*. Today, *L* is concentrated in South Asia, and spills over into Central Asia and parts of the Middle East (**Color Plate 203**). Unlike haplogroup *T*, haplogroup *L* does not have a distribution suggestive of an indigenous Middle Eastern lineage. In fact, the distributions of *L* and *T* are mostly non-overlapping (**Color Plate 204**). Where they occur together, one haplogroup exists at levels 2 to 8 times higher than the other. Otherwise, they reside in separate locations.

Nevertheless, at one point both *T* and *L* were in the same location. They must have been since they are genetically linked (see **Color Plate 202**). Then, in the 2200s B.C. to 1900s B.C. (**Color Plate 202**), something caused *T* and *L* to disperse.

But what? The history of the patriarchs suggests a number of possible explanations. Each of the patriarchs had sons who went their separate ways and who could have ended up living far from the Middle East. Abraham's son Ishmael founded tribes of his own; the Ishmaelites and Israelites (through Abraham's son Isaac) mostly kept to themselves. Isaac's son Esau founded the Edomites. The Edomites largely maintained a separate identity from the Israelites who came through Isaac's other son, Jacob. Jacob's twelve sons originally lived as part of a unified nation. But after Solomon's death, the 10 northern tribes separated from the southern ones. Division between north and south became permanent when the Assyrians conquered the northern tribes and resettled them elsewhere.

In each of these scenarios, *T* could have belonged to the line eventually leading to the southern tribes of Israel. In other words, *T* could have been the line of Abraham, Isaac, and Jacob. Haplogroup *L* could have represented the splinter population — the Ishmaelites, Edomites, or Lost Tribes of Israel (i.e., the northern tribes conquered by Assyria).

In the context of these scenarios, the South/Central Asian distribution of haplogroup *L* contained an unexpected hint. Today, *L* exists among the peoples of Afghanistan at levels between 6% and 7% (see **Color Plate 203** and supplemental online data). The major ethnic group of Afghanistan, the *Pashtun* people, also possesses *L* at a similar frequency.[13] With regards to their own origins, the Pashtuns claim descent from King Saul of ancient Israel through a purported grandson named *Afghana* (hence, the name of their country, *Afghanistan*).[14] Perhaps *L* does indeed connect to the line of Abraham.

How can we know whether this connection is real? Though we've traced *T* and *L* back to the time of Abraham, we haven't yet reached the beginning of the *T-L* lineage.

The deepest history of *T-L* revealed a spectacular confirmation of the connection to Abraham's genealogy.

It also moved us one step closer to uncovering the beginning of the story of the rest of the world.

In the following sections, the discussion wades a bit into the weeds of genetics. Normally, I would move such technical discussions into an appendix or into the endnotes. However, the implications of these details are so profound that I've left them in the main text. They hold the most explosive insights to the beginning of human history.

The Deepest Genetic Relationships

On the Y chromosome tree, the *T-L* lineage eventually joins with the ancestor of the *N-O* lineage (chapter 10), the *K-M-S* lineage (chapter 11), and the *Q-R* lineage (chapters 7, 9, 12). This fact holds a key clue to the history of Israel and of the world, but in **Color Plate 22**, it's hard to see. The display in **Color Plate 22** is zoomed out too far to see how the branches connect deep in history.

Let's reset our visual bearings via an alternate display of the same tree.

Color Plate 205 is the same as **Color Plate 22**, but with four changes to how I've displayed the data. I've rotated the tree 90 degrees (compare the direction of the Time arrow in **Color Plate 205** to

---

13. Di Cristofaro et al. (2013).
14. https://www.britannica.com/topic/Pashtun, accessed May 10, 2021.

the direction in **Color Plate 22**). I've also collapsed the details of the branches into shaded triangles. Effectively, this brings the deep roots of each haplogroup into closer visual proximity. I've also zoomed in on the early branches, which cuts off the long lengths of haplogroups *C, B, A, D, E2, E1a, E1b1b,* and *E1b1a* in **Color Plate 205**. Unlike **Color Plate 22**, I've also displayed the number of DNA differences along each branch in **Color Plate 205** — a change which will become critical shortly. For the moment, it should now be obvious in **Color Plate 205** that the nearest genealogical neighbors to haplogroup *T-L* are haplogroups *N-O, K-M-S,* and *Q-R*.

In a sense, we could have inferred this fact from the observations we made in previous chapters. We discovered that the deep roots of haplogroup *H* are genealogically close to the deep roots of haplogroup *I-J* (chapter 9). We also discovered that the deep roots of *N-O* are genealogically close to the deep roots of *H* and *I-J* (chapter 10). In fact, **Color Plate 149** included *T* and *L* in the display. **Color Plate 149** showed a connection between *T-L* and *N-O*, and this connection occurred before the combined *T-L* and *N-O* lineages linked back to *I-J* and *H*.

With our new visual bearings in hand, we can dive once again into the earliest history of *T-L*.

However, as soon as we attempt to do so, we run into another technical hurdle that we'll need to clear before we proceed. Notice in **Color Plate 205** that precise numbers of DNA differences separate the various haplogroups. These DNA differences conceal a surprising connection to the history of ancient Israel. To pull back the curtain on what these DNA differences mean, let's again regain our bearings. But this time we'll need, not new visual bearings, but a new perspective on the details of Y chromosome copying errors.

Let's acquire this perspective in several steps.

As a first step, let's derive a new perspective on the timescale embedded in the Y chromosome tree. Recall from chapter 6 that we put the beginning of the Y chromosome tree about 4,500 years ago with Noah. For the last 4,500 years, let's assume that men were around 30 years old when they fathered the next generation. If we divide 4,500 years by 30 years per generation, then about 150 generations have elapsed since Noah.

As a second step, let's consider how many mutations — Y chromosome copying errors — occurred from the beginning of the

Y chromosome tree until now. In **Color Plate 22**, notice how the total number of DNA differences from the start of the tree to the present varies by haplogroup. The branches for haplogroups *F, G, H, J2, J1, I, L, T, O, N, M, K, S, Q, R2, R1b,* and *R1a* are shorter than those for haplogroups *C, B, A, D, E2, E1a, E1b1b,* and *E1b1a* (see **Color Plate 22**). (This is one reason I had to truncate the display in **Color Plate 205**.) However, if you look carefully at **Color Plate 22** or at **Color Plate 205**, you'll notice that the branches for haplogroups *F, G, H, J2, J1, I, L, T, O, N, M, K, S, Q, R2, R1b,* and *R1a* end in roughly the same physical location. On average, about 435 to 440 DNA differences separate the beginning of the tree from the tips of these haplogroups (see supplemental online tables and data for full justification for this statement).

These hundreds of DNA differences imply a rate at which Y chromosome copying errors occur.

As a third step, let's calculate this rate. Take the number of generations since Noah (i.e., 150; see above) and divide it into 440 Y chromosome DNA differences: 440 DNA differences / 150 generations = 2.9 DNA differences per generation. This number represents the predicted number of Y chromosome DNA mutations per generation. Since mutations happen as whole numbers, let's round 2.9 to 3. The Y chromosome mutation rate adds three DNA differences to the Y chromosome tree every generation.

In chapter 6, we discussed empirical measurements of the rate of Y chromosome mutations (copying errors) per generation. We explored how many mutations fathers pass on to their sons. In chapter 6, I presented the conclusion: That the rate implies a recent origin for humanity. What I didn't state is the absolute value of the empirically discovered rate. The two high quality DNA mutation rate measurements uncovered a rate of 3 to 5 Y chromosome mutations per generation.

This is exactly in line with the predicted number of mutations based on the DNA differences in the Y chromosome tree.[15] In other words, the

---

15. Again, for the longer branches, these results imply that their mutation rates were or are faster than this. For the longest branches (i.e., the *Mbo* individuals in haplogroup A in the Karmin et al. (2015) study), I expect their rate to still be highly elevated. For branches shorter than the longest haplogroup A individuals, but still longer than 440 DNA letters (i.e., the branches in haplogroups *C, D, B, E,* and subgroups within *A*), I'm suspicious that their mutation rates were higher in the past but have since slowed down to something along the lines of 3 to 5 mutations per generation.

predicted number of mutations per generation (3) is also the lower end of the range of empirically measured mutations per generation.

Now we have the tools by which to understand the meaning of the DNA differences in the deepest part of the tree.

Let's begin by finding the part of the tree that leads to haplogroups *T-L, N-O, K-M-S,* and *Q-R* in **Color Plate 205**. You should see the number 16 above the branch that leads from the beginning of the tree to the first branching division. On one side of this division, you'll find branches that lead to haplogroups *N-O, K-M-S,* and *Q-R*. On the other side of this division, you should see 24 DNA differences on a branch leading to haplogroups *T* and *L*.

Now apply the mutation rate: 16 DNA differences / 3 DNA mutations per generation = 5.3 generations. Let's round this to a whole number: 5 generations. Now apply the mutation rate to the second number: 24 DNA differences / 3 DNA mutations per generation = 8 generations.

In other words, 5 generations after the beginning of human history, the ancestor of a purportedly Jewish lineage (*T*) also gave rise to an East Asian lineage (*N-O*), a New Guinea/Australian Aboriginal lineage (*K-M-S*), and a Central Asian/American lineage (*Q-R*). Then, 8 generations later, the *T* lineage split from *L*, with the *T* men staying in the Middle East for a period of time, while the *L* men eventually landed in Central/South Asia.

What could possibly explain this history? It turns out that the ancient Israelite records contained a genealogical tree with a near-identical match to this genetic history. The match also uncovered the answer to the question of how humanity arose.

In the next few sections, the level of biblical and scientific detail that we'll engage is high. But with a little patience, I think you'll find the outcome to be well worth the effort.

History According to Israel

Similar to our approach to the deep history in the Y chromosome tree, we'll start by reorienting our perspective on Israel's history and on the echo of this history in the Y chromosome tree. We'll identify big-picture parallels between the two. Then we'll dive into the fine details of each record and compare the match between them.

The Israelite documents most relevant to their earliest history are found in the Torah, in the book of Genesis. Genesis traces Abraham's line through his father Terah back to Noah's son Shem in nine genealogical steps (see **Color Plate 206**; in **Color Plate 206**, I've broken the generation numbering scheme into two parts for reasons that will become clear in the following paragraphs).

Genesis 11 gives the genealogy in narrow father-son terms back to Noah's son Shem. Genesis 10 details some of Abraham's early relatives who were not in his direct ancestral line. *These early relatives of Abraham gave rise to the peoples in the rest of the world*. Genesis 9 makes this claim explicit: "Now the sons of Noah who went out of the ark were Shem, Ham, and Japheth. And Ham was the father of Canaan. **These three were the sons of Noah, and from these the whole earth was populated**." (emphasis added, v. 18–19). Genesis 10 lists the offspring of Shem, Ham, and Japheth — the men from whom the whole earth was populated.

I have reproduced the Genesis 10 family tree in **Color Plate 207**. In **Color Plate 207** and in subsequent color plates, you'll find a consistent color scheme: Blue for Shem's line and for genetic candidates for Shem's line; green for Japheth's line and for genetic candidates for Japheth's line; pink for Ham's line and for genetic candidates for Ham's line.

At a minimum, Genesis 10 implies that the paternal genealogical tree of the world would have three original branches — one each for Shem, Ham, and Japheth. Since all three boys inherited their Y chromosomes from the same father, Noah, these three branches would also collapse into a single ancestor. *This is what the Y chromosome tree reveals* (**Color Plate 208**; see also **Color Plate 209** where I zoomed in on "the beginning" section of **Color Plate 205**).

While this result doesn't directly connect haplogroup *T-L* to Abraham, it gets us one step closer to doing so. A deeper look at the names in Genesis 10 makes the link even more likely.

After Genesis 10, the rest of the Old Testament focuses heavily on Israel and its neighbors (see the shaded blue area in **Color Plate 210**). Many of the neighbors are explicitly associated with their Genesis 10 ancestors. The *Canaanites* (descendants of Ham) are mentioned repeatedly. Assyrians (descendants of Shem via *Asshur*), Egyptians (descendants of Ham via *Mizraim*), Ethiopians/Kushites (descendants of Ham via *Cush*), Medes (descendants of Japheth via *Madai*), and even

Greeks (see Daniel 8; descendants of Japheth via *Javan*) all play a role in the history of the Israelites and are identified in the Old Testament text (**Color Plate 211**).

The partitions in the Y chromosome tree replicate these biblical identifications. In chapter 8, we saw that haplogroup *I-J* makes a good candidate for the Indo-European peoples. Greeks are classified as Indo-Europeans, and Greeks descended from Japheth. Notice the partition into which haplogroup *I-J* falls on the Y chromosome tree — one to which we can tentatively assign the label *Japheth* (**Color Plate 212**). Chapters 5 and 6 associated several haplogroups (*E1a, E1b1a, E1b1b, E2,* and possibly *A* and *B*) with ancient Egypt/ancient Ethiopia, both descendants of Ham. Notice how these haplogroups belong to a separate partition on the Y chromosome tree — one to which we can tentatively assign the label *Ham* (**Color Plate 212**). Earlier in this chapter, we identified haplogroup *T* as a good candidate for the lineage of the Jews. Notice how this haplogroup falls into a third partition on the Y chromosome tree (**Color Plate 212**), exactly as expected from the biblical text. We can tentatively assign the label *Shem* to this partition.

The associations between sons of Noah and Y chromosome tree partitions become even stronger in light of what the Bible does *not* say about the men in Genesis 10. For example, many of Joktan's sons are mentioned in Genesis 10 and nowhere else, apart from a repetition of the Genesis 10 genealogy found in 1 Chronicles 1. This latter reference adds no information on who these sons of Joktan gave rise to.

Conversely, many parts of the world receive little to no mention in the Bible. Primarily, these regions are all at a significant distance from the Near Eastern sphere of the ancient Israelites. The Old Testament is almost completely silent on the post-Genesis 10 events in sub-Saharan Africa, South Asia, Central Asia, Siberia, the Far East, New Guinea, Australia, the Pacific, and the Americas (see the stars in **Color Plate 210**).

Putting these two facts together, we can identify candidate ancestors for the peoples who arose at great distances from the Near East. Those Genesis 10 names on which Scripture is silent are good candidates for giving rise to peoples in regions of the globe on which Scripture is also silent.

Among the three sons of Noah, Japheth has the fewest candidates for giving rise to peoples at a significant distance from the Near

Eastern sphere of the ancient Israelites. Shem and Ham have the most candidates — more than twice as many as Japheth (**Color Plate 213**).

Previous chapters in this book have already associated major Y chromosome haplogroups to these far-flung regions, and we did so independent of these biblical observations. In chapters 5 and 6, we found the dominant haplogroups of Africa, including of sub-Saharan Africa (*A, B, E*). In chapter 7, we began to identify the haplogroups of Central Asia (*R1b, R1a*). Chapters 8 (Turkic *G*), 9 (South Asian *R2*), and 12 (American *Q*) added to the list of originally Central Asian haplogroups. Chapter 9 uncovered a good candidate for the earliest South Asian lineage (*H*). Chapter 10 described the major lineages of the Far East and of Siberia (*O, N*). In chapter 11, we observed several lineages that are dominant in East Asia, Siberia, and the Pacific (*D, C, K, M, S*).

All of these lineages belong to the candidate lines of Shem and Ham and not to the candidate line of Japheth (**Color Plate 214**). The lineages (*I, J1, J2*) of the candidate line of Japheth all seem to be focused on the Near Eastern sphere of ancient Israel (**Color Plate 215**), whereas the lineages of Japheth's brothers — Shem and Ham — reached the far-flung corners of the earth (**Color Plate 215**).

These results imply specific origins for each of the major haplogroups. The association between haplogroup *T* and the Jews suggests that haplogroups *T, L, O, N, S, K, M, Q, R2, R1b*, and *R1a* all descended from Shem (**Color Plates 212, 214**). The association between haplogroup *I* and the ancient Greeks implies that haplogroups *I, J1*, and *J2* are all descendants of Japheth (**Color Plates 212, 214**). The link between haplogroup *E* (and possibly *A* and *B*) and Egypt/Ethiopia intimates that haplogroups *H, G, F, C, B, A*, and *E* are all descendants of Ham (**Color Plates 212, 214**).

Together, these results suggested that the big-picture elements of the early biblical history of Israel found an echo in the Y chromosome tree.

The fine details of this history made the echo loud and clear.

Step by Genealogical Step

Let's return to the rate of Y chromosome mutations that we explored earlier.

Recall that, on average, three Y chromosome mutations represent a single generation. Up to five mutations might as well. But *three* is the number common between two independent studies,[16] and it is precisely the number needed to explain the length of the branches on the Y chromosome tree. We just observed that this rate implies a specific number of generations between the beginning of human history and the origin of the putative Jewish lineage, haplogroup *T*. Five generations — sixteen mutations — elapsed between the beginning of human history and the first major haplogroup division (see **Color Plate 209**). Another eight generations — twenty-four mutations — elapsed before haplogroup *T* separated from haplogroup *L* (see **Color Plate 209**).

Scripture seems to tell a slightly different story. In Shem's line, the sons of Joktan represent some of the best candidates for the distant peoples of the world (**Color Plate 213**). However, the Jewish line separated from the rest of Shem's lineage via Peleg, Joktan's brother (**Color Plates 206, 216**). The father of Peleg and Joktan, *Eber*, represents the last generation born before the major split between the Jewish line and the candidate lineages of many far-flung peoples (**Color Plates 213, 216**). Yet Eber was the fourth generation to be born after Noah, not the fifth (**Color Plates 213, 216**).

This result implies a slight discrepancy. The Y chromosome tree suggests an extra generation than the biblical record. The 16 mutations from the beginning to the separation of *T-L* from *N-O-K-M-S-Q-R* represents the fifth generation, not the fourth (see **Color Plate 216**). The results are close — just one generation off. But the extra generation is cause for pause.

Recent research suggests an explanation for the discrepancy. Several independent studies have uncovered a relationship between the age of the father and the number of mutations that he passes on to his offspring.[17] The older the father, the more mutations he gives his children.

Noah is the oldest father we have on record. "And **Noah was five hundred years old**, and Noah begot Shem, Ham, and Japheth" (emphasis added, Genesis 5:32). Perhaps Noah passed on more than three Y chromosome mutations to his sons.

But how many more than three? Unfortunately, the only published results we have at the moment revolve around mutations in the rest of the DNA — not in the Y chromosome. No one has yet published a

---

16. Jeanson (2019).
17. E.g., see Maretty et al. (2017).

study on the relationship between a father's age and the number of Y chromosome mutations that he passes on to his sons. Furthermore, no one has — or will — publish empirical findings on what a *500-year-old* father will pass on to his sons. No one lives this long anymore.

A further complication to this question is the nature of the pre-Flood world. This was the world in which Noah was born, and into which his three sons were born. These considerations dampen our elevated mutation expectations.

Prior to Noah, the men in the biblical record lived for almost a millennium (see table below). The reason for this longevity is unknown. Presumably, since these men were just a few generations

	Patriarch	Lifespan
Pre-Flood	Adam	930
	Seth	912
	Enosh	905
	Cainan	910
	Mahalalel	895
	Jared	962
	Enoch	365
	Methuselah	969
	Lamech	777
	Noah	950
Post-Flood	Shem	600
	Arphaxad	438
	Salah	433
	Eber	464
	Peleg	239
	Reu	239
	Serug	230
	Nahor	119
	Terah	205
	Abraham	175
	Isaac	180
	Jacob	147

removed from Adam's genome, which was created without error, these men harbored fewer mutations than we do. Perhaps they passed on fewer mutations as well. Furthermore, the geologic record indicates that the pre-Flood environment was dramatically different from the post-Flood environment.[18] It seems to have been more conducive to human existence. This may have also played a role in the longevity of fathers. Either way, it's entirely possible that these ancient men passed on *fewer* mutations than do fathers in the post-Flood world.

Consistent with these considerations, the lifespans of fathers dropped off dramatically after the Flood (see table at left). This result fits the possibility that post-Flood men had a more corrupted genetic state, which could have arisen via a sudden increase of the rate of mutations.

In light of these theoretical concerns, what can we conclude about how many mutations Noah passed on to his sons? Theory pulls us in both directions, toward higher and lower mutational expectations. How can we decide between these two opposing lines of thought? Instead of relying on theory, let's try to derive the mutation number from the Y chromosome tree. Then we'll explore whether the number gives internally consistent results. Internal inconsistencies would suggest we're on the wrong track. Internal consistency would encourage our pursuit.

On the putative Hamitic[19] side of the tree (see pink box in **Color Plate 217**), four major lineages separated early in the history of the Hamitic line: Haplogroup *H*, haplogroup *G*, haplogroup *F*, and haplogroup *A-B-C-D-E*. These four Y chromosome lineages might represent Ham's four sons.[20] Even if they don't, 7 mutations preceded this splitting event (see lower red arrow in **Color Plate 217**). These 7

---

18. See Snelling, A. 2009. *Earth's Catastrophic Past: Geology, Creation and the Flood*. Dallas, TX: Institute for Creation Research.

19. I.e., the side descending from Noah's son Ham.

20. A technical caveat: In **Color Plate 217**, a single mutation separates *G* from *H*, and three mutations separate *G* from *F* and *A-B-C-D-E*. At a minimum, this would seem to imply that a generation or two elapsed between the origin of some of these lineages. If so, then these four major branches would not seem to be the four sons of Ham. Perhaps a son and some grandsons, but not four separate sons. However, the precise structure at the base of these lineages varies from study to study (e.g., compare it to the tree in the Supplementary Figure 14 in Poznik et al. (2016); also, see the tree in Figure 1 of Francalacci et al. (2013)). I'm suspicious that more intense sequencing of men in these haplogroups will result in four sibling lineages.

mutations represent the upper limit for mutations that Noah would have passed on to Ham.[21]

Now apply these 7 mutations to Shem's side of the tree. Presumably, if Noah passed on 7 mutations to Ham, then he also passed on 7 mutations to Shem. On Shem's side of the tree, sixteen mutations separate the beginning from the split between *T-L* and *N-O-K-M-S-Q-R*. If we subtract 7 mutations from 16 total mutations (to account for the mutations from Noah to Shem), we're left with 9 mutations. At 3 mutations per generation, 9 mutations represent three generations (**Color Plate 217**). This implies a total of only four generations between the beginning and the split between *T-L* and *N-O-K-M-S-Q-R*. It also resolves our earlier discrepancy.

Take a look at another genealogical detail on Shem's side of the tree. Notice how 1 mutation, then 4 mutations, separate the *N-O* lineage and the *K-M-S* and *Q-R* lineages from the *T-L* lineage (see the two red arrows at the top of **Color Plate 217**). The precise relationship among these three major lineages — *N-O*, *K-M-S*, and *Q-R* — varies from study to study (which is why I put an asterisk by the 4 in **Color Plate 218**).[22] But in each case, it seems that one round of 3 or 4 mutations — which is a single generational step as per the measured mutation rate of 3 to 5 mutations (per generation) — transpired after *T-L* broke away from these three groups.

So far, the evidence we've uncovered is in remarkable alignment with the early history of the descendants of Shem. When we factor in the extra mutations between Noah and Shem, the timing of the *T-L* split aligns with the genealogies of Genesis 10 and 11 (**Color Plate 218**). The mutational steps also imply that the *N-O*, *K-M-S*, and *Q-R* lineages may have been descendants of Eber, or perhaps Joktan (**Color Plate 218**). Each of these three lineages lead to people living in the lands of East Asia, New Guinea/Australia, and Central Asia/Americas, respectively — lands that are all far from the Middle East. This is consistent with our biblical expectations about the fate of the sons of Shem (**Color Plates 213, 218**).

Together, all of these lines of evidence are consistent with individuals in haplogroup *T* being descendants of Abraham, Isaac, and Jacob.

---

21. If haplogroup *H* arose from, say, a grandson of Noah, then 7 mutations are the mutations that Noah passed on to Ham *and* mutations that Ham passed on to his son.

22. E.g., see the tree in the Supplementary Figure 14 in Poznik et al. (2016).

These results are also consistent with haplogroup *L* being the Lost Tribes of Israel. Notice how the 8 generational steps from the origin of *T-L* (i.e., its separation from *N-O, K-M-S,* and *Q-R*) to the origin of *L* falls right in line with the timing of the split in Jacob's 12 sons (**Color Plate 218**).

One caveat: A separate Y chromosome study identified only 21 mutations — 7 generations — from the origin of *T-L* (i.e., its separation from *N-O, K-M-S,* and *Q-R*) to the origin of *L*.[23] This would make the *L* men Edomites — descendants of Esau — rather than descendants of Jacob. Either way, the evidence is consistent with *L* also being in the line of Abraham.

Consider the far-reaching implications of these results. If all that we've explored is true, then *the blood of Abraham can be found in the dark-skinned peoples of Southern Africa* (**Color Plate 200**), *the lighter-skinned peoples of Western Europe* (**Color Plate 200**), *and the olive-skinned peoples of Thailand and Central Asia* (**Color Plate 203**).

Beyond the implications for Israel, these results also touched the beginning of the whole world.

How It Started

As we discussed in an earlier section, Genesis 9 and 10 claim that all the peoples of the earth descended from Shem, Ham, and Japheth. We've just observed a tight and detailed correlation between the biblical genealogical record for Shem and the Y chromosome tree (**Color Plate 218**). We also observed correlations between the biblical expectations for Ham and Japheth and the Y chromosome tree (**Color Plates 207–215**). Unfortunately, the biblical record for many of these people goes silent after Genesis 10.[24]

Genesis 11 tells us why. It also contains a critical clue to understanding why and how the beginning of human history transpired:

> Now the whole earth had one language and one speech. And it came to pass, as they journeyed from the east, that they found a plain in the land of Shinar, and they dwelt there. Then they said to one another, "Come, let us make bricks and

---

23. See the tree in the Supplementary Figure 14 in Poznik et al. (2016).
24. First Chronicles 1 is a later book, but the names in Genesis 10 are repeated there almost verbatim. No additional historical detail is provided for many of the Genesis 10 names in 1 Chronicles 1.

bake them thoroughly." They had brick for stone, and they had asphalt for mortar. And they said, "Come, let us build ourselves a city, and a tower whose top is in the heavens; let us make a name for ourselves, lest we be scattered abroad over the face of the whole earth."

But the LORD came down to see the city and the tower which the sons of men had built. And the LORD said, "Indeed the people are one and they all have one language, and this is what they begin to do; now nothing that they propose to do will be withheld from them. Come, let Us go down and there confuse their language, that they may not understand one another's speech." So the LORD scattered them abroad from there over the face of all the earth, and they ceased building the city. Therefore its name is called Babel, because there the LORD confused the language of all the earth; and from there the LORD scattered them abroad over the face of all the earth. (Genesis 11:1–11).

In other words, the people listed in Genesis 10 were part of the activity at Babel described in Genesis 11. The descendants of Noah's three sons were the builders of the city and tower at Babel. They all originally spoke a single language, but their evil designs precipitated the judgment of God. This verdict took a specific form: God supernaturally gave them different languages. The verdict also had a specific purpose: *To prevent their progress on the city and tower that they were building.*

Let's reflect on these observations. The earliest peoples were likely a small group; the short list of names in Genesis 10 (see **Color Plate 207**) implies as much. Yet, despite their small numbers, these people were technologically advanced enough to build a city and a tower. Their purpose in doing so was at odds with God's commands, and His judgment was *designed to inhibit their ability to work together.*

This would naturally shatter whatever cultural advances they had achieved to date. I don't say this simply in light of what we observed in the Americas in chapter 12. I say it because cultural shattering *was part of the stated purpose of the judgment.*

This shattering happened shortly after the beginning of human history. Genesis 10 places the event within the lifetime of Peleg: "To

Eber were born two sons: the name of one was Peleg [a Hebrew word meaning *division*], for in his days the earth was divided" (v. 25).[25] Peleg was born around 101 years after the Flood, and he lived for a total of 239 years. Therefore, the shattering occurred within the first four centuries after the beginning.

After the shattering, people would have moved away from Babel. The precise location of Babel is debated among biblical scholars, but it seems to have been somewhere in the Middle East. As people moved away from this Middle Eastern site, they would have settled in new locations, some of which were at great distances from Babel — locations like China, New Guinea, Australia, and the Americas.

Consistent with this history-and-spread-from-Babel, the earliest cradles of civilization arose in close proximity to the Near East. Those at greater distances arose later (**Color Plate 219**). There, these dispersed families would have restarted their lives with only a portion of the technological knowledge they once had as a larger community at Babel. They also would have had to start economically from scratch without any prior infrastructure, manufacturing, planted fields, or other aids to their survival. Hunting and gathering becomes a necessity when you're fleeing to an uninhabited place. In other words, once they landed in a new place, their immediate way of life would have been simple, or "primitive."

In **Color Plate 219**, I've given the dates for the cradles of civilization as mainstream science has assigned them. I've done this for two reasons, even though these dates will eventually be adjusted in light of the genetic results that we discussed in chapter 6. Though the absolute values are incorrect, these dates depict the relative relationship between geographic distance from the Middle East and time of origin. The absolute dates also provide context[26] for understanding history assigned to even earlier eras in the mainstream science temporal framework.

Presumably, these cradles arose shortly after Babel. This would have placed them within a few centuries after the beginning of human history. Therefore, events dated even earlier in the mainstream version of history, such as the rise and fall of the Neanderthals, the Stone Age,

---

25. In the context of Genesis 11:1–9 (see quote above), which describes how the *earth* was originally one language before it was divided by language, the *earth* in 10:25 seems to refer to humanity, not to the crust of our planet.

26. This line of reasoning was inspired by archaeology and geology collaborators in mainstream academia who graciously provided input on the research.

and the Agricultural Revolution, all would have transpired within these early centuries.

Viewed from this perspective, the slow-and-gradual narrative for human history disappears. Humanity still progresses from "primitive" to advanced, but the transition is a rapid one, consistent with the needs and trials of recently dispersed bands of people arriving in previously uninhabited areas.[27]

Finishing the Story

So far, we've left one major aspect of the human narrative unaddressed: What about the huge technological leap that we've witnessed since A.D. 1400? How does this fit the revised account of human history that we just derived? The history of human population growth suggests an explanation (**Color Plate 220**). The last 600 years experienced a rise in human population size unlike the previous 2,400 years combined. More people naturally entail more hands and more minds to innovate and do work. In turn, more innovation and more work tend to result in technological progress.

Given the contrast between the growth of the last 600 years and the growth of the prior 2,400 years, I would be tempted to refer to the recent centuries of human population growth as *unprecedented* — but only tempted to label them as such. From A.D. 1400 to now, the world population has increased quickly, but it hasn't doubled every generation. The earliest era of human history — the era before God's judgment at Babel — saw an even greater rate of increase.

Take a close look at **Color Plate 207** once again. Count the number of men in each generation. Starting with Shem, Ham, and Japheth, the male population increases from 3 (in generation 1) to 16 (in generation 2) to 36 (in generation 3). The average rate of increase across these generations isn't population doubling; it's population *tripling*.[28] Each generation entailed more hands and minds and work. No wonder they talked of building a city and a tower.

And then their purposes were thwarted. At the dawn of human history, mankind's cooperative advance was broken. And it's taken four thousand years to recover.

---

27. To be clear, I'm not espousing a view that evolution of apes to people occurred. I see a clear break and no common ancestry between the two. See Appendix B for more discussion.
28. Technically, it's even higher. The cube root of 36 is 3.3.

Chapter 13 Summary:

- Mainstream science invokes a single explanation for all of human pre-history and history: Slow and gradual evolution from simple to complex. In this view, the last 600 years (A.D. 1400 to the present) of rapid technological advancement are the culmination of millions of years of progress.
- The temporal framework for this mainstream narrative is inconsistent with the timescale implied by Y chromosome mutation rates. This raises the question anew of how human history began.
- Based on historical precedence in the Americas (chapter 12), humanity could have started in an advanced state, regressed to a more primitive state, and then progressed back to an advanced state.
- The ancient Israelites kept careful records of their own origins, and these records connect the ancestors of the ancient Israelites to the history of the rest of the world.
- The mainstream candidate for an ancient Israelite Y chromosome haplogroup, *J2*, is Indo-European in origin, not Semitic.
- Haplogroup *T* makes a compelling candidate for an ancient Jewish lineage based on its geographic distribution and its enrichment in modern Jewish populations.
- Genesis 10 and 11 detail the origin of the Abrahamic line, and the early Y chromosome history leading to the origin of haplogroup *T* is a point-for-point match to this biblical history:
  - * Genesis 10 implies that the paternal family tree of humanity has three fundamental branches. This is also what the Y chromosome tree reveals.
  - * The rest of the Old Testament reveals specific nation-state associations with specific names in Genesis 10. The partitions in the Y chromosome tree bear out these associations as expected from the biblical text.
  - * The rest of the Old Testament also suggests candidates from Genesis 10 as ancestors of peoples living at great distances from the Near East. Most of these candidates come from the lines of Shem and Ham, not from the

line of Japheth. The Y chromosome tree aligns with these expectations.

* Genesis 10 and 11 describe a specific, step-by-step sequence of genealogical events (1) leading to the line of Abraham and (2) separating the line of Abraham from a lineage with many candidates for ancestors of peoples living at great distances from the Near East. The DNA differences deep in the Y chromosome tree exactly match this genealogical sequence. The match is strongest when we include the possibility that Noah passed on extra Y chromosome copying errors/mutations to his sons, due to his advanced paternal age.

- This correlation implies that haplogroup L, the sister lineage to haplogroup T, is also Abrahamic in origin. It represents either the descendants of Esau (Abraham's grandson through Isaac) or the Lost Tribes of Israel.
- One of the deepest events in Israel's history points toward an explanation for the beginning of all of human history.
- At the dawn of human history, humanity was in an advanced state. The people spoke a single language and, together, they set about to build a city and a tall tower.
- Divine judgment, in the form of language confusion, was handed down for the express purpose of shattering their collaborative cultural advances — advances which had an evil intent.
- This judgment was also designed to scatter the people over the earth. Consequently, these migratory bands would have entered a short period of cultural primitiveness, from which they eventually emerged to progress forward.
- The most recent 600 years of human history have witnessed a sharp increase in human technological progress, but this technological growth has paralleled the sharp increase in the global human population. Only near the beginning of human history, when humanity was in an advanced state, has the global population grown faster.
- Thus, the history of Israel reveals that humanity began in an advanced state, regressed briefly into primitive one, and then took 4,000 years to recover.

14

Finding Out

England, centuries after the fall of the western Roman Empire (as described by the Anglo-Saxon Chronicle)

A.D. 787. In [the days of King Bertric] came first three ships of the Northmen from the land of robbers. The [sheriff] then rode thereto, and would drive them to the king's town; for he knew not what they were; and there was he slain. These were the first ships of the Danish men that sought the land of the English nation.

A.D. 793. This year came dreadful fore-warnings over the land of the Northumbrians [i.e., northeast England], terrifying the people most woefully: these were immense sheets of light rushing through the air, and whirlwinds, and fiery, dragons flying across the firmament. These tremendous tokens were soon followed by a great famine: and not long after, on the sixth day before the ides of January in the same year, the harrowing inroads of heathen men made lamentable havoc in the church of God in Holy-island, by rapine and slaughter.

A.D. 794. The heathen armies spread devastation among the Northumbrians, and plundered the monastery of King Everth at the mouth of the Wear. There, however, some of their leaders were slain; and some of their ships also were shattered to pieces by the violence of the weather; many of the crew were drowned; and some, who escaped alive to the shore, were soon dispatched at the mouth of the river.[1]

So began the time of terror unleashed by the people described above as the *Danish men*, the *heathen men*, and the *heathen armies*. Today, we know these Scandinavian invaders as the *Vikings*.

Their travels took them to places as distant as Russia and the New World (**Color Plate 221**). Their settlements reached nearly as far (**Color Plate 221**). From the late A.D. 700s through the A.D. 1000s, the Vikings held sway over Northern Europe. Then their era closed.

What happened to these ferocious people?

History books say that the original Vikings simply merged into the populations of their subject peoples. Do descendants of the Vikings still exist in those locations? Are modern Frenchmen, British, Russians, and especially Scandinavians related to these warriors?

At this stage in our journey, the fate of the Viking people touches more than meets the eye. Yes, the question of the Vikings holds its own intrigue and represents a worthy pursuit. But pursuing this question now, instead of earlier in this book, illuminates a larger omission in the preceding chapters.

When exploring the history of Europe in chapter 7, the Vikings were but one of many European peoples whose fates we didn't cover. The Franks were a European people who were contemporaries of the Vikings, but we haven't explicitly said anything about their genealogical heritage either. Nor have we traced the history of the Bulgars, the Slavs, the Avars, the Minoans, the Mycenaeans, the Etruscans, the Celts, the Picts, the Basques, the Thracians, or any of the many other peoples supposedly ancestral to Europe.

We followed a similarly narrow path elsewhere on the globe. In the Middle East, we left the fate of the ancient Assyrians and Babylonians unresolved. We didn't trace the heritage of the Canaanites, the *Urartians*, the *Hurrians*, the *Kassites*, or the *Mitanni*. In sub-Saharan Africa, we bypassed the *Soninke* of the kingdom of ancient Ghana, as well as the people of the state of *Takrur* and the of the empire of *Kanem*.

---

1. *The Anglo-Saxon Chronicle: Eighth Century*. https://avalon.law.yale.edu/medieval/ang08.asp, accessed February 1, 2021.

Around the rest of the globe, we've overlooked countless stories for early peoples known by their archaeology.

At the earliest stages of history, we were equally neglectful. In chapter 13, we observed a family tree depicting the male population at the dawn of human history (**Color Plate 207**). Each of these men — roughly 70 in total — would have given rise to an ancient group of people. Yet the deepest part of the Y chromosome tree reveals only around 10 branches, not 70 (**Color Plates 205, 209**). What happened to the other 60?

In short, it's as if the previous chapters have shown us the highlight reel of history, not the full movie. To raise the question of the fate of the Vikings at this juncture is to underline how much world history we've missed.

In this chapter, we'll discover even more secrets in the Y chromosome tree that have been hidden in plain sight. Our journey will take us full circle — back to where we started. It will also take us back to the beginning of human history, and then into the future.

We'll begin by digging deep into the question of the fate of the Vikings. But as you'll see, we'll soon find that the clues we uncover for this corner of the European world apply to peoples around the globe.

Hidden in the Numbers

If we wanted to find a candidate Viking lineage, where would be the best place to look? What part of the Y chromosome tree might hold the critical clues? What branches of the tree are left to investigate? The ground that we've covered in previous chapters casts a long shadow over these questions. The vast majority of men alive today belong to the Y chromosome haplogroups that we've already discussed.

For visual proof, take a look at **Color Plate 222**. In this display, I've taken representative populations from each of the continents and regions that we've explored in previous chapters. I've then tallied the frequency at which various Y chromosome haplogroups exist in these peoples. Notice the percent of each population that these haplogroups explain. The twenty-six haplogroups from chapters 5 through 13 define almost 100% of the men in each of these modern populations (**Color Plate 222**).

This would seem to leave us few options for a Viking lineage. Almost nothing in the Y chromosome tree remains unresolved. It's as if the genetic results in preceding chapters imply that the Vikings — and so many other earlier European peoples — went extinct.

Did they? Probably not. To see why, let's go back to where we started our exploration of human history in chapter 2.

Recall that the world population has recently spiked. Europe was no exception to this rule. Since A.D. 1400, the number of Europeans has jumped 12-fold. In A.D. 1400, it was 60 million; now it's 740 million.[2] Or, to turn the equation around, the 740 million Europeans alive today arose from just 60 million ancestors.

The branches on the European family tree reflect this math. Today, 740 million branches exist. In A.D. 1400, only 60 million existed. To reduce 740 million to 60 million, you have to connect a whole bunch of branches.

In terms of percentages, 60 million is just 8% of 740 million. Consequently, by A.D. 1400, you have to connect 92% of today's branches. Prior to A.D. 1400 is when the remaining 8% of the branches connect.

In **Color Plate 222**, this is why existing haplogroups "explain" so much of each population's males. The vast majority of the branches on the European — and global — family tree have arisen within the last 600 years. The most recent branches alone tell over 90% of their stories. Less than 10% is all that's available to tell the story of the earlier millennia of human history.

This reality becomes even more profound when we view it through the lens of absolute numbers rather than just percentages. Let's say that you have a group of 500 living European males. Today, 500 branches will lead to them. In A.D. 1400, 92% of them will have connected. This means just 40 branches will remain that go deeper into the past.

What if you want to access additional history prior to A.D. 1400? What if you have more than 40 European people groups who lived in the millennia prior? How can you access their history when your sample consists of just 500 men? The short answer is . . . you can't.

Well, you can't with DNA from just 500 men.

To interrogate this history, you need only a sporting mathematical chance. All you do is increase the absolute value of your original sample of males. Let's say that, instead of 500 males, you get the Y chromosomes from 50,000 males. Today, 50,000 branches will lead to these

---

2. United Nations, Department of Economic and Social Affairs, Population Division 2019.

men. In A.D. 1400, this number reduces by 92%. This time, however, the result is not 40 branches but *4,000* branches.

In summary, many more haplogroups remain to be discovered. The more men that you sample in the present, the greater your ability to look deep into the past. The more living men whose DNA you obtain, the more branches you will have in ancient history.

This mathematical framework constrains our ability to find an ancient Viking lineage. The details within this framework make the search even more difficult.

Finding the Vikings?

In A.D. 800, 29 million people roamed Europe.[3] Just 800,000 — or 2% of the total — lived in Scandinavia.[4] If we're looking on the Y chromosome tree for a Viking lineage from this time period, we're already at a mathematical disadvantage. Ninety-eight percent of the European lineages present back then would probably *not* have belonged to the Vikings.

But that's not the end of the story. We've just seen that the way to dig into the deeper past is to sequence the DNA of more men in the present. Let's estimate how far back we can go with existing Y chromosome sequences.

Right now, the three major global studies of the Y chromosome tree involve just over 2,000 men. In these studies, men of European descent number around 400. We can use the history of European population growth to estimate how many branches we can expect to find in A.D. 800.

Today, 400 branches connect to these 400 European men. In A.D. 800, the population of Europe (29 million) was 25-fold smaller than it is today (around 740 million). Therefore, in A.D. 800, the number of European Y chromosome branches must be 25-fold fewer than they are today. In other words, in A.D. 800 these 400 modern European men will have only 16 branches connecting them (400 / 25 = 16).

In theory, the Viking (Scandinavian) branches would represent 2% this total. Two percent of 16 branches is less than one branch. In short, with existing Y chromosome sequences, we might not have even a single Viking branch.

---

3. McEvedy and Jones (1975).
4. McEvedy and Jones (1975).

One way to check our conclusions is to compare them to other regions of the globe. The Dark Ages (early Middle Ages) in Europe were parallel to the Arab Muslim conquests. While the Vikings were plundering Europe, the Arab Muslims were rushing through North Africa and the Middle East. Yet we didn't do any theoretical calculations for the Arab Muslims. We did not reflect on why it would be so difficult to detect the genetic signature of their lineage. Instead, in chapters 5 and 8, we identified two good candidates for the Arab Muslim people — haplogroups *E1b1b* and *J1*.

Why was it easy to find the Arab Muslims, whereas it's hard to identify a Viking lineage? Once again, the answer is found in the math of human population growth.

Scandinavians represented 2% of the total population of Europe in A.D. 800. By contrast, the people of the Arabian Peninsula represented *over one-fourth* of total population of the Middle East.[5] For their region of the globe, Arabs were over *ten times more abundant* than the Vikings were for theirs. The math of human population growth keeps the fate of the Vikings obscure.

Hidden World History

What we've just witnessed in the preceding paragraphs is but one example of a larger global principle. It's not just the Viking history that remains hidden. It's also much of the early history of the entire world.

Since A.D. 1400, the global population has jumped, not 12-fold, but 20-fold. In A.D. 1400, it was 350 million; now it's more than 7 *billion*. The 7 to 8 billion people alive today arose from just 350 million ancestors. Again, the branches on the global family tree reflect this math. Today, 7–8 billion branches exist. In A.D. 1400, only 350 million existed. To reduce 7 billion to 350 million, you have to connect 95% of the branches.

Prior to A.D. 1400 is when the remaining 5% of the branches join. In A.D. 1, the world population was only 170 million, or just 2.4% of 7 billion. Consequently, by A.D. 1, 97.6% of today's branches will have joined.

Again, percentages tell only part of the story. Absolute values reveal even more. In this book, we've surveyed the cutting edge of Y

---

5. Calculation from data in McEvedy and Jones (1975), as per their reported numbers for *Turkey-in-Asia, Syria and Lebanon, Palestine and Jordan, Arabia, Iraq,* and *Iran.*

chromosome research. The three major studies[6] that revealed Y chromosome trees from men around the globe include just over 2,000 men. Today, 2,000 branches lead to these men. In A.D. 1, around 40 to 60 branches (2% to 3% of 2,000 branches) exist.[7]

Were only 50 male lineages[8] present in A.D. 1? Is this all we have to work with when we go deeper into the past? Must the ancient Assyrians, Babylonians, Canaanites, Urartians, Hurrians, Kassites, Mitanni, and so many more ancient peoples be located on just 50 lineages? The answer to all three questions is no. Two thousand years ago, around 85 *million* males were alive. This means 85 *million* Y chromosome branches existed back then. We don't see them right now because, at this point, we've sampled only a tiny fraction of today's males.

With these facts in hand, let's revisit the percentages in **Color Plate 222**. In our previous discussion of this color plate, I chose to omit a key detail. When I tallied the percentages of various haplogroups among modern male populations, I rounded off the results to the ones place. For example, the British haplogroups added up to 100%, but 100% is a rounded number. It could be 99.75%, leaving 0.25% to be explained.

This tiny detail has large ramifications. A number less than 1% might not seem like much. But when you have a million Y chromosomes, it becomes significant (0.25% of 1 million = 2,500).

Mathematically, the key to the deepest human history resides in the less-than-1%.

Dawn of the Dark Ages

Mathematical theory notwithstanding, let's return to the practical side of European history — and to the fate of the Vikings. The genetic history of Europe has left us a tantalizing hint of what happened to these ferocious Scandinavian warriors.

In chapter 8, one of the haplogroups we explored was haplogroup *I*. Recall that we concluded that *I* was a good candidate for an indigenous European lineage. In the 800s B.C. to 500s B.C., haplogroup *I* split into

---

6. Karmin et al. (2015); Poznik et al. (2016); Bergström et al. (2020).
7. Percentages were drawn from the dates for branches for these three studies; details of the dates can be found in online supplemental tables and data.
8. Fifty is the average of 40 and 60 male lineages.

two subgroups (**Color Plates 107**). I chose not to disclose the names of these subgroups until now: Haplogroup *I1* and haplogroup *I2* (**Color Plate 223**). Today, haplogroup *I2* is distributed across Europe (**Color Plate 224**). Haplogroup *I1* is as well (**Color Plate 225**).

But the highest levels of *I1* are found in Scandinavia (**Color Plate 225**). Could *I1* be the echo of the Vikings? Let's explore this possibility by retracing the history in haplogroup *I*.

The split in *I* overlaps the time of the Greeks and/or Romans. It's not hard to imagine that some sort of internal or external crisis sent a subgroup of Mediterranean *I* individuals fleeing north to Scandinavia.

Centuries later, at least one Scandinavian group — the Goths — would return to the Mediterranean. In the early A.D. era the Goths were one of many tribes that overthrew the western Roman Empire (**Color Plate 60**). Perhaps a subset of Goths remained in Scandinavia and eventually gave rise to the Vikings.

Looking from the present backward in time, haplogroup *I1* is consistent with Scandinavian population history. Recall that Scandinavians made up just 2% of the total European population in A.D. 800. Haplogroup *I1* shows evidence of having a historically small population size. If you look at its branching structure, *I1* has multiplied only in the recent past (**Color Plate 223**). Prior to the A.D. 1400s (**Color Plate 223**), it's just a long flat line. This is consistent with a historically small population size.

How can we know if *I1* was indeed a Viking lineage? This narrow question of European history is wider than it seems.

Haplogroup *I1* isn't the only haplogroup whose history I've left unresolved. In **Color Plate 22**, you may have noticed another haplogroup that, thus far, I've chosen to overlook. Today, haplogroup *F* is found as far afield as Italy and Southeast Asia (**Color Plate 226**). In these places, haplogroup *F* levels do not exceed 6%. Everywhere else, *F* is undetectable.

On the Y chromosome tree, the roots of haplogroup *F* run deep — to the beginning of human history (**Color Plate 227**; see also **Color Plates 205, 209**). From this perspective, haplogroup *F* makes an ideal candidate lineage for one of the ancient peoples that we've ignored to this point.

Conversely, haplogroup *H* is one we've discussed before (chapter 9), but whose fine details I decided to omit until now. In our earlier discussion, I didn't disclose a deep split within *H*. Haplogroup[9] *H0* broke away from haplogroup *H1/H2* somewhere between 2400 B.C. and the 1900s B.C. (**Color Plate 228**). Haplogroup *H0* represents another candidate for one of the ancient peoples we've neglected.

I didn't describe haplogroups *I1, F,* and *H0* in earlier chapters because I don't yet have an explanation for them. Neither haplogroup *F* nor haplogroup *H0* have an abundance of published detail. The early history of haplogroup *I1* is also understudied. It's hard to know the history to which these haplogroups correspond when so few clues exist. Nevertheless, the fact that these haplogroups occur means that they represent some aspect of human history yet unaccounted for. Though we've neglected the fate of many ancient peoples, their stories will still come to light. They must, for *someone* must have given rise to these haplogroups.

For other ancient peoples, a more sinister fate may have befallen them.

The Dark Side of History

Recent history has given us a taste of the more unpleasant facts of human existence. In chapter 12, we found that, after Europeans arrived, close to 90% of the pre-Columbian American population died. This wasn't the end of the tragedy. The indigenous American Y chromosome lineages that survived might still be on the decline.

Today, Latin American men overwhelmingly belong to Y chromosome haplogroups that do *not* look like indigenous American lineages. Almost 60% belong to haplogroups that were brought to the Americas by Europeans — haplogroups such as *R1b, R1a, I, J, G,* and even *T*. Around 12% belong to haplogroup *E1b1b*, which could have arrived in the Americas via Europeans or Africans. Another 6% belong to originally African haplogroups like *B, E1a,* and *E1b1a*. Together, these lineages account for more than three-fourths of all Latin American males. In other words, less than 25% of Latin American males belong to lineages that arrived from Central Asia in the early A.D. era — lineages such as haplogroup *Q* or early *R1b* (i.e., see **Color Plate 195** and chapter 12).[10]

---

9. For these splits in haplogroup *H*, I'm following the haplogroup nomenclature of Poznik et al. (2016).
10. See Poznik et al. (2016) for data behind the percentages in these two paragraphs.

Among peoples such as the Maya of Guatemala[11] or the Navajo of the southwestern United States, haplogroup Q can still be found at high levels.[12] But these communities are isolated. When Native Americans intermingle with the Latin American or European American communities, frequencies of Q and early $R1b$ drop. For example, among Puerto Rican men, haplogroups Q and early $R1b$ have almost entirely disappeared.[13]

The indigenous American Y chromosome lineage might eventually cease to exist.

Extinction may have already occurred to the west of the Americas in the Pacific. In A.D. 1777, three thousand Easter Islanders roamed Rapa Nui. Just one century later, the population was 96% smaller; only 111 people remained (**Color Plate 229**). The numbers themselves might not relate the full extent of the Easter Island population collapse. Seven years prior to the population nadir of A.D. 1877, settlers from the island of Tahiti had arrived on Rapa Nui. Today, Easter Islanders belong to haplogroup C — but so do more than 70% of Tahitian males (see **Color Plate 161** and supplemental online data). The "Easter Islanders" of today might be the descendants of the A.D. 1870 Tahitian immigrants, not the original settlers of Rapa Nui. Offspring of the latter might no longer exist.

Disease and violent conflict aren't the only means of population replacement that we've witnessed in the recent past. I realized this acutely when engaging an African-American man on his personal Y chromosome history. He shared with me that he belonged to haplogroup $R1b$. My own paternal ancestry is also $R1b$, and I exulted in our new-found familial relationship. He didn't seem to reciprocate my enthusiasm for our new genealogical link, and I later realized why — to my shame. It concerns the actions of our common $R1b$ male relative — a man who was likely a European-American slave owner, and who likely had a female African-American slave. I suspect that the latter was an unwilling participant in the conjugal affair.

Sadly, this history seems to apply to almost a fourth of African-American men alive today.[14]

---

11. E.g., see Söchtig et al. (2015).
12. E.g., see Malhi et al. (2008).
13. See data in Poznik et al. (2016).
14. See Figure 1 of Hammer et al. (2006b) for the frequencies of haplogroups I, J, and $R1b$ among African-Americans.

Each of these tragedies has occurred within the last few centuries. I can relate these awful facts to you because we have access to historical records that provide the documentation. Imagine how much population replacement occurred in the ancient past, an era for which we have much less historical documentation.

This point becomes even more relevant in the context of ancient population sizes. Today, China can field an army of 1 million men, lose them all on the battlefield, and still be left with more than 99.9% of its national population. Conversely, small communities in ancient times might have mustered armies of only a few thousand. Their populations were much smaller than China's is today, and the slaughter of these ancient armies could have spelled the doom of their ancient paternal lineages.

In this respect, the Vikings again provide helpful perspective. The reason we're even talking about them is that they were military victors. They defeated their enemies, and so we know their name. What about all the losers in human history, whose names are unknown because they never succeeded in battle?

The lineages of some ancient peoples might be permanently lost to history.

The Future

Currently, we have at least partial Y chromosome sequence information from fewer than 100,000 men. In a world of nearly 4 billion males, the Y chromosomes of 99.75% of the male population have yet to be explored. With DNA sequencing technology improving at a breakneck pace, it's only a matter of time before many more clues, many more lineages, and many more haplogroups will be revealed.

When this day comes, we'll have a much better sense of whether haplogroup *I1* is the Viking lineage. We'll also know which peoples gave rise to haplogroups *F, H0*, and *H1/H2*. For that matter, we'll have far more than the 28 haplogroups that we've explored in this book. The math of human population growth demands it.

We'll also get a much better sense of which ancient peoples went extinct, and which ones managed to leave descendants. We'll know which of the 70 ancient patriarchs (**Color Plate 207**) defied the odds and persisted.

I, for one, can't wait to find out.

Chapter 14 Summary:

- This book has identified only a handful of lineages from the innumerable people groups of history. For example, I never described the genetic fate of the Vikings, nor did I reveal the fate of the ancient Assyrians, Babylonians, Urartians, and many others.

- This is because the number of Y chromosome lineages in the global family tree is a function of human population growth.

  * Since A.D. 1400, the population of Europe has grown 12-fold. This massive increase has put the lineages from ancient European history at a mathematical disadvantage when compared to the lineages from recent European history — 92% of today's European lineages connect by A.D. 1400.

  * Since A.D. 1400, the world population has grown 20-fold. This massive increase has put the lineages from ancient world history at a mathematical disadvantage when compared to the lineages from recent world history — 95% of today's lineages connect by A.D. 1400.

- The solution to these mathematical challenges is to sequence the Y chromosomes from more men today. Once we sample the DNA from millions of men, we should have a much more complete picture of who we came from and of what happened to all the peoples of the ancient past. Until then, much of human history remains hidden.

Epilogue

15

The Lost Civilization

Six thousand years ago, a civilization arose unlike any the world had ever seen before.[1] Or since. No other civilization has ever achieved or experienced what this early civilization felt and touched. Nor can any other civilization reach the peak of this early civilization's heights.

Six days into speaking the universe into existence, the all-knowing, all-seeing, all-powerful, and glorious God completed His creation by crowning the first king and queen. He created Adam from dust and Eve from Adam's side, granting them rule of the entire earth. No natural disasters threatened their lordship. No humans plotted their downfall. No other humans existed.

The crown jewel of this kingdom was a garden paradise — Eden. The Hebrew word *Eden* literally means *pleasure*. The king and queen were granted a domain more idyllic than any we've ever seen. They had no pain to thwart their joy. No diseases or illnesses stole their happiness. No aging and approaching death dampened their enthusiasm. This paradise was the epitome of perfection.

Then a serpent entered this paradise. This serpent was the devil himself, in snake form. He tempted the queen to seek greater glory and dominion. He offered the hope of higher rule, equality with God Himself. Eve took the offer. Adam followed her lead.

---

1. Our knowledge of this civilization comes from the Bible. Some might view this as a flaw. In my experience, it's a feature. The genetic history we've seen in this book is based on it. Or, to put it more bluntly, apart from the biblical timescale, we wouldn't have been able to see the genetic echo of the known history of civilization. I see no reason to abandon the Bible when it speaks of the earliest civilization.

At the heart of this proposition was a lie. The serpent was living it. In the beginning, he had been an exalted angel. Yet he, too, sought equality with God, and God cast him down. On the earth, the serpent sought to bring humanity with him in his fall. Eve believed the lie, and Adam followed her example.

Equality with God was never a possibility. No created thing can speak back to, and gain power over, its Creator. Adam and Eve owed their existence, as well as every breath they took, to the kind and gracious hand of God. God had breathed Adam's first breath into Adam's nostrils. In response to Adam's rebellion, God promised to eventually remove his breath. Nine-hundred and thirty years after Adam's creation from dust, Adam died.

Before he died, Adam fathered numerous sons and daughters. We are his descendants.

Since Eden, kings and kingdoms have come and gone, some majestic, others oppressive. None were as magnificent as Adam and Eve's. Since then, all rulers have lived under the expectation of eventual death. All have succumbed to disease, illness, and age. All have had to defend against usurpers to the throne. All eventually fell — or will fall.

When God punished Adam and Eve for their rebellion, God also showed them mercy. He promised to send a male offspring of Eve who would crush the serpent and one day restore Paradise.

Two thousand years ago, God fulfilled part of His promise. He sent the supreme Ruler to earth:

> Jesus came to Galilee, preaching the gospel of the kingdom of God, and saying, "The time is fulfilled, and the kingdom of God is at hand. Repent, and believe in the gospel" (Mark 1:14–15).

Jesus, the God-Man, did not crush all other human kingdoms during His time on earth. Instead, He crushed death itself.

After announcing the coming kingdom of God, Jesus died on a cross at the hands of His own people, the Jews, who were aided by the Romans. Yet His death was not just an act of human cruelty. It was also divine judgment. Unlike those who murdered Him, Jesus did no wrong. God the Father punished God the Son — Jesus — for the sins of others. Jesus took on Himself God's wrath toward sinners. He was a substitute, dying in the place of those who should have suffered God's eternal torment.

God was satisfied with this act. He showed His approval by raising Jesus from the dead. Still, Jesus did not crush the kingdoms of His day. Instead, He ascended into heaven, where:

> God also has highly exalted Him and given Him the name which is above every name, that at the name of Jesus every knee should bow, of those in heaven, and of those on earth, and of those under the earth, and that every tongue should confess that Jesus Christ is Lord, to the glory of God the Father (Phil. 2:9–11).

Before He left earth, Jesus promised to return. He is the Ruler of the kingdom that will never pass away. His kingdom will one day crush all others. He will restore the lost kingdom of Paradise. God revealed this to one of Jesus' contemporaries, the apostle John:

> Now I saw a new heaven and a new earth, for the first heaven and the first earth had passed away. Also there was no more sea. Then I, John, saw the holy city, New Jerusalem, coming down out of heaven from God, prepared as a bride adorned for her husband. And I heard a loud voice from heaven saying, "Behold, the tabernacle of God is with men, and He will dwell with them, and they shall be His people. God Himself will be with them and be their God. And God will wipe away every tear from their eyes; there shall be no more death, nor sorrow, nor crying. There shall be no more pain, for the former things have passed away."
>
> Then He who sat on the throne said, "Behold, I make all things new." And He said to me, "Write, for these words are true and faithful" . . . (Revelation 21:1–5).

> Then one of the seven angels . . . came to me and talked with me, saying, "Come, I will show you the bride, the Lamb's wife." And he carried me away in the Spirit to a great and high mountain, and showed me the great city, the holy Jerusalem, descending out of heaven from God, having the glory

of God. Her light was like a most precious stone, like a jasper stone, clear as crystal. Also she had a great and high wall with twelve gates, and twelve angels at the gates, and names written on them, which are the names of the twelve tribes of the children of Israel: three gates on the east, three gates on the north, three gates on the south, and three gates on the west.

Now the wall of the city had twelve foundations, and on them were the names of the twelve apostles of the Lamb. And he who talked with me had a gold reed to measure the city, its gates, and its wall. The city is laid out as a square; its length is as great as its breadth. And he measured the city with the reed: twelve thousand furlongs. Its length, breadth, and height are equal. Then he measured its wall: one hundred and forty-four cubits, according to the measure of a man, that is, of an angel. The construction of its wall was of jasper; and the city was pure gold, like clear glass. The foundations of the wall of the city were adorned with all kinds of precious stones: the first foundation was jasper, the second sapphire, the third chalcedony, the fourth emerald, the fifth sardonyx, the sixth sardius, the seventh chrysolite, the eighth beryl, the ninth topaz, the tenth chrysoprase, the eleventh jacinth, and the twelfth amethyst. The twelve gates were twelve pearls: each individual gate was of one pearl. And the street of the city was pure gold, like transparent glass.

But I saw no temple in it, for the Lord God Almighty and the Lamb are its temple. The city had no need of the sun or of the moon to shine in it, for the glory of God illuminated it. The Lamb is its light. And the nations of those who are saved shall walk in its light, and the kings of the earth bring their glory and honor into it. Its gates shall not be shut at all by day (there shall be no night there). And they shall bring the glory and the honor of the nations into it. But there shall by no means enter it anything that defiles, or causes an abomination or a lie, but only those who are written in the Lamb's Book of Life (Revelation 21:9–27).

And he showed me a pure river of water of life, clear as crystal, proceeding from the throne of God and of the Lamb.

In the middle of its street, and on either side of the river, was the tree of life, which bore twelve fruits, each tree yielding its fruit every month. The leaves of the tree were for the healing of the nations. And there shall be no more curse, but the throne of God and of the Lamb shall be in it, and His servants shall serve Him. They shall see His face, and His name shall be on their foreheads. There shall be no night there: They need no lamp nor light of the sun, for the Lord God gives them light (Revelation 22:1–5a).

Jesus won't be the only ruler in this restored Paradise:

And they [His servants] shall **reign** forever and ever. (Revelation 22:5b; emphasis added)

The rule that Adam and Eve lost will one day be restored. But only to a select few:

And [He who sat on the throne] said to me, "It is done! I am the Alpha and the Omega, the Beginning and the End. I will give of the fountain of the water of life freely to him who thirsts. He who overcomes shall inherit all things, and I will be his God and he shall be My son. But the cowardly, unbelieving, abominable, murderers, sexually immoral, sorcerers, idolaters, and all liars shall have their part in the lake which burns with fire and brimstone, which is the second death" (Revelation 21:6–8).

Blessed are those who do His commandments, that they may have the right to the tree of life, and may enter through the gates into the city. But outside are dogs and sorcerers and sexually immoral and murderers and idolaters, and whoever loves and practices a lie (Revelation 22:14–15).

All of us have loved and practiced the same lie that Adam and Eve believed. We have not exalted our Creator, giving Him the glory that He is due. He gave Adam and Eve their breath, and He gives us ours. Yet we have not lived lives of gratitude. God gave Adam and Eve one prohibition, and they disobeyed it. God has given us a book, the Bible, that is full of commands — exhortations and prohibitions that we might appropriately reflect His glory. Like Adam and Eve, we have rejected God's commands, seeking to rule our own lives. In essence, we have all lived as our own little gods, not in submission to the one true God, whose kingdom will never pass away. We have not acknowledged that the Most High rules in the kingdom of men, and gives it to whomever He chooses.[2]

As a result, all of us will one day lose the breath that God gave us. After death, God has promised an eternity of punishment in the fires of hell.

However, God has also made a way to escape this fate.

Jesus' perfect life and substitutionary death is our way out. He has done what Adam and Eve could not do — He has perfectly obeyed God's commands. In His death, He has taken the penalty for sin that we deserve; in His perfect life, we receive the credit for His faithfulness. Those who repent of seeking to be their own god, who accept Jesus' death in their place, and who submit to the reality that the Most High rules in the kingdom of men and gives it to whomever He chooses, God promises the restoration of Paradise.

I've confessed my self-seeking, accepted God's offer of this kingdom, and repented of seeking my own. It's my sincere desire that you do the same. Will you?

---

2. Partial quote from Daniel 4:32.

Appendix A
Technical Methods

Online Supplemental Data

See <AnswersInGenesis.org/go/traced> for access to **Supplemental Tables 1-7**, and **Supplemental Figure 1**.

Population Sizes

Historical population sizes were drawn from several sources. The primary source was McEvedy and Jones (1975), as their publication contained the most temporal and geographic detail. For population sizes in very recent history, United Nations, Department of Economic and Social Affairs, Population Division (2019) was also consulted. For select populations (e.g., the recent population history of Rapa Nui), Encyclopedia Britannica was the source. For the maps of population density, Goldewijk, Beusen, and Janssen (2010) was the basis. Finally, Maddison (2001) was also utilized to set a range of historical population sizes, as per Jeanson (2019).

For population sizes inferred from the Y chromosome tree, see below.

Y Chromosome Analyses

Datasets

Full Y chromosome sequences

In this book, full-sequence Y chromosome data was drawn from three primary sources. The first dataset was Karmin et al. (2015). The second dataset was Bergström et al. (2020). Rob Carter requested the vcf file from the authors, converted it to a FASTA file, and then shared it with me. I removed three individuals from the dataset that looked like outliers based on their high numbers of missing data [HGDP00725 (Palestinian15-G); HGDP00644 (Bedouin22-J); HGDP01179 (Yi6-O)], leaving a total of 600 men in the final dataset.

The third dataset was the tree in Supplementary Figure 14 [pages 16 to 20 of Supplementary Material] in Poznik et al (2016).

Y chromosome typing studies and haplogroup definitions

For global Y chromosome haplogroup frequency data, see **online Supplemental Table 1** which contains (1) the list of studies from which the data was extracted; (2) the details on the populations examined; and (3) the raw data that was used to draw the circles on the maps used throughout this book. The Excel formula for converting the frequency of a haplogroup in a given population (reported in percent of the population) to circle diameter is as follows:

$$2*(SQRT((([frequency]/100*0.785398163397/(PI())))))$$

This formula is also embedded in individual cells in **online Supplemental Table 1**.

I reported haplogroup labels as per the International Society of Genetic Genealogy (ISOGG) 2019 haplogroup definitions (https://isogg.org/tree/). Where studies used older or alternate designations, I first converted to the ISOGG 2019 labels, and then entered the values in **online Supplemental Table 1**. In most cases, conversion of haplogroup labels was done via reported Y chromosome markers. The markers from the study were entered into the ISOGG database, and then the resultant haplogroup labels were used for analysis in **online Supplemental Table 1**. The Karmin et al. (2015) and Poznik et al. (2016) datasets either embedded the markers in the tree itself or reported them in online tables associated with the paper. For Karmin et al. (2015) Table S1, I had to curate the reported results (see **online Supplemental Table 2** for details). For the Bergström et al. (2020) dataset, the haplogroup inference was either taken as reported or inferred by comparing their reported labels and populations to labels and populations in other datasets.

Not all studies tested for every single haplogroup. However, given the haplogroups that were tested, it was possible to estimate the maximum possible value a particular (untested) haplogroup might have in a population. Hence, these "<1%" and other such designations in **online Supplemental Table 1**.

I chose 1% as the cutoff value for displaying haplogroup percentages. Any haplogroup with a reported value of less than 1% in a population was not displayed in the maps in this book.

The typing data from one additional study (Myres et al. 2011) that focused specifically on *R1b* was treated separately. The details of how I parsed and analyzed this dataset can be found in **online Supplemental Table 3**.

Tree building from full Y chromosome sequences

For Karmin et al. (2015), branch length data were extracted from the tree in Figure S3 and Table S7 as per Jeanson (2019) for the "Epsilon" root, with modifications as described in the next section. Details can be found in **online Supplemental Table 4**.

For Bergström et al. (2020), trees were built from the FASTA file (see above) with MEGA7 software (Kumar, Stecher, and Tamura 2016). The neighbor-joining tree option was chosen; gaps/missing data were treated with the "Pairwise deletion" option. Other parameters were left default. The resultant tree can be found in **online Supplemental Figure 1**. Branch length data were manually extracted from the resultant files and deposited in **online Supplemental Table 5**. See next section for details.

For Poznik et al. (2016), the branch length data were manually extracted from the tree in Supplementary Figure 14 [pages 16 to 20 of Supplementary Material in Poznik et al. (2016)] and deposited in **online Supplemental Table 6**. See next section for details.

Derivation of dates and population growth curves from tree data

Overview

In this book, the derivation of dates for branch points for the various Y chromosome trees, as well as the derivation for population growth curves based on these dates, follows much the same approach as the one taken for the "Epsilon" root in Jeanson (2019), with notable exceptions.

Overall, the precise position for the "Epsilon" root — and for the position of Shem, Ham, and Japheth in the tree — changes slightly in light of the new findings reported in chapter 13. These absolute base pair adjustments are minor; they have minor effects on dates in haplogroups *F, G, H, I, J, K, L, M, N, O, P, Q, R, S, T*; and they are described in more detail below.

A larger change stems from an alternative approach to the history embedded in haplogroups *A, B, C, D*, and *E*. Several lines of evidence suggested that one or more branches in this group had undergone mutational slowdown in the past. As compared to the rest of the haplogroups in the tree, the branches for these five haplogroups are noticeably longer (i.e., see **Color Plate 22**). At a minimum, this would suggest that these branches have or once had a faster mutation rate then the rest of the branches.

The unusual nature of these five branches can be seen, not just in the tips of the branches, but also at the base. The separation among haplogroups *A, B, C, D,* and *E* is one of the latest in the tree, as measured in terms of branch length (i.e., see **Color Plate 205**). It's even later than the separation between *Q* and *R* (see **Color Plate 205**). This is also consistent with all five haplogroups sharing an early, high rate of mutation.

However, it's visually apparent that haplogroups *A, B, C, D,* and *E* differ in their overall branch lengths relative to one another. The branches in haplogroup *A* are the longest; branches in haplogroup *B* are shorter than those in *A*; and branches in haplogroups *C, D,* and *E* are all roughly the same length, a length which is shorter than the branches in *B* and *A*. A plausible explanation for these hierarchy is as follows:

- All five haplogroups started off at a high rate of mutation.
- Then something happened in haplogroups *C, D,* and *E* to slow the mutation rate down. This could have occurred around the points at which *C* and *D-E* separated from *A-B*.
- After this point, the high rate would have continued in haplogroups *A* and *B*.
- Eventually, the rate slowed down in *B* as well, perhaps at the point at which it broke away from *A*.
- Even within *A*, it seems that mutation rates have eventually slowed down, with perhaps only the longest branches still mutating at a high rate.

Currently, the longest branches on record are found in the *Mbo* men of the Karmin et al. (2015) study. I used their branches as the basis for inferring what a theoretically high rate of mutation might be. However, I recognize that the discovery of men with even longer branches would require an adjustment in the details of the analysis described in the following section.

Details

For all three datasets (Karmin et al. (2015), Bergström et al. (2020), and Poznik et al. (2016)), dates for nodes in haplogroups *F* through *T* were derived as follows:

1) Roots were defined:

All three studies had a point at which the tree separated into three main branches (e.g., see **Color Plate 208**). These three main branches contained haplogroups (i) *A* through *H*, (ii) *I* and *J*, and (iii) *K* through *T*. These three main branches were also treated as the lineages of Noah's sons Ham, Japheth, and Shem, respectively.

For the Karmin et al. (2015) tree, the root or "Noah" position was node 8 in Figure S3. For the Bergström et al. (2020) tree (see **online Supplemental Figure 1**), the root or "Noah" position was node 1077. The root or "Noah" position for the Poznik et al. (2016) tree was node 258 on p.18 of their Supplementary Information.

2) Mutations from Noah to each of his sons, due to Noah's advanced paternal age, were derived from the tree. These were used to define the effective start points for the post-Flood time period.

For the Karmin et al. (2015) tree, Noah's mutational contribution was treated as the distance from node 8 (their Figure S3) to node 7 (their Figure S3). This distance was reported in units of *years*, and this time length was treated as a surrogate for molecular distances (i.e., similar to Jeanson (2019)). Node 7 was treated as the effective start for the post-Flood time period for Ham's lineage. For Japheth's lineage, the same temporal "distance" was subtracted from the distance between node 8 (their Figure S3) and node 193 (their Figure S3). The resultant point was treated as the effective start for the post-Flood time period for Japheth's lineage. For Shem's lineage, the same temporal "distance" was subtracted from the distance between node 8 (their Figure S3) and node 9 (their Figure S3). The resultant point was treated as the effective start for the post-Flood time period for Shem's lineage. (See **online Supplemental Table 4** for details.)

For the Bergström et al. (2020) tree (see **online Supplemental Figure 1**), Noah's mutational contribution was treated as the distance from node 1077 to node 1076, and it was 7 base pairs. Node 1076 was treated as the effective start for the post-Flood time period for Ham's lineage. For Japheth's lineage, 7 base pairs were subtracted from the distance between node 1077 and node 1051. The resultant point was treated as the effective start for the post-Flood time period for Japheth's lineage. For Shem's lineage, 7 base pairs were subtracted from the distance between node 1077 and node 1081. The resultant point was treated as the effective start for the post-Flood time period for Shem's lineage. (See **online Supplemental Table 5** for details.)

For the Poznik et al. (2016) tree, Noah's mutational contribution was treated as the distance from node 258 (on p.18 of their Supplementary Information) to node 128 (on p.17 of their Supplementary Information), and it was 7 base pairs. Node 128 was treated as the effective start for the post-Flood time period for Ham's lineage. For Japheth's lineage, 7 base pairs were subtracted from the distance between node 258 (on p.18 of their Supplementary Information) and node 257 (on p.18 of their Supplementary Information). The resultant point was treated as the effective start for the post-Flood time period for Japheth's lineage. For Shem's lineage, 7 base pairs were subtracted from the distance between node 258 (on p.18 of their Supplementary Information) and node 340 (on p.19 of their Supplementary Information). The resultant point was treated as the effective start for the post-Flood time period for Shem's lineage. (See **online Supplemental Table 6** for details.)

3) The distance from the effective start points to various nodes was measured:

For haplogroups *F* through *T*, the root to tip ("R2T") distances and the root to node ("R2N") distances were measured from the effective start points to the tips of each branch for each individual in the dataset. See **online Supplemental Tables 4–6** for details.

This step was performed slightly differently for the early nodes leading to haplogroups *A, B, C, D*, and *E*. For these haplogroups, I modeled a mutational slowdown in calculating dates. This model was derived via the following steps:

(i) Identification of candidate branch for fast mutation rate.

In each of the three studies, an early, long branch leads to these five haplogroups before they separate from one another. In the Karmin et al. (2015) tree, this branch represents the distance between nodes 5 and 6 (their Figure S3). For the Bergström et al. (2020) tree, this branch represents the distance between nodes 1073 and 1015 (see **online Supplemental Figure 1**). In the Poznik et al. (2016) tree, this branch represents the distance between node 72 (p.16 of Supplementary Information) and node 168 (p.17 of Supplementary Information).

(ii) Identification of longest overall branches.

The Karmin et al. (2015) study had men belonging to haplogroup *A00* (i.e., the longest branches on record), whereas the other two studies did not. Thus, I used the data from Karmin et al. (2015) to calculate a date for when the separation among haplogroups *A, B, C, D*, and *E* occurred.

(iii) Derivation of fast mutation rate.

From Supplemental Figure 3 of Jeanson and Holland (2019) (which uses the primary data from Karmin et al. (2015)), I extracted the distance (i.e., 124 base pairs) from the early, long branch connecting nodes 483 and 511. I also extracted the total branch lengths for the two haplogroup *A00* Mbo men. Finally, I calculated the theoretical number of generations that transpired in the post-Flood time period. I then divided the total Mbo branch lengths by this number of generations to calculate a theoretical fast mutation rate. (See **online Supplemental Table 7** for details.)

(iv) Derivation of date for end of long branch/beginning of mutational slowdown for haplogroups *C, D*, and *E*.

I used this calculated mutation rate from step (iii) to calculate a range of dates for the time of separation between haplogroup *C* and haplogroup *A-B-D-E*. (See **online Supplemental Table 7** for details.) I applied this range of dates across all three studies. (See **online Supplemental Tables 4–6** for details.)

(v) Re-derivation of R2N and R2T distances.

For haplogroups *C*, *D*, and *E*, I used the split point between haplogroup *C* and haplogroup *A-B-D-E* as the effective start point — in a sense, the root — to measure R2N and R2T distances. (See **online Supplemental Tables 4–6** for details.)

(vi) Assessment of additional fast mutation steps for remaining haplogroup *A* and *B* branches.

I repeated steps (i)-(v) for the branch leading to the split between *A* and *B*. (See **online Supplemental Tables 4–6** for details.)

In theory, my model requires the repetition of this all the way down to the point at which only equally-long *A00* branches remain. But I stopped at the branch point between *A* and *B* because the findings would have been harder to transfer across studies, due to the low number of *A* individuals in each one.

4) A range of dates was calculated for each node position.

The R2N distance was divided into either the minimum ("MIN") or maximum ("MAX") distance of the individuals for whom the node in question was ancestral. Then this ratio was multiplied by the total time since the beginning (TTB). As per Jeanson (2019) and Hardy and Carter (2014), I used 4,206 years (for MIN calculations) or 4,636 years (for MAX calculations) for TTB for haplogroups *F* through *T*. For nodes within haplogroups *C* through *E*, I used 4,026 years (for MIN calculations) or 4,441 years (for MAX calculations) for TTB, because I modeled mutational slowdown in these lineages (see **online Supplemental Table 7** for details.). For nodes within haplogroups *A* and *B*, I used 3,762 years (for MIN calculations) or 4,153 years (for MAX calculations) for TTB, because I modeled mutational slowdown in these lineages (see **online Supplemental Table 7** for details).

The result was subtracted from the TTB. Then this value was subtracted from a calendar date approximating the birth year (BY) of study participants (A.D. 1950 for MIN calculations; A.D. 1990 for MAX calculations). In summary, the dates were determined with the following formula:

Calendar date for node = BY – (TTB – (R2N/R2T*TTB))

See **online Supplemental Tables 4–6** for details.

5) If population growth curves were drawn, dates for nodes were sorted to draw the curve.

Again, this step closely follows the methods of Jeanson (2019): "After performing these calculations for all [or relevant, if focusing on a specific haplogroup or lineage] branch points [nodes], the time points were then sorted by date, and then plotted sequentially. Time points for minimum values were sorted by date and kept separate from time points for maximum values, which were also sorted independently by date. For simplicity of viewing, B.C. calendar dates in my figures were treated as negative numbers; A.D. dates, as positive numbers. . . . Again, because my results contained uncertainties in the range of hundreds of years, I did not bother to correct my time scales for absence of a "year zero" (i.e., the abrupt transition from 1 B.C. to A.D. 1)."[1]

Because of the small sample size of several of these reconstructions, I added a step to avoid bias: After sorting the nodes by date from smallest to largest, I made sure the graph of the dates for these nodes did not step up to the next value until the new date was reached.

See **online Supplemental Tables 4–6** for details.

Determination of branches in A.D. 1

The total number of branches present by A.D. 1 were counted from the Karmin et al. (2015), Bergström et al. (2020), and Poznik et al. (2016) studies. See details in **Supplemental Table 8**. The data in each Excel sheet were taken from **Supplemental Tables 4–6**.

---

1. Jeanson, 2019, p. 409.

History methods and notes

The sources for the non-genetic historical information in this book can be found in the references section.

Determination of biblical fates of peoples listed in Genesis 10

For this analysis, my primary goal was to establish what Scripture alone said about the fates of each of the men that are listed in Genesis 10.[2] In my view, each of the Genesis 10 men were heads of ethnolinguistic groups that separated due to the events of Genesis 11:1–9. Therefore, in searching for the fates of the men in Genesis 10, I was also searching for the fates of their descendants.

I used Blue Letter Bible (https://www.blueletterbible.org/) to perform Strong's Concordance searches for each name. The names listed in the color plates are taken from the KJV.

For names that showed up only in Genesis 10 and in 1 Chronicles 1 (which simply repeats the Genesis 10 list), I treated them as "no further information." Names in this category were, to me, peoples for whom the Scripture was silent on their fates.

I also lumped into the "no further information" category any name whose only reference was in an eschatologically disputed passage. For example, two of Japheth's sons, Gomer and Magog, appear in Ezekiel 38 and 39. However, the interpretation of these two chapters of Ezekiel depends on one's eschatological position. Rather than take a specific eschatological position, and rather than give a complicated set of if-then statements about the fates of peoples descending from Gomer and Magog, I conservatively placed them in the "no further information" category. And I left the determination of their biblical fates to proponents of each specific eschatological position.

Scripture is also silent on a number of regions of the globe that have been inhabited from early times. For example, China, New Guinea/Australia, South Asia, and the Americas all have cradles of civilization or archaeological evidence for early settlement. Yet Scripture does not explicitly speak of these locations. I treated the Genesis 10 names in the "no further information category" as candidates for giving rise to these peoples in these distant locations.

---

2. Terry Mortenson and Simon Turpin have been especially helpful in assisting with the concordance searches of the names in Genesis 10.

The second category of results from my concordance search were names on which Scripture *did* give clues to their fate. Some names were explicitly translated with recognizable nation-state names (e.g., "Javan" as "Greece" in Daniel 8:21, NKJV; "Asshur" as "Assyria" several times in 2 Kings 18, NKJV). Other names were transliterated from Hebrew into English without recognizable nation-state names, but Scripture gave indirect clues on their geographic location. For example, a number of names from Genesis 10 occur in Ezekiel 27. In context, the chapter represents a condemnation of Tyre. The Genesis 10 names are mentioned in Ezekiel 27 as part of the list of deeds, business transactions, and military relationships that Tyre had with surrounding nations.

For example, see Ezekiel 27:12–13.

> Tarshish was your merchant because of your many luxury goods. They gave you silver, iron, tin, and lead for your goods. Javan, Tubal, and Meshech were your traders. They bartered human lives and vessels of bronze for your merchandise.

"Tarshish," "Javan," "Tubal," and "Meshech" are all listed in Genesis 10 as sons or grandsons of Japheth. But by the era in which Ezekiel — and the city of Tyre — existed, the peoples descending from these four men must have remained in close enough geographic proximity to the Near East (i.e., the location of Tyre) to do business with Tyre. This is indirect evidence that the peoples descending from Tarshish, Javan, Tubal, and Meshech did *not* give rise to peoples at lands at great distances from Tyre. China, New Guinea/Australia, South Asia, and the Americas all seem too far away to have been engaging with Tyre in the same way that Tarshish, Javan, Tubal, and Meshech did. Therefore, Tarshish, Javan, Tubal, and Meshech are *not* good candidates for giving rise to the early peoples of China, New Guinea/Australia, South Asia, and the Americas.

This analysis represents an initial attempt to identify the biblical fates of the men in Genesis 10. A more rigorous analysis would include concordance searches for Hebrew cognates of the names listed in Genesis 10. It also would also attempt to explain outstanding puzzles in the text of Genesis 10. For example, it would determine the precise relationship among the Casluhim, Philistim, and Caphtorim; the translators of the NKJV and NASB differ in their treatment of these relationships. A more rigorous analysis would also explain why some names in Genesis 10 are singular nouns and other names are plural. Until these analyses are performed, the results in this book should be treated as first-pass attempts to elucidate the biblical fates of the men (and peoples) of Genesis 10.

Appendix B
Y Chromosome Adam and Evolution

It's been said that extraordinary claims require extraordinary evidence. Compared to mainstream science, my claims about Y chromosome Adam (Noah) are extraordinary.

But they're not unusual. Dissenters from mainstream science have been advancing claims for decades. One of the most prominent battles, the creation-evolution conflict, has been fought for more than a century.

For many of these years, dissent has focused on shortcomings in mainstream scientific views. In other words, the arguments have largely been negative and *against* mainstream views rather than positive and *for* new, non-mainstream views.

Members of the mainstream scientific community are aware of this. They view it as a fatal weakness of the opposition.[1] They've also codified this position into U.S. federal court decisions.[2]

In short, for at least 40 years, proponents of mainstream science have held to a specific standard for claims they view as *extraordinary*: These dissenting claims must not simply advance negative arguments; they must also propose testable, empirically falsifiable predictions. In other words, these claims must make predictions that future experiments can reveal to be true or false.

My claims about Y chromosome Adam/Noah are extraordinary on two counts. The first has been explicit in this book: I've claimed that the history of civilization spans only 4,500 years back to the Flood, and a total of only 6,000 years if we trace history back to the first man, Adam. I'm denying that human history reaches back 200,000 years. Implicitly, I'm also denying the longer timescale associated with this view. If God created Adam 6,000 years ago on the sixth day of creation, I'm implying that the universe is only a few thousand years old as well.

The second claim follows from the first. It's more implicit than explicit. If human history is only 6,000 years long, and if the universe is only a few thousand years old, then humans did not evolve from

---

1. Futuyma and Kirkpatrick, 2017.
2. *McLean v. Arkansas Board of Education*, 1982.

ape-like creatures. Wholesale evolution of all species from single-celled creatures is also out of the question.

In this book, I've advanced the most important line of evidence in favor of my view. For the most part, I haven't advanced negative arguments about mainstream views; I've said hardly a word about evolution. Instead, I've built a positive case for my timescale. I've also put testable predictions in print. Most importantly, in this book, I've shown the *fulfillment* of testable predictions that I published earlier.

6,000 Years

One of the main predictions that flows from my timescale is technical in nature. But it's worth exploring, slowly and in detail.

As we observed in the main text of this book, the global family tree of humanity has recorded more than ancestor-descendant relationships. It has also recorded the rises and falls in human population sizes throughout the millennia.

If humans originated a few thousand years ago (as opposed to hundreds of thousands of years ago), how would we expect the human family tree to look? From historical and archaeological records, we know the rises and falls in the human population for the last 3,000 years.[3] The rises and falls should also be reflected in genetics. Specifically, they should be reflected in the branches of the global family tree of humanity based on genetics.

Before we test this prediction, we have to make one adjustment. In a perfect world, we would have access to DNA from people all throughout history. In the real world, however, we usually reconstruct our family trees based on the DNA from living people. Living people are the *survivors* of the rises and falls in human population sizes over the millennia. Their DNA-based family tree reflects the *minimum* human population size over the years. The branches from those people who died out or left no descendants won't be reflected in the Y chromosome DNA of living people.

How would this look? The difference between the total and the minimum human population history isn't as strong as we might expect. In **Color Plate 230**, the solid line represents the total history of human population growth; the dashed line, the minimum. In **Color Plate 231**, I show the same data, but this time zooming in on the pre-spike history

---

3. See Jeanson, 2019, and references therein for further justification and explanation.

of human population growth. As you can see in **Color Plates 230–231**, the minimum human population growth curve still has a hockey stick shape to it. In fact, its shape is smoother than the curve for the total human population.[4]

How does this compare to the history recorded in the family tree based on the Y chromosome? When we attempt to reconstruct human population history from the Y chromosome-based family tree, it has a hockey stick shape. More importantly, it matches more than 90% of the known human population history (**Color Plate 232**). In **Color Plate 232**, the dashed lines represent the known history of human population growth; the solid (filled-in) area, the history based on the Y chromosome.[5]

What's remarkable about these results is that they are based on the Y chromosomes from just over 300 men. From just 300 men, we can reconstruct *thousands of years of population history for billions of people.*

What's also remarkable is that this result does not follow from a start position in the Y chromosome tree that is based on evolution. According to evolution, humanity arose first in Africa. However, if we assign the beginning of the Y chromsome tree to the African branches of the tree, the resultant reconstruction of human population history misses about 60% of the human population growth curve.[6]

This prediction-and-fulfillment is something that I've published elsewhere.[7] In a sense, it's old news.

However, this success leads to even more predictions. For example, one prediction is that the Y chromosome tree should accurately depict the population history for specific regions of the globe. In April of 2020, I showed this to be true for the post-Columbian history of Native Americans. **Color Plate 193** independently confirms these results.

At the time I published my global population history studies,[8] I had no access to the family trees of North Africans. A recent study of around 600 men from around the globe included North Africans. In this book, you've already encountered them: The *Mozabites* from Algeria.

---

4. Again, see Jeanson, 2019, and references therein for further justification and explanation.
5. Adapted from Jeanson, 2019.
6. Jeanson, 2019.
7. Prediction: Jeanson, 2017c.; Fulfillment: Jeanson, 2019.
8. Jeanson, 2019.

Take a look at the known population history of Algeria (**Color Plate 233**). (Again, the solid line represents total population growth; the dashed, minimum population growth.) Notice how Algerian population growth underwent a steep uptick beginning in the A.D. 1700s and 1800s (**Color Plate 233**). From A.D. 1700 to 1990, the Algerian population increased 15-fold.

Now take a look at the shape of the growth curve based solely on Mozabite branches (**Color Plate 234**). Notice how the curve shoots upward right around A.D. 1800 (**Color Plate 234**). Notice that it is also preceded by a long flat line of no population growth from around A.D. 600 to A.D. 1400. Overall, the match between the known population history of Algeria and the history derived from the Y chromosome is extraordinary. It's even more astonishing when you consider that it's based on genetic data from just 19 men.

In short, my timescale is *working*. It has made — and is making — testable predictions that have been fulfilled and are being fulfilled. It meets the decades-old standard that mainstream science has put in place for extraordinary claims.

It also happens to find independent corroboration in the rest of our DNA. The maternally-inherited DNA, *mitochondrial DNA*, also has a clock that ticks off just a few thousand years of history. The history embedded in the DNA that we inherit from both parents also finds confirmation in multiple, independent lines of evidence. I've documented these findings elsewhere, both in technical paper format[9] and in book form.[10]

Evolution

With respect to evolution, the question of human-ape common ancestry hits on a multitude of topics, on multiple fields of science, and on the evidence from multiple species. To attempt to address all of this in a single appendix would be an injustice to the question. Instead, I've written a full-length book treatment of the topic. In it, my focus was on a positive, predictive, falsifiable argument that meets long-standing standards for extraordinary claims. I gave the book a title consistent with this purpose: Instead of *Rebutting Darwin*, I called it *Replacing*

---

9. Jeanson, 2013; Jeanson, 2015b; Jeanson, 2017a; Jeanson, 2017b; Jeanson and Lisle, 2016.
10. Jeanson, 2017c. See also Jeanson, 2018a and Jeanson, 2018b.

Darwin. If you're reading this as a skeptic, I especially encourage you to read *Replacing Darwin*. I wrote the book specifically with a skeptic in mind.[11]

As a side note, *Replacing Darwin* also addresses side questions that might come to your mind regarding the timescale of the universe. By training, I'm not a geologist or an astronomer; I can't walk you through the technical details of methods used to estimate the age of the earth and of the universe. But in *Replacing Darwin,* I point the reader to resources that do. These resources show geologic and astronomical methods that point toward a 6,000-year age for the earth and universe.

The best evaluation of my claims won't be in *Replacing Darwin* or in this appendix. The hallmark of scientific claims is what they say with respect to the future. I've put several claims in print that future observations will reveal to be true or false. In fact, the main claim of this book is, itself, a testable prediction. I've claimed that future studies will reveal even more branches that go deeper in the tree. In one of my published papers, I've put this prediction in precise mathematical terms.[12]

Specifically, I've described how I expect future experiments to play out:

> The strong confirmation of the YEC [i.e., 6,000-year] timescale across much of the Y chromosome tree leads to additional testable hypotheses by which my model can be further examined. The simplest is a predictive mathematical formula for Y chromosome lineage discovery. This formula predicts the frequency with which deep-rooting Y chromosome lineages will be discovered in the future, and it derives from the multiplicative relationships among the known historical population sizes. As figs. 3-5 show [i.e., figs. 3-5 that are found in the published paper[13]], the multiplicative relationships among this historical population sizes match the multiplicative relationships among deep and shallow Y chromosome lineages. Thus, historical population sizes can be used to predict the discovery of deep Y chromosome lineages.

---

11. Jeanson, 2017c.
12. Jeanson, 2019.
13. Jeanson, 2019.

Whether my ideas stand or fall is something we'll have to wait to find out. Good science demands nothing less.

Appendix C
Can I Find My Ancestors
with Genetic Testing?

Who did you come from? Can genetic testing reveal the answer? If you've made it this far in this book, you're probably wondering about the answers to these questions.

The most helpful genetic test that you can take is the Y chromosome test. Several genetic testing companies offer it, and the process of data collection is simple. These companies typically ask you to provide a saliva sample or cheek swab, both of which contain samples of your DNA.

Once these companies receive your saliva or cheek swab, they extract the DNA from the cells in these samples and then sequence the Y chromosome.

The specifics of the sequencing vary from company to company, and the amount of Y chromosome detail generally depends on how much you're willing to pay. If all you want to know is the Y chromosome haplogroup to which you belong, the cheapest test will likely suffice. If you want very specific detail on where your Y chromosome lineage falls on the global Y chromosome tree, a more expensive test will be appropriate. I recommend contacting the genetic testing company's customer service department to confirm before you make your choice.

Once you have the results, you can use **Color Plate 235** as a guide to figure out your history. **Color Plate 235** gives you a quick overview of your history, and then points you to the relevant chapters where you can dig deeper.

It's likely that you won't find the full name of your specific haplogroup in **Color Plate 235**. If I tried to create a comprehensive table for every single specific haplogroup label, the table would fill a small book. **Color Plate 235** is simply an attempt to paint a picture with broad brushstrokes.

"What if I Don't Have a Y Chromosome?"

If you're a woman, you might be wondering how Y chromosome tests could be applicable to you. Men have the Y chromosome. Women do not. And it's not just women who need to wrestle with this question of Y chromosome tests. Men need to know the answer, too.

Consider the limits of the Y chromosome test. If I have my Y chromosome sequenced, I learn the *paternal* lineage to which I belong. In other words, I learn about the history on my dad's side of the family. The Y chromosome test tells me nothing about my mother's side.

You could say that the Y chromosome test tells only half the story.

How can I learn about my mother's side? If I find one of her male relatives (e.g., her brother/my uncle, or the son of my uncle/my male cousin), I can ask him to have his Y chromosome sequenced. The result will tell me part of the story of my mother's side.

Again, this step won't fill in the entire picture. Because the Y chromosome test is limited to revealing male ancestry, it will never tell the full story. But it can successively peel away the layers of mystery.

For example, let's say that I had my Y chromosome sequenced, and my mother's brother had his Y chromosome sequenced. The results reveal only part of each of my parents' ancestry — and, therefore, only part of my total ancestry. My Y chromosome lineage will be the same as my dad's. My uncle's Y chromosome lineage reveals the *paternal* ancestry of my mother's family. Neither test reveals the *maternal* ancestry of my mom or of my dad.

To expand the story of my parents' ancestry, I would need to obtain the Y chromosome sequences of males on the maternal sides of their family trees. I would need the Y chromosome sequences of two "grand"-relatives: My maternal grandfather, and the brother of my paternal grandmother.

If this is starting to make your head swim, just draw out your own family tree on a piece of paper. Fill in as much detail as you can. Then circle all the males in the tree. Follow their male descendants to see how many unique lineages exist. If two lineages eventually join, discard one of them. Sequencing the Y chromosome from both would be redundant. Focus only on those which do not connect. These are the lineages whose Y chromosome sequences you will want to identify. These lineages (haplogroups) will fill in the details of your ancestry.

We've begun this process in my own family. I've had my Y chromosome sequenced, and my father-in-law has had his Y chromosome sequenced. You could say that these results have begun to fill in the ancestry picture for my *children*. The results have revealed some of the history coming through their paternal (i.e., me) and maternal (i.e., my wife's) sides of their family. Turns out that my father-in-law and I belong to different Y chromosome haplogroups.

I'm hoping that we can fill in even more of my family tree. Some of the women in my wider family tree have begun to catch the vision for this, and we're exploring who else might be willing to be tested.

This is the way forward for anyone who's interested in his or her family history. With more Y chromosome sequences from wider and wider branches of your family tree, you'll begin to collect the large and complex picture that tells the story for each of us.

But I should warn you: Eventually, you'll probably find some close connections — closer than you might be comfortable with. The history of human population growth demands this. Go back just 600 years, and the family tree of humanity is 95% smaller than it is today. Branches *must* connect. It's the only way to make the math work.

I haven't yet found the connections on my own family tree. But, then again, I've just started looking.

Regardless of where you are in the process, I can guarantee that the results will surprise you. They've definitely surprised me.

References

Abu-Amero, K.K., et al. 2009. "Saudi Arabian Y-Chromosome Diversity and Its Relationship with Nearby Regions." *BMC Genet.* 10:59.

Addison, D.J., and Matisoo-Smith, E. 2010. "Rethinking Polynesians Origins: a West-Polynesia Triple-I Model." *Archaeol. Oceania.* 45:1–12.

Axworthy, M. 2008. *A History of Iran.* New York: Basic Books.

Balanovsky, O., et al. 2008. "Two Sources of the Russian Patrilineal Heritage in their Eurasian Context." *Am J Hum Genet* 82. (1):236–250.

Balanovsky, O., et al. 2011. "Parallel Evolution of Genes and Languages in the Caucasus Region." *Mol Biol Evol* 28. (10):2905–2920.

Balanovsky, O., et al. 2015. "Deep Phylogenetic Analysis of Haplogroup G1 Provides Estimates of SNP and STR Mutation Rates on the Human Y-Chromosome and Reveals Migrations of Iranic Speakers." *PLoS One* 10(4):e0122968.

Balinova, N., et al. 2019. "Y-Chromosomal Analysis of Clan Structure of Kalmyks, the Only European Mongol People, and Their Relationship to Oirat-Mongols of Inner Asia." *Eur J Hum Genet* 27(9):1466–1474.

Batini, C., et al. 2015. "Large-scale Recent Expansion of European Patrilineages Shown by Population Resequencing." *Nat Commun* 6:7152.

Battaglia, V., et al. 2009. "Y-chromosomal Evidence of the Cultural Diffusion of Agriculture in Southeast Europe." *Eur J Hum Genet* 17(6):820–830.

Baumer, C. 2012. *The History of Central Asia: The Age of the Steppe Warriors.* New York: I.B. Tauris & Co. Ltd.

Baumer, C. 2014. *The History of Central Asia: The Age of the Silk Roads.* New York: I.B. Tauris & Co. Ltd.

Baumer, C. 2016. *The History of Central Asia: The Age of Islam and the Mongols.* New York: I.B. Tauris & Co. Ltd.

Baumer, C. 2018. *The History of Central Asia: The Age of Decline and Revival.* New York: I.B. Tauris & Co. Ltd.

Beckwith, C.I. 2009. *Empires of the Silk Road.* Princeton, NJ: Princeton University Press.

Bekada, A., et al. 2013. "Introducing the Algerian Mitochondrial DNA and Y-Chromosome Profiles into the North African Landscape." *PLoS One* 8(2):e56775.

Berger, B., et al. 2013. "High Resolution Mapping of Y Haplogroup G in Tyrol (Austria)." *Forensic Sci Int Genet* 7(5):529–536.

Bergström, A., et al. 2016. "Deep Roots for Aboriginal Australian Y Chromosomes." *Curr Biol* 26(6):809–813.

Bergström, A., et al. 2017. "A Neolithic Expansion, but Strong Genetic Structure, in the Independent History of New Guinea." *Science* 357(6356):1160–1163.

Bergström, A., et al. 2020. "Insights into Human Genetic Variation and Population History from 929 Diverse Genomes." *Science* 367(6484):eaay5012.

Berniell-Lee, G., et al. 2009. "Genetic and Demographic Implications of the Bantu Expansion: Insights from Human Paternal Lineages." *Mol Biol Evol* 26(7):1581–1589.

Bogucki, P.I. 2017. *The Barbarians*. London: Reaktion Books.

Bortolini, M.-C., et al. 2003. "Y-Chromosome Evidence for Differing Ancient Demographic Histories in the Americas." *Am J Hum Genet* 73(3):524–539.

Bourke, S., chief consultant. 2008. *The Middle East: The Cradle of Civilization Revealed*. NSW, Australia: Global Book Publishing.

Brewer, D.J., and Teeter, E. 2007. *Egypt and the Egyptians*. New York: Cambridge University Press.

Bronk Ramsey, C., et al. 2010. "Radiocarbon-based Chronology for Dynastic Egypt." *Science* 328(5985):1554–1557.

Burns, T. 1984. *A History of the Ostrogoths*. Bloomington, IN: Indiana University Press.

Caciagli, L., et al. 2009. "The Key Role of Patrilineal Inheritance in Shaping the Genetic Variation of Dagestan Highlanders." *J Hum Genet* 54(12):689–694.

Cadenas, A.M., et al. 2008. "Y-Chromosome Diversity Characterizes the Gulf of Oman." *Eur J Hum Genet* 16(3):374–386.

Carlsen, W. 2017. *Jungle of Stone: The Extraordinary Journey of John L. Stephens and Frederick Catherwood and the Discovery of the Lost Civilization of the Maya*. New York: William Morrow (HarperCollins).

Canuto, M.A., et al. 2018. "Ancient Lowland Maya Complexity as Revealed by Airborne Laser Scanning of Northern Guatemala." *Science* 361(6409):eaau0137.

Chambers, G.K. 2013. "Genetics and the Origins of the Polynesians." In: eLS. John Wiley & Sons, Ltd: Chichester.

Chiaroni, J., Underhill, P.A., Cavalli-Sforza, L.L. 2009. "Y Chromosome Diversity, Human Expansion, Drift, and Cultural Evolution." *Proc Natl Acad Sci U.S.A.* 106(48):20174–20179.

Coe, M.D. 2003. *Angkor and the Khmer Civilization*. New York: Thames & Hudson Inc.

Coe, M.D., and Houston, S. 2015. *The Maya*. New York: Thames & Hudson Inc.

Coe, M.D., and Koontz, R. 2013. *Mexico: From the Olmecs to the Aztecs.* New York: Thames & Hudson Inc.

Cohen, S.J.D. 2000. *The Beginnings of Jewishness: Boundaries, Varieties, Uncertainties.* Berkeley, CA: University of California Press.

Cox, M.P., and Mirazòn Lahr, M. 2006. "Y-Chromosome Diversity Is Inversely Associated with Language Affiliation in Paired Austronesian- and Papuan-speaking Communities from Solomon Islands." *Am J Hum Biol* 18(1):35–50.

Cox, M.P., et al. 2007. "A Polynesian Motif on the Y Chromosome: Population Structure in Remote Oceania." *Human Biology* 79(5):525–535.

Cozzens, P. 2016. *The Earth Is Weeping: The Epic Story of the Indian Wars for the American West.* New York: Alfred A. Knopf.

Cruciani, F., et al. 2007. "Tracing Past Human Male Movements in Northern/Eastern Africa and Western Eurasia: New Clues from Y-Chromosomal Haplogroups E-M78 and J-M12." *Mol Biol Evol* 24(6):1300–1311.

Cruciani, F., et al. 2010. "Human Y Chromosome Haplogroup R-V88: a Paternal Genetic Record of Early Mid Holocene Trans-Saharan Connections and the Spread of Chadic Languages." *Eur J Hum Genet* 18(7):800–807.

Cruciani, F., et al. 2011. "Strong Intra- and Inter-continental Differentiation Revealed by Y Chromosome SNPs M269, U106 and U152." *Forensic Sci Int Genet* 5(3):e49–52.

Cunliffe, B. 1997. *The Ancient Celts.* New York: Oxford University Press.

Cunliffe, B. 2019. *The Scythians: Nomad Warriors of the Steppe.* New York: Oxford University Press.

D'Atanasio, E., et al. 2018. "The Peopling of the Last Green Sahara Revealed by High-coverage Resequencing of Trans-Saharan Patrilineages." *Genome Biol* 19(1):20.

Daryaee, T. 2012. *The Oxford Handbook of Iranian History.* New York: Oxford University Press.

Davies, N. 1998. *Europe: A History.* New York: Harper Perennial.

de Filippo, C., et al. 2011. "Y-Chromosomal Variation in Sub-Saharan Africa: Insights into the History of Niger-Congo Groups." *Mol Biol Evol* 28(3):1255–1269.

de Souza, J.G., et al. 2018. "Pre-Columbian Earth-builders Settled Along the Entire Southern Rim of the Amazon." *Nat Commun* 9(1125): doi:10.1038/s41467-018-03510-7.

Denevan, W.M., ed. 1992. *The Native Population of the Americas in 1492.* Madison, WI: The University of Wisconsin Press.

Derenko, M., et al. 2006. "Contrasting Patterns of Y-chromosome Variation in South Siberian Populations from Baikal and Altai-Sayan Regions." *Hum Genet* 118(5):591–604.

Di Cosmo, N. 2004. *Ancient China and its Enemies: The rise of nomadic power in east Asian history.* New York: Cambridge University Press.

Di Cosmo, N., Frank, A.J., and Golden, P.B., eds. 2015. *Inner Asia: The Chinggisid Age.* Cambridge, UK: Cambridge University Press.

Di Cristofaro, J., et al. 2013. "Afghan Hindu Kush: Where Eurasian Subcontinent Gene Flows Converge." *PLoS One* 8(10):e76748.

Di Cristofaro, J., et al. 2018. "Prehistoric Migrations Through the Mediterranean Basin Shaped Corsican Y-Chromosome Diversity." *PLoS One* 13(8):e0200641.

Dulik, M.C., et al. 2012. "Mitochondrial DNA and Y Chromosome Variation Provides Evidence for a Recent Common Ancestry Between Native Americans and Indigenous Altaians." *Am J Hum Genet* 90(2):229–246.

Engel, P. 2005. *The Realm of St Stephen: A History of Medieval Hungary 895–1526.* New York: I.B. Tauris & Co. Ltd.

Fagan, B. 2011. *World Prehistory: A Brief Introduction.* Upper Saddle River, NJ: Prentice Hall.

Feder, K.L. 2011. *The Past in Perspective: An Introduction to Human Prehistory.* New York: Oxford University Press, Inc.

Feng, L. 2013. *Early China: A Social and Cultural History.* New York: Cambridge University Press.

Fischer, S.R. 2013. *A History of the Pacific Islands.* New York: Palgrave and Macmillan.

Fornarino, S., et al. 2009. "Mitochondrial and Y-Chromosome Diversity of the Tharus (Nepal): A Reservoir of Genetic Variation." *BMC Evol Biol* 9:154.

Francalacci, P., et al. 2013. "Low-pass DNA Sequencing of 1200 Sardinians Reconstructs European Y-Chromosome Phylogeny." *Science* 341(6145):565–569.

Futuyma, D., and Kirkpatrick, M. 2017. *Evolution.* Sunderland, MA: Sinauer Associates, Inc.

Gelber, H.G. 2007. *The Dragon and the Foreign Devils: China and the World, 1100 B.C. to the Present.* New York: Walker & Company.

Golden, P.B. 2011. *Central Asia in World History.* New York: Oxford University Press.

Gomes, V., et al. 2010. "Digging Deeper into East African Human Y Chromosome Lineages." *Hum Genet* 127(5):603–613.

GenomeAsia100K Consortium. 2019. "The GenomeAsia 100K Project Enables Genetic Discoveries across Asia." *Nature* 576(7785):106–111.

Goldewijk, K.K., Beusen, A., and Janssen, P. 2010. "Long-term Dynamic Modeling of Global Population and Built-up Area in a Spatially Explicit Way: HYDE 3.1." *The Holocene* 20(4):565–573.

Grugni, V., et al. 2012. "Ancient Migratory Events in the Middle East: New Clues from the Y-Chromosome Variation of Modern Iranians." *PLoS One* 7(7):e41252.

Gwynn, D.M. 2017. *The Goths*. London: Reaktion Books.

Gwynne, S.C. 2010. *Empire of the Summer Moon*. New York: Scribner.

Haber, M., et al. 2019. "A Rare Deep-Rooting D0 African Y-Chromosomal Haplogroup and Its Implications for the Expansion of Modern Humans Out of Africa." *Genetics* 212(4):1421–1428.

Haber, M., et al. 2016. "Chad Genetic Diversity Reveals an African History Marked by Multiple Holocene Eurasian Migrations." *Am J Hum Genet* 99(6):1316–1324.

Hall, R. 2007. *The World of the Vikings*. New York: Thames & Hudson Inc.

Hamilton, M.B. 2009. *Population Genetics*. Chichester, West Sussex, UK: Wiley-Blackwell.

Hammer, M.F., et al. 2006a. "Dual Origins of the Japanese: Common Ground for Hunter-Gatherer and Farmer Y Chromosomes." *J Hum Genet* 51(1):47–58.

Hammer, M.F., et al. 2006b. "Population Structure of Y Chromosome SNP Haplogroups in the United States and Forensic Implications for Constructing Y Chromosome STR Databases." *Forensic Sci Int* 164(1):45–55.

Hammer, M.F., et al. 2009. "Extended Y Chromosome Haplotypes Resolve Multiple and Unique Lineages of the Jewish Priesthood." *Hum Genet* 126(5):707–717.

Hardy, C., and R. Carter. 2014. "The Biblical Minimum and Maximum Age of the Earth." *Journal of Creation* 28(2):89–96.

Hassan, H.Y., et al. 2008. "Y-Chromosome Variation among Sudanese: Restricted Gene Flow, Concordance with Language, Geography, and History." *Am J Phys Anthropol* 137(3):316–323.

Helgason, A., et al. 2015. "The Y-Chromosome Point Mutation Rate in Humans." *Nat Genet.* 47(5):453–457.

Henn, B.M., et al. 2008. "Y-Chromosomal Evidence of a Pastoralist Migration through Tanzania to Southern Africa." *Proc Natl Acad Sci U.S.A* 105(31):10693–10698.

Herrera, K.J., et al. 2012. "Neolithic Patrilineal Signals Indicate That the Armenian Plateau Was Repopulated by Agriculturalists." *Eur J Hum Genet* 20(3):313–320.

Holcombe, C. 2017. *A History of East Asia*. Cambridge, UK: Cambridge University Press.

Hudjashov, G., et al. 2007. "Revealing the Prehistoric Settlement of Australia by Y Chromosome and mtDNA Analysis." *Proc Natl Acad Sci U.S.A* 104(21):8726–8730.

Hudjashov, G., et al. 2018. "Investigating the Origins of Eastern Polynesians Using Genome-wide Data from the Leeward Society Isles." *Sci Rep* 8(1):1823.

Ilumäe, A.-M., et al. 2016. "Human Y Chromosome Haplogroup N: A Non-trivial Time-Resolved Phylogeography that Cuts across Language Families." *Am J Hum Genet* 99(1):163–173.

Jeanson, N.T. 2013. "Recent, Functionally Diverse Origin for Mitochondrial Genes from ~2700 Metazoan Species." *Answers Research Journal* 6:467–501.

Jeanson, N.T. 2015a. "Mitochondrial DNA Clocks Imply Linear Speciation Rates within 'kinds'. " *Answers Research Journal* 8:273–304.

Jeanson, N.T. 2015b. "A Young-earth Creation Human Mitochondrial DNA 'Clock': Whole Mitochondrial Genome Mutation Rate Confirms D-loop Results." *Answers Research Journal* 8:375–378.

Jeanson, N.T. 2016. "On the Origin of Human Mitochondrial DNA Differences, New Generation Time Data Both Suggest a Unified Young-Earth Creation Model and Challenge the Evolutionary Out-of-Africa Model." *Answers Research Journal* 9:123–130.

Jeanson, N.T. 2017a. "Response to 'On the Creationist View on mtDNA.' " *Answers Research Journal* 10:183–186.

Jeanson, N.T. 2017b. "Response to 'Reply to Response to "On the Creationist View on mtDNA." ' " *Answers Research Journal* 10:239–240.

Jeanson, N.T. 2017c. *Replacing Darwin: The New Origin of Species*. Green Forest, AR: Master Books.

Jeanson, N.T. 2018a. "Response to 'No Replacement of Darwin: A Review of *Replacing Darwin — The New Origin of Species*.' " *Answers Research Journal* 11:63–83.

Jeanson, N.T. 2018b. "Response to 'Still No Replacement of Darwin: A Reply to Nathaniel Jeanson's Response to My Review of *Replacing Darwin — The New Origin of Species*.' " *Answers Research Journal* 11:275–279.

Jeanson, N.T. 2019. "Testing the Predictions of the Young-Earth Y Chromosome Molecular Clock: Population Growth Curves Confirm the Recent Origin of Human Y Chromosome Differences." *Answers Research Journal* 12:405–423.

Jeanson, N.T. 2020. "Young-Earth Y Chromosome Clocks Confirm Known Post-Columbian Amerindian Population History and Suggest Pre-Columbian Population Replacement in the Americas." *Answers Research Journal* 13:23–33.

Jeanson, N.T., and Holland, A.D. 2019. "Evidence for a Human Y Chromosome Molecular Clock: Pedigree-Based Mutation Rates Suggest a 4,500-Year History for Human Paternal Inheritance." *Answers Research Journal* 12:393–404.

Jeanson, N.T., and Lisle, J. 2016. "On the Origin of Eukaryotic Species' Genotypic and Phenotypic Diversity: Genetic Clocks, Population Growth Curves, and Comparative Nuclear Genome Analyses Suggest Created Heterozygosity in Combination with Natural Processes as a Major Mechanism." *Answers Research Journal* 9:81–122.

Jin, G.Y., et al. 2012. "An Important Military City of the Early Western Zhou Dynasty: Archaeobotanical Evidence from the Chenzhuang Site, Gaoqing, Shandong Province." *Chinese Science Bulletin* 57:253–260.

Karafet, T.M., et al. 2008. "New Binary Polymorphisms Reshape and Increase Resolution of the Human Y Chromosomal Haplogroup Tree." *Genome Res* 18(5):830–838.

Karafet, T.M., et al. 2018. "Siberian Genetic Diversity Reveals Complex Origins of the Samoyedic-speaking Populations." *Am J Hum Biol* 30(6):e23194.

Karlsson, A., et al. 2006. "Y-Chromosome Diversity in Sweden — a Longtime Perspective." *Eur J Hum Genet* 14(8):963–970.

Karmin, M., et al. 2015. "A Recent Bottleneck of Y Chromosome Diversity Coincides with a Global Change in Culture." *Genome Res.* 25(4):459–466.

Kayser, M., et al. 2006. "Melanesian and Asian Origins of Polynesians: mtDNA and Y Chromosome Gradients Across the Pacific." *Mol Biol Evol* 23(11):2234–2244.

Keay, J. 2000. *India: A History.* New York: Atlantic Monthly Press.

Kelleher, J., et al. 2016. "Spread of Pedigree Versus Genetic Ancestry in Spatially Distributed Populations." *Theor Popul Biol* 108:1–12.

Kennedy, H. 2007. *The Great Arab Conquests.* Philadelphia, PA: Da Capo Press.

King, R.J., et al. 2008. "Differential Y-Chromosome Anatolian Influences on the Greek and Cretan Neolithic." *Ann Hum Genet* 72(Pt 2):205–214.

King, R.J., et al. 2011. "The Coming of the Greeks to Provence and Corsica: Y-Chromosome Models of Archaic Greek Colonization of the Western Mediterranean." *BMC Evol Biol* 11:69.

Kumar, S., Stecher, G., and Tamura, K. 2016. "MEGA7: Molecular Evolutionary Genetics Analysis Version 7.0 for Bigger Datasets." *Molecular Biology and Evolution* 33(7):1870–1874.

Kutanan, W., et al. 2020. "Cultural Variation Impacts Paternal and Maternal Genetic Lineages of the Hmong-Mien and Sino-Tibetan Groups from Thailand." *Eur J Hum Genet* 28(11):1563–1579.

Lappalainen, T., et al. 2008. "Migration Waves to the Baltic Sea Region." *Ann Hum Genet* 72(Pt 3):337–348.

Lockard, C.A. 2009. *Southeast Asia in World History.* New York: Oxford University Press.

Loughlin, N.J.D., et al. 2018. "Ecological Consequences of Post-Columbian Indigenous Depopulation in the Andean-Amazonian Corridor." *Nature Ecology & Evolution* 2(8):1233–1236.

Li, H., et al. 2008. "Paternal Genetic Affinity between Western Austronesians and Daic Populations." *BMC Evol Biol* 8:146.

Macholdt, E., et al. 2020. "The Paternal and Maternal Genetic History of Vietnamese Populations." *Eur J Hum Genet* 28(5):636–645.

Maddison, A. 2001. *The World Economy: A Millennial Perspective (Development Centre Studies)*. Organization for Economic Cooperation and Development.

Malhi, R.S., et al. 2008. "Distribution of Y Chromosomes among Native North Americans: A Study of Athapaskan Population History." *Am J Phys Anthropol* 137(4):412–424.

Malyarchuk, B., et al. 2013. "Y-Chromosome Diversity in the Kalmyks at the Ethnical and Tribal Levels." *J Hum Genet* 58(12):804–811.

Mann, C. 2005. *1491*. New York: Alfred A. Knopf.

Maretty, L., et al. 2017. "Sequencing and *de novo* Assembly of 150 Genomes from Denmark as a Population Reference." *Nature* 548(7665):87–91.

Matyszak, P. 2020. *Forgotten Peoples of the Ancient World*. New York: Thames & Hudson Inc.

McCutchen, D., trans. 1993. *The Red Record: The Wallam Olum*. Garden City Park, NY: Avery Publishing.

McEvedy, C., and Jones, R. 1978. *Atlas of World Population History*. Middlesex, England: Penguin Books.

McLean v. Arkansas Board of Education. 1982. https://law.justia.com/cases/federal/district-courts/FSupp/529/1255/2354824/.

Mendez, F.L., et al. 2011. "Increased Resolution of Y Chromosome Haplogroup T Defines Relationships among Populations of the Near East, Europe, and Africa." *Hum Biol* 83(1):39–53.

Mendez, F.L., et al. 2013. "An African American Paternal Lineage Adds an Extremely Ancient Root to the Human Y Chromosome Phylogenetic Tree." *Am J Hum Genet* 92(3):454–459.

Mitchell, P., and Lane, P., eds. *The Oxford Handbook of African Archaeology*. New York: Oxford University Press.

Mona, S., et al. 2007. "Patterns of Y-Chromosome Diversity Intersect with the Trans-New Guinea Hypothesis." *Mol Biol Evol* 24(11):2546–2555.

Mondal, M., et al. 2017. "Y-Chromosomal Sequences of Diverse Indian Populations and the Ancestry of the Andamanese." *Hum Genet* 136(5):499–510.

Moore, J.D. 2014. *A Prehistory of South America: Ancient Cultural Diversity on the Least Known Continent*. Boulder, CO: University Press of Colorado.

Morgan, D. 2007. *The Mongols*. Malden, MA: Blackwell Publishing.

Morris, C., and von Hagen, A. 2011. *The Incas*. New York: Thames & Hudson Inc.

Mulrooney, M.A., et al. 2011. "High-precision Dating of Colonization and Settlement in East Polynesia." *Proc Natl Acad Sci U.S.A.* 108(23):E192–E194.

Myres, N.M., et al. 2011. "A Major Y-Chromosome Haplogroup R1b Holocene Era Founder Effect in Central and Western Europe." *Eur J Hum Genet* 19(1):95–101.

Nagle, N., et al. 2016. "Antiquity and Diversity of Aboriginal Australian Y-Chromosomes." *Am J Phys Anthropol* 159(3):367–381.

Naidoo, T., et al. 2010. "Development of a Single Base Extension Method to Resolve Y Chromosome Haplogroups in Sub-Saharan African Populations." *Investig Genet* 1(1):6.

Ochsenwald, W., and Fisher, S.N. 2011. *The Middle East: A History*. New York: McGraw-Hill.

Oestreicher, D.M. 1995. *The Anatomy of the Walam Olum: A 19th Century Anthropological Hoax*. Ph.D. dissertation, Rutgers University. New Brunswick, New Jersey.

Pagani, L., et al. 2015. "Tracing the Route of Modern Humans Out of Africa by Using 225 Human Genome Sequences from Ethiopians and Egyptians." *Am J Hum Genet* 96(6):986–991.

Perez-Benedico, D., et al. 2016. "Mayans: A Y Chromosome Perspective." *European Journal of Human Genetics* 24:1352–1358.

Pierron, D., et al. 2017. "Genomic Landscape of Human Diversity across Madagascar." *Proc Natl Acad Sci U.S.A.* 114(32):E6498–E6506.

Pinotti, T., et al. 2019. "Y Chromosome Sequences Reveal a Short Beringian Standstill, Rapid Expansion, and early Population structure of Native American Founders." *Curr Biol.* 29(1):149–157.

Phillipson, D.W. 2005. *African Archaeology*. New York: Cambridge University Press.

Plog, S. 2008. *Ancient Peoples of the American Southwest*. London: Thames & Hudson.

Potter, B.A., et al. 2018. "Current Evidence Allows Multiple Models for the Peopling of the Americas." *Science Advances* 4(8):eaat5473.

Poznik, G.D., et al. 2013. "Sequencing Y Chromosomes Resolves Discrepancy in Time to Common Ancestor of Males Versus Females." *Science* 341(6145):562–565.

Poznik, G.D., et al. 2016. "Punctuated Bursts in Human Male Demography Inferred from 1,244 Worldwide Y-Chromosome Sequences." *Nat Genet.* 48(6):593-599.

Rębała, K., et al. 2013. "Contemporary Paternal Genetic Landscape of Polish and German Populations: From Early Medieval Slavic Expansion to Post-World War II Resettlements." *Eur J Hum Genet* 21(4):415–422.

Richards, J.F. 1993. *The Mughal Empire*. Cambridge, UK: Cambridge University Press.

Rieth, T.M., and Hunt, T.L. 2008. "A Radiocarbon Chronology for Sāmoan Prehistory." *Journal of Archaeological Science* 35:1901–1927.

Rohde, D.L.T., Olson, S., and Chang, J.T. 2004. "Modelling the Recent Common Ancestry of All Living Humans." *Nature* 431(7008):562–566.

Roewer, L. et al. 2013. "Continent-wide Decoupling of Y-Chromosomal Genetic Variation from Language and Geography in Native South Americans." *PLoS Genet* 9(4):e1003460.

Roggeveen, M.J. 1721–2. (Extract from the official log.) Published in: *The Voyage of Captain Don Felipe Gonzalez to Easter Island, 1770–1*. Corney, B.G., Ed. Trans. Accessed from https://www.easterisland.travel/easter-island-facts-and-info/history/ship-logs-and-journals/hakluyt-society-gonzalez-w-roggeveen-extract.pdf.

Rootsi, S., et al. 2007. "A Counter-clockwise Northern Route of the Y-chromosome Haplogroup N from Southeast Asia Towards Europe." *Eur J Hum Genet* 15(2):204–211.

Rowold, D.J., et al. 2019. "Investigating the Genetic Diversity and Affinities of Historical Populations of Tibet." *Gene* 682:81–91.

Sachar, A.L. 1965. *A History of the Jews*. New York: Alfred A. Knopf, Inc.

Scarre, C., Ed. 2009. *The Human Past*. New York: Thames & Hudson.

Segal, R. 2001. *Islam's Black Slaves*. New York: Farrar, Straus and Giroux.

Šehović, E., et al. 2018. "A Glance of Genetic Relations in the Balkan Populations Utilizing Network Analysis Based on in Silico Assigned Y-DNA Haplogroups." *Anthropological Review* 81(3):252–268.

Semino, O., et al. 2004. "Origin, Diffusion, and Differentiation of Y-Chromosome Haplogroups E and J: Inferences on the Neolithization of Europe and Later Migratory Events in the Mediterranean Area." *Am J Hum Genet* 74(5):1023–1034.

Skorecki, K., et al. 1997. "Y Chromosomes of Jewish Priests." *Nature* 385:32.

Shi, H., et al. 2008. "Y Chromosome Evidence of Earliest Modern Human Settlement in East Asia and Multiple Origins of Tibetan and Japanese Populations." *BMC Biol* 6:45.

Shillington, K. 2019. *History of Africa*. London: Red Globe Press.

Shou, W.-H., et al. 2010. "Y-Chromosome Distributions among Populations in Northwest China Identify Significant Contribution from Central Asian Pastoralists and Lesser Influence of Western Eurasians." *J Hum Genet* 55(5):314–322.

References

Signor, D. 1990. *The Cambridge History of Early Inner Asia*. Cambridge, UK: Cambridge University Press.

Simons, G.F., and Fennig, C.D., eds. 2018a. *Ethnologue: Languages of Asia*. Dallas, TX: SIL International Publications.

Simons, G.F., and Fennig, C.D., eds. 2018b. *Ethnologue: Languages of the Americas and the Pacific*. Dallas, TX: SIL International Publications.

Simons, G.F., and Fennig, C.D., eds. 2018c. *Ethnologue: Languages of Africa and Europe*. Dallas, TX: SIL International Publications.

Singh, U. 2009. *A History of Ancient and Early Medieval India: From the Stone Age to the 12th Century*. Uttar Pradesh, India: Pearson India Education Services Pvt. Ltd.

Söchtig, J., et al. 2015. "Genomic Insights on the Ethno-history of the Maya and the 'Ladinos' from Guatemala." *BMC Genomics* 16(1):131.

Solé-Morata, N., et al. 2017. "Whole Y-Chromosome Sequences Reveal an Extremely Recent Origin of the Most Common North African Paternal Lineage E-M183 (M81)." *Sci Rep* 7(1):15941.

Soodyall, H. 2013. "Lemba Origins Revisited: Tracing the Ancestry of Y Chromosomes in South African and Zimbabwean Lemba." *S Afr Med J* 103(12 Suppl 1):1009–1013.

Stark, R. 2014. *How the West Won*. Wilmington, DE: ISI Books.

Sturtevant, W.C., Gen. Ed. 1978-2004. *Handbook of North American Indians*. Washington, DC: Smithsonian Institution.

Tajima, A., et al. 2004. "Genetic Origins of the Ainu Inferred from Combined DNA Analyses of Maternal and Paternal Lineages." *J Hum Genet* 49(4):187–193.

Thangaraj, K., et al. 2003. "Genetic Affinities of the Andaman Islanders, a Vanishing Human Population." *Curr Biol* 13(2):86–93.

Thapar, R. 2004. *Early India: From the Origins to A.D. 1300*. Berkeley, CA: University of California Press.

Thomas, H. 1993. *Conquest: Montezuma, Cortés, and the fall of old Mexico*. New York: Simon & Schuster.

Tishkoff, S., et al. 2007. "History of Click-Speaking Populations of Africa Inferred from mtDNA and Y Chromosome Genetic Variation." *Mol Biol Evol* 24(10):2180–2195.

Trejaut, J.A., et al. 2014. "Taiwan Y-Chromosomal DNA Variation and Its Relationship with Island Southeast Asia." *BMC Genet* 15:77.

Trombetta, B., et al. 2015. "Phylogeographic Refinement and Large Scale Genotyping of Human Y Chromosome Haplogroup E Provide New Insights into the Dispersal of Early Pastoralists in the African Continent." *Genome Biol Evol* 7(7):1940-1950.

Underhill, P.A., et al. 2015. "The Phylogenetic and Geographic Structure of Y-Chromosome Haplogroup R1a." *Eur J Hum Genet* 23(1):124–131.

Unger, M.F., Harrison, R.K., Vos, H.F., and Barber, C.J., eds. 1988. *The New Unger's Bible Dictionary*. Chicago: Moody Press.

United Nations, Department of Economic and Social Affairs, Population Division. 2019. *World Population Prospects 2019, Online Edition. Rev. 1.*, accessed July 1, 2019.

van de Mieroop, M. 2016. *A History of the Ancient Near East: ca. 3000–323 B.C.* West Sussex, UK: Wiley Blackwell.

van de Mieroop, M. 2021. *A History of Ancient Egypt*. Hoboken, NJ: Wiley Blackwell.

van Oven, M., et al. 2014. "Seeing the Wood for the Trees: A Minimal Reference Phylogeny for the Human Y Chromosome." *Hum Mutat* 35(2):187–191.

Wang, C.-C., et al. 2014. "Genetic Structure of Qiangic Populations Residing in the Western Sichuan Corridor." *PLoS One* 9(8):e103772.

Watanabe, Y., et al. 2019. "Analysis of Whole Y-Chromosome Sequences Reveals the Japanese Population History in the Jomon Period." *Sci Rep* 9(1):8556.

Weatherford, J. 2004. *Genghis Khan and the Making of the Modern World*. New York: Broadway Books.

Webster, D. 2002. *The Fall of the Ancient Maya: Solving the Mystery of the Maya Collapse*. New York: Thames & Hudson Inc.

Wen, S.-Q., et al. 2020. "Y-Chromosome Evidence Confirmed the Kerei-Abakh origin of Aksay Kazakhs." *J Hum Genet* 65(9):797–803.

Wilmshurst, J.M., et al. 2011. "High-precision Radiocarbon Dating Shows Recent and Rapid Initial Human Colonization of East Polynesia." *Proc Natl Acad Sci U.S.A.* 108(5):1815–1820.

Wolfram, H. 1988. *History of the Goths*. Berkeley, CA: University of California Press.

Xue, Y., et al. 2009. "Human Y Chromosome Base-substitution Mutation Rate Measured by Direct Sequencing in a Deep-rooting Pedigree." *Curr Biol.* 19(17):1453-1457.

Y Chromosome Consortium. 2002. "A Nomenclature System for the Tree of Human Y-chromosomal Binary Haplogroups." *Genome Res* 12(2):339–348.

Young, R. http://www.rcyoung.org/.

Yunusbayev, B., et al. 2012. "The Caucasus as an Asymmetric Semipermeable Barrier to Ancient Human Migrations." *Mol Biol Evol* 29(1):359–365.

Zegura, S.L., et al. 2004. "High-resolution SNPs and Microsatellite Haplotypes Point to a Single, Recent Entry of Native American Y Chromosomes into the Americas." *Mol Biol Evol* 21(1):164–175.

References

Zhabagin, M., et al. 2017. "The Connection of the Genetic, Cultural and Geographic Landscapes of Transoxiana." *Sci Rep* 7(1):3085.

Zhong, H., et al. 2010. "Global Distribution of Y-Chromosome Haplogroup C Reveals the Prehistoric Migration Routes of African Exodus and Early Settlement in East Asia." *J Hum Genet* 55(7):428–435.

Zhong, H., et al. 2011. "Extended Y Chromosome Investigation Suggests Postglacial Migrations of Modern Humans into East Asia Via the Northern Route." *Mol Biol Evol* 28(1):717–727.

Zhou, R., et al. 2007. "Testing the Hypothesis of an Ancient Roman Soldier Origin of the Liqian People in Northwest China: A Y-Chromosome Perspective." *J Hum Genet* 52(7):584–591.

The Encyclopedia Britannica (https://www.britannica.com/) was also heavily consulted for historical information.

Glossary of Key Terms

Arabian Peninsula — includes the modern lands of Saudi Arabia, Kuwait, Bahrain, Qatar, United Arab Emirates, Oman, and Yemen.

Central Asia — includes the modern lands of Kazakhstan, Kyrgyzstan, Uzbekistan, Turkmenistan, and Tajikistan.

Cradle of civilization — earliest site of human state formation. Egypt and Sumer are two examples.

Haplogroup — a subdivision within the Y chromosome family tree. Essentially, within the tree, it's a branch and all of its descendant branches.

Language family — a formal category of language classification. The category of language *family* is one of the larger groupings of languages. As an example, the *Indo-European* language family, the family to which the English language belongs, contains more than 400 languages.

Mutation — a copying error in DNA.

New World — the Americas.

Old World — Europe, Africa, and Asia.

Pre-Columbian — the time prior to the arrival of Columbus in the Americas.

Y chromosome — DNA found only in males and, therefore, inherited only through males.

Y chromosome lineage — a branch within the Y chromosome family tree. I use it almost synonymously with *haplogroup*, though some lineages may not yet have formal haplogroup names.

Acknowledgments

For much of 2020, my life was filled with stories from human history. I sat with the accounts of peoples gone by, circumstances much different from mine, opportunities and challenges a world apart from my own.

I've also had much time to reflect and compare my circumstances to others'. I was born and raised in the United States in a stable, middle-class family to two parents who stayed together and raised their children in an era of unprecedented economic, educational, financial, medical, and academic opportunity. I wasn't born in Syria or Iraq in the midst of violent political or military turmoil. I wasn't born in the slums where successful education meant discovering creative ways to stave off hunger pangs rather than discovering aspects of DNA. I wasn't born in Central America on the eve of the arrival of Europeans where my life would likely have ended up as a statistic, one of the 80% to 90% of the population who disappeared with hardly a trace. I wasn't born into my circumstances through any act or willpower of my own. These circumstances were chosen for me.

Consequently, I am grateful, first and foremost, to God for the opportunity to explore the past in ways few people anywhere in the world or at any other time in history have been able to do. I recognize that the advances I've made are not because of my own cleverness or insight. It's due to the mercy of God giving me breath for each day and a sound mind to comprehend what I encounter. He has already given me far more than I deserve — the future hope of heaven, a clean conscience, and trustworthy promises of Scripture. Any discoveries I have made are the gracious and kind result of His enabling.

I am also grateful to my long-suffering wife who endured long hours of nerdy discussion and speculation all while supporting the pursuit of happiness in our four children.

I cannot overstate the contribution of Rob Carter at Creation Ministries International. He and I have spent countless hours on the phone and in person crunching numbers, bouncing research ideas off one another, and provoking each other to new hypotheses and pursuits. I have learned much from these interactions.

The AiG librarian, Walt Stumper, has been an enormous help in promptly tracking down critical papers. His aid to my research cannot be overstated.

Several years ago, Les Bruce and I started a research collaboration on human history. I don't think either of us anticipated where our efforts would lead. Looking back, I can see that the questions that we grappled with, the conclusions that we reached, and the further questions that we raised were foundational to the discoveries made in this book. I'm all the more grateful for his partnership.

Cameron Suter has done a massive work in preparing the illustrations and diagrams for this book. His efforts are not limited just to what you see in print in this work. He's been a tremendous help in thinking through the theoretical side of visual communication and on how to lay out the illustrations for maximum impact. I have put him on the title page of this book as big public *thank you* for his efforts.

With regards to the Y chromosome echo of the Tower of Babel, discussions with Terry Mortenson, Bodie Hodge, and Simon Turpin have been a great aid to working through the parallels between biblical text and Y chromosome branches.

I owe a debt of gratitude to the many reviewers of this work. Scientists, historians, a linguist, and laymen alike have all made this work dramatically better than what it was when they received it. Some I will name in particular (David Boyd, Les Bruce, Paweł Chojecki and his colleagues, Joe Deweese, Ola Hössjer, Nagy Iskander, Yingguang Liu, Tom McMullen, Bryan Osborne, Joe Owen, Georgia Purdom, Rick Roberts, Simon Turpin, Ryan Vogel, Richard Weikart, Steve Woodworth); others will remain anonymous, as public association with this work may jeopardize their careers. Any errors which remain are my own and not theirs.

I want to especially thank David Sparks whose early feedback was invaluable in setting the direction and tone of the book.

Special thanks to Garry Knussman for grammar editing and suggestions. Again, any errors which remain are my own and not his.

This book would not have been possible without the support of Ken Ham, of Answers in Genesis (AiG), and of AiG's research director, Andrew Snelling. Dr. Snelling's guidance in my navigation of the publishing process was a huge help.

Credits and Sources for Photos, Illustrations, and Color Plates

Color Plate 2 — Getty Images, credit: pop_jop

Color Plate 3 — Based on Scarre 2009, p.195, Figure 5.11.

Color Plate 4 — Redrawn from: Long-term dynamic modeling of global population and built-up area in a spatially explicit way: HYDE 3.1. Kees Klein Goldewijk, Arthur Beusen, Peter Janssen. 2010. *The Holocene*. Volume: 20 issue: 4, page(s): 565–573

Color Plate 5 — Redrawn from: Long-term dynamic modeling of global population and built-up area in a spatially explicit way: HYDE 3.1. Kees Klein Goldewijk, Arthur Beusen, Peter Janssen. 2010. *The Holocene*. Volume: 20 issue: 4, page(s): 565–573

Color Plate 6 — Source: Robert A. Rohde / Berkeley Earth https://en.wikipedia.org/wiki/File:Annual_Average_Temperature_Map.png

Color Plate 7 — Getty Images, credit: FrankRamspott

Color Plate 8 — Redrawn from: Long-term dynamic modeling of global population and built-up area in a spatially explicit way: HYDE 3.1. Kees Klein Goldewijk, Arthur Beusen, Peter Janssen. 2010. *The Holocene*. Volume: 20 issue: 4, page(s): 565–573

Color Plate 9 — Redrawn from: Long-term dynamic modeling of global population and built-up area in a spatially explicit way: HYDE 3.1. Kees Klein Goldewijk, Arthur Beusen, Peter Janssen. 2010. *The Holocene*. Volume: 20 issue: 4, page(s): 565–573.

Color Plate 10 — Graph based on a combination of McEvedy and Jones 1975 (for time points through A.D. 1975) and United Nations, Department of Economic and Social Affairs, Population Division 2019 (for time points after A.D. 1975).

Color Plate 14 — Getty Images, credit: Digital Vision.

Color Plate 15 — Getty Images, credit: tanukiphoto

Color Plate 16 — Getty Images, credit: poco_bw

Color Plate 17 — Getty Images, credit: kali9

Color Plate 21 — Getty Images, credit: sanchesnet1

Color Plate 25 — Redrawn from Ochsenwald and Fisher 2011, p.54.

Color Plate 26 — Redrawn from https://cdn.britannica.com/83/1983-050-705E524C/locations-languages-Indo-European-Eurasia.jpg.

Color Plate 27 — Redrawn from https://cdn.britannica.com/71/23871-050-8758B1E1/Distribution-Afro-Asiatic-languages.jpg.

Color Plate 28 — Redrawn from: Savelyev, Alexander & Robbeets, Martine. (2020). Bayesian phylolinguistics infers the internal structure and the time-depth of the Turkic language family. Journal of Language Evolution. 5. 10.1093/jole/lzz010.

Color Plate 29 — Redrawn from https://cdn.britannica.com/s:1500x-700,q:85/88/4788-004-A4A301A2/Rum-Seljuq-sultanate-Inset-empire.jpg.

Color Plate 30 — Redrawn from https://en.wikipedia.org/wiki/Mongol_Empire#/media/File:Mongol_Empire_(greatest_extent).svg and Baumer 2016, p.180–181.

Color Plate 31 — Redrawn from Daryaee 2012, p. xvi.

Color Plate 32 — Redrawn from https://cdn.britannica.com/89/4789-050-B6176F52/Expansion-Ottoman-Empire.jpg.

Color Plate 33 — Afro-Asiatic language distribution redrawn from https://cdn.britannica.com/71/23871-050-8758B1E1/Distribution-Afro-Asiatic-languages.jpg.

Color Plate 34 — Redrawn from https://cdn.britannica.com/61/127261-050-E09E43D0/languages-peoples-Africa.jpg.

Color Plate 36 — African language map redrawn from https://cdn.britannica.com/61/127261-050-E09E43D0/languages-peoples-Africa.jpg.

Color Plate 39 — Redrawn from https://www.slavevoyages.org/static/images/assessment/intro-maps/01.jpg.

Color Plate 40 — Graph drawn from data at https://www.slavevoyages.org/assessment/estimates. I used the "Embarked" metric.

Color Plate 43 — Redrawn from Shillington 2019, p.61, Map 3.3.

Color Plate 45 — Getty Images, credit: guenterguni

Color Plate 46 — Redrawn from Shillington 2019, p.20, Map 1.2.

Color Plate 48 — African language map redrawn from https://cdn.britannica.com/61/127261-050-E09E43D0/languages-peoples-Africa.jpg.

Color Plate 58 — Satellite base map from NASA (https://commons.wikimedia.org/wiki/File:Africa_satellite_orthographic.jpg).

Color Plate 59 — Redrawn from https://cdn.britannica.com/43/1043-050-CA993CCB/extent-Roman-Empire-117-ce.jpg.

Color Plate 60 — Redrawn from https://cdn.britannica.com/44/1044-050-A36E58D3/invasions.jpg.

Color Plate 61 — Redrawn from https://cdn.britannica.com/46/64946-050-3D7FE219/Byzantine-Empire.jpg.

Color Plate 62 — Basemap from Getty Images, credit: FrankRamspott

Color Plate 75 — Basemap from Getty Images, credit: FrankRamspott

Color Plate 76 — Redrawn from Baumer 2016, p.54–55.

Color Plate 77 — Redrawn from https://cdn.britannica.com/83/1983-050-705E524C/locations-languages-Indo-European-Eurasia.jpg and https://cdn.britannica.com/s:1500x700,q:85/30/2030-004-41A16422/Distribution-Uralic-languages.jpg.

Color Plate 78 — Redrawn from Baumer 2016, p.224–225.

Color Plate 82 — Redrawn from https://cdn.britannica.com/50/3850-050-01023ADD/Russian-expansion-Asia.jpg.

Color Plate 83 — Redrawn from Baumer 2018, p.49.

Color Plate 86 — Redrawn from Daryaee 2012, p. xiv.

Color Plate 87 — Basemap from Getty Images, credit: FrankRamspott

Color Plate 88 — Redrawn from https://cdn.britannica.com/54/64954-050-A9948889/Alexander-the-Great-conquests-rule-menace-culture.jpg.

Color Plate 89 — Redrawn from Daryaee 2012, p. xiv.

Color Plate 90 — Redrawn from Daryaee 2012, p. xv.

Color Plate 91 — Redrawn from Daryaee 2012, p. xvi.

Color Plate 94 — Redrawn from Baumer 2016, p.175.

Color Plate 101 — Graph based on a combination of McEvedy and Jones 1975 (for time points through A.D. 1975) and United Nations, Department of Economic and Social Affairs, Population Division 2019 (for time points after A.D. 1975).

Color Plate 102 — Graph based on a combination of McEvedy and Jones 1975 (for time points through A.D. 1975) and United Nations, Department of Economic and Social Affairs, Population Division 2019 (for time points after A.D. 1975).

Color Plate 105 — Graph based on a combination of McEvedy and Jones 1975 (for time points through A.D. 1975) and United Nations, Department of Economic and Social Affairs, Population Division 2019 (for time points after A.D. 1975).

Color Plate 110 (Hittite) — Redrawn from Scarre 2009, p.455, Figure 12.34.

Color Plate 112 — Getty Images, credit: somchaisom

Color Plate 113 — Basemap from Getty Images, credit: FrankRamspott

Color Plate 114 — Redrawn from Baumer 2014, p.10.

Color Plate 117 — Redrawn from https://cdn.britannica.com/64/67964-050-A70268B3/Distribution-languages-Dravidian.jpg.

Color Plate 118 — Redrawn from https://cdn.britannica.com/01/1601-050-CF76EF3D/empire-India-Ashoka-extent-c-250-bce.jpg.

Color Plate 119 — Redrawn from https://cdn.britannica.com/03/1603-050-E28C4592/Gupta-empire.jpg.

Color Plate 124 — Getty Images, credit: aphotostory

Color Plate 125 — Getty Images, credit: loonger

Color Plate 126 — Redrawn from several sources:

https://cdn.britannica.com/83/1983-050-705E524C/locations-languages-Indo-European-Eurasia.jpg.

Savelyev, Alexander & Robbeets, Martine. (2020). Bayesian phylolinguistics infers the internal structure and the time-depth of the Turkic language family. *Journal of Language Evolution*. 5. 10.1093/jole/lzz010.

Simons and Fennig 2018a.

Simons and Fennig 2018b.

Simons and Fennig 2018c.

https://cdn.britannica.com/s:1500x700,q:85/32/2032-004-9433820F/Distribution-Sino-Tibetan-languages.jpg.

https://cdn.britannica.com/s:1500x700,q:85/04/2004-004-7102F813/divisions-Austronesian-languages.jpg.

https://cdn.britannica.com/43/2043-050-F64DBB90/divisions-languages-Tai.jpg.

https://cdn.britannica.com/s:1500x700,q:85/31/2031-004-47AD0C57/Distribution-Austroasiatic-languages.jpg.

https://cdn.britannica.com/s:1500x700,q:85/82/98382-004-3780512B/Distribution-language-family-Hmong-Mien-China-Southeast-Asia.jpg.

Color Plate 127 — Basemap from Getty Images, credit: FrankRamspott

Color Plate 128 — Redrawn from https://cdn.britannica.com/05/19805-050-75597A75/Great-Wall-of-China-Asia-World-Heritage-1987.jpg.

Color Plate 129 — Redrawn from https://cdn.britannica.com/93/7493-050-2729B310/China-emperor-Han-Wudi-Chunqiu-Period.jpg.

Color Plate 130 — Getty Images, credits:

Дмитрий Седаков, Rawpixel, Bim, JGalione, yanjf, MediaProduction, LeoPatrizi, hadynyah, Kadek Bonit Permadi

Color Plate 135 — Redrawn from several sources:
https://cdn.britannica.com/43/2043-050-F64DBB90/divisions-languages-Tai.jpg.
https://cdn.britannica.com/s:1500x700,q:85/31/2031-004-47AD0C57/Distribution-Austroasiatic-languages.jpg.
https://cdn.britannica.com/s:1500x700,q:85/82/98382-004-3780512B/Distribution-language-family-Hmong-Mien-China-Southeast-Asia.jpg.
Color Plate 136 — Language maps redrawn from several sources:
https://cdn.britannica.com/43/2043-050-F64DBB90/divisions-languages-Tai.jpg.
https://cdn.britannica.com/s:1500x700,q:85/31/2031-004-47AD0C57/Distribution-Austroasiatic-languages.jpg.
https://cdn.britannica.com/s:1500x700,q:85/82/98382-004-3780512B/Distribution-language-family-Hmong-Mien-China-Southeast-Asia.jpg.
Color Plate 137 — Redrawn from https://cdn.britannica.com/s:1500x700,q:85/04/2004-004-7102F813/divisions-Austronesian-languages.jpg.
Color Plate 140 — Redrawn from Baumer 2016, p.224-225 and https://cdn.britannica.com/38/64938-050-FA3FE2DD/China-Qing-dynasty.jpg.
Color Plate 142 — Redrawn from Holcombe 2017, p.35, Map 2.1.
Color Plate 146 — Based on Feng 2013, p.114, Map 6.1.
Color Plate 147 — Redrawn from Holcombe 2017, p.46, Map 2.2.
Color Plate 148 — Based on Feng 2013, p.130, Map 6.3.
Color Plate 151 — Getty Images, credit: Mlenny
Color Plate 152 — Redrawn from https://cdn.britannica.com/57/126157-050-7F6512BB/Culture-areas-Pacific-Islands.jpg.
Color Plate 153 — Getty Images, credits: yanjf, LeoPatrizi, MollyNZ chameleonseye
Color Plate 155 — Getty Images, credits: SolStock, blendshapes, hadynyah, JohnnyGreig
Color Plate 157 — Redrawn from the following:
https://cdn.britannica.com/s:1500x700,q:85/04/2004-004-7102F813/divisions-Austronesian-languages.jpg.
https://cdn.britannica.com/s:1500x700,q:85/59/22959-004-70091ED7/Distribution-Australian-Aboriginal-languages.jpg.
Simons and Fennig 2018b.

Color Plate 159 — Getty Images, credit: ZU_09

Color Plate 160 — Getty Images, credits: blendshapes, JohnnyGreig

Color Plate 162 — Getty Images, credits: yanjf, LeoPatrizi, MollyNZ, chameleonseye, Дмитрий Седаков, Rawpixel

Color Plate 163 — Getty Images, credits: Rawpixel, JGalione,Deepak Sethi, blendshapes

Color Plate 167 — Getty Images, credits: JGalione, Bim, duncan1890, ZU_09

Color Plate 168 — Getty Images, credits: duncan1890, JohnnyGreig, Rawpixel, poco_bw

Color Plate 169 — Getty Images, credits: yanjf, MollyNZ, SolStock, poco_bw, LeoPatrizi, chameleonseye, blendshapes, JohnnyGreig

Color Plate 170 — Redrawn based on Simons and Fennig 2018b.

Color Plate 171 — Redrawn from https://cdn.britannica.com/55/128355-050-493DB764/Distribution-languages-Athabaskan.jpg.

Color Plate 172 — Image sources:
https://commons.wikimedia.org/wiki/File:Custer_Bvt_MG_Geo_A_1865_LC-BH831-365-crop.jpg
https://commons.wikimedia.org/wiki/File:Sitting_Bull_by_D_F_Barry_ca_1883_Dakota_Territory.jpg.

Color Plate 173 — Redrawn based on: Coe and Koontz 2013, p.199, Figure 144. Morris and von Hagen 2011, p.13, Figure 1.

Color Plate 174 Redrawn based on Coe and Houston 2015, p.12, Figure 1.

Color Plate 175 — Getty Images, credit: diegograndi

Color Plate 176 — Getty Images, credit: SimonDannhauer

Color Plate 177 — Getty Images, credit: ferrantraite

Color Plate 178 — Getty Images, credit: diegocardini

Color Plate 179 — Getty Images, credit: javarman3

Color Plate 180 — Getty Images, credit: diegograndi

Color Plate 181 — Getty Images, credit: ferrantraite

Color Plate 182 — Getty Images, credit: SL_Photography

Color Plate 183 — Getty Images, credit: Photo Beto

Color Plate 184 — Getty Images, credit: Starcevic

Color Plate 185 — Getty Images, credit: RobertoGennaro

Color Plate 186 — Getty Images, credit: arturogi

Color Plate 196 — Redrawn from Unger, Harrison, Vos, and Barber 1988, map 7 (at the back of the book).

Color Plate 197 — Redrawn from Bourke 2008, p.160.

Color Plate 198 — Redrawn from Unger, Harrison, Vos, and Barber 1988, map 5 (at the back of the book).

Color Plate 199 — Redrawn from https://www.jewishpublicaffairs. org/political-map-of-israel/.

Color Plate 219 — Geographic locations of cradles of civilization based on Scarre 2009, p.195, Figure 5.11.

Color Plate 220 — Graph based on a combination of McEvedy and Jones 1975 (for time points through A.D. 1975) and United Nations, Department of Economic and Social Affairs, Population Division 2019 (for time points after A.D. 1975).

Color Plate 221 — Redrawn from https://cdn.britannica. com/s:1500x700,q:85/19/69619-004-F8DE34BF/Routes-travel-settlements-Vikings.jpg.

Color Plate 229 — Graph based on data found at: https://www. britannica.com/place/Easter-Island/People#ref54067.

Color Plate 230 — Graph based on a combination of McEvedy and Jones 1975 (for time points through A.D. 1975) and United Nations, Department of Economic and Social Affairs, Population Division 2019 (for time points after A.D. 1975).

Color Plate 231 — Graph based on a combination of McEvedy and Jones 1975 (for time points through A.D. 1975) and United Nations, Department of Economic and Social Affairs, Population Division 2019 (for time points after A.D. 1975).

Color Plate 232 — Based on methods in Jeanson 2019. See Appendix A and online supplemental tables and data for details.

Color Plate 233 — Graph based on a combination of McEvedy and Jones 1975 (for time points through A.D. 1975) and United Nations, Department of Economic and Social Affairs, Population Division 2019 (for time points after A.D. 1975).

Color Plate 234 — Based on methods in Jeanson 2019. See Appendix A and online supplemental tables and data for details.